STUDIES IN AMERICAN LITERATURE

Volume XXVI

☆☆☆☆☆☆☆☆☆☆☆☆☆☆☆☆☆☆☆☆☆☆☆☆☆☆☆☆☆☆☆

THE AMERICAN
LITERARY REVIEW
A CRITICAL HISTORY 1920-1950

by

G. A. M. JANSSENS

University of Nijmegen

1968

MOUTON

THE HAGUE · PARIS

LIBRARY OF CONGRESS CATALOG CARD NUMBER: 68-23198

Printed in The Netherlands by Mouton & Co. Printers, The Hague.

for Uta

ACKNOWLEDGEMENTS

This book is to a considerable extent based upon unpublished manuscript materials: the *Dial*, the *Hound & Horn*, the *Southern Review*, and the Alfred Stieglitz collections at Yale University; the Allen Tate and the Samuel Putnam collections at Princeton University; the Richard Aldington, the Louis Zukofsky, and the Ronald Bottrall collections at the University of Texas at Austin; the *Poetry* and the Ronald Latimer collections at the University of Chicago; the Sherwood Anderson and the Malcolm Cowley collections in the Newberry Library at Chicago; and the Merrill Moore collection in the Library of Congress at Washington D.C. These collections are described more fully in the bibliography. For granting or procuring permission to use them my thanks are due to Donald Gallup, Alexander Clark, Mary Hirth, Robert Rosenthal, Lawrence Towner, and John Broderick. I am grateful also to Andrew Lytle who gave me access to the editorial correspondence of *The Sewanee Review*, and to Felix Pollak who made available to me the magnificent Marvin Sukov collection of little magazines at the University of Wisconsin at Madison. James Burnham, Marjory Clary, Franklin Gary, Andrew Lytle, Hildegard Nagel, John Palmer, Ellen Thayer, Philip Wheelwright, and Yvor Winters all talked to me about the past. Their reminiscences clarified a number of episodes in the histories of the magazines with which they had been associated. Nicholas Joost and Felix Pollak read part of the manuscript and suggested improvements.

I am under a great obligation to the Commonwealth Fund which awarded me a Harkness Fellowship starting in September

1963. A grant-in-aid of the Newberry Library of Chicago enabled me to continue my research in the United States in the summer of 1965. I wish to thank the staffs of both the Fund and the Library for their invariable kindness. I am indebted to the University of Nijmegen for a two-year leave of absence. The Netherlands Organisation for the Advancement of Pure Research (Z.W.O.) has generously contributed towards the costs of publication.

My debt to Professor T. A. Birrell cannot be acknowledged adequately in a few words. He has been my friend and mentor for over a decade. To him may be traced the virtues of this book, but none of its shortcomings.

My wife actively participated in my research from the very beginning. Her assistance and encouragement have been invaluable.

CONTENTS

ABBREVIATIONS

H & H	*The Hound & Horn*
KR	*The Kenyon Review*
PR	*Partisan Review*
SR	*The Sewanee Review*
SoR	*The Southern Review*

1

THE TRADITION OF THE LITERARY REVIEW

I

The publication of the refurbished *Dial* in New York in 1920 inaugurated a new chapter in the history of American literary periodicals. It was the first of an interrelated group of magazines which will be the subject of this book. Although the circulation of the individual magazines of this group was exceedingly small, their aggregate influence on the formation of literary taste in the twentieth century has been profound. This discrepancy between circulation and influence must be explained in terms of the high literary standards of these magazines. They were virtually impervious to the pressure exerted by the vested interests of the publishing world, whose standards are largely dictated by commercial interests; on the other hand, they did not succumb to an uncritical admiration for the literary products of the *avant-garde*. Their intelligent critical detachment resulted in an authoritative evaluation of the literature of both the present and the past which was rivalled by no other comparable group of American magazines in the twentieth century. They provided a common meeting-ground for a great many poets, novelists, and men of letters whom they numbered among their readers and contributors. Their crucial importance for literary history has been recognized in recent specialized studies of three of them – two books on *The Dial* (1963 and 1964), a book on *The Hound & Horn* (1966, first presented as a doctoral dissertation in 1963), and a doctoral dissertation on *The Southern Review* (1955) – but nobody has as yet attempted a serious integrated study of the tradition which these magazines constitute. There can be little doubt that this tradition has been more influential than any other highbrow magazine tradition of this century in the United States, and that it reached its peak some twenty years ago and has been declining since. A study of its definitive achievement would seem a worthwhile undertaking.

Although the magazines under discussion are differentiated from other literary periodicals by a number of special traits, they obviously did not appear out of nowhere. Their roots must be sought in Europe as well as in America. This chapter will investigate their European parentage and offer a short introduction to the American tradition. Chapter II will examine the achievement of *The Dial* (1920-1929) and will emphasize those interests and characteristics which would decisively influence the careers of its successors. Chapters III, IV, and V will, in a similar fashion, deal with *The Hound & Horn* (1927-1934), *The Symposium* (1930-1933), and *The Southern Review* (1935-1942). The final chapter will examine the early careers of *The Kenyon Review* (1939-), *The Sewanee Review* (1892 [1942]-), and *Partisan Review* (1934 [1937]-) in the light of the tradition established in the preceding two decades; it will close with a short discussion of the trend of literary magazines in the 'Fifties and 'Sixties.

A literary magazine is a highly complex organism. It does not offer us the opinions and imaginative writings of one man: it confronts us with different interests, different sensibilities, and, sometimes, with contrasting opinions. But a good magazine is more than a miscellany; it is also a form of criticism. Editors and contributors share a point of view, a conglomerate of basic principles and interests, which sets the tone of the magazine but does not limit the intellectual freedom of any one contributor. Our task will be to catch this tone, to separate the representative from the idiosyncratic, the shared principles from the personal opinions. But this study must be more than a series of intellectual biographies of the individual magazines; it must attempt to trace the individual contributions of each magazine to the tradition of the group and to delimit its abiding interests and attitudes. Consequently, whereas the unique character of each magazine will be our central concern, our interpretation and evaluation must never lose sight of the larger context of the tradition.

Our task, then, will be one of rigorous selection; firstly, to impose an order upon the vast number of contributions to each individual magazine and to distil those elements which from the vantage point of history may be seen to have been its *raison d'être*; and, secondly, to relate the character and achievement of the individual magazines to the development of the tradition in the United States. A study of this kind cannot hope to do justice to all the variegated aspects of the different magazines. Our main endeavour will be to ensure the readability of the individual chapters and the continuity of the narrative as a whole. The interested reader will find a good deal of additional information in the footnotes which, it is hoped, will redress somewhat the effect of the inevitable selectiveness of the different chapters.

The genealogy of the magazines under discussion has been a matter of virtually instantaneous recognition and unanimous agreement. It was duly recorded in the official history of *The Little Magazine* in 1946,[1] but there are innumerable earlier references to family resemblances. Already by 1932, for instance, the similarity between *The Hound & Horn* and *The Dial* had become so generally recognized that an ordinary Boston newspaper called the one "the spiritual descendant" of the other,[2] and such specialized magazines as *Poetry* and *The Criterion*, in their reviews of fellow periodicals, often compared the achievements of the individual members of the group. Not only did comparative outsiders notice the inherited resemblances of the successive magazines, the editors themselves were often consciously following in the tracks of their predecessors. In the course of this study we shall have occasion to examine some of the more significant references to the genealogy of these magazines. We shall start from the presupposition that *The Dial, The Hound & Horn, The Symposium, The Southern Review, The*

[1] Frederick Hoffman, Charles Allen, and Caroline Ulrich, *The Little Magazine: A History and a Bibliography* (Princeton, 1946; 2nd rev. ed., 1947).
[2] K. S., review of Lincoln Kirstein, *Flesh is Heir*, in *Boston Evening Transcript* (March 23, 1932), Part IV, p. 2.

Kenyon Review, The Sewanee Review and, in some respects, *Partisan Review* have enough traits in common to warrant a comparative discussion.

II

When John Crowe Ransom was laying plans for *The Kenyon Review* in 1938, he drew inspiration from the example of both the contemporary *Southern Review* and of the earlier *Dial*; and when Allen Tate took over the reconstructed *Sewanee Review* in 1944 he explicitly stated that *The Sewanee Review* hoped to be a worthy successor of *The Southern Review* and to continue in the tradition of *The Dial*. Now the *Kenyon* and *Sewanee* reviews of the 'Forties show obvious resemblances to *The Southern Review* of the late 'Thirties, but they must strike the modern reader as very different magazines from *The Dial* of the 'Twenties. This does not mean that their intentions were necessarily very different; rather they were products of different literary and cultural eras. For the sake of convenience we shall call all members of the group "literary reviews", although numerous magazines of very different complexion have laid claims to this title.

As a descriptive term, however, the name "literary review" is more than arbitrary. For one thing it differentiates the magazines under discussion from "little magazines". Although they have a number of characteristics in common, a literary review, in our sense of the word, is not a little magazine. The distinction is relevant if we want to understand fully the continuity of the tradition from *The Dial* onwards. Objections to the denomination "little magazine" as applied to the literary reviews under discussion have been numerous. It is not surprising that these objections have been more frequent in discussions of the later "critical quarterlies" like *The Kenyon Review* and *The Sewanee Review* than in discussions of the earlier "literary magazines" like *The Dial* and *The Hound & Horn*. This must be explained in terms of the historical development of our group of "literary reviews", a term which covers both the earlier and the later representatives. But even those critics who have discussed the first review of the group, *The Dial,* in the context of little magazines, have granted it a special position. Lionel Trilling, for instance, examined the genus "little magazine" from "the elegant and brilliant *Dial* to the latest little scrub from the provinces", and Harold Loeb spoke of "the august *Dial*".[3] Matthew Josephson observed that *The Dial* was "pursuing an educational function", which is hardly an aspect of our accepted image of a little magazine, and Samuel Putnam described it as "the most influential organ of the day among intellectuals".[4] Ezra Pound, who was closely associated with *The Dial* in its early years, was "not sure that the *Dial* would like to see itself listed among little reviews" [in Pound's vocabulary "small magazine", "little review", and "little magazine" were interchangeable].[5]

Nor were *The Dial*'s successors universally described as little magazines; many critics called them "little" only with reference to their circulation and non-profit character. Lincoln Kirstein, an editor of *The Hound & Horn,* remembered that his magazine "never considered" itself little, although "others may have thought so", and an editor of the little magazine *Direction* described *The Seven Arts* [in some respects a forerunner of *The Dial*], *The Dial, The Hound & Horn,* and *The Symposium* as "reviews in the European manner".[6] Indeed, if a little magazine is, as it has recently been defined, a magazine that customarily prints "the unknown writers and kinds of writing", that does not "come out on time or even, to surprise you", does not come out at all, that appears "often on cheap paper with type hard to read", that publishes "what the big ones won't", and pays contributors "little or nothing", then such a magazine is not identical with a high-brow literary review.[7]

[3] Trilling, *The Liberal Imagination* (New York, 1950), p. 97; Loeb, *The Way It Was* (New York, 1959), p. 6.
[4] Josephson, *Life among the Surrealists: A Memoir* (New York, 1962), 188; Putnam, *Paris Was Our Mistress* (New York, 1947), p. 26.
[5] Pound, "Small Magazines", *The English Journal,* XIX, 9 (November 1930), 697.
[6] Kirstein, "*The Hound & Horn,* 1927-1934", *The Harvard Advocate,* CXXI, 2 (Christmas 1934), 8; H. R[ivers], "Editorial: Literature Without Money", *Direction* (special issue), I, 3 (1938), 7.
[7] W. G. Rogers, *Wise Men Fish Here: The Story of Frances Steloff and the Gotham Book Mart* (New York, 1965), p. 109.

What, then, were the salient characteristics exemplified, in different degrees, by all the highbrow literary reviews under discussion? They were all serious and "disinterested". They refused to compromise in literary and intellectual matters. Their approach was invariably highbrow and they were continually on the alert to detect signs of intellectual simplification, dishonesty or surrender. Ideally, they had, in the words of T. S. Eliot, a "tendency" rather than a "programme".[8] Although their excellence depended to a considerable extent on a body of regular contributors, they were not coterie publications. They appealed to a national audience and their interests transcended national borders in so far as they published the work of foreign writers and commented on the foreign literary and cultural scene. They were interested in the past as it bore on the present, but the present was their proper territory. They were primarily interested in literature, but as literature "does not exist in a vacuum",[9] they were concerned with those aspects of contemporary culture, politics and thought which influenced the literature they published and discussed. They tried to give an accurate and critical picture of the contemporary state of literature and culture and to predict and influence their future development. They were most often quarterly publications – although *The Dial* was a monthly and *Partisan Review* at different times a monthly, a bi-monthly and a quarterly – and were, therefore, able to transcend journalistic reportage and be truly detached and critical. Their success depended upon the publication of imaginative and critical writing which had been selected from a mature, informed point of view and which was arranged in such a fashion as to be truly representative of its time. Each successful issue was a reflection and an interpretation of the "best that is known and thought" at the time and the bound volumes of a successful review presented an invaluable critical

---

[8]   "The Idea of a Literary Review", *The Criterion*, IV, 1 (January 1926), 3.
[9]   Ezra Pound, *ABC of Reading* (London, 1934), p. 32. Pound had used this phrase on a number of earlier occasions (see, for instance, Pound's "The First Year of 'Pagany' and the Possibility of Criteria", *Pagany*, II, 1 [Winter 1931], 104). Cf. also Richard Aldington's "Literature cannot exist *in vacuo*" ("Notes: Literature and the 'Honnête Homme' ", *The Criterion*, I, 4 [July 1923], 421).

commentary on its era. Indeed, although they were "catholic" they were not miscellaneous; the critical acumen of the editors and their closest contributors defined the character and the importance of the review.

Like little magazines, the reviews under discussion were non-commercial publications, but they have proved so much more influential because they were all assured of a solid financial backing.[10] Some were wealthier than others, but they all appeared regularly and in a uniform format. Their struggle for survival was never as fierce and desperate as, for instance, the fight which the best little magazine of this century, *The Little Review*, had to put up; in 1916 it told its readers: "we may have to come out on tissue paper pretty soon, but we shall *keep on coming out*! Nothing can stop us now." [11] The reviews were also able to pay for their contributions. Their rates of payment enabled them to solicit manuscripts from writers of their own choice; this enlarged their range and made them less dependent upon the occasional acceptable manuscript in the mails. They could suggest topics for critical articles, they could plan each issue as a unit and they could carry on a discussion through several issues. In this way they did not merely record their own time, but also exerted a profound influence on it. They were undemocratic in that they believed that high culture is transmitted by a very small number of individuals – certain great editors of this century like T. S. Eliot, Allen Tate, F. R. Leavis and, after his earlier revolutionist period, Dwight Macdonald, have spoken of an intellectual *élite*; others have used the more picturesque concept of

---

[10] Cf. Delmore Schwartz, "An Unpleasant and Important Fact: The Misery and Necessity of the Quarterly", *The American Scholar*, XV, 4 (Autumn 1946), 554: "The risk of depending upon the good will of the patron can be illustrated by extremes: the man who supported one of the best literary reviews in America is now in an insane asylum; the state official who supported another one was a demagogue who was assassinated, and the man who continued this support turned out to be a thief who had to be put in a penitentiary." Schwartz clearly referred to *The Dial* and *The Southern Review*, but although the facts quoted had some bearing on the career of these magazines, they were discontinued for very different reasons.

[11] "To Our Readers", *The Little Review*, III, 7 (November 1916), 21.

the *avant-garde* – and their achievement is largely due to their uncompromising temper. They did not believe in the "common reader"; they addressed themselves to a highbrow audience in a lowbrow and middlebrow society. It is therefore nostalgic rather than helpful to regard the early nineteenth century English reviews, like the *Edinburgh Review* or *Blackwood's Magazine*, as the direct precursors of the twentieth century reviews. However much we may prefer to our own the cultural situation of which the nineteenth century reviews were the products, different times create different reviews. It is instructive to remember that in the twentieth century the highbrow literary quarterly has preeminently flourished in the United States; and a major reason would seem to be that in the United States the split between the intellectuals and artists and the general public has been wider than in Europe.

The preceding description is general enough to allow for the inclusion of all the magazines under discussion, but the largest common denominator is often less interesting than the parts from which it is abstracted. It does not explain why *The Kenyon Review* is so profoundly different from *The Dial* and in which respects. But it is obvious that a resuscitation of *The Dial* in the late 'Thirties would have produced a different magazine from *The Dial* of the 'Twenties. The reason is plain: as the literary reviews are primarily concerned with the present, they are exceedingly susceptible to the literary climate of their day.[12] That is why it is so difficult to devise a very precise rationale for the highbrow literary review. It also explains why revivals of once famous magazines are almost invariably failures if they try to follow their models too closely.

III

After these general remarks, a quick summary of the tradition of the literary review should prove a useful introduction to the

[12] When, in 1948, Herbert Muller wrote: "Today we have no literary review as good as the *Dial*, and I see no reason why we could not have", he ignored the crucial differences between the 'Twenties and the 'Forties ("The Function of a Critical Review", *Arizona Quarterly*, IV, 1 [Spring 1948], 15).

detailed chapters on the individual magazines. We have pointed out earlier that the American literary reviews were to a considerable extent indebted to European examples. By far the most important initial influence was *La Nouvelle Revue Française*. Virtually all important reviews in England and America have at one time or other recognized the excellence and the influence of this French periodical. Its success was primarily due to two factors. Firstly, its tone was set by a small group of persons, "qu'unissaient, en même temps qu'une étroite amitié, de communes préoccupations esthétiques",[13] and, secondly, it was the product of a flourishing, self-confident literary culture. In the years after World War I, when Paris was considered by many the cultural centre of the world, this second factor undoubtedly contributed to its prestige in England and America. It also accounts for a curious provincialism. The *Revue's* interests did not often reach beyond French borders, and when they did, they were restricted to two or three European countries. Valéry Larbaud wrote occasional "Lettres Anglaises", but one cannot avoid the impression that the interest in the English scene was more often a reflection of the admiration of a group of prominent English-speaking writers for *La Nouvelle Revue Française* and French literature than *vice versa*. The Proust memorial number of January 1923, for instance, featured an "Hommage d'un Groupe d'Ecrivains Anglais", and when one discovers that the December 1924 number was an "Hommage à Joseph Conrad 1857-1924", one is tempted to suspect the influence of Ford Madox Ford who was a Francophile and a friend and admirer of Conrad and who lived in Paris at the time as editor of *The Transatlantic Review*. This supposition does not seem too far-fetched if we remember that Ford had strongly influenced *The Dial's* admiration for Conrad and that *The Transatlantic Review* had featured a Conrad supplement in September 1924, with contributions by Ford, Ernest Hemingway, Robert McAlmon and others. The *Revue* carried an early notice of *The Criterion*, "une jeune revue, que

---

[13] Jacques Rivière, "La Nouvelle Revue Française", *La Nouvelle Revue Française*, VIe Année, No. 69 (Nouvelle Série, June 1919), 1.

vient de fonder à Londres notre collaborateur T. S. Eliot"[14] (Eliot contributed an occasional "Lettre d'Angleterre"), but it never once mentioned *The Dial,* which had close connections with T. S. Eliot and *The Criterion,* nor any other American magazine of the 'Twenties. The *N.R.F.* failed entirely to recognize the importance of the modern movement in America, but it is only fair to point out that so many American writers of the early 'Twenties were equally blind; in their onslaught on Babbittry they were often impervious to the vitality of the American ambience. The derisive comments on their native country by the voluntary exiles from the United States cannot but have strengthened the native French chauvinism; they may be partly responsible for the blind spot of the *Nouvelle Revue Française.*

The *Revue* was first edited in early 1909 by seven writers: André Gide, Michel Arnauld, Jacques Copeau, Henri Ghéon, Jacques Rivière, André Ruyters, and Jean Schlumberger. It was suspended during the first World War and it reappeared in June 1919. The monthly issues of this "Nouvelle Série" counted some one hundred and sixty pages during the first year and dwindled down to an average of one hundred and thirty pages in subsequent years. Its main contributors during the first few years, apart from the editors, included Paul Valéry, Charles Péguy, Jules Romains, Albert Thibaudet, Valéry Larbaud, Paul Morand (in later years the French correspondent of *The Dial*), and Georges Duhamel. Its make-up was very much like that of *The Dial.* It carried foreign letters, chronicles of the theatre and of music, and its reviews were long, well-reasoned and strategic:

La *Nouvelle Revue Française* ne prétend pas embrasser par sa critique l'ensemble de la production contemporaine. Elle y fait un choix très réfléchi et ne s'impose aucun compte rendu de pure courtoisie. Ses notes ont toujours pour but, soit de définir et de classer brièvement une œuvre que l'actualité ou sa propre valeur mettent au premier plan, soit de marquer, à propos d'un livre ou d'une manifestation artistique, qui peuvent être parfois de second ordre, un point de vue ou une idée dont ses collaborateurs sont pénétrés.[15]

[14] "Les Revues", *La Nouvelle Revue Française,* Xe Année, No. 111 (Nouvelle Série, December 1922).
[15] "Notes", *La Nouvelle Revue Française,* VIe Année, No. 69 (Nouvelle Série, June 1919), 143.

The editorial for the first issue of the *Nouvelle Série* was written by Jacques Rivière. It is of unusual interest to our discussion because on first reading it appears to be an archetypal description of the function of the literary review, but at the same time it proves to be – and inevitably – a statement written at a particular time and for a particular occasion. The *Revue* would attempt above all to be "un terrain propice à la création, qu'une critique intelligente maintiendrait constamment ameubli". Rivière's editorial stressed the autonomy of the artistic order:

... la guerre a pu changer bien des choses, mais pas celle-ci, que la littérature est la littérature, que l'art est l'art. ... Aujourd'hui comme hier, et malgré des millions de morts, il reste vrai qu'une œuvre est belle pour des raisons absolument intrinsèques, qu'on ne peut pas démêler que par une étude directe, que par une sorte de corps à corps avec elle. Aujourd'hui comme hier, et malgré des monceaux de ruines, il reste vrai que la création artistique est un act original, que créer c'est peut-être avant tout ne rien sentir, ne rien vouloir d'autre que ce qu'on fait. Aujourd'hui, par conséquent, comme hier, et malgré les scrupules qu'on serait tenté d'éprouver, il reste nécessaire de purifier et de maintenir exempte de toute influence étrangère, l'atmosphère esthétique.[16]

It is hard to think of a more eloquent introduction to the aestheticism of the 'Twenties, born of political and social disillusionment, than the above statement. It sets the scene for the exuberant reception of the work of Proust and Joyce, and retrospectively, of Flaubert. It epitomizes the literary climate in which *The Dial* was conceived. It exalts the Artist as conscious craftsman. "Nous accueillerons la revendication de l'intelligence qui cherche visiblement aujourd'hui à reprendre ses droits en art; non pas pour supplanter entièrement la sensibilité, mais pour la pénétrer, pour l'analyser et pour régner sur elle." Although Rivière maintained that the *Revue* would not advocate the "tour d'ivoire", it was with some reluctance that he recognized the necessity "de contribuer personnellement à la solution des grands problèmes posés par la guerre". But the task of reconstruction and the activity of the artist would be kept entirely separate: "Le seul point que

---

16   Rivière, "La Nouvelle Revue Française" (see above, note 13), 2, 3.

nous nous défendions, c'est de laisser les unes déteindre sur les autres, pensant que ce ne pourrait arriver qu'a leur mutuel désavantage." [17]

Another item in the first issue of the reconstructed *Nouvelle Revue Française* which may be brought to bear on the present discussion, is the leading review, also written by Jacques Rivière, of Julien Benda's *Belphégor*. The tenor and the conclusions of Benda's inquiry into the contemporary literary situation were very pessimistic. Although his criticisms were mainly inspired by the French literary scene, they were more widely applicable. Two foreign admirers of Benda's aestheticism and classicism were T. S. Eliot and Ezra Pound. The latter thought Benda's ideas indeed so relevant to the American scene that he sent an English translation to *The Dial* which published it in instalments. Jacques Rivière, however, challenged Benda's pessimism although he was in essential agreement with his literary ideas. He reproached Benda for being behind the times: "Il faut, au moment où les plus belles qualités françaises semblent se réveiller, que nous retrouvions le secret de la transcendance et le goût de l'analyse. Mais justement je suis persuadé que ce renouveau est déjà commencé et je reproche vivement à M. Benda d'y fermer les yeux." Rivière detected numerous indications of a new analytical intellectual awareness which indeed, he pointed out, had been exemplified by *La Nouvelle Revue Française* from its inception. If anybody had worked "à désembourber la littérature du symbolisme, à la faire sortir du lyricisme pur et inarticulé, à rendre de la faveur aux genres qui exigent du raisonnement, de la composition et de l'artifice, c'est bien nous." [18]

Rivière's editorial and review in the first issue of the resuscitated *Nouvelle Revue Française* expressed a belief in the autonomy of art and a suspicion of belletrism which was to be the central creed of the American literary reviews. The *Revue*'s formative influence can indeed hardly be overrated but it is uncertain in how far this influence was direct or was transmitted through

---

[17]   *Ibid.*, 8, 10.
[18]   *La Nouvelle Revue Française*, VIe Année, No. 69 (Nouvelle Série, June 1919), 152.

English magazines. Names like *The English Review* and *The Egoist* come to mind, but their endeavours were finally consolidated and made effective by T. S. Eliot's *Criterion* (1922-1939) whose achievement we shall discuss presently.[19] Another French magazine which has been claimed as a shaping influence on the English and American literary reviews, was the *Mercure de France*. Richard Aldington, for instance, wrote: "From its foundation in 1890 until the war, the *Mercure de France* was one of the best, if not the best, of the independent literary periodicals in France. Nothing like it has existed in England and America, though the *English Review* under Ford, the *Dial* under Scofield Thayer, and T. S. Eliot's *Criterion* did succeed in reproducing some of the *Mercure*'s features."[20] Ezra Pound claimed an even more direct influence for the *Mercure* when he wrote: "As nearly as I can now discern, the *Dial* wanted to be in America what the *Mercure* had been in France."[21] But by 1920, the year the new *Dial* was first published, the *Mercure* had undergone radical changes which Pound was among the first to deplore. For one thing, it had become even more obviously than before a general magazine as much as a literary review. It seems therefore likely that Pound was rather referring to *The Dial*'s aspiration to rival the *Mercure*'s influence than to follow its editorial direction. While the appearance and lay-out of the *Nouvelle Revue Française* in the early 'Twenties was very much like *The Dial*'s, the *Mercure* published three issues per month

---

[19] Herbert Read has proposed the short-lived magazine *Art and Letters* as a predecessor of *The Criterion*: see *Annals of Innocence and Experience* (London, 1940), 178. Eliot himself has confirmed that "the general intention was that it [*The Criterion*] should serve as a kind of successor to the defunct *Art and Letters*" ("Last Words", *The Criterion*, XVIII, 71 [January 1939], 270).

[20] *Life for Life's Sake: Reminiscences* (New York, 1940), p. 174.

[21] "Small Magazines", 696. Pound was evidently confusing his own hopes for *The Dial* and the aspirations of the *Dial* editors, as is apparent from a letter which he wrote to Carlo Linati on 9 June 1920: "I *want* (with some immoderation) the Dial to do what the Mercure de France used to do. But God knows if there is the least chance of success in this enterprise" (*Letters of James Joyce*, Vol. II, ed. Richard Ellmann [London, 1966], p. 470).

of almost three hundred pages each. Consequently, it covered a number of areas, like politics, which *The Dial* left alone. Its huge size made an occasional chronicle about contemporary American writing possible. In common with the *N.R.F.* and *The Criterion* it published a regular column on fellow literary periodicals.

Two American magazines which have been repeatedly mentioned as formative influences on the tradition of the highbrow American literary review are *The Seven Arts* and *The Harvard Monthly*. There is indeed a viable connection between *The Seven Arts* and *The Dial* but the influence of the former has been overrated. We shall try to define it in some detail in our discussion of *The Dial*. The influence of *The Harvard Monthly* was most persuasively claimed by Malcolm Cowley: "The Dial was perhaps the last of the magazines that sprang more or less directly from the old Harvard Monthly, a college magazine with many offspring. From 1890 till 1916, Harvard was the most literary of American universities, and The Monthly was Harvard at its most literary." Cowley maintained that the "esthetic tradition of The Harvard Monthly was later revived by The Dial".[22] It would seem, however, that the significance of the *Monthly* is primarily to be sought in the fact that it brought a number of later *Dial* regulars together and that it gave them an early opportunity of getting their work published. James Sibley Watson, Gilbert Seldes, E. E. Cummings, Conrad Aiken, John Dos Passos, and Herbert Seligmann were all connected with the *Monthly* in the years just previous to World War I. Their early association and experiences are of some importance to the history of the

[22] "Midsummer Medley", *The New Republic*, LXXX (August 15, 1934), 25. Matthew Josephson remembers that "some wag called it [*The Dial*] 'a sort of postgraduate version of the *Harvard Literary Monthly*'" (*Life Among the Surrealists: A Memoir* [New York, 1962], p. 92). Varian Fry, an early editor of *The Hound & Horn*, described how his magazine had also been inspired by *The Harvard Monthly*: "We knew about the *Monthly*, had looked over the files of it in the Widener, and had lamented its untimely death. We thought that Harvard deserved a mature magazine like the *Monthly* ..." (Letter appended as a Note to Lincoln Kirstein, "*The Hound & Horn*, 1927-1934", *The Harvard Advocate*, CXXI, 2 [Christmas 1934], 93).

later *Dial,* but *The Harvard Monthly* can hardly be said to have served as its model.

Allen Tate has called *The Criterion* "the best quarterly of our time",[23] and it is appropriate to recall this statement because its later issues have been so widely condemned as dull and unconstructive that the achievement of *The Criterion* as a literary review has occasionally been obscured. As a review it was truly cosmopolitan and intellectually alert; the wide range of its interests was ordered by a consistent point of view. A detailed study of *The Criterion* would constitute a highly interesting literary and cultural history of the 'Twenties and 'Thirties.[24] The American magazine which perhaps approached nearest to *The Criterion*'s intellectual poise was *The Symposium,* but a comparison of the two will illumine Eliot's superb editorship. *The Symposium* was the happy outcome of the editorial cooperation of two different sensibilities, but it soon perished from resulting tension.

The tremendous influence of *The Criterion* on the tradition of the American literary review was undoubtedly due in part to the fact that although – as Ezra Pound so aptly worded it – it was "not strictly a magazine '*in* the United States', it emerged definitely from American racial sources"; and, Pound added, "the story of American letters cannot be told without mention of it".[25] Where, then, did the crucial influence of *The Criterion* lie? Eliot's prestige as a poet certainly heightened its influence, but the answer to the question must ultimately be sought in the width of its scope and in its sustained point of view. Whereas the early *Nouvelle Revue Française,* in its rebellion against the confusion of literature and "life", had battled for an autonomous aestheticism and a classicism, *The Criterion* kept a vigilant watch

---

[23]   "The Function of the Critical Quarterly", *SoR,* I, 3 (Winter 1936), 558.
[24]   The best introduction to *The Criterion* is Malcolm Bradbury, "*The Criterion*: A Literary Review in Retrospect", *London Magazine,* V, 2 (February 1958), 41-54. An early article on *The Criterion* was written by Delmore Schwartz ("*The Criterion,* 1922-1939", *Purpose,* XI, 4 [Oct.-Dec. 1939], 225-237). See also Herbert Howarth, *Notes on Some Figures behind T. S. Eliot* (Boston, 1964), *passim.*
[25]   "Small Magazines", 698.

over both the making of literature and the conditions which influenced it.

Eliot was in essential agreement with the aestheticism and the classicism propagated by the *N.R.F.* In an early editorial in defence of the autonomy of literature, he wrote: "A literary review should maintain the application, in literature, of principles which have their consequences also in politics and in private conduct; and it should maintain them without tolerating any confusion of the purposes of pure literature with the purposes of politics or ethics." A work of literature, then, is autonomous; nothing must be read into it. But it is the function of the literary review not only to maintain "the autonomy and disinterestedness of literature", but at the same time to exhibit the relations of literature "to all the other activities, which, together with literature, are the components of life".[26] This editorial, incidentally, was quoted with approval by the editors of *The Dial*. Three years later, after *The Criterion* had loosened its ties with its benefactress, Viscountess Rothermere, Eliot wrote a more confident and outspoken statement of the function of the literary review, which is worth quoting from at some length:

I have seen the birth and death of several purely literary periodicals; and I say of all of them that in isolating the concept of literature they destroy the life of literature. It is not merely that there is not enough good literature, even good second-rate literature, to fill the pages of *any* review; or that in a *purely* literary review the work of a man of genius may appear almost side by side with some miserable counterfeit of his own style. The profounder objection is the impossibility of defining the frontiers, or limiting the context of 'literature'. ... We will not include irrelevant information, subjects of technical and limited interest, or subjects of current political and economic controversy. We must include besides 'creative' work and literary criticism, any material which should be operative on general ideas – the results of contemporary work in history, archeology, anthropology, even of the more technical sciences when those results are of such a nature to be valuable to the man of general culture and when they can be made intelligible to him.[27]

[26] "Notes: The Function of a Literary Review", *The Criterion*, I, 4 (July 1923), 421.
[27] "The Idea of a Literary Review", *The Criterion*, IV, 1 (January 1926), 3, 4. Two years earlier Eliot had written an interesting letter of advice to

Another literary review edited in England which showed an affinity to the American tradition was F. R. Leavis's *Scrutiny* (1932-1953). If we would compare the best years of this review, the 'Thirties, with the corresponding declining years of *The Criterion,* we would very probably find a higher percentage of first-rate critical articles per issue in *Scrutiny,* but there is an equally strong probability that, as a literary review, *Scrutiny* would strike us as insular. It is also true that in the later 'Thirties *Scrutiny* exerted the greater influence on its American contemporaries. The decline from the high ideals of the literary review which *The Criterion* had tried to live up to was unavoidable. A similar trend is noticeable in the United States where the cosmopolitan *Dial* was followed by the more specialized, academic *Southern Review. The Criterion* had been an international magazine; it had attempted "to provide in London a local forum of international thought".[28] Changing conditions made this increasingly difficult. They are described in Eliot's last editorial of January 1939:

Gradually communications became more difficult, contributions more uncertain, and new and important foreign contributors more difficult to discover. The 'European mind', which one had mistakenly thought might be renewed and fortified, disappeared from view: there were fewer writers in any country who seemed to have anything to say to the intellectual public of another. Divisions of political theory became more important; alien minds took alien ways, and Britain and France appeared to be progressively nowhere. Here in England, a definitely post-war generation began to speak. At this stage, our efforts turned to what was possible in a situation of enforced insularity. . . .[29]

The effect of the changing political and intellectual conditions

---

The Transatlantic Review: "But a review is not measured by the number of stars and scoops that it gets. Good literature is produced by a few queer people in odd corners; the use of a review is not to force talent, but to create a favourable atmosphere. ... In *The Criterion* we have endeavoured not to discriminate in favour of either youth or age, but to find good work which either could not appear elsewhere at all, or would not appear elsewhere to such advantage" ("Communications", *The Transatlantic Review,* I, 1 [January 1924], 96).
[28] "Last Words", *The Criterion,* XVIII, 71 (January 1939), 271.
[29] *Ibid.,* 271-272.

on the different American reviews will be traced in due course. We shall also at different points investigate the specific resemblances between *The Criterion* and *Scrutiny* and their American fellow journals. The effect of other English magazines, such as *The Athenaeum, The Adelphi,* and *The Calendar of Modern Letters,* on the American tradition has been negligible, except perhaps indirectly through *The Criterion* and *Scrutiny*.

It is inherent in the nature of the highbrow literary review that it prints criticism as well as creative writing. The amount of the criticism published in the different American magazines varied greatly, as did their interest in various non-literary matters, but they all eschewed the danger, which Eliot warned against, of the purely literary periodical. They were all, in different degrees, magazines of engagement, political or otherwise. A review has a larger potential influence than a literary miscellany. Even the most "literary" of the American reviews, *The Dial,* was more than a miscellany. Its reviews, chronicles and foreign letters, the choice of its poetry and fiction, and the composition of the individual issues spoke for a definite and consistent editorial policy. Its success was largely due to the productivity of the literary *avant-garde* of the early 'Twenties and to its close bonds with Europe. But when in the later 'Twenties literary creativity declined, *The Dial* failed to adjust itself to the changing scene; the result was ineffectuality and preciousness.

Its successor, *The Hound & Horn,* was more adaptable. It was alive to the intellectual and artistic movements of its time; its success must indeed be sought in its versatility. It was a magazine of the early 'Thirties, and the political and economic pressures of that era influenced it profoundly. It examined a number of literary programmes with political overtones, such as humanism, agrarianism, and Marxism, only to be confirmed in its conviction that the partisan critic cannot be trusted to give an objective judgment. It therefore advocated a technical criticism – which did not tolerate the belletristic approach of some of the older contributors to *The Dial* – which would ideally result in a combined verdict on both the artistry and the content of a work of literature. Its contemporary, *The Symposium,* started out as a magazine entirely devoted to criticism and its essentially critical character was hardly affected by the imaginative writing in its later issues. Although, in contrast to *The Hound & Horn,* it refused to allot space to contemporary movements merely because they were contemporary, it constitutes perhaps a more profound commentary on the intellectual vitality of the age. Because of its astute editorship – and partly because most of its contents were critical – it achieved an unparalleled intellectual unity in its individual numbers and a continuing discussion from issue to issue. But its career was a short one. It died after a short but intense discussion of the Marxist ideology; the editors could not agree upon the politics of their magazine.

In a later chapter we shall trace in which ways *The Symposium* combined traits of the temper of both *Partisan Review* and *The Southern Review.* These magazines continued the tradition of the literary review later in the 'Thirties, but there cannot be any doubt that *The Southern Review* was the closer heir to that tradition. Although it was edited in the South it appealed to a national audience. Its temper was conservative but its pages were open to dissenting views if they were intelligently and persuasively expressed. The strength of *The Southern Review* lay in its consolidated body of contributors and in its unobtrusive but intelligent editorship. Its point of view was centred in an opposition to the ever increasing strength of what it called "positivism" – the application of rational, scientific criteria to all human activities and faculties including the imagination. It became known as an organ of the new criticism, but it was more than that. To a greater extent, however, than its predecessors it appealed to an academic audience. It exercised an extraordinary influence not only on critical writing but also on the teaching of literature in the universities.

The companion magazine of its later years and its legitimate successor was *The Kenyon Review.* For almost a quarter of a century this magazine was edited from Gambier, Ohio, by John Crowe Ransom, a friend of the *Southern Review* editors, Cleanth Brooks and Robert Penn Warren. It continued the propagation of the new criticism but it was less satisfactory as a literary review in as far as it operated on a narrower intellectual basis. It was joined by *The Sewanee Review* which, under a new editorship, was completely refurbished in the early 'Forties. The final chapter of this study will investigate the close personal and ideological bonds between the *Southern, Kenyon,* and *Sewanee* reviews and compare their achievement to that of a somewhat different magazine, *Partisan Review.*

In retrospect, with a view to the literary situation of the 1960's, *Partisan Review* appears to have been the most important review of the 'Forties although, at the time, the influence of *The Kenyon Review* was perhaps more pervasively felt. *Partisan Review* had started out as a Marxist magazine and it was the only one of a host of Marxist contemporaries that had sufficient intellectual resilience to adapt itself successfully to the rapid political changes of the later 'Thirties without sacrificing its radical temper. In the 'Forties, its literary point of view moved closer to that of its fellow reviews, the *Southern, Kenyon,* and *Sewanee,* but its rationalistic and positivistic temper remained unchanged. It kept a closer, more belligerent watch over its surroundings than its contemporaries.

One way of characterizing the difference between *Partisan Review* and, say, *The Kenyon Review* is Eric Bentley's distinction between "journalistic" and "academic". "In breaking the barriers between past and present, it is the function of the 'journalistic' magazine to march with the moment, to make us aware what the present is. The function of the 'academic' magazine is to show that *all* the past is 'usable' if we learn how to use it." [30] We should also bear in mind that *Partisan Review* was edited from New York and that its contemporaries were edited away from the larger urban centres and were mainly identified with the South. But whatever valuable work is still being done, the Southern "renaissance" is past and regionalism in literature is declining. The new criticism, which was sponsored by the reviews and which must be considered the most important critical movement of the century, is now more important for the effect

---

[30]   "Little Magazines", *KR*, IX, 1 (Spring 1947), 285.

it has had on our critical awareness than as a critical method. A number of other critical approaches which in its campaign for the recognition of fundamentals the new criticism had rejected too confidently, have been rehabilitated. It would appear that the urban, "journalistic" branch of the literary review is more relevant to the 'Sixties than the more detached "academic" branch. The relative historical contributions of the individual reviews can only be assessed in a detailed study of their files.

IV

The preceding remarks are offered by way of introduction. They suggest some general notions which will be worked out in the following chapters. They are necessarily sketchy but, it is hoped, will acquaint the reader with the objectives of this study. This is not a history of modern American literature, although few aspects of it were left unrepresented or unexplored in the reviews. Nor is it a history of modern American criticism, although some of the major developments in that criticism issued from the reviews. This study will follow through the interests of the different magazines, be they literary, cultural or political, and, in the light of the common tradition, assess their achievements as literary reviews.

2

THE DIAL (1920–1929)

I

The Dial is a name of considerable distinction in the history of American literature. It is associated with Ralph Waldo Emerson and Margaret Fuller and the New England transcendentalists in the early 1840's and it appeared again on the cover of a Chicago fortnightly magazine in 1880.[1] For our purposes it will be sufficient to give a quick summary of the events preceding the publication of the reconstructed *Dial* in January 1920 under the editorship of Scofield Thayer and James Sibley Watson. A detailed account of the events may be found in Nicholas Joost's recent history of *The Dial*, 1912-1920.[2] Joost details the story of *The Dial*'s move to New York in the summer of 1918; the subsequent editorial dissent which primarily reflected the split between John Dewey and his pupil Randolph Bourne over American participation in the first World War; Scofield Thayer's financial support of the magazine and the tensions that led him to disengage himself from it in December 1918; and the protracted death-struggle of the fortnightly liberal *Dial* during the

---

[1] For further information, see Fredric Mosher, "Chicago's 'Saving Remnant': Francis Fisher Browne, William Morton Payne, and the *Dial* (1880-1892)" (unpublished doctoral dissertation), University of Illinois, 1950.

[2] *Years of Transition: The Dial, 1912-1920* (Barre, Mass., 1967). See also Joost's account of *The Dial* of the 1920's, *Scofield Thayer and 'The Dial', An Illustrated History* (Carbondale and Edwardsville, 1964), and G. A. M. Janssens, "*The Dial* and the 'Twenties", *The Yale Review*, LIV, 2 (Winter 1965), 282-284. The contemporary interest in *The Dial* and its era was underscored by the publication of another, less interesting book, William Wasserstrom's *The Time of 'The Dial'* (Syracuse, N.Y., 1963).

first ten months of 1919. During these months Scofield Thayer laid plans with James Sibley Watson, who had contributed some reviews to the fortnightly *Dial,* to buy out Martyn Johnson, the then editor. This was accomplished in November 1919. The first monthly *Dial* under the editorship of Scofield Thayer, with Stewart Mitchell as Managing Editor and Dr. Watson as President of the Dial Publishing Company, appeared in January 1920. Thayer had come to see "the anomaly of putting up money for a paper and letting others have the fun of running it".[3]

Who were these two friends, Thayer and Watson, who combined to fight "the immortal battle of beauty against ugliness?" [4] Though both were Harvard graduates and men of independent wealth, and though both were devoted to art and literature and generous in their support of artists and their causes, they struck their contemporaries as very different personalities. "To see Dr. Watson and Mr. Scofield Thayer together was something to remember", wrote their friend Llewelyn Powys, and he continued characteristically: "It would have required a Henry James to tabulate and record each interesting tarot card of this astounding association." [5] Powys's wife, Alyse Gregory, *The Dial*'s Managing Editor during 1924 and half of 1925, had this to say about editorial conferences:

Like Parliament after some public scandal, the staff held post mortem meetings each month following the publication of the magazine. Scofield would arrive with a long sheet of paper on which he had meticulously noted down every error, and each would be remorselessly tracked to the guilty person. These were painful occasions, redeemed by the presence of Dr. Watson, whose quick and indulgent understanding offered balm to all. The most tangled problem he could unravel, the most ruffled feelings appease.[6]

Thayer was highstrung and moody; Watson tolerant and modest. Their different personalities are mirrored in their common enterprise. *The Dial*'s setting at 152 West 13th Street, "the three-storey brick building with carpeted stairs, fireplace and white mantelpiece rooms, business office in the first storey front par-

---

3 Robert Morss Lovett, *All Our Years* (New York, 1948), p. 155.
4 E. E. Cummings, *Six Non-Lectures* (Cambridge, Mass., 1953), p. 50.
5 *The Verdict of Bridlegoose* (New York, 1926), p. 165.
6 *The Day is Gone* (New York, 1948), p. 211.

lour" and the "constant atmosphere of excited triumph" among
the staff, have been depicted by Marianne Moore in her charming
reminiscences of the years 1925 to 1929 when she edited *The
Dial*.[7]

By January 1920 the course of the "new" *Dial* was set, and
from then till its demise in July 1929 it appeared regularly every
month. Its regularity and its uniform, sober appearance were
external characteristics which immediately set it off from the
host of little magazines which sprang up and faded and were
rekindled during the 'Twenties. But it was *The Dial*'s payment
of contributors that did more than anything to gain it a unique
position. Its generous remuneration of $20 a page for poetry,
two cents a word for prose,[8] and $2 for Briefer Mentions (*The
Dial*'s very short reviews of an average length of 120 words) was
matched by no other comparable magazine of the time. *The
Dial*'s policy of payment did not allow "special prices for special
contributors − a phase of chivalry towards beginners", Marianne
Moore remembers, "that certain of them suspiciously disbelieved
in".[9] The staff themselves were not remunerated for their contributions.

It was indeed the rule that there were to be no special prices
for special contributors, and certainly during the editorship of
Marianne Moore this rule was strictly enforced, but in the earlier
years of the magazine there were exceptions which drew criticism
from several quarters. "Different people have complained to us",
Thayer wrote to Sherwood Anderson on 17 July 1920, "because
we have not paid absolutely all our contributors at the same
rate. We have now determined henceforth to pay everybody our

[7]   "The Dial", *Life and Letters Today*, XXVII, 40 (December 1940), 175-
176, 178. Marianne Moore received the *Dial* Award for 1924, became
"Acting Editor" in June 1925, and Editor in January 1927.
[8]   Scofield Thayer to Sherwood Anderson, September 15, 1920: "You
will, I trust, be glad to hear that we are now able to raise our rates for
prose, though to nothing such as we should be at one with you in wishing
they were. Our rate for prose is henceforth two cents the word" (Anderson
papers, Newberry Library). The rate for poetry was $10 a page during the
first two years instead of $20 in later years.
[9]   "The Dial" (Part Two), *Life and Letters Today*, XXVIII, 41 (January
1941), 9.

regular rates;" but a few months later, on 15 September 1920, Thayer, after announcing that the rates for prose would be raised, contradicted his earlier determination: "On exceptional occasions we may pay something above this new rate." [10] Although these occasions were few and far between, they drew the resentment of an important contributor, Ezra Pound, who thought it "ridic. for Sher. Anderson and old washbasket Geo. Moore to get paid a higher rate than we do." [11] Pound's remark was probably prompted by the *cause célèbre* in this matter, Thayer's negotiations with Eliot about publication of *The Waste Land* in *The Dial*. On 29 January 1921, Thayer offered Eliot $150 for the poem which would cover some eleven pages. *The Dial's* rates for poetry were then apparently still only $10 a page, so that this offer of a "round sum" slightly exceeded these rates. Eliot, however, flatly requested £856; he felt Thayer's offer to be "inadequate for my poem, considering the amount of work that I had put into it and also considering the vast amount of verse, which in comparison with most writers, I refrained from writing".[12] Thayer, on the other hand, thought *The Waste Land* "very disappointing" and would rather have secured for *The Dial* "the work of such recognised American authors as Edith Wharton".[13] Negotiations continued and thanks to the mediation of Dr. Watson and Ezra Pound, the manuscript was in the possession of the editors by mid-August 1922. Eliot was paid $130 for thirteen printed pages and was promised the *Dial* Award of $2000 for 1922.

This episode illustrates the difficulties the editors experienced in carrying out their policy of equal payment to all contributors. As was to be expected, it was often the better established writers who chafed against this strict house-rule. George Moore, for instance, wrote: "I hope the *Dial* has given up the notion of paying

[10]   Anderson papers.
[11]   Letter to Richard Aldington, March 16, 1922 (marked "second letter"): Aldington papers, University of Texas Library at Austin.
[12]   Letter to Richard Aldington, July 4, 1922, Aldington papers.
[13]   Letter to Alyse Gregory, October 22, 1922, quoted in Joost, *Scofield Thayer and 'The Dial'*, p. 111. For a full description of *The Waste Land* episode, see Joost, pp. 157-165.

all contributors the same price, a notion which seems to me unreasonable, for one contributor is worth ten times as much as another;" [14] for today's reader this statement but underlines the irony of the rise and fall of literary reputations. For the majority of the contributors, however, the rates of payment were royal remuneration, and the favourable exchange-rate of the dollar in post-war Europe was undoubtedly responsible for *The Dial*'s distinguished array of foreign contributions.

The Dial's manner of payment for contributions shows that it was the intention of the editors not only to secure the best contemporary writing for their magazine but also to support deserving artists. It must be borne in mind that, according to Dr. Watson's recollection, Thayer had initially approached him with the vague general plan either of starting a magazine or of setting up a fund for artists. [15] When in 1919 Thayer heard that James Joyce was in straitened circumstances he immediately cabled seven hundred dollars and within a fortnight Watson added three hundred more. [16] During the time of *The Dial* both Thayer and Watson contributed to a fund to support the painter John Marin, and Watson's generosity to a rival magazine, *The Little Review,* is gratefully recorded in Margaret Anderson's *My Thirty Years' War*. [17] Thayer's idea of a fund for artists was realized in connection with the magazine when the editors established the *Dial Award*. It was described in the following terms: "The DIAL an-

[14] Letter to Marianne Moore, March 1, 1926, *Dial* papers, Yale University Library.
[15] Charles Norman, *E. E. Cummings: The Magic-Maker* (New York, 1964), p. 115.
[16] Cf. Richard Ellmann, *James Joyce* (New York, 1959), p. 471. Wyndham Lewis possibly alluded to the same occasion when he wrote that it was through Ezra Pound that "a very considerable sum of money was put at Joyce's disposal, at the critical moment" ("Early London Environment", *T. S. Eliot: A Symposium*, compiled by Tambimuttu and Richard March [London, 1965 (1948)], p. 31). Ellmann writes that Thayer heard about Joyce's plight from his friends Padraic and Mary Colum.
[17] *My Thirty Years' War* (New York, 1930), pp. 188-189. Marin was one of Alfred Stieglitz's *protégés*. Edmund Wilson suspected Stieglitz of "having rather unduly inflated" Marin's reputation; "I might have discovered this if I had been left alone with the pictures" (*The American Earthquake: A Documentary of the Twenties and Thirties* [Garden City, N.J., 1958], p. 102).

nounces that on January the first of each year it will acknowledge the service to letters of some one of those who have, during the twelvemonth, contributed to its pages by the payment to him of two thousand dollars." [18] "It is simply an additional payment, recognizing the writer's service to letters", wrote Gilbert Seldes, Stewart Mitchell's successor as Managing Editor, to George Saintsbury,[19] and the editors in "Comment" after "Comment" (*The Dial*'s editorials) emphasized that it was their aim to give an American artist leisure from the struggle for his daily bread. "Our insistence that the Dial's award is not a prize is frequently taken to be a characteristic pedantry on our part", they wrote in their August 1923 "Comment", but they insisted that they were using words in their accurate and accepted sense; that a prize was something contested for and that an award was a gift. Since the advent of the *Dial* Award was an important event on the American literary scene and since, at the same time, it proclaimed the editors' vote of confidence in an American writer, it was well advertised. The project was announced to three hundred newspaper editors who gave it "space, headlines, preferred position, and comment to a gratifying degree", and Seldes frankly told the first recipient Sherwood Anderson that he wanted "to get as much publicity to the award as can decently be got".[20]

Another external characteristic which distinguished *The Dial* from contemporary little magazines was its circulation. It did not take long for the magazine to outstrip its competitors, and it reached its peak, when, for January 1923, 18000 copies were printed. At that time the editors had fond hopes that the magazine might become financially self-supporting, but circulation gradually dropped, to 10000 copies in late 1925, and eventually back to 4000. Towards the end of the 'Twenties this seemed to Dr. Watson "a natural number". But although *The Dial* had a remarkable circulation for a magazine of its type, Watson remembered that the "annual deficit was usually around thirty

---

[18]   "Announcement", *Dial*, LXX, 6 (June 1921), 730.
[19]   October 10, 1922, *Dial* papers.
[20]   "Comment", *Dial*, LXXI, 2 (August 1921), 250; letter, Seldes to Anderson, October 26, 1921, Anderson papers, Newberry Library.

thousand dollars; but some years it was fifty thousand dollars".[21]
This was the price for bringing out a magazine of arts and letters
whose monthly size ranged from a maximum 138 pages in its
earliest days to a regular ninety pages in later years.

II

The preceding remarks constitute the barest outline of the physical setting of the magazine and the mechanics of its operation.
We shall now turn to the files of the magazine itself, examine its
attitudes to its cultural and literary environment, and try to trace
some of the major influences which shaped these attitudes. First
a word about its general editorial policy.

The Dial's editorial taste was wider than the editorial taste of
any of its successors. It was not militantly *avant-garde* nor did
it merely flaunt established names. "The inevitable and 'impossible' pieces of work", the editors wrote in their "Comment" of
March 1920, "give the special tone to a magazine which must,
in the interest of completeness, publish a number of other things
which are, in any case, predestined for publication". Consequently, they were grateful for the rebuke that they were printing
things no other magazine would print, as well as for the praise that
they were bringing into the light work that any publication would
be proud of. *The Dial* hoped always to deserve both comments.
This editorial policy, or perhaps rather, this catholic taste, was
proclaimed with remarkable consistency throughout the files of
The Dial. Two months later, in May 1920, the editors wrote that
the place of a contributor in any "movement" – backward or
forward – did not concern them, and this open attitude was
reinforced in the first issue of *The Dial*'s second year: "Also the
whole point of The Dial was to give exponents of both the accepted and the unaccepted an agreeable carpet whereon they
could fitly and cheek by jowl and in their very different ways

[21]   Norman, *E. E. Cummings*, p. 116; I have taken my circulation figures
from Joost, *op. cit.*, pp. 42, 91. In a letter to Norman, Watson remembered
twenty-two thousand as "the high watermark".

perform. To cage off either group was almost to turn the show into a farce." [22]

This generous attitude to the old and the new in literature would suggest a lack of direction to which, perhaps, Van Wyck Brooks alluded when he wrote that "only good taste unified the contents of *The Dial*".[23] "Good taste" is a misleading term which would indicate that *The Dial* was a mere miscellany – Brooks actually used this designation – and which discounts the fact that taste is a conglomerate of prejudices and predilections which very rarely escapes the shaping influence of contemporary ideas, vogues and movements. Thayer and Watson, although of independent minds, were very much of their time, and their choice of contributions and contributors is a fair index to the influences that inspired it.

The Dial has often been called the successor of *The Seven Arts, "a Seven Arts* without politics".[24] As this notion has become a maxim of modern magazine lore it will bear some looking into.[25] *The Seven Arts* had a run of twelve issues during the years 1916 and 1917; closely associated with it are the names of James Oppenheim, Waldo Frank, Van Wyck Brooks, Paul Rosenfeld, and Randolph Bourne. Its demise was precipitated by Bourne's outspokenly pacifist ideas after the United States had declared war; these ideas gained the magazine an anti-patriotic reputation which prompted its "angel", Mrs. A. K. Rankine, to withdraw her subsidy.

The Seven Arts' editors were very specific about the nature of their venture, the flavour of which is best conveyed in the peculiar blend of aggressive and prophetic rhetoric which, from the be-

---

[22] "Comment", *Dial*, LXX, 1 (January 1921), 123.

[23] *Days of the Phoenix* (New York, 1957), p. 66.

[24] S. Foster Damon, *Amy Lowell, A Chronicle* (Boston and New York, 1935), p. 519. The following pages will appear in essay form as "*The Dial* and *The Seven Arts*" in *Papers on Language & Literature*, IV, 1968.

[25] This notion reached its extreme form in Wasserstrom's *The Time of 'The Dial'* (Syracuse, N.Y., 1963), for a sober reply to which, see Lewis Mumford's review in *The New York Review of Books*, II, 1 (February 20, 1964), 3-5; see also Wasserstrom's reply, *The New York Review of Books*, II, 5 (April 16, 1964), 19.

ginning, gave the magazine its characteristic tone. Both ideas and tone are exemplified in the "Announcement" of the magazine which was issued as a circular after its first number had appeared:

American artists like Whistler, American writers like Henry James, gave up America in despair and did their work abroad. Even today there is a feeling among artists that this country is provincial, and that their work is not appreciated here until it has been approved by foreign authority.

Against this attitude *The Seven Arts* appears: it is a magazine of American artists, American authors, American critics for America – possibly for a new America, an America waking up to that self-consciousness which is the first step toward national greatness. In this faith *The Seven Arts* was conceived . . .

It would seem as if we had appeared at the psychological moment, to become a part of the forces which are giving America a new light and a new leadership.

It is instructive to compare the first paragraph of this statement with a sentence from the "Announcement" of the *Dial* Award which Thayer and Watson issued in *The Dial* of June 1921: "Too many Mary Gardens and Henry Jameses had had to go abroad for recognition; we found it high time somebody set up to recognize good work at home." The editors, there seems little doubt, were furthering an objective of the earlier *Seven Arts,* but the two subsequent paragraphs of that magazine's "Announcement" must needs sound very alien to a reader of *The Dial.* The blatant cultural nationalism of the second paragraph and the starry-eyed faith of the third are clearly anachronistic in almost any discussion of the 'Twenties, when so many young artists turned their back on their native country and when the word "reformer" had virtually disappeared from the highbrow's vocabulary.

This is not to say that the *Dial* Award was the only viable connection with *The Seven Arts*; some of the idealism that fired that magazine lay at the root of the new *Dial* and the central inspiration behind both magazines was Randolph Bourne.[26] "His

---

[26] Cf. Lewis Mumford, "The Image of Randolph Bourne", *The New Republic*, LXIV (September 24, 1930), 151. Recently Gorham Munson

coming was the greatest thing that happened to *The Seven Arts*", wrote its editor James Oppenheim,[27] and the first item of *The Dial*'s January 1920 number was Bourne's posthumous "Autobiographical Chapter" which appears rather an act of homage on the part of the editors than a discriminating literary choice. Thayer had been an admirer of *The Seven Arts* – he had offered financial assistance when the magazine was about to fold up [28] – and he had also been a close friend of Bourne's. Indeed, had Bourne lived, the new *Dial* would have looked quite different. "When Thayer had first laid plans for a magazine", Watson wrote to Charles Allen, "it was his intention, in which I concurred, to divide the magazine into two sections, literary and political", and Bourne was to have had a completely free hand with the political section.[29] This plan seems to fit in with Bourne's idea that art and politics could be separated only at each other's peril.[30] It is very difficult, however, to imagine *The Dial* in an activist political position after the debacle of Bourne's fight against American participation in World War I.

Thayer's (and Alyse Gregory's) close connection with Bourne and the *Seven Arts* group, the Young Generation of the second decade, is very noticeable in the early issues of *The Dial,* but we immediately find a counter influence at work, the influence of Ezra Pound and T. S. Eliot, and the influence of the even younger generation of Gilbert Seldes, Malcolm Cowley, Kenneth Burke, and perhaps Edmund Wilson, which was largely related to the editorial influence of James Sibley Watson. It will be instructive to trace the reputations of some of the closest

---

has drawn a somewhat lugubrious picture of the organizational "behind-the-throne-power" of Dr. Beatrice Hinkle, "a pioneer psychoanalyst of the Jungian persuasion". Both Oppenheim and Mrs. Rankine were her patients ("Herald of the Twenties", *Forum*, III, 8 [Autumn 1961], 7).

[27] "The Story of *The Seven Arts*", *American Mercury*, XX, 78 (June 1930), 163.
[28] Cf. Waldo Frank, "Symposium on the Little Magazines", *Golden Goose*, III, 1 (1951), 21.
[29] Allen, "The Dial", *The University Review*, X, 2 (Winter 1943), 101.
[30] Bourne, *War and the Intellectuals, Essays 1915-1919*, edited and with an Introduction by Carl Resek (Harper Torchbook, 1964), p. xii.

associates of *The Seven Arts* in the pages of *The Dial* in order
to arrive at a more precise estimate of the influence of the earlier
magazine.

The most optimistic and the most naive of these was James
Oppenheim, whose gushy, Whitmanesque rhetoric and indiscrim-
inate nativism are fairly exemplified in his antithesis of "Europa":

Whither goest thou, Europa, whither goest thou
      dusty and grown aged and
withering at the breasts?

and "My Land":

Not for long can I be angry with the most beautiful − I look out of
my vengefulness, and see her so young, so vastly young. . . .[31]

In February 1920 Oppenheim contributed a short article to *The
Dial* with the characteristic title "Poetry − Our First National
Art" but when, in August of the following year, Kenneth Burke
reviewed his autobiographical novel, *The Mystic Warrior,* it was
in terms which indicated a completely different conception of
literature; Burke criticized its lack of form: "The real objection
to the frankly autobiographical 'fiction' is that the editing of
one's accidental experience offers so little opportunity for an
imaginative aggressiveness, a sense of line, mass, organization,
and the like." [32] Waldo Frank, another *Seven Arts* regular, suffered a very similar fate at the pen of Burke when the latter
reviewed *Rahab* and *City Block*. Burke found the two books "not
finally beautiful. They lack just that element of cold carving, that
bloodless autopsy of the emotions, which allows Mallarmé so
near an approach to perfection." He proceeded with a quite outspoken statement of preference which sets the tone of a new era:
"Mr. Frank is as serious as Buddha, which is a dangerous thing
to be in an age which could produce Ulysses. If we have to
choose between an artist who is passionless and clever, and an

---

[31] *The Solitary* (New York, 1919), pp. 87, 123.
[32] "The Editing of Oneself", *Dial*, LXXI, 2 (August 1921), 234.

artist who is tumultuous and non-clever, it is a sad pair to choose from, but the former would be nearer to art." [33]

Oppenheim and Frank were minor contributors. The *Seven Arts* tradition in the pages of *The Dial* was mainly continued by Van Wyck Brooks and Paul Rosenfeld and by *The Seven Arts'* favourite living author, Sherwood Anderson.[34] Both Brooks and Anderson received the *Dial* Award, and Rosenfeld was the magazine's music critic. They appeared most frequently in the early issues of *The Dial*; later on their reputations declined till Anderson and Rosenfeld were virtually eclipsed in the era of the new criticism, while Brooks began his investigation of the American past, not as in his studies of Twain and James to expose its cultural shallowness, but to cherish its Americanness.

Brooks's early contributions to *The Dial* were two parts of *The Ordeal of Mark Twain,* his highly personal, psychological interpretation of Twain's fight against the ambience of 19th century America. Robert Morss Lovett's review of Brooks's book, in the September 1920 *Dial,* was more descriptive than evaluative but it ended by saying that Brooks had not only recounted the Ordeal of Mark Twain but had also written a morality which might be called Every American.[35] More stringently formulated expressions of the disenchantment of *The Dial* with Brooks, and of Brooks with *The Dial,* were not long in appearing. "One reads many of the strange experiments in *The Dial* and the *Little Review,* for example (many, but by no means all) with a sense of nothing but confusion and bafflement", wrote Brooks as editor of *The Freeman* in September 1920,[36] and Watson, under the pseudonym W. C. Blum, countered this criticism by saying that Brooks had been criticizing modern literature without naming

---

[33] "The Consequences of Idealism", *Dial*, LXXIII, 4 (October 1922), 451, 452. Towards the end of the decade Frank still wrote: "To our tragic artists there remains only the apocalyptic method" (*The Re-Discovery of America* [New York, 1929], p. 140).

[34] Cf. James Oppenheim, "The Story of *The Seven Arts*", 161: "It so happened that we were paying him [Anderson] more than our other contributors, because his work was so good and because he needed it."

[35] "An American Morality", *Dial*, LXIX, 3 (September 1920), 299.

[36] "A Reviewer's Notebook", *The Freeman*, II, 27 (September 15, 1920), 22.

work or author. Watson, who was not speaking in an editorial capacity, attacked the entire *Seven Arts* group in the same article: "The Seven Arts group was too ready to disregard and despise as un-American very admirable and very American poets like Ezra Pound, Marianne Moore, and William Carlos Williams for one to have much faith in their affection for art." [37] During 1923, however, Brooks contributed to *The Dial* parts of his book on Henry James and the January 1924 "Comment" announced Brooks as the recipient of the third *Dial* Award in recognition of his labours as "a critic whose chief interest it is that American writers should occur, should be able, in the American society, to exist and to create". But the editors were careful to add that they recognized the supreme importance of such a figure without necessarily agreeing with the whole body of his doctrine. Mary Colum's essay "An American Critic: Van Wyck Brooks", published in the same issue, emphasized in similar fashion Brooks's role as a pathfinder for the artist.

There is little doubt that this public recognition of Brooks was made at Thayer's suggestion and that it was probably half-nostalgic.[38] Watson, it is true, admired Brooks's editorial talents, but he had little use for his criticism. When Gorham Munson published his essay on Brooks in *The Dial* of January 1925 (exactly one year after the announcement of the Award), his strictures and censure of Brooks's critical position were nothing more than a systematic expression of the feeling against Brooks's criticism that had been building up in the pages of *The Dial* during the preceding years. In September 1925 appeared Alyse Gregory's review of *The Pilgrimage of Henry James*; her friendship with Brooks and her general sense of decorum are probably responsible for what is easily the most astonishing backhanded compliment in the reviewing pages of *The Dial*: "If one can bring to the reading of Mr. Brooks's study, however, a mind purged of preconceptions, washed quite clean indeed of any pre-

---

[37] "American Letter", *Dial*, LXX, 5 (May 1921), 563.
[38] Cf. Susan Turner, *A History of 'The Freeman'* (New York, 1963), p. 97. Miss Turner suggests that the *Dial* Award to Eliot was so phrased as to be a rebuke to Brooks and *The Freeman*.

vious knowledge of the subject, one's admiration will remain unshaken to the end." [39]

The history of Sherwood Anderson's reputation in *The Dial* shows a similar downward curve; the reader can trace it from the first *Dial* Award in January 1922 to an unfavourable 'Briefer Mention' of his *Notebook* in January 1927.[40] The decline of the reputations of Brooks and Anderson in the pages of *The Dial* as well as in the general context of the 'Twenties, was indeed so rapid and effective that their connection with the magazine has been totally obscured in the minds of some modern critics. When one of them, Charles Norman, enumerated the writers who received the *Dial* Award prior to Ezra Pound, he failed to mention both Anderson and Brooks.[41]

Anderson was *The Dial*'s favourite American story writer during its first year. At the time the regular contributor's rate for prose was $5 a page, but *The Dial* paid Anderson $100 for each of his early stories, "partly", as Thayer wrote, "because of a misunderstanding existing between us".[42] In a letter of introduc-

[39]   "A Superb Brief", *Dial*, LXXIX, 3 (September 1925), 238.

[40]   "The epitome of ultimate avant-garde response to Anderson is best seen in the pages of the *Dial*, which published him frequently, printed laudatory statements, and early in 1922 bestowed upon him the first *Dial* award for distinguished service to American letters, then in the next few years directly and allusively in reviews and other forms of comment gradually formulated a negative attitude toward him" (Brom Weber, *Sherwood Anderson*, University of Minnesota Pamphlets on American Writers, No. 43 [1964], p. 43).

[41]   Charles Norman, *Ezra Pound* (New York, 1960), p. 290: "The first recipient had been Eliot . . . , the second Marianne Moore . . . , the third E. E. Cummings . . . , and the fourth William Carlos Williams." For a more recent example, cf. Josephine Herbst's "Only the Best", *KR*, XXVII, 2 (Spring 1965), 355, which mentions Anderson, but leaves out Brooks and Cummings.

[42]   Letter to Anderson, July 17, 1920, Anderson papers. This misunderstanding had come about when Gilbert Cannan boasted, in Anderson's presence, that *The Dial* had paid him $200 for his story, "A Tragic End", which was published in the January 1920 *Dial*. According to Thayer this statement was untrue. "We paid Mr. Cannan one hundred dollars. We paid him one hundred and not fifty because we had no fiction ready for the January number and were forced to ask Mr. Cannan to write a story especially for us . . ." (Thayer to Anderson, October 8, 1920, Anderson papers).

tion to T. S. Eliot, Thayer called Anderson "our most distinguished writer of fiction",[43] and in later years Gilbert Seldes
wanted to film one of Anderson's most popular *Dial* stories,
"I'm A Fool". The eulogy on the occasion of the *Dial* Award to
Anderson in January 1922 was appropriately sung by Paul
Rosenfeld: "Sherwood Anderson is one in whom the power of
feeling has not been broken. He is one in whom the love of the
growing green in men, so mortally injured in most of us, has
found a way of healing itself of the wounds dealt it by the callous
society in which he sprung." [44] The underlying notion that most
modern men are intellectually well developed but emotionally
stunted, is in the best *Seven Arts* tradition, and the prose which
expresses it is a fair example of Rosenfeld's impressionistic, con-
voluted style. In the same issue of *The Dial* Robert Morss Lovett
reviewed Anderson's *The Triumph of the Egg,* a volume of short
stories which had then just come out, and praised his "persistent
effort to come to close grips with life" although he was not yet
completely successful in subduing his material. But in October
of that same year 1922 *The Dial* published the first instalment
of *Many Marriages* which ran on, seemingly interminably, till
March 1923 and marked the beginning of Anderson's failure.
When Edmund Wilson reviewed it in the following month he
could only state that Anderson's repetitions were becoming ter-
ribly boring.[45] The definitive, though mildly phrased verdict on

[43]   May 7, 1921, Anderson papers. Sometime later in the same year, however, Watson rejected the first of a series of "experimental things" entitled
"A Testament" (Seldes to Anderson, November 10, 1921, Anderson papers).
[44]   "Sherwood Anderson", *Dial*, LXXII, 1 (January 1922), 38. Anderson's
early attitude to Thayer and *The Dial* was singularly ungracious. See
Letters of Sherwood Anderson, selected and edited with an Introduction
and Notes by Howard Mumford Jones and Walter B. Rideout (Boston,
1953), p. 51. At the time of the *Dial* Award, however, Anderson's attitude
had substantially changed: "After all, the *Dial* is the one thing we have,
they are sincerely trying for something the rest of us are after also. How
could I be anything but pleased and flattered" (undated letter to Paul
Rosenfeld, published in *Paul Rosenfeld: Voyager in the Arts*, ed. Jerome
Mellquist and Lucie Wiese [New York, 1948], pp. 207-208).
[45]   "Many Marriages", *Dial*, LXXIV, 4 (April 1923), 399. Thayer's dissatisfaction is evident from a letter which he wrote to Gilbert Seldes on

Anderson was passed five months later by Alyse Gregory when she weighed the achievement of Anderson's four novels, two books of short stories, and a collection of poems, and found that Anderson had turned to more articulate authors in search of new methods and had "permitted his own native talent to become blighted by inattention, to wilt under the glaze formed over it by the betraying phrases, thought processes, and attitudes of others".[46]

The most important representative of the *Seven Arts* ethos in *The Dial* was Paul Rosenfeld and the magazine, even if it was not invariably enthusiastic about all of his contributions, remained loyal to him till the end. Rosenfeld was, in Brooks's words, "an absolute worshipper of art",[47] who in his use of language tried to recreate and to communicate some of the feeling, the intrinsic qualities, of the work of art he was discussing, be it painting, literature or music. His criticism was frankly impressionistic and his style florid, rhapsodic and sometimes exotic. It reminded an acquaintance of Llewelyn Powys of a

---

October 24, 1922, parts of which are quoted by Joost, *op. cit.*, p. 196: "to Thayer, to run 'any serials from the pen of Sherwood Anderson, certainly in the course of the next few years,' would be 'catastrophical for The Dial ... He is a good short story writer and we must have his best short stories; otherwise we require nothing from his pen. We only want serials when they are by masters'."

[46] "Sherwood Anderson", *Dial*, LXXV, 3 (September 1923), 244. The following passage from a letter of Alyse Gregory to Anderson, dated January 29, 1924, reveals one of the problems that face a contributing editor: "I have been looking, ever since I came to The Dial for a story from your pen, hoping that it might just suddenly be discovered in our mail. I am sure that if you read my article on your writing you must know that I do genuinely like and appreciate your work. I think I have always said that you were the most interesting and important American writing fiction today" (Anderson papers). Anderson expressed his annoyance at Miss Gregory's review in a letter to Paul Rosenfeld on January 15, 1924: "Can I be blamed for having an impersonal feeling about *Dial*? They seem to be always apologizing for me. I don't want particularly to be apologized for. The Gregory seems to be afraid to either praise or blame. The effort to keep her balance makes her, in my eyes, appear like one who has her feet on just nothing" (letter published in *Paul Rosenfeld: Voyager in the Arts*, p. 220).

[47] *Days of the Phoenix* (New York, 1957), p. 7.

"merchant of Samarkand unrolling with slow deliberation sashes of silk".[48] Rosenfeld's romantic temperament and his impressionistic approach did not endear him to the rising generation of exact formalist critics and he soon became the easy butt of the brassier writers in contemporary little magazines. "Criticism in New York", wrote jh (Jane Heap), in *The Little Review*, "is one of the allied fashion-designing trades. . . . Every smart journal has its Well-Dressed Man and its well-dressed artist feature. *The Dial* has Paul Rosenfeld." [49] An early vitriolic attack on Rosenfeld appeared in the third issue of *Secession,* in August 1922, under the title "Mr. Blunderbuss". Its author was Matthew Josephson and it probably inspired Edmund Wilson's "An Imaginary Conversation, Mr. Paul Rosenfeld and Mr. Matthew Josephson" which appeared in *The New Republic* on 9 April 1924, and which perfectly caught the tone of the dispute between the two generations:

The day for rhapsody [Wilson's Josephson asserted] as a substitute for exact analysis has long gone by. . . . We who have been lately in Germany and France and have had the advantage of an acquaintance with some of the more tonic figures of the younger generation such as Tzara and the other Dadaists realize that Eliot and Schoenberg and Joyce are as dead for the purposes of the present as Shakespeare, Wagner and Flaubert . . . it is commercialism, it is industrialism which has created this astounding world; if you would interpret it you must take it on its own terms. . . . And it is the vaudeville comedian or the comic artist who can catch the excitement of its hilarious brutality, the gusto of its gargantuan appetite. (XXXVIII, 181)

Rosenfeld, in Wilson's spoof, responds to this and similar tirades with a sober "Yes, I see: that is the real difference between us, I suppose. For me it is a serious matter but for you it is only a game." Ezra Pound who seems to have had a particular grudge against Rosenfeld, called him "Mr. Rosie Field"; "HAVE you ever met Rosie?", he asked *The Hound & Horn*'s editor Lincoln Kirstein, "The Dial's critik of mooZeek?" [50]

---

[48]   Llewelyn Powys, *op. cit.,* p. 139.
[49]   "The 'Art Season' ", *The Little Review*, VIII, 2 ("Picabia Number": Spring 1922), 59.
[50]   October 26, 1930: *Hound & Horn* papers, Yale University Library.

But although the hostility of the literary climate increasingly obscured Rosenfeld's reputation and impaired his confidence, he always had a number of admiring friends even after the time of *The Dial*,[51] and only recently Sherman Paul wrote a glowing introduction to a new edition of Rosenfeld's *Port of New York*, a collection of portraits of contemporary American artists and writers, several of which had first appeared in *The Dial*.[52] Rosenfeld's most important contribution to *The Dial* was his monthly "Musical Chronicle", which was not just a chatty catalogue of the musical events of the preceding month but often developed into a small-scale essay on a particular composer or *œuvre*. The "Musical Chronicle" was one of the three regular departments of *The Dial* – the other two were "The Theatre" and "Modern Art" – and has perhaps the most durable interest of the three, although the others were more representative of *The Dial*.

It will be clear that Rosenfeld's criticism was not of a type that could retain the sympathy of the editors for long. Indeed, several of his essays or suggestions for essays were rejected, and there are indications that his "Musical Chronicle" did not always meet with whole-hearted editorial approval. But although most of his contributions, like those of the others of the *Seven Arts* remnant, appeared in the early years of *The Dial*, his reputation in the reviewing pages did not fall off as spectacularly as those of Brooks and Anderson. Herbert J. Seligmann's review of *Port of New York* was laudatory throughout: "Paul Rosenfeld is a fortunate gift to American critical literature. Into our boneyard of erudition and theoretical writing he pours the excitement of

---

[51]   See the memorial volume *Paul Rosenfeld: Voyager in the Arts*, ed. Jerome Mellquist and Lucie Wiese (New York, 1948).
[52]   Urbana, Ill., 1961. Especially the essay on American painting (*Port of New York* title "Albert P. Ryder") drew much praise when it appeared in *The Dial* in December 1921. See, for instance, *The Letters of Hart Crane*, ed. Brom Weber (New York, 1952), p. 57 and undated letter of Sherwood Anderson to Paul Rosenfeld in *Paul Rosenfeld: Voyager in the Arts*, pp. 201-202. William Carlos Williams was no less enthusiastic: "I am admiring Paul Rosenfeld's article. ... I hope some day he will do something on American poets such as he did in that case on the painters" (Williams to Harriet Monroe, December 1921, *Poetry* papers, Chicago University Library).

music and paint, of sounds and colours and words joyfully apprehended. These are his life." [53] Seligmann praised Rosenfeld as the most variously cultivated among contemporary critics, thus concurring with the opinion of many of Rosenfeld's friends. Lewis Mumford and John Peale Bishop, in their reviews respectively of *Musical Chronicle (1917-1923)* and *Men Seen,* showed a similar respect and appreciation, and William Carlos Williams, in *The Dial* of November 1928, praised Rosenfeld's "ceaseless impersonal activity in the New York field for what he believes fine".[54] It should be pointed out that these four critics all remarked upon Rosenfeld's style, Mumford defending it energetically: "I see no occasion", he wrote, "to be irritated . . . in the failure of his prose to duplicate the plodding beat of those grey syllables that drop in an even pall over our thoughts. When Mr. Rosenfeld reminds words it is often with a great gain in colour and clearness."

The fortunes of Oppenheim, Frank, Brooks, Anderson, and Rosenfeld in the pages of *The Dial* clearly indicate the rapid decline of the *Seven Arts* ethos in the magazine. *The Seven Arts* has its place in any discussion of *The Dial* as a significant initial influence, which quickly lost force when it was countered by a new conception of the function and the importance of literature as literature rather than as a means towards "the emotional development of the race".[55] A further discussion of the contents of *The Dial* will bear this out. Whitman whom the *Seven Arts* critics had called their "Homer" [56] was no longer the central

---

[53]   "Port of New York", *Dial,* LXXVI, 6 (June 1924), 544. When Rosenfeld did not want to accept the burden of the "Musical Chronicle" for another season, in September 1927, he proposed Seligmann as one of three possible candidates for the job. Rosenfeld was again invited to do the Chronicle, but again declined.

[54]   Mumford, "Beyond Musical Criticism", *Dial,* LXXVIII, 5 (May 1925), 411-413; Bishop, "A Humanistic Critic", *Dial,* LXXIX, 2 (August 1925), 157-161; Williams, "Impasse and Imagery" (review of Rosenfeld's novel *The Boy in the Sun*), *Dial,* LXXXV, 5 (November 1928), 432.

[55]   "Editorial", *The Seven Arts,* I, 1 (November 1916), 56.

[56]   This epithet was first used in Romain Rolland's declaration "America and the Arts" (*The Seven Arts,* I, 1 [November 1916], 51); his "Your Homer" became Van Wyck Brooks's "Our Homer" (*The Seven Arts,* I, 3 [January 1917], 272). In the early 'Twenties, Waldo Frank proclaimed

inspiration. A young and influential *Dial* critic, Kenneth Burke, attacked "our neo-Whitmanite hoax, which strives to make art explode like a blunderbuss" and D. H. Lawrence stated quite simply: "Whitman's 'you' doesn't get me." [57]

The strongest factor which worked against *The Seven Arts'* influence was the association with *The Dial* of Kenneth Burke, Ezra Pound and T. S. Eliot. Burke's attitude to the *Seven Arts* group is exemplified by the quotations from his articles in the preceding paragraphs. He did not only contribute to *The Dial*; he also served it, off and on, in subordinate editorial capacities. His position is illumined by a letter he wrote offering his editorial services just before Marianne Moore was appointed managing editor in 1925: "I should not feel justified in doing this had I not, on so many occasions, talked of avoiding permanent jobs – a policy which, as I see it now, was designed more to convince myself than others yet can have the opposite effect of convincing others more than myself. As for credentials, I suppose I possess neither more nor less of them than during the three months I worked with you previously at The Dial. . . ." [58] Three and a half years later Burke wrote to Gilbert Seldes from the office of *The Dial*: "I am now celebrating my twenty-seventh substitution under this roof." [59] In 1928 his importance for contemporary American letters was honoured by the *Dial* Award. Both Eliot and Pound had received the same award, for 1922 and 1927 respectively, and the careers of both of them were closely connected with the first years of *The Dial*. Pound occasionally reported on the Paris scene and Eliot did the same for London. *The Waste Land* was *The Dial's* most spectacular *coup* but the magazine also published parts of *Hugh Selwyn Mauberley* and some early *Cantos*.

---

confidently: "The whole world can claim Walt Whitman best" (*The New America* [London, 1922], p. 221) and a decade later he recalled: "Our 'master' was Walt Whitman" ("How I Came to Communism: A Symposium", *New Masses*, VIII, 3 [September 1932], 6).

[57] Burke, "The Modern English Novel Plus", *Dial*, LXX, 5 (May 1921), 575; Lawrence, "Model Americans", *Dial*, LXXIV, 5 (May 1923), 509.

[58] Burke to Alyse Gregory, February 25, 1925, *Dial* papers.

[59] September 14, 1928, *Dial* papers.

Pound had the stronger direct influence of the two on editorial matters. Already in 1916 or at the end of 1915 Thayer had been in England and had been on the point of contributing a small sum towards the starting costs of an independent review under the editorship of Eliot and Pound,[60] but that plan had fallen through before any definite suggestion had been made. In January 1920 Thayer started *The Dial* and three months later he offered Pound a job as foreign agent at $750 a year[61] and soon Pound was writing on notepaper which proclaimed *The Dial*'s agency to be at 5 Holland Place Chambers, London W. 8, which was Pound's private address and which had in earlier days appeared on the contents page of *The Little Review*. His position was, however, an uneasy one because, as he himself wrote later, "*The Dial* stated that it could not expect to be my spiritual home";[62] which is another way of saying that the editors of *The Dial* held the opinion that it was Pound's function to collect suitable manuscripts rather than to dictate editorial policy. "The Dial was always hell", he wrote to Harriet Monroe, "or nearly always, endured on the principle 'faim [fait?] saillir le loup du bois'!"[63] His connection with *The Dial* came to an end in April 1923 when Thayer fired him.[64]

During the three years of his association with the magazine, however, Pound exerted a considerable influence. He brought many distinguished Europeans to it, including Rémy de Gourmont, Julien Benda and W. B. Yeats, but a less concrete but perhaps more important aspect of his influence was the fact that he helped to shape and to formulate more overtly certain editorial attitudes, especially with regard to the function and the meaning of literature. Pound's connections with little magazines

[60] Cf. Pound, "Small Magazines", *The English Journal*, XIX, 9 (November 1930), 696.
[61] Cf. Joost, *op. cit.*, p. 166. It should be noted that Pound had received the same salary ($750) as foreign editor of *The Little Review*, but this money, according to Pound, was also used as "payment of foreign contributors" ("Small Magazines", 696).
[62] "Small Magazines", p. 696.
[63] Probably early March 1931, *Poetry* papers.
[64] Joost, *op. cit.*, p. 170.

is a subject in itself; in the following chapter we shall look somewhat deeper into his association with *The Hound & Horn* to get
an insight into the bustle and, often, the acrimony of such an
association. That Pound took his work for *The Dial* seriously
is apparent from a letter he wrote to Harriet Monroe on 11
October 1920. He offered Miss Monroe a poem of Ford Madox
Hueffer's for her magazine *Poetry* because *The Dial* was "full
up for the next six months. . . . It is the first mss. lost to the Dial
which has caused me any deep regret, and I do not in the least
like letting it go elsewhere; though you, in view of having printed
On Heaven are certainly entitled to next shot at it." [65] If there is
reason to compare *The Dial* to *The Seven Arts* or perhaps even
to *Others,* it is also feasible to point out that Pound's influence
strengthened its family resemblance to *The Little Review* and
The Egoist.[66]

Pound's admirer on the staff of *The Dial* and in its pages was
Dr. Watson who, in Scofield Thayer's words, exerted a "con-
stant and subterranean pull to the left. I myself detest all
Modern Art".[67] This remark clearly reflects the difference in
editorial tastes, which is also illustrated in "W. C. Blum's"
(Watson's) "American Letter", in *The Dial* of May 1921, in
praise of Pound and of the then less well-known American poets
William Carlos Williams, E. E. Cummings, and Marianne
Moore. Watson not only admired the *Cantos* but also defended

---

[65] *Poetry* papers. Ford's *Collected Poems* (Oxford, 1936) has the following note: "On Heaven, written in 1913 was first published in *Poetry* of
Chicago and was to have appeared simultaneously in *Fortnightly Review*
but was withdrawn at the instance of the Home Secretary as being blas-
phemous. During the late war it was circulated by H.M. Department of
Propaganda as being likely to make soldiers take a cheerful view of
Death." "On Heaven" appeared in *Poetry* in June 1914; a few lines were
omitted in *Collected Poems.*
[66] Cf. Charles Allen, *"Glebe* and *Others", College English,* XV, 8 (May
1944), 423. At the end of the decade, in his essay "Small Magazines",
Pound wrote: "The *Dial* . . . requested me to collect manuscripts from a
number of European authors, essentially the *Little Review* list with
George Moore and Alice Meynell added, plus certain writers with 'names'
– Anatole France, etc." (p. 696).
[67] Thayer to Alyse Gregory, January 1, 1925, quoted in Joost, *op. cit.,*
p. 83.

Pound's stop-gap prose against detractors who, in Pound's own words, "want such things wrapped up in 'an article' ": [68]

All this is intended as an explanation of Mr. Pound's failure to impress the multitudes who ask for "constructive criticism". If he would wrap up his prejudices in cosmic tendencies and add a little sensational gossip to his technical discussion, he might put over those very unpopular causes, classical learning and modern literature, to a somewhat larger public. But he agrees too well with that public's avowed belief in the necessity for good schoolteaching, to do his work in other than schoolmasterly fashion.[69]

Watson's admiration for the *Cantos* was not shared whole-heartedly by all other contributors to *The Dial*. Edmund Wilson, in his review of *The Waste Land*, considered the *Eight Cantos* of Eliot's "imitator" extremely ill-focussed, merely "a bewildering mosaic with no central emotion to provide a key".[70] Glenway Wescott expressed a similar sense of confusion in his review of *A Draft of Sixteen Cantos*: "Singly, they astounded the reader with tough magnificence; the group is an almost impenetrable mass, for they give each other little aid. The structure of the individual cantos is too subtle to be enjoyed; or perhaps there is no structure, perhaps this is a ragbag like Sordello. . . . The common reader is confused . . . by a Tower of Babel medley." [71]

In January 1928 *The Dial* announced its Award to Pound which at his own request was given in recognition of the poetry,

[68]   "Simplicities", *The Exile*, No. 4 (Autumn 1928), 1.

[69]   "W C. Blum", "Super Schoolmaster", *Dial*, LXIX, 4 (October 1920), 423. Pound criticized this statement although he acknowledged that Watson was "well disposed toward me, personally" ("Historical Survey", *The Little Review*, VIII, 1 ["Brancusi Number", Autumn 1921], 40).

[70]   "The Poetry of Drouth", *Dial*, LXXIII, 6 (December 1922), 616. Eliot objected to Wilson's disparaging remarks about Ezra Pound: "While I wish to express my appreciation of Mr. Wilson's praise, as well as your own, there is one point in Mr. Wilson's article to which I must strongly take exception. I do very much object to be made use of by anyone for the purpose of disparaging the work of Ezra Pound. I am infinitely in his debt as a poet, as well as a personal friend, and I do resent being praised at his expense" (Eliot to Gilbert Seldes, December 27, 1922, quoted by Daniel Woodward, "Notes on the Publishing History and Text of 'The Waste Land' ", *The Papers of the Bibliographical Society of America*, LVIII [Third Quarter 1964], 258).

[71]   "A Courtly Poet", *Dial*, LXXIX, 6 (December 1925), 501, 502.

not the prose. The editorial on the occasion, however, emphasized in no uncertain terms that apart entirely from the influence
of his verse, Pound was one of the most valuable forces in contemporary letters. As the editors, or, in this case, Watson for the
editors, could hardly have escaped selfpraise in commenting
upon Pound's earlier association with their own magazine, they
acknowledged his services in this respect by stating that when
"he was foreign editor of The Little Review, The Little Review
was the most interesting magazine of a quarter century".[72]

Although T. S. Eliot's association with *The Dial* was not as
influential as Pound's, it was close and intricate, and the magazine's generosity helped Eliot through a difficult period in the
early 'Twenties. Pound mentions that "Thayer made an amazingly generous offer to Eliot" some time during the early
months of 1921 but that Eliot's indecision shipwrecked further
discussion.[73] Pound probably refers here to negotiations between Thayer, Eliot, and Lady Rothermere to explore the possibilities of an English branch of *The Dial* with Eliot as editor.
These negotiations fell through, but on 16 August 1921 Eliot
wrote to Richard Aldington that there was "a possibility of a
new literary venture, to be financed up to a certain (too certain)
point, in which (if it comes off) I shall be deeply involved",
and three weeks later Eliot spoke of "the Hypothetical Review".[74] This review was finally christened *The Criterion* [75] at
the suggestion of Eliot's wife and its first issue appeared in
October 1922. It had no formal ties with *The Dial*, although its
regular section "Foreign Reviews" was mostly kind to *The Dial*.

But before the actual appearance of *The Criterion*, Eliot had
a serious breakdown, and on the advice of his doctor, spent
October to December 1921 in complete isolation, partly in England and partly in Switzerland. It was during these months that
most of *The Waste Land* was written. Eliot's condition prompted

---

[72] "Announcement", *Dial*, LXXXIV, 1 (January 1928), 90.
[73] Letter to Richard Aldington (probably March 12, 1922), Aldington
papers, University of Texas Library at Austin.
[74] Letter to Aldington, September 8, 1921, Aldington papers.
[75] "Have decided on *The Criterion* on Vivien's suggestion"; pencil scrawl
on back of letter, Eliot to Aldington, July 4, 1922, Aldington papers.

Richard Aldington to write to Pound asking him "for Christ's
sake to do something"; Pound's answer was "Bel Esprit", a fund
for artists, "a general movement, in which T. is merely the first
man to be freed".[76] The organization would give Eliot and, possibly, subsequent candidates an income for life. "We are not",
Pound wrote in a circular especially printed for the occasion,
"a home for sick animals. We want the work of certain men. We
want a better grade of work. . . ." The absolute minimum for
Eliot which Pound thought acceptable was £300 a year, but
there would be ways of adding to this subsidy: "The Dial will
take something from him every month and that wd. make easily
the fourth hundred. Also if he can hold out until Dec. I dare
say the Dial's prize might be made to land on him." [77]

Since the early months of 1920 Eliot had indeed drawn a
small subsidy from *The Dial* in the form of payments for poems,
articles, and, most regularly, his "London Letter", and as we
have recounted earlier, the fracas over his remuneration for *The
Waste Land* was settled when Eliot was promised the *Dial* Award
for 1922. "Bel Esprit" was hotly discussed during most of 1922
and several pledges of regular subsidies were registered. John
Quinn, that indefatigable patron of *avant-garde* ventures, was
again "the white hope of the affair",[78] and Pound who was "Bel
Esprit's" agent in Paris sent a flow of suggestions to Aldington
who was managing the English end of the line. But the campaign
bore no final fruit. Eliot himself was hesitantly sympathetic
towards the idea, but as he wrote to Aldington on 30 June 1922,
"the situation is embarrassing and fatiguing to me in spite of the
motives which I appreciate".[79] A note in the *Liverpool Post* of
16 November 1922, to the effect that *The Waste Land* was "the

[76]   Pound to Aldington, Spring 1922 and March 14, 1922, Aldington
papers.
[77]   Pound to Aldington, probably March 12, 1922, Aldington papers.
[78]   Cf. Pound to Aldington, Spring 1922, Aldington papers. "Quinn is
giving, as I think I wrote you, 350 bones (or MyrKhn dollars, pieces of 8)
for five years." Probably the last project Quinn subsidized was Ford
Madox Ford's *Transatlantic Review*. Quinn died in the summer of 1924
(cf. Frank MacShane, "The Transatlantic Review", *The Dalhousie Review*,
XLI, 3 [Autumn 1961], 303-313).
[79]   Aldington papers.

initial result of what must be regarded as a considerate and generous scheme with excellent possibilities", finally convinced Eliot that the scheme had no future.

The *Dial* Award, although it was no subsidy for life, achieved at least for one year what "Bel Esprit" had set out to accomplish. Incidentally, whereas Aldington was mainly interested in "Bel Esprit" for the possibilities it offered to help Eliot, Pound had much grander plans. "I am not quite so exclusive as you are", he wrote to Aldington on 20 March 1922; "I shd like Bill to have a year off; and even Marianne might bloom under the influence of a vacation. An old man's home for myself in ten years time, may possibly be avoided by a trip to the orient." [80] The bearing of this passage on the history of *The Dial* will be clear: William Carlos Williams, Marianne Moore, and Pound himself, poets whom Dr. Watson had praised in his "American Letter" in *The Dial* one year earlier, all received the *Dial* Award in subsequent years.

Eliot's *Poems* and *The Sacred Wood* drew high praise from their reviewers, E. E. Cummings and Marianne Moore. In November 1922 *The Dial* published *The Waste Land,* a poem which, in Gilbert Seldes' opinion, joined *Ulysses* as the complete expression of the spirit which would be "modern" for the next generation.[81] It was reviewed by Edmund Wilson who remarked that the poem was Eliot's most considerable claim to eminence; that it not only recapitulated all his earlier and already familiar motifs, but that it sounded "for the first time in all their intensity, untempered by irony or disguise, the hunger for beauty and the anguish at living which lie at the bottom of all his work".[82] The editorial eulogy (written by Gilbert Seldes) on the occasion of the *Dial* Award concentrated specifically on Eliot's criticism, and it is again a comment on the incompatibility of the Awards to Eliot and to Brooks that Mary Colum, when she praised the

---

[80]   Six days earlier (March 14, 1922) Pound had told Aldington: "We are restarting civilization, and have devised a new modus of making art and lit. possible."

[81]   "Nineties – Twenties – Thirties", *Dial*, LXXIII, 5 (November 1922), 577.

[82]   "The Poetry of Drouth", *Dial*, LXXIII, 6 (December 1922), 611.

latter as a pathfinder for the artist, inevitably contrasted him with Eliot who, in her opinion, was pleading for a literary dictatorship.[83] Apart from occasional similar dissonances Eliot's reputation was secure with *The Dial* till, in its last year, 1929, Conrad Aiken wrote an adverse review of *For Lancelot Andrewes*. Aiken had been a great admirer of Eliot's early work but now Eliot seemed to be "definitely and defeatedly in retreat from the present and all that it implies".[84]

III

In the preceding pages we have examined *The Dial*'s attitude towards a number of writers and movements that influenced its career. We shall now broaden the scope of the discussion by trying to gauge the magazine's reactions to more general literary and cultural problems of its time.

We have seen that it was *The Dial*'s policy to favour neither the established nor the new experimental writers. In much the same fashion it published both American and European authors, manifesting in its selectiveness a sophisticated cosmopolitanism which was matched in no other journal of the time. The relative superiority of the American or the European cultural scene was, of course, a much debated issue in the 'Twenties; it ranged from the hopeful cultural nationalism of the *Seven Arts* group to the much more vocal cultural anti-Americanism of the exiles who considered Paris the art centre of the world. Many of the contemporary little magazines took an uncompromising stand in this cultural debate, which was often their main reason for existence. *The Dial*'s position in the midst of this *mêlée* was curiously uncommitted; its pages were open to quite opposing points of view. In a way the editors refused to recognize the issue as an issue at all: "We have published European work not as exotics and not as exemplars; only because we feel that Americans are at

[83] "An American Critic: Van Wyck Brooks", *Dial*, LXXVI, 1 (January 1924), 34.
[84] "Retreat", *Dial*, LXXXVI, 7 (July 1929), 629.

work in the same *milieu* and in the same tradition of letters as the Europeans – that we are all in the Western-civilized-Christian-European-American tradition, and that American letters have their independent existence and their separate, precious character, within that circle, just as German and Italian letters have." [85]

But although the editors believed that the love of letters knows no frontiers and although they tried to secure the best European writers for their magazine, they felt especially committed to the American artist. The most impressive manifestation of this commitment was, of course, the *Dial* Award. They felt that in most cases there was no need for the American writer to go abroad: "The lonely thinker", they wrote in their March 1922 "Comment", "if he thinks, can entertain himself more nobly at home, destroying Franklin, Emerson, and Louisa M. Alcott, than in the arms of the newest dadaist, despising Voltaire." In this same "Comment" they praised Mencken for his newly rewritten *The American Language,* because his studies indicated "what Americans so wilfully forget, that they have a tradition," the materials for a culture of their own. They praised the free intellectual interchange in art circles in Paris only to insist that Americans must try once more to establish this association of creative minds at home.[86] The editors wanted indeed to be of as much help to American writers and artists as they possibly could, but they were in no way provincially narrow in their standards of criticism. Indeed, patriotism in literary criticism was to them intolerable.[87]

This cosmopolitan view of literature gathered to the magazine a wide variety of reviewers with a great many different opinions and prejudices, and this makes a discussion of the cultural debate between "old" Europe and "young" America particularly interesting and appropriate. John Dewey, in an early issue of *The Dial*, pleaded that writers should dig deep down in a specific

[85]   "Comment", *Dial,* LXXIV, 6 (June 1923), 638.
[86]   "Comment", *Dial,* LXXII, 3 (March 1922), 344.
[87]   "Comment", *Dial,* LXXI, 3 (September 1921), 377. *The Dial* was in no way chauvinistically American, but, as Thayer wrote to Alfred Stieglitz, "we like to keep up such American traditions as we can" (November 12, 1923, Stieglitz papers, Yale University Library).

American locality to get away from mere local colour. "We have
been too anxious to get away from home", he wrote; "naturally
that took us to Europe even though we fancied we were going
around America. When we explore our neighbourhood, its forces
and not just its characters and colour, we shall find what we
sought." [88] Thayer's teacher and friend, George Santayana, on
the other hand, asserted that America did not afford material
opportunities for the poet, but he refused to follow the authors
of *Civilization in the United States* all the way in their negativism:
a man like William James at least had left an indelible furrow.[89]

The America-Europe antithesis found different manifestations
in the discussions of the different arts, but the overall impression
is that the debate, through the years, moved towards a greater
confidence in America. We have of course to allow for the idio-
syncrasies of the different critics. It is not surprising that Paul
Rosenfeld, who often felt compelled to censure the insensitiveness
and the snobbery of American music audiences, already in 1921
rebelled against the "Jamesesque sentiment of herd-inferiority
[which] has caused men to see Europe and her music-makers
through stained-glass spectacles." [90] Or that the ebullient Wyndham Lewis, as early as July 1921, set out to pierce through that
" 'French painting against the world' stuff" by dryly observing
that "the most famous French painters to-day, those whose work
was the chief attraction of the French shows, are principally
Spaniards, Belgians, Greeks, Germans, or Jews. French *race* or
birth is the last thing, it would appear, to qualify an artist for
inclusion in an elect community of impeccable geniuses." [91] But

[88]   "Americanism and Localism", *Dial*, LXVIII, 6 (June 1920), 688.
[89]   "Marginal Notes on Civilization in the United States", *Dial*, LXXII, 6
(June 1922), 564. The thirty debunking essays of *Civilization in the United
States* were edited by Harold Stearns, who immediately after delivering the
completed manuscript to the publisher left for France. "Reporters came to
the gangplank to jot down his last words. Everywhere young men were
preparing to follow his example." In Paris people "used to look down at
him sleeping on a café terrace and say 'There lies civilization in the
United States' " (Malcolm Cowley, *Exile's Return* [Compass Books, 1962
(1951)], pp. 79, 105 [Note]).
[90]   "Musical Chronicle", *Dial*, LXXI, 5 (November 1921), 616.
[91]   "Paris versus the World", *Dial*, LXXI, 1 (July 1921), 24.

a Francophile like Ford Madox Hueffer stated categorically that the English had no art as a national characteristic, whereas "the French have everything".[92]

The last two quotations are taken from articles by an American born expatriate living in England and an Englishman; a loquacious American protagonist in the debate was *The Dial*'s art critic, Henry McBride. McBride was the only one of *The Dial*'s three chroniclers who stayed with the magazine for nine years without interruption. Consequently his monthly art chronicle, "Modern Art", was to a considerable extent responsible for the tone of art criticism in *The Dial*. It is unfortunate that McBride's high spirits were sometimes expended on baiting the American art public rather than on discussing works of art proper. However, there is no denying the liveliness of McBride's chronicle or its interest; it is almost an exact gauge of *The Dial*'s taste in art. Even if it was sometimes repetitious it was never boring. Although McBride paid homage to Alfred Stieglitz's protégés among the American artists and sincerely encouraged them, he still considered France the artist's paradise. "The European visitor to the exhibition of the New Society of Artists might imagine that the court language of the world still was French", he wrote in January 1921; "the nasal accent of Uncle Sam is not heard in those precincts".[93] But by 1929 he had reversed his position: " ... the centre of the world has shifted", he then proclaimed; "Paris is no longer the capital of Cosmopolis. All the intelligence of the world is focussed on New York; it has become the battleground of modern civilization; all the roads now lead in this direction, and all the world knows this save the misguided artists who are jeopardizing their careers for the dubious *consommations* of the Café de la Rotonde." [94] By that time McBride felt that even the New York "market" for modern art had vastly improved, and that the auctionroom followers had become intelligent on the subject.[95]

92 "Thus to revisit ...", *Dial*, LXX, 1 (January 1921), 20.
93 "Modern Art", *Dial*, LXX, 1 (January 1921), 112.
94 "Modern Art", *Dial*, LXXXVI, 4 (April 1929), 354.
95 "Modern Art", *Dial*, LXXXVI, 6 (June 1929), 535-536.

The files of *The Dial* provide innumerable comments on the Europe-America dispute but even the few examples quoted above indicate that the terms of the dispute were often chiselled down to France (or rather Paris) over against America. In a similar fashion Paris was often opposed to London mainly by observers in these two cities themselves. "Viewed from Paris", wrote Raymond Mortimer, "London still slumbers in a Victorian complacency".[96] But whereas the cross-Atlantic debate gradually turned towards America's advantage, London remained a scapegoat till the end, although in later years it became a less prominent issue.

As the interest in Europe in the pages of *The Dial*'s successors largely confined itself to England, it appears appropriate to pay special attention to *The Dial*'s attitude to England. The most articulate attacks on the London literary scene to appear in its pages were written by T. S. Eliot and Ezra Pound. The latter's Anglophobia after he had finally turned his back on London is well-known: "One has to keep going east", he told Mary Colum, "to keep one's mind alive".[97] It expressed itself mainly in general attacks on "Bloomsbuggers" and other personalities and on the pernicious influence of publishing houses on literary reviewing: "Young ladies are sought for docility, elderly gentlemen for the faculty of never grasping an idea, and the result is what we all know: Spectator, Times Lit. Sup., Nation-aeum, London Mercury, all there with their publishers' ads." [98] T. S. Eliot's irritation with London's literary climate was more convincing because he wrote his reports on the spot and was less liable to let his anger provoke him to reiterated commonplaces. The acerbity of his observations is illustrated in the following passage:

There is certainly, in the atmosphere of literary London, something which may provisionally be called a moral cowardice. It is not simply

[96]   "London Letter", *Dial*, LXXVIII, 5 (May 1925), 406.
[97]   Mary Colum, *Life and the Dream* (New York, 1947), p. 307. At the time he made this remark Pound had moved from London via Paris to Rapallo.
[98]   "Paris Letter", *Dial*, LXXI, 4 (October 1921), 456. Pound's haphazard attacks on the "establishment" are reminiscent of the more organized campaign of the later English magazine *Scrutiny*.

cowardice, but a caution, a sort of worldly prudence which believes implicitly that English literature is so good as it is that adventure and experiment involve only unjustified risk; lack of ambition, laziness, and refusal to recognize foreign competition; a tolerance which is no better than torpid indifference. ... Other cities decay, and extend a rich odour of putrefaction; London merely shrivels, like a little book-keeper grown old.[99]

The ire of Eliot's "London Letters" in the early *Dial* was mainly provoked by a literature without any critical sense, especially the very popular Georgian poetry. Indeed, in the pages of *The Dial* the epithets "Georgian" and "Victorian" eventually vied for the highest degree of intrinsic rebuke. In the first few issues the magazine's attitude towards the Georgians was still non-committal. *The Dial* of January 1920 contained two fairly lauda-tory reviews of poetry and criticism of J. C. Squire, and Edward Shanks in his "London Letter" of April of that year commented noncommittally on the increasing popularity of the Georgian poets of whom he himself was one. This same April issue, how-ever, also contained a "Briefer Mention" of *A Miscellany of British Poetry, 1919* which presented the more innocuous of the Georgian poets and which was criticized for the omission of D. H. Lawrence, J. C. Squire, and Siegfried Sassoon – the more robust members of the group. But if there had been any doubt of *The Dial*'s position towards the Georgians, it was effectively dispelled by Malcolm Cowley in May 1920: "Eight years ago when the Georgians first appeared as a group, it seemed that they were discovering more strident harmonies, subtler disso-nances. But with the publication of each new anthology, the dis-appointment is cumulative. Every two years a volume bound in fresh brown boards, printed on fresh paper, but with the contents so familiar, so delicately trite, reaching with such skill to new heights of inanity." [100] Squire, Lawrence and Sassoon were again singled out for praise. When, five months later, Amy Lowell

[99] "London Letter", *Dial*, LXXII, 5 (May 1922), 510.
[100] "Against Nightingales", *Dial*, LXVIII, 5 (May 1920), 621. "Out of all the group, one metaphysician who slips between the boundaries of the unreal and the real; one passionate consumptive; one forthright satirist – Siegfried Sassoon – and the rest nightingales".

reviewed *Georgian Poetry 1918-1919,* she found it "pale and spectre-like, haunted by the ghosts of England's vanished bards", but she mentioned Sassoon, Graves, Lawrence and Squire as notable exceptions.[101] But even among these chosen few Squire's verses soon seemed more interminable than eternal and Sassoon's war-poetry was outstripped by Wilfrid Owen's.[102]

If British poetry, apart from the work of W. B. Yeats, did not provoke much enthusiasm among *The Dial'*s contributors, nor did English fiction, although the earlier criticism tended to detect some promise – which was on the whole not fulfilled – especially in the work of some women novelists. Katherine Mansfield was foremost among them. Malcolm Cowley thought the descriptions in her collection of stories, *Bliss,* so fine that he had to fight back the temptation to quote whole pages of them; but *The Garden Party and Other Stories* mitigated his enthusiasm: "It is almost as good as Bliss, but not much different; from Katherine Mansfield it is immensely disappointing." [103] None of the stories or journals which John Middleton Murry, who was no friend of the editors, published after her death met with the approval of *The Dial'*s reviewers; they all felt that he was doing injury to his wife's reputation by publishing every scrap of paper she chanced to have written on. Another promising English novelist was May Sinclair. When Raymond Mortimer compared Miss Sinclair to Katherine Mansfield he defined the difference between them as between great talent and something rather more; but this talent again left its promise unfulfilled, and five years later, in a "Briefer Mention" of May Sinclair's *The Allinghams,* the reviewer's respect remained unwarmed by enthusiasm.[104]

Katherine Mansfield, May Sinclair and, also, Rebecca West were among English women novelists most frequently discussed

[101]   "Weary Verse", *Dial,* LXIX, 4 (October 1920), 425.
[102]   "Briefer Mention", *Dial,* LXXVI, 1 (January 1924), 93; "Briefer Mention", *Dial,* LXXI, 1 (July 1921), 120.
[103]   "Page Dr. Blum!", *Dial,* LXXI, 3 (September 1921), 366; "The Author of Bliss", *Dial,* LXXIII, 2 (August 1922), 232.
[104]   "Miss Sinclair Again", *Dial,* LXXII, 5 (May 1922), 534. "Briefer Mention", *Dial,* LXXXIII, 4 (October 1927), 353. This "Briefer Mention" was written by Alyse Gregory who also influenced *The Dial'*s attitude to the posthumously published work of Katherine Mansfield.

in the early *Dial*, but its favourite, no doubt, was Virginia Woolf. But as half of the criticism of her work was written by such writers as Clive Bell, David Garnett and Raymond Mortimer, her reputation is perhaps less a relevant indication of the taste of *The Dial* than a comment on the influence which the Bloomsbury group exerted in America through its pages. By far the best criticism of Virginia Woolf was written by Conrad Aiken in his article "The Novel as Work of Art". Aiken wondered whether, because of a kind of "self-consciousness of adroitness . . . she might not lose her way and give us a mere series of virtuosities or *tours de force*". However, in his opinion, her new novel, *To the Lighthouse,* relieved one's doubts on that score almost entirely.[105] Almost, but not completely, because it was just her cleverness which, in Aiken's judgment, two years later spoiled the perfection of *Orlando*.[106]

The Bloomsbury group was not only responsible for much of the tone of the criticism of Virginia Woolf but it also influenced the tone of the criticism of D. H. Lawrence. One ought not, however, to emphasize the influence of this group too strongly because, without it, *The Dial's* criticism of these two authors would probably have been different merely in the degree of its praise and censure. This argument really anticipates our discussion of some of the aesthetic considerations which lay at the root of *The Dial's* taste; we shall therefore postpone the discussion of *The Dial's* attitude towards Lawrence and also towards James Joyce, because Lawrence soon became the antithesis of all that Joyce stood for. It is sufficient, at this point, to call attention to Raymond Mortimer's statement that he was "entirely in sympathy" with Virginia Woolf, Duncan Grant and Lytton Strachey, but "when faced, say, with Mr. Lawrence's farouche imaginings, I dislike even while I admire."[107]

Let us turn to some other English novelists whose work was discussed in *The Dial*. In a review of E. M. Forster's *Howards End*, Hamish Miles praised the consummate civilized quality of

105   *Dial*, LXXXIII, 1 (July 1927), 42, 43.
106   "Orlando", *Dial*, LXXXVI, 2 (February 1929), 147-149.
107   "London Letter", *Dial*, LXXVIII, 5 (May 1925), 408.

Forster's work,[108] but as *Passage to India* was the only new novel which Forster brought out during the time of *The Dial*, his work did not attract much attention otherwise. T. F. Powys received favourable notice but it ought to be pointed out that the "Briefer Mention" of his *Mark Only* was written by his brother John Cowper Powys; that several of the stories which he submitted for publication were turned down, because *The Dial* found them "not in harmony with its contents";[109] and that his brother Llewelyn married *The Dial*'s business manager Alyse Gregory. Of the older generation of English novelists only Conrad was consistently admired. In this connection a most illuminating remark was made by Kenneth Burke, in a review of Virginia Woolf's *Night and Day* and *The Voyage Out*, to the effect that in England "letters since the 'Nineties seem to have been maintained by one Pole, two Americans [undoubtedly Eliot and Pound], and a horde of Irishmen [including Joyce and Yeats]".[110]

After the preceding paragraphs about *The Dial*'s attitude to Europe and particularly to England, we must now discuss its more immediate environment. It will not be surprising that the most frequent and the most stringent criticism of modern society is to be found in those departments of the magazine that dealt specifically and directly with the present: the letters of the foreign contributors, the editorials, and the monthly chronicles of the theatre, of music, and of modern art. Some of the problems posed by the foreign contributors have already been described in discussing the antithesis Europe-America. We shall be specifically concerned here with *The Dial*'s attitude towards the American environment.

A few general observations may be made at the outset. There

---

[108] "E. M. Forster", *Dial*, LXXVI, 5 (May 1924), 453.

[109] Marianne Moore to D. Choules [for T. F. Powys], September 1, 1927, in connection with "The White Pater Noster", *Dial* papers.

[110] "The Modern British Novel Plus", *Dial*, LXX, 5 (May 1921), 572. Yeats was to the editors "the most distinguished of living practicers of the Art of English Poesy" ("Comment", *Dial*, LXXVII, 6 [December 1924], 535), and his own countryman and admirer, W. K. Magee ["John Eglinton"], considered him Ireland's "principal ornament" ("Yeats and his Story", *Dial*, LXXX, 5 [May 1926], 366).

was relatively little undefined anti-Babbittry in *The Dial* and the magazine seldom engaged in a controversy unless it was specifically provoked by an outside criticism. If controversy occurred it generally took place in "Comment", the editors' column. We are speaking here of *The Dial* under Thayer's editorship. Thayer was very touchy and personally saw to it that the magazine's detractors met the scorn of his curiously high-spirited, tortuous "Comments". When Marianne Moore became editor in 1925, her "Comments" tended more and more towards little prose poems, often about a seventeenth century author or a book which had caught her interest in the preceding month. Controversy virtually disappeared; indeed, as Miss Moore told an Italian correspondent, "our tendency is against controversy".[111] *The Dial* only paid attention to local affairs in so far as they came within the province of one of the regular departments. It did not have editorials on such topics as "Motor Buses on Chicago Boulevards" as was featured in *The Little Review* in 1916, nor did it have anything like that magazine's regular column "The Reader Critic". *The Dial,* therefore, lacked some of the exciting contemporaneity of its fellow little magazines but, on the other hand, it did not waste space on the kind of information which has hardly retained even a touch of quaintness for the modern reader. The "Theatre Chronicle" suffers most heavily in this respect as it tends to deal with more ephemeral subject-matter than either the art or the music department. Gilbert Seldes was the regular chronicler although he was not, like Henry McBride in the art department, the only one; during his rather frequent travels abroad the Chronicle was written in turn by Scofield Thayer, E. E Cummings, and Edmund Wilson, and, towards the end, Padraic Colum became the regular theatre critic.

The problem of modern civilization in the most general terms expressed itself in a distrust of the rise of the machine and the consequent atrophy and loss of individuality. "And should man surround himself with a wilderness of thought-saving machines", Slater Brown wrote, "with an efficient social order to limit his

[111]   Letter to Raffaello Piccoli, August 17, 1928, *Dial* papers.

desires and enlarge contentment, then even intelligence, lacking the stimulus of a struggle, may atrophy. Man, with all the futility of an ant, may come to revolve in endless and ridiculous circles." [112] Probably the most eloquent and forceful champion of cultural regeneration was Ezra Pound. His fulminations against a democratic mass-culture and in favour of an intellectual *élite* will be familiar. "Is it possible", he asked, "to establish some spot of civilization, or some geographically scattered association of civilized creatures? One is up against this problem in a decadent wallow like London, in an enervated centre like Paris, in a reawakening Italy, in an inchoate America." [113] Thomas Mann faced the same problem in Germany which was infested with "the kind of youth that thinks it has dispensed with the concept of humanity for good and all and has sewn the swastika of exultant brutality on its banner".[114] The general apathy and lack of culture of New York audiences was often noticed and commented upon in the monthly Chronicles. "Music in America is a rich cloak men wear for a few hours each week, and then throw off again", Rosenfeld wrote in exasperation and Seldes stated categorically that it was "necessary to destroy not the theatre but the audience".[115]

The gloomy view of contemporary society which emerges from the preceding paragraphs is more characteristic of general highbrow dissatisfaction and disillusionment than of any one magazine of the period. In *The Dial,* however, the complaint rose above the mere *cliché* and it did not lose itself in romantic yearnings for the past. *The Dial* was very much aware of the present, and many contributors felt with Gilbert Seldes that "if we are not to separate ourselves from the world, if we are to live complete lives, not as Thoreau, but in the crowd, we can appreciate, value correctly, and subdue to our uses everything from fast

---

[112] "The Mystic Finger-Post", *Dial*, LXX, 4 (April 1921), 465. Brown, incidentally, lived on the top floor of the same building that housed *The Dial.*
[113] "Paris Letter", *Dial*, LXXIII, 5 (November 1922), 549.
[114] "German Letter", *Dial*, LXXXIII, 1 (July 1927), 55.
[115] "Musical Chronicle", *Dial*, LXIX, 5 (November 1920), 550. "The Theatre'", *Dial*, LXXI, 5 (November 1921), 620.

motor cars to quantum theory." [116] Seldes, especially, was susceptible to the excitement of the times and to the native qualities
of what he termed the "Seven Lively Arts". Indeed, some of the
antagonism which Edmund Wilson had observed between the
ideas of Paul Rosenfeld and Matthew Josephson existed in the
pages of *The Dial* itself. Wilson, who himself had sung the praises
of Ring Lardner in *The Dial,* was best qualified to review Seldes's
book *The Seven Lively Arts.* His review is particularly interesting in that it considered Seldes's book "a genuine contribution
to America's new orientation in the arts which was inaugurated
by America's Coming of Age, in 1915 . . ." [117] It is unlikely that
the author of *America's Coming of Age,* Van Wyck Brooks, or
Seldes's fellow chronicler, Paul Rosenfeld, would have been very
pleased with Wilson's comparison. Wilson was a representative
of a new generation of American writers and his interpretation
of Brooks's position is characteristic of one of the main currents
in *The Dial.* Some time earlier Wilson had characterized Seldes's
flaming prophetic enthusiasm for the lively arts as a little exces-
sive; [118] yet writing the "Theatre Chronicle" during 1923 had
brought Wilson's views in rather close sympathy with Seldes's.
The latter himself confessed to "having been confused and having
caused confusion, largely because it is tiresome always to repeat
simple and essential things". The theatre, he went on to say,
"does not appear in my mind as a unit; there are several theatres,
and the highest praise of one is not nearly so rich a commenda-
tion as a moderately adverse report on another".[119]

Some of Seldes's admiration for the lively arts was also shared
by other *Dial* regulars, including Thayer and Watson and Cummings. Watson's enthusiasm for the film grew apace in the pages
of *The Dial* and in later years he was to make some experimental
films himself. In September 1921 he still felt that the question

---

[116] "The Golden Day", *Dial*, LXXXII, 6 (June 1927), 521.
[117] "The Seven Low-Brow Arts", *Dial*, LXXVII, 3 (September 1924), 250.
[118] "The Theatre", *Dial*, LXXV, 5 (November 1923), 514. Some thirty
years later, Lawrence Langton remembered Gilbert Seldes as "an argu-
mentative young aesthete with a time sense which led him in easy steps
from literature to television" (*The Magic Curtain* [London, 1952], p. 71).
[119] "The Theatre", *Dial*, LXXIX, 5 (November 1925), 435.

of the movies being a new art or anything like it had to be answered in the negative; however, "if producers spend more money on film and speed up their cameras, the movies will indubitably quit hopping and start becoming." [120] But in his February 1927 "Comment" Watson professed himself "shocked to see a very able paper in The Dial by Mr. Craven withering the movies root and branch," and he was dissatisfied with the all too tame rejoinder of Ralph Block in the following issue.[121] Thayer shared Cummings's enthusiasm for George Herriman's cartoons of Krazy Kat: "Here is a veritable creation", he wrote enthusiastically, "standing cheek by jowl with all the incredible vulgar and stupid work of our comic artists".[122] Cummings himself was one of the few moderns for whom Thayer had an unstinting admiration; he was as Pound wrote "the white-haired boy for that outfit".[123] Thayer's taste for Krazy Kat may well have been whetted by Cummings's cartoon-like drawings, several of which were reproduced in *The Dial*. When Cummings received the *Dial* Award for 1925, he was characterized as "one of this generation's great poets", but the "Announcement" was not so much the usual eulogy as an essay in explanation of his genius: a clear indication that the editors realized that Cummings was as yet but little known outside the pages of *The Dial*.

One of the few persistent preoccupations of the editors in their "Comment" was with the ethics of publishers and their influence on the state of criticism and of literary reviewing.

[120] "American Letter", *Dial*, LXXI, 3 (September 1921), 348.
[121] The mildness of Block's reply was in complete agreement with Marianne Moore's editorial views. On 5 November 1926 she wrote to Thomas Craven: "We are inviting Mr. Block to write us an article, to come out early in the year, presenting the favourable view which he naturally holds in respect to motion pictures, but in no sense to be controversial ... a debate – on this or any subject – would be contrary to The Dial's intention" (*Dial* papers).
[122] "Comment", *Dial*, LXIX, 1 (July 1920), 108. Later on, Cummings wrote an introduction to an edition of Krazy Kat which first appeared in *The Sewanee Review*, LIV, 2 (April-June, 1946).
[123] Quoted by Charles Norman, *Ezra Pound*, p. 225. Norman also observed the strong personal link of Thayer with Cummings (Cummings married Thayer's former wife, Elaine Orr); Cummings knew Watson and Seldes at Harvard (Norman, *E. E. Cummings*, p. 123).

Already in August 1920, they remarked ironically that "the engines for accelerating and predisposing favourable opinion are grown remarkably in our time. . . . Merely to confess that you are trying to distinguish for yourself between good and shoddy has become the sign of an inferior mind – the mind which cannot recognize a great thing simply because it happens also to be popular." In this same "Comment" the editors urged that criticism hold on to its independence at all costs; it must fight everlastingly against the gentle and insinuating voice of propaganda.[124] The critic has a most important function to fulfil: he must create an intellectual situation, an informed audience, as a setting for the artist. "What has happened in America over and over again is this: the potential artist has stopped halfway because no critic and certainly no public demanded of him the last item of his strength as an artist. The American critic has hit soft and the American writer has gone soft." [125] Editors of newspapers and magazines are intimidated by the publishers because they often need the advertising. "But", the editors wrote hopefully in August 1923, "the number of individuals who are growing sceptical and who are caring for independent intelligence, is growing".

An examination of the contents of The Dial shows that, although its contributors formed less of a "school" than those of its successors, its interest in criticism and its emphasis on high-standard book reviewing crystallized certain assumptions about literature and its place in the cultural environment of the time. The furtherance of these assumptions and the evaluation of different literary works and their authors in accordance with them constituted The Dial's most direct influence. But although the editors had specific ideas of what criticism should be like, these ideas never prejudiced their tolerance of the different critical approaches of their contributors. There is indeed a great discrepancy between the more or less official critical line of The Dial and some of the criticism in its pages, but the ideas were vigorously promoted in at least a substantial number of contributions. Although The Dial was not the only magazine to sponsor

124 Dial, LXIX, 2 (August 1920), 217.
125 "Comment", Dial, LXXII, 2 (February 1922), 234.

modern modes in criticism, none of its contemporaries was as consistent or as influential. The first few issues show an uncertain and ambiguous attitude towards the function of the literary critic. Maxwell Bodenheim felt that it was the critic's job to discuss only writers he respected and to explain the trend of their work rather than to chide them for what they were not.[126] Evelyn Scott agreed that one "does not waste a ream of good paper to damn a man's works".[127] It is curious, incidentally, to note how closely this attitude fits Marianne Moore's conception of the function of the reviewer: "Our wish to review only such books as would seem to a reviewer valuable and enticing, is well known and when a book is asked it is our hope always that the review will be an exposition of the merits of the book", she wrote as editor of *The Dial*.[128] In his "London Letter" published in the April 1920 issue, Edward Shanks showed a typical diffidence of literary discrimination when he quoted Rupert Brooke's "What we want, of course, is a volume of initial essays by God." [129] In another "London Letter" four months later, Shanks reported that "at this moment in England we are talking, all together and most of us at the top of our voices, about criticism". He welcomed the possible effect of greater astringency in curbing the free-flowing stream of mediocre literature and especially commended Eliot's concern for making a useful distinction between criticism and reviewing.[130] It was in their "Comment" of this same August issue that the editors pleaded for independent and disinterested criticism.

By December 1920 there was little doubt as to which line the magazine would follow. In the issue of that month, the fourth instalment of Julien Benda's "Essay on the Aesthetics of Contemporary French Society" preceded Eliot's important essay "The Second-Order Mind." Benda attacked his contemporaries who "have willed that the business of criticism should consist in

---

[126]   "Selfglorification and Art", *Dial*, LXVIII, 1 (January 1920), 92-94.
[127]   "Gilbert Cannan: Inquisitor", *Dial*, LXVIII, 2 (February 1920), 184.
[128]   Letter to Leo Stein, March 13, 1928, *Dial* papers.
[129]   *Dial*, LXVIII, 4 (April 1920), 490.
[130]   *Dial*, LXIX, 2 (August 1920), 152, 153.

'sympathizing' with the subject", and then denounced them for considering works *"in relation to the personality of the author, and never in themselves,"* and also for considering *"souls* rather than *works"*.[131] In general, his anger was directed against subjective and impressionistic criticism which did not concentrate exclusively on the work it discussed. Eliot, in "The Second-Order Mind", criticized Matthew Arnold for having attacked the uncritical rather than established a criticism, and also for having squandered his energies in attacking extra-literary, often political activities. What was needed, according to Eliot, were more "second-order minds" – "(I do not say 'second-rate', the word is too derogatory)" – which were difficult to come by but which were necessary for that "current of ideas", that "society permeated by fresh thought", of which Arnold had spoken.[132]

The Dial, then, was looking for critics who would introduce no extraneous information into their discussion of a work of art which was not strictly relevant to it. The editors felt indeed that interest in aesthetic perfection had "dwindled to such an extent that there are moments when one feels inclined to forego the moral type of criticism entirely and to say that the only value of comparative literature is to make us interested in the incomparable".[133] This quotation is taken from the editorial "Comment" of August 1922 which indicated a belief in the uniqueness of the work of art and in the value of the artist's personal experiences as subject-matter for his work. Two months later, Gilbert Seldes, as "Sebastien Cauliflower" writing from the vantage-point of "Dante, Va.", remarked that some of the literary criticism in the press was indeed illuminating, "but we find that it illuminates nearly everything except letters". This type of criticism, Seldes wrote, issued from "critics not of literature, but of economics, sociology, psychoanalysis, morality – and so on".[134]

---

[131]   *Dial,* LXIX, 6 (December 1920), 568, 570, 569. Benda blamed the subjectivity of French literary criticism on the fact that women are the only readers: "nobody else reads any more" (p. 580).

[132]   *Dial,* LXIX, 6 (December 1920), 588.

[133]   "Comment", *Dial,* LXXIII, 2 (August 1922), 240.

[134]   "American Letter", *Dial,* LXXIII, 5 (November 1922), 555, 556.

The *Dial* Award to Eliot in 1922 acknowledged from whom these new directions in criticism primarily emanated. Eliot had published *The Sacred Wood* in 1920 and Marianne Moore had immediately discovered its value "in what it reveals as a definition of criticism".[135] When the editors announced their Award to Eliot they emphasized that it was given as much in recognition of the criticism as of the poetry. "It is impossible", they stated, "to read the opening essays of The Sacred Wood without recognizing that it is from these pages that the attack upon perverted criticism is rising. The journalists who wish critics to be forever concerned with social laws, economic fundamentals, and the science of psychoanalysis, and never by any chance with the erection into laws of those personal impressions which are the great pleasure of appreciation, would do well to destroy Mr. Eliot first." [136]

The editors' interest in criticism culminated in their "Comment" of October 1923 in which they proposed three "phases" in which criticism might manifest itself: interpretation, orientation, and judgment. By interpretation they understood tracing "the author's purpose and the means utilized for effecting that purpose. This phase of criticism tends towards the technical approach, and is usually done best by critics who are themselves poets." Orientation is the use of disciplines other than literary and of information gleaned from sources outside the work of art. This method is more useful as a source of added insight than as a method to gauge excellence. The third phase, judgment, seeks to establish and to justify objective criteria for evaluation. This phase, the editors pointed out, "is the most far-reaching aspect of criticism, and has always been the one which has proved the most disastrous to its devotees. It requires the critic to assert some clear relationship between art and life, entangling him in ethics, and even metaphysics".[137]

The editors, in other words, advocated a technical criticism which arrives at a clear evaluation, and this kind of criticism was

---

[135] "The Sacred Wood", *Dial*, LXX, 3 (March 1921), 336.
[136] "Comment", *Dial*, LXXIII, 6 (December 1922), 686.
[137] *Dial*, LXXV, 4 (October 1923), 402-403.

practised by many of the younger generation. If in later issues the debate about criticism tended to lose its urgency, this went hand in hand with a general withdrawal from controversy and editorial commitment. But aesthetic criticism was not the only kind of criticism practised in *The Dial*; indeed, the kind of belletristic essay as written by Llewelyn Powys or Logan Pearsall Smith appeared quite as frequently as spare, formalist criticism. The latter kind of criticism, however, was in the ascendant, and as it was felt to be a new departure, it imparted a sense of excitement to the magazine especially in the early 1920's.

The interest in aesthetic criticism was concomitant with new departures in techniques of composition or, in other words, with the modernism of contemporary literature. As late as 1927, Seldes complained that "critics are few who understand the new terms which artists use".[138] For Seldes the solution was simple: modern criticism should be preoccupied with technique and method, with form in the technical sense, rather than with content. It is obvious that this conception of form was much simpler than Eliot's, but it proved an adequate weapon in the arsenal of many of the younger contributors who tended to make a fetish out of Art and modernism.[139] Their idols were Flaubert, Proust (and to a lesser extent, James), and Joyce. The Flaubert cult did not remain unchallenged. "There are two Flauberts", John Middleton Murry wrote in *The Dial* of December 1921. "One was born on the 12th of this month a hundred years ago in the surgeon's house at Rouen hospital; the other in enthusiastic minds in the last quarter of the nineteenth century."[140] Murry's, however, was a

---

[138] "An Enquiry into the Present State of Letters", *Dial*, LXXXIII, 5 (November 1927), 436.

[139] Kenneth Burke, however, discovered that Gertrude Stein's method leaves the reader so little to feed upon, that "one might almost say that it argues for the insignificance of significant form" ("Engineering with Words", *Dial*, LXXIV, 4 [April 1923], 411) and Djuna Barnes's *A Book* had, according to Burke, "no interior designs, no 'functioning' sentences" to recommend it, so that "we must situate the appeal of this book precisely in the vigour of her attitudes, in her immersion" (Kenneth Burke, "Immersion", *Dial*, LXXVI, 5 [May 1924], 460).

[140] "Gustave Flaubert", *Dial*, LXXI, 6 (December 1921), 625.

minority opinion which was held up to ridicule by Ezra Pound in his "Paris Letter" of April 1922.[141] But Murry was not intimidated and he reopened his attack on Flaubert, the symbol and party cry, with greater pugnacity two years later in *The Yale Review*. There were Flaubert and Flaubart, he said, the latter a creation of Englishmen and Americans (especially Americans), not Frenchmen. "But in this again the Flaubartians showed their wisdom. It was to their advantage that Flaubart (to be for ever distinguished from Gustave Flaubert the novelist) should have delivered his oracles in a foreign tongue." Murry explained this thriving trade in literary superstition in terms of the conception of the Art of literature as something totally mysterious, which had resulted in a cult of incomprehensibility.[142]

In the same *Yale Review* article Murry attacked the poetry of E. E. Cummings, and whatever the editors thought of his attack on Flaubert's critics, they resented his derogatory remarks about Cummings. Thayer answered in a vigorous editorial and in a personal letter severed the relations of *The Dial* with Murry.[143] But Murry was not the only contributor to *The Dial* who was dubious about the legitimacy of Flaubert's reputation. When Kenneth Burke discussed Flaubert's letters he remarked that "the most striking implication of the letters with respect to his art-methods is that his emotions are paralyzed by his intelligence".[144] And Hermann Hesse expected that the youngest generation would

---

[141] Pound's "Paris Letter" began: "We have enough dullards, dunces in America; there's no need of importing them, but the Murry article is so fine a specimen, so typical a slide that it is worth examining" (*Dial*, LXXII, 4 [April 1922], 401).

[142] "Flaubert and Flaubart", *The Yale Review*, XIII, 2 (January 1924), 347-364.

[143] Thayer's letter to Murry read in part: "I did not feel the manner of your comment to be legitimate. I have felt it incumbent upon me to defend Mr. Cummings in what seems to me injustice. Feeling as you do about the work of so important and characteristic a contributor to The Dial as Mr. Cummings I should not think you would care to write further for The Dial. I also fear that my answer to your pages in The Yale Review may erect a further barrier between yourself and my magazine" (January 24, 1924, *Dial* papers).

[144] "The Correspondence of Flaubert", *Dial*, LXXII, 2 (February 1922), 151.

shortly turn against Flaubert "if only as a punishment for the exaggerated patronage of their fathers".[145]

Proust and Joyce were, in Glenway Wescott's words, "the two most striking writers of this period", and in March 1922 Gilbert Seldes prophesied that James Joyce, Marcel Proust and Dorothy Richardson would control the novel for a decade.[146] Joyce's *Ulysses* became the measure of all contemporary novels. "All men should 'Unite to give praise to Ulysses' ", Pound wrote from Paris in June 1922 in his habitual dogmatic manner; "Those who will not, may content themselves with a place in the lower intellectual orders." [147] In that same issue, however, *The Dial*'s Irish correspondent "John Eglinton" [W. K. Magee] expressed a very different opinion. He noticed "a growing divergence between the literary ideals of our artists and the books which human beings want to read", and the editors, evidently mediating between their Paris and Dublin correspondents, hastened to point out that they had no "wish, at this moment, to declare an official attitude towards Ulysses". They thought it sufficient to take note of the quickening of the life of the mind which *Ulysses* had effected.[148] But Eglinton was undoubtedly on the losing side. *Ulysses* recurred periodically in his "Dublin Letter" as a ghost that had to be laid, but the best he could say for this "mephistophelian" work was that it had "every characteristic of a masterpiece except a *raison d'être*".[149] But if *Ulysses* was the work of a different generation, Eglinton faithfully registered Joyce's influence on the young men of the new Ireland.[150]

[145] "The Brothers Karamazov – the Downfall of Europe", *Dial*, LXXII, 6 (June 1922), 617.

[146] "Concerning Miss Moore's Observations", *Dial*, LXXVIII, 1 (January 1925), 4; "The Art of the Novel", *Dial*, LXXII, 3 (March 1922), 320. It is instructive to compare Wescott's evaluation with a statement written nine years later, in the 'Thirties: "James Joyce and Marcel Proust are the leading representatives of the literature of the decadent bourgeois culture of the West" (D. S. Mirsky, "Joyce and Irish Literature", *The New Masses*, XI, 1 [April 3, 1934], 31).

[147] "Paris Letter", *Dial*, LXXII, 6 (June 1922), 623.

[148] "Dublin Letter", *Dial*, LXXII, 6 (June 1922), 622; "Comment", *Dial*, LXXII, 6 (June 1922), 662.

[149] "Dublin Letter", *Dial*, LXXV, 2 (August 1923), 180.

[150] "Irish Letter", *Dial*, LXXXVI, 5 (May 1929), 419.

The official review of *Ulysses* in *The Dial* was written by
T. S. Eliot, but it only appeared in November 1923, after the
magazine had witnessed a heated discussion already. "I am
struggling with a notice of Ulysses myself which I have promised
to the 'Dial' ", Eliot wrote to Richard Aldington a year before
the review finally appeared; "I find it extremely difficult to put
my opinion of the book intelligently, in as much as I have little
sympathy with the majority of either its admirers or its detractors." [151] In his review Eliot praised *Ulysses* as "the most important expression which the present age has found; it is a book
to which we are all indebted, and from which none of us can
escape." These were his postulates for any further discussion.
But he also warned against the very real danger that "a very
great book may have a very bad influence indeed".[152]

Joyce, then, was generally considered the greatest force in
modern literature but this did not mean that editorial admiration
for his work was uncritical. When Sylvia Beach offered *The Dial*
a long episode from Joyce's *Work in Progress,* it was accepted
by telegram, but – evidently after editorial deliberation, and
after Joyce had sent three separate sheets of corrections – *The
Dial* changed its mind and proposed to print only parts of it.
Miss Beach's reply was a telegram cancelling publication. Already
in an editorial before Eliot's review had come out, the editors
had expressed their opinion that *Ulysses* marked "the snapping
of a contact. A second Joyce could merely prospect for the
watery oil which is left." They characterized the contemporary
stage in the history of art as decadence which only left the choice
between *Ersatz* and *retour*. "*Ersatz* demands ingenuity, and there
is much ingenious work being done. *Retour* means classicism."
The editors thought it not unlikely that the next phase of European thought would be away from "the recent religion of 'pure
creation' " to classicism.[153]

[151]   November 8, 1922, Aldington papers, University of Texas Library.
[152]   "Ulysses, Order and Myth", *Dial*, LXXV, 5 (November 1923), 481.
Joyce himself liked the review (cf. *Letters of James Joyce*, Vol. III,
ed. Richard Ellmann [London, 1966], p. 83).
[153]   "Comment", *Dial*, LXXV, 1 (July 1923), 103. Marianne Moore explained the confusion of *The Dial*'s initial acceptance and subsequent

IV

The limited space of a chapter will hardly do justice to all the
diverse interests of a monthly magazine with a run of nine years.
The preceding remarks seek to single out and to exemplify some
of *The Dial*'s interests and preoccupations which may be considered representative of the magazine and which will also form
a setting for the discussion of its successors. Selectiveness of this
kind, however, cannot escape a certain arbitrariness. The present
chapter, for instance, gives only the faintest indication of the
variety and the number of European contributions – apart from
the English ones – because the attention of the later magazines
confined itself more and more to the English speaking world,
and it emphasizes the more experimental younger writers and
critics rather than the slightly older generation, who were frequently represented in the pages of *The Dial,* because these
younger writers monopolized much of the discussion of the later
reviews.

At this point an examination of *The Dial*'s reputation, among
its contemporaries as well as in later years, will serve to give
perspective to the foregoing discussion. It will not only bring out
some of the weaknesses of the magazine, but also present a more
balanced picture of its preoccupations and its place in the 'Twenties. Such an examination would seem all the more profitable,

---

rejection of Joyce's manuscript in a letter to Sylvia Beach of September 28,
1926: "The letter which I wrote to you accepting the manuscript was not
held as I had asked that it should be until a final conference would be
held" (*Dial* papers). The telegram cancelling publication – "Unpermissible
to publish Joyce verbatim" (September 17, 1926) – may indicate that the
editors were afraid of a possible conflict with the censor. Five years earlier John Quinn had called Thayer as a witness in the famous *Ulysses* trial
of *The Little Review.* "Thayer praised the book but conceded that he would
probably not have published the Nausicaa episode in the *Dial*" (Richard
Ellmann, *James Joyce* [New York, 1959], p. 518). The part of *Finnegans
Wake* submitted to *The Dial* is commonly referred to as "Anna Livia
Plurabelle" (cf., e.g., Sylvia Beach, *Shakespeare and Company* [New York,
1959], p. 170), but Joyce's published letters seem to refer to different
sections (cf. *Letters of James Joyce,* Vol. I, ed. Stuart Gilbert [London,
1957], pp. 243, 245, 246; Vol. III, ed. Ellmann [London, 1966], pp. 121,
144).

as *The Dial* has attracted more numerous and also more outspoken comments than any of the magazines under discussion,
and for that matter, than any other little magazine of this century
with the possible exception of *Poetry* and *The Little Review*.
Early praise for *The Dial* came from England as well as from
the United States. *The London Mercury* welcomed the first
number of the new *Dial*: "We await its development with interest." [154] In 1921 A. R. Orage, who was always held in high
esteem by little magazine editors including Ezra Pound, called
The Dial "perhaps the most fully realized of all the promising
literary magazines now current in the world", and G. K. Chesterton always found the magazine "full of articles and illustrations
of more than ordinary interest".[155] Among American magazines,
Time launched its career in 1923 with a characteristic jibe at
The Dial.[156] A year earlier *The Double Dealer* of New Orleans
had mentioned *The Dial* as one of the two existing serious magazines in America (the second being *The Yale Review*) but had
added that "even *The Dial* seems only too likely to print many
a thing, not because it is inherently excellent, but because it is
new".[157] This was unusual censure for a magazine which, as we
shall see, was more often attacked for its caution than for its
avant-gardism. The *Dial* Award drew much favourable attention
when it was first announced, but the awardees did not always
meet with approval. When Van Wyck Brooks was announced as
the recipient, for instance, Ernest Hemingway wrote: "For every
writer produced in America there are produced eleven critics.

---

[154] "Literary Intelligence", *The London Mercury*, I, 4 (February 1920),
392. We have seen how the reputation of *Mercury*'s editor, J. C. Squire,
quickly declined in *The Dial*; the same happened to *The London Mercury*
which later in 1920 met with *The Dial*'s wrath when it published Francis
Hackett's "A Letter from America" (II, 10 [August 1920]); Hackett wrote
that the editors were "determined, if they can afford it, to lead America
to art – by the ear, if necessary" (p. 472).
[155] *Readers and Writers (1917-1921)* (New York, 1922), p. 165; *The New
Witness*, XIX, 483 (February 10, 1922), 94. Gilbert Seldes thanked Chesterton for "the frequent favourable and highly gratifying notices which The
New Witness has given to *The Dial*" (undated letter among *Dial* papers).
[156] *Time*, I, 1 (March 3, 1923), 12.
[157] "Editorials: The Magazine in America", *The Double Dealer*, I, 3
(March 1921), 82.

Now that the *Dial* prize has gone to a critic the ratio may be expected to increase to 1/55 or over. As I have always regarded critics as the eunuchs of literature . . . But there is no use finishing that sentence." [158]

Although such a magazine as *The Nation* kept publishing gracious notices, *The Dial*, especially towards the end, drew more censure than praise. Early opposition came especially from the side of some experimental little magazines like *The Little Review, Secession,* and *Broom. "Dial*-baiting", as Bernard Smith has pointed out, became their "sport".[159] *Secession* accused *The Dial* of irresolution and diffuseness: "It would be less compromising to go one way or the other. Stay on dry land like the *Atlantic Monthly* or leap head first into the contemporary stream. *If you wish a good swim take off your life-belt!*" *Secession* was made necessary by the existence of "this *Yale-Review*-in-a-Harvard-Blazer".[160] This was not simply a Bohemian pose or an attack merely prompted by the jealousy of an impecunious little magazine for a distinguished, prosperous review. Munson, who was *Secession*'s editor, voiced the same sentiment in a private letter soliciting material for his magazine from Malcolm Cowley: "I would be particularly interested", he wrote, "in seeing the work which you may possibly value highly but which magazines like *The Dial* are reluctant to accept".[161] Indeed *The Dial*'s catholicity of taste and its alleged opposition to experimentalism attracted ever increasing censure during its life-time. The following letter from "I.S." in New York, was published in *The*

---

[158] "Chroniques III: And to the United States", *The Transatlantic Review*, I, 5 (May 1924), 355.

[159] *Forces in American Criticism* (New York, 1939), p. 357. In 1953, *The Dial*'s friend, E. E. Cummings, wrote a vigorous defence of the magazine (see *Six Non-Lectures*, p. 50), but by 1927, even *The Criterion* felt that *The Dial* seemed "to have grown a little tired" (H[erbert] R[ead], "Periodical Reviews", *The Criterion*, V, 3 [June 1927], 372).

[160] G[orham] B. M[unson], "Exposé No. 1", *Secession*, No. 1 (Spring 1922), 24.

[161] January 23, 1922: Anderson papers. Munson's opinion of *The Dial* seems to have changed radically since the 1920's; in 1962 he described it as "the most exciting magazine of the arts in the Twenties" ("Greenwich Village That Was: Seedbed of the Twenties", *The Literary Review: An International Journal of Contemporary Writing*, V, 3 [Spring 1962], 320).

Little Review, in its Spring issue for 1925, and may be taken as a representative attack:

The Dial is an endowed institution; and, in addition, its heart is in the right place – both fatal diseases. It is indulgent with art and artists beyond reason, taste and discretion; its patience is inexhaustible; and not only is it infinitely patient with art and artists, but it is even patient with its own patience. It is determined that when the roll will be called up yonder it shall be among those present. And this, not being themselves dirt artists, is for them a most trying resolution to live up to and with. For they can never feel quite certain that they are not being hoaxed or imposed upon, which they must dread above all things. Consequently, they must buy only sure things, and must help only those who can well help themselves. Inevitably, their final product is sane, sound and substantial. They must give good value for the money, even though they are never quite sure that they are getting it.

The attitude towards *The Dial* of Harold Loeb and Matthew Josephson, the editors of the little magazine *Broom,* did not change with the years. In 1959, Loeb remembered that *The Dial* "tended to repeat the same names over and over again. No longer was there novelty in publishing T. S. Eliot or James Joyce, Mina Loy or Marianne Moore." [162] This must indeed seem extreme modernism, but it explains the underlying motives of much "*Dial* baiting". Matthew Josephson, whose imaginary conversation with Paul Rosenfeld we discussed earlier in this chapter, rebuked *The Dial*, in 1962, for its preference for "old authors of international renown, such as Anatole France and Arthur Schnitzler".[163]

This reference to *The Dial*'s European contributors exemplifies another frequent criticism of the magazine. A number of American contemporaries felt that *The Dial* was patronizing the older generation of European writers to the detriment of young native Americans. William Carlos Williams was among such critics.

[162]   *The Way It Was* (New York, 1959), p. 6.
[163]   *Life among the Surrealists: A Memoir* (New York, 1962), p. 101. Cf., also, Eugene Jolas and Eliott Paul, "A Review", *transition*, No. 12 (March 1928), 146: "*The Dial* ... continues to purr, when Anatole France is mentioned, and up to a short time ago thought of German literature in terms of Hauptmann, Schnitzler and von Hoffmannsthal."

Although Williams had been very grateful for the *Dial* Award for 1926 – he had written a poem for the occasion, "Lines on the Receiving The Dial Award" – he told Ezra Pound in August 1928 that *The Dial* was "a dead letter among the publisher crowd. It almost means that if you are 'one of *The Dial* crowd' you are automatically excluded from perlite society as far as influence in N.Y. goes. And yet I myself feel so disgusted with *The Dial* for its halfhearted ways that I am almost ready to agree with anyone concerning its worthlessness."[164] Four years later, when he reviewed the state of the magazines in the first issue of his revived *Contact,* he complained that *The Dial* had tried "to 'bring in Europe' for our good", but had left "us timidly unprinted".[165]

Indeed the magazine's "foreign accent became so thick"[166] that, in later years, it alienated many of its earlier sympathizers. An early and ill-advised attack on the magazine's interest in European literature, one which drew a reply from *The Dial* itself, was launched by Henry Seidel Canby in his editorial column in *The Literary Review* of *The New York Evening Post.* Canby had made mention of *The Dial* before, but in 1923 he devoted a full editorial to it. His main complaint was that *The Dial* would like to have Americans write like Europeans: "Bring Europe to us by all means and in every measure . . . but don't tell us to write like Schnitzler, D. H. Lawrence, or Paul Fort, or anyone else whose environment and tradition are utterly different from our own."[167] Thayer was in Germany at the time and in his absence Kenneth Burke wrote a letter to *The Literary Review* which

[164] August 11, 1928, *The Selected Letters of William Carlos Williams,* ed. John C. Thirlwall (New York, 1957), p. 103. But the *Dial* Award was very welcome although the money was spent in a sad way: "then in 1926 *The Dial* gave me its award, two thousand dollars. Unfortunately I had just been sued for fifteen thousand dollars for a short story of mine printed in another magazine. It had been settled out of court for five thousand, so that the *Dial*'s money came in handy" (*Autobiography* [New York, 1951], pp. 241-242).
[165] "The Advance Guard Magazine", *Contact,* I, 1 (February 1932), 89.
[166] William Troy, "The Story of the Little Magazines", *The Bookman,* LXX, 5 (January 1930), 481.
[167] "Longfellow Junior", *The Literary Review* of *The New York Evening Post,* III, 26 (March 13, 1923), 497.

registered due thanks for the kind things Canby had said about
The Dial but challenged his criticism. The editors, Burke wrote,
considered "the value of the contribution more important than
the arbitrary national lines", but they saw no reason "why Americans should be expected to write like Europeans – or unlike
them, for that matter". That *The Dial* should have been mis-
construed in such a manner seemed to Burke unnecessary.[168]
The attack had indeed misrepresented such an essential trait of
the magazine that the editors, to reinforce Burke's refutation,
devoted their "Comment" for June 1923 to yet another defence
of their editorial ideas: "It has been our fear, precisely, that too
many young Americans would begin writing like James Joyce." [169]

We have remarked earlier that it was especially the later *Dial*
that was criticized most frequently and most severely; this was
during the editorship of Marianne Moore. Since Seldes had left
The Dial in December 1923, Alyse Gregory had been managing
editor. In September 1924, however, she moved away from New
York City to Montoma in Ulster County in the company of
Llewelyn Powys for whose delicate health country air was essential. She married Powys in the end of that same month and did
not return to New York City before the end of February 1925, in
the meantime directing most of the *Dial* business by correspondence
with the New York office. Already on 15 August 1924 Marianne
Moore had offered her services to *The Dial* to relieve Alyse
Gregory, and in March 1925 she accepted *The Dial*'s invitation
to succeed Miss Gregory as managing editor. In June 1925,
Thayer announced the appointment of Marianne Moore as
Acting Editor, who "will then include among her duties, in addition to those of Managing Editor, many of those hitherto belonging to the Editor himself".[170] Thayer wanted more leisure
to write for *The Dial*. Since some time before Miss Moore's
appointment, however, his health had not been good, and even-

---

[168] "Correspondence: *The Dial*'s Policy", *The Literary Review*, III, 31
(April 7, 1923), 594.
[169] *Dial*, LXXIV, 6 (June 1923), 638.
[170] "Announcement", *Dial*, LXXVIII, 6 (June 1925), 533. Alyse Gregory
had been Thayer's first choice for editor (Van Wyck Brooks had also been
considered), but Powys persuaded her to return to England with him. Cf.

tually he had a complete breakdown. Watson had moved to Rochester, N.Y., and Alyse Gregory went to live in England. Much of the editors' enthusiasm had waned; the exciting days of the earlier *Dial* were over. No literary work of the later 1920's was to create the same stir as *The Waste Land* and *Ulysses,* except perhaps the fiction of Hemingway – and *The Dial*'s treatment of Hemingway was rather ambiguous.[171] The influence on *The Dial* of these internal as well as external developments was very noticeable; with the new editorial policy controversy was so completely banned from its pages that, apart from the *Dial* Awards, the magazine seemed to move in a vacuum, a world completely its own. Especially the European contributions became more and more insignificant.

The remoteness and preciosity of the later *Dial* was undoubtedly partly due to the change in editorship, but many contemporary critics of the magazine did not take sufficient account of the more general changes in editorial enthusiasm as well as in the literary climate of the time. They wondered at the discrepancy between Marianne Moore's talents as an editor and as a poet. Gorham Munson pondered on the "qualifications of a first order editor, who is so much rarer than a good poet".[172] But there were others such as William Carlos Williams and Ezra Pound who never doubted Miss Moore's editorial talents, although they were

---

also the following remark of William Carlos Williams: "Scofield Thayer, so the rumor ran, had proposed to Marianne Moore who had begged off, though continuing to work at the *Dial* office" (*Autobiography,* pp. 163-164).
[171] In October 1924, Edmund Wilson reviewed *Three Stories and Ten Poems* and *In Our Time* and praised Hemingway's prose. *The Sun Also Rises,* however, received only a "Briefer Mention" in January 1927, and was characterized as assuming "the rhythm, the monotony, and the absence of colour which one associates with a six-day bicycle race". This judgment was reversed in "Comment" of September 1927, presumably written by Watson or Burke. When in March 1925, Thayer, Watson, and Miss Gregory disagreed about a Hemingway story, Marianne Moore was asked for a final verdict. She turned it down. This was the second and last story Hemingway submitted to *The Dial.* Some of his poems had been rejected earlier. Cf., also, N. Joost's article on Hemingway & *The Dial* in *Neophilologus,* April-August 1968.
[172] *Destinations: A Canvas of American Literature since 1900* (New York, 1928), p. 100.

highly critical of the later *Dial*. We have related earlier that Williams told Pound that he was "disgusted with *The Dial*", but he went on to say: "Marianne, however, is never included by me in my condemnations; she is doing quietly all she can to warp things toward a better policy – but she will not succeed. . . ." [173] Pound also retained his faith in Miss Moore's editorial capacities; when Harriet Monroe was looking for a possible successor as editor of *Poetry,* Pound suggested Marianne Moore. She had, Pound felt, the "necessary irreproachable respectability, the that against which no lousy ploot can object on the grounds of her not bein' a lady or bein' likely to pervert the growing school child, etc.".[174]

An aspect of Miss Moore's editorship which gained perhaps widest publicity, and which was blown up out of all proportions, was the fact that she proposed alterations in manuscripts. When he interviewed Miss Moore for *The Paris Review* in 1963, Donald Hall mentioned Hart Crane's complaint that she had rearranged his poem "The Wine Menagerie" and changed the title to "Again". "I would never have conceded to such an outrageous joke if I had not desperately needed the twenty dollars", Crane had written.[175] Marianne Moore, however, remembered – and the *Dial* papers bear her out – that Crane's "gratitude was ardent

---

[173] August 11, 1928, *The Selected Letters of William Carlos Williams,* p. 104.

[174] October 6, 1931, *The Letters of Ezra Pound, 1907-1941,* ed. D. D. Paige (New York, 1950), p. 235.

[175] Letter to Charlotte and Richard Rychtarik, December 1, 1925: *The Letters of Hart Crane,* ed. Brom Weber (New York, 1952), p. 220. About the earlier editorial procedure concerning alterations Alyse Gregory wrote: "When I was associated with the *Dial* it was our editiorial policy never to make corrections or alterations in the work of our contributors, but if we found some passage too obscure for our understanding, some punctuation that confused the sense, some error in grammar, to call it to the attention of the author and get his advice" ("*Dial* Days", *Paul Rosenfeld: Voyager in the Arts,* p. 24). Marianne Moore described her editorial dilemma in a letter to Robert Hillyer (June 7, 1926): "I am so desirous of maintaining the standard of style of writing which Doctor Watson and Mr. Thayer regard as essential and realizing that they decline contributions rather than request changes, I am exceedingly unhappy in harassing contributors and in certain instances, close friends of theirs; but on the other hand, there is work that I could not easily relinquish" (*Dial* papers).

and later his repudiation commensurate".[176] Crane's cordial letters to Miss Moore and his criticism of her to his friends seem to indicate a private frustration which prevented objectivity. Miss Moore did propose alterations to different writers on several occasions, but so did (and do) editors of many magazines, including the editors of *The Hound & Horn* and *The Southern Review*.

However often and however severely *The Dial* was criticized, it went its own way; as Marianne Moore remarked: "We didn't care what other people said. I never knew a magazine which was so selfpropulsive." [177] On several occasions Miss Moore has commented on "the ferocity of contributors ... toward editors", but she felt that "anything in the way of ill-wishing fulminations was constantly neutralized by over-justice to us from other quarters".[178] *The Dial*, indeed, had its admirers till the end. When it finally ceased publication in July 1929, many contributors professed their regret. Thomas Mann's homage is representative and exemplifies the feeling of many that *The Dial* had been given less than its due: "Die Nachricht von dem Verschwinden des 'Dial' aus dem literarischen Leben Amerikas hat mich sehr betrübt. Diese so fein geleitete Zeitschrift hätte wirklich eine lebhaftere Beteiligung des Publikums verdient." [179] Not only contributors, however, found praise for *The Dial*. *This Quarter*, for instance, which just then after a silence of two years resumed

---

[176] *Writers at Work: The Paris Review Interviews*, Second Series, edited and with an Introduction by Van Wyck Brooks (New York, 1963), p. 80. Marianne Moore had proposed the alterations with the greatest reluctance and Crane's reply – which he had signed "Gratefully yours" – had shown no signs of exasperation (both letters dated November 10, 1925, *Dial* papers).

[177] *Writers at Work*, p. 78. A decade earlier Miss Moore had written: "to have disliked *The Dial* from the inside would have been impossible" ("Symposium on the Little Magazine", *Golden Goose*, III, 1 [1951], 18); cf., also, letter, Marianne Moore to Gordon Craig: "I have to admit that the welfare of The Dial has become a passion with me that nothing supersedes. ... The Dial is my supreme concern" (September 26, 1927, *Dial* papers).

[178] "Symposium on the Little Magazines", 18; "The Dial" (Part II), *Life and Letters Today*, XXVIII, 41 (January 1941), 5.

[179] Letter to Marianne Moore, June 8, 1929, *Dial* papers.

publication, "profoundly regrets the passing of this pioneer 'pure' literary magazine, and freely acknowledges the debt of its good example. *The Dial* showed, as no current American magazine has done, that taste exists in America, and that trans-Atlantic creative writing can stand alongside its European counterpart with no need to lower its head." [180] Several of its enemies, however, "had prepared its obituary long before July 1929".[181]

The fact that *The Dial* bought eleven poems of D. H. Lawrence as late as 28 March 1929 for its October issue, seems to indicate that the decision to suspend the magazine was taken some time towards the middle of 1929. There were no financial worries: *The Dial* died a natural death because, as Miss Moore wrote to Harriet Monroe three years afterwards, "we each felt the mechanical obstacle to our continuing the magazine, all but insuperable. Mr. Thayer was out of town and able to give advice only occasionally; Doctor Watson was living in Rochester; and we did not wish to publish material – text or pictures – without consultation. You can imagine the amount of correspondence involved." [182] The weariness of these remarks was the result of burnt-out editorial enthusiasm, but there was also a more general feeling abroad that 1929 was the end of an era, symbolized by the death of both *The Dial* and *The Little Review* in that year.[183] "Contemporary art has come into its own", the editors of *The Little Review* proclaimed in a special circular announcing the final issue; "today there is only emulation . . . there will be repetition for a hundred years".

[180] "Sic Transit", *This Quarter*, II, 1 (Summer 1929), 176.
[181] William Troy, "The Story of the Little Magazines", *The Bookman*, LXX, 5 (January 1930), 481.
[182] February 22, 1932, *Poetry* papers, Chicago University Library.
[183] In his obituary on these two magazines, Morton Dauwen Zabel wrote: "With their last issues . . . we are made to feel quite clearly the passing of a period which furnished both its partisans and its astonished observers with enough excitement to establish it as one of the most colorful chapters in our literary history" ("The Way of Periodicals", *Poetry*, XXXIV, 6 [September 1929], 330). A year later *The Nation* reminisced about the "despairing comment that accompanied the death last year of the *Little Review* and the *Dial*, the lament that America could not support experimental literary magazines and that the old ardor of revolt was dying" ("Editorial: The New Magazines", *The Nation*, CXXX [January 29, 1930], 116).

The years to follow would depart very sharply from the tenets and tastes of *The Dial* and the 'Twenties. The tone of those years is exemplified by the following words of Michael Gold which were published just one year after the suspension of *The Dial*: "There is something symbolic about this death of every literary vestige of the pre-war period in America; *Dial, Little Review, transition*. The cards are being shuffled for a new deal; a bigger game is being prepared, may we all find ourselves ready to play it." [184] Already during its life-time *The Dial* had been rebuked for its lack of social commitment, and in the age of Marxism "the solipsistic aestheticism of the *Dial* school and the inane eclecticism of the liberal and individualistic critics" were indeed at a low ebb. [185] It was only after Marxism had been discredited and the university English departments had institutionalized modern literature, that the reputation of *The Dial* rose to its present-day zenith.

Although *The Dial* closed down with a minimum of fuss, rumours of its continuance or revival were abroad for some time. Malcolm Cowley thought that "The Dial may possibly continue under Orage", and two years later the editor of *The Hound & Horn,* Lincoln Kirstein, wrote to Roger Sessions: "Watson, who put up the money for The Dial, is now backing Kenneth Burke, Matthew Josephson, Malcolm Cowley and I suppose Paul Rosenfeld, on another Dial." [186] This editorial list would probably have met with Watson's approval, but a month later when Kirstein met Cowley for lunch it turned out that the latter "seemed to know nothing about it, and yet the rumor persists". [187] But *The Dial* had definitely breathed its last in July 1929, though its influence was to persist.

[184] Michael Gold, "Notes of the Month", *The New Masses*, VI, 2 (July 1930), 5. *transition* was only suspended temporarily.

[185] Cf. Richel North (pseudonym for A. D. Emmart), "The Limitations of American Magazines", *Modern Quarterly*, I, 1 (March 1923), 2-12; I, 3 (September 1923), 17-25; Newton Arvin, "Discussion", *PR*, II, 7 (April-May 1935), 25.

[186] Cowley to Allen Tate, June 3, 1929: Tate papers, Princeton University Library. Kirstein to Sessions, June 8, 1931, *Hound & Horn* papers, Yale University Library.

[187] Kirstein to Kenneth White, July 8, 1931, *Hound & Horn* papers.

3

THE HOUND & HORN (1927-1934) *

I

Already during the life-time of *The Dial,* there appeared an undergraduate magazine at Harvard which set out to "supply a fresh medium for creative expression to all members of the University who desire it".[1] Its rather exotic name, *The Hound & Horn,* was derived from Ezra Pound's poem *The White Stag,*[2] and this initial homage proved prophetic of a close, if short-lived collaboration with Pound in later years. In its early days, however, the magazine was, as its subtitle indicated, "A Harvard Miscellany". It was initially edited by two undergraduates, Lincoln Kirstein, who was to be the magazine's mainstay till the end, and Varian Fry; they had little hope of making the board of *The Harvard Advocate* and consequently decided to edit a magazine of their own. Later associates with varying degrees of editorial influence included R. P. Blackmur, Bernard Bandler II,

---

* All quotations from personal correspondence in this chapter are taken from letters in the *Hound & Horn* Collection in the Beinecke Library of Yale University, unless it is stated otherwise. For a description of the collection, see Leonard Greenbaum, "The *Hound & Horn* Archive", *The Yale University Library Gazette,* XXXIX, 3 (January 1965), 137-146.

[1] "Announcement", *H & H,* I, 1 (September 1927), 5.

[2] " 'Tis the white stag, Fame, we're a-hunting,
   Bid the world's hounds come to horn!' "
   (Ezra Pound, *Personae* [London, 1952], p. 39).
Also quoted, with slight inaccuracies, by Lincoln Kirstein, "The Hound & Horn, 1927-1934" (with a Letter from Varian Fry as a Note), *The Harvard Advocate,* CXXI, 2 (Christmas 1934), 6 (hereafter cited as Kirstein). Kirstein remembers that "even up to seven years later confused people would send us advertisements of prize beagles and airdales [sic], thinking we were a hunting magazine" (p. 7).

A. Hyatt Mayor, Dudley Fitts, Francis Fergusson, Ezra Pound, Allen Tate, and Yvor Winters.

From the start, the roots of the magazine were clearly exposed; it was started as "a college paper based on the London *Criterion*", and it considered itself, "in some respects", the successor of *The Dial*.[3] The influence of *The Criterion*'s editor, T. S. Eliot, was apparent to friends and enemies alike and was often commented upon. *The Hound & Horn*, in the words of William Carlos Williams, "took the hint from Eliot in determining the tone of its material", and *This Quarter* detected "the marks of a sinister influence exercised . . . by Mr. T. S. Eliot".[4] Early issues of the magazine were very complimentary about *The Criterion*. "Periodical Reviews" – a quarterly department of the early *Hound & Horn* clearly inspired by a similar column in *The Criterion* – described it as "the most refreshing and at the same time the soundest review published in English", although it was not oblivious to an undefined "atmosphere of officialdom and heaviness".[5] The editorial "Comment" of the third issue expressed unrestrained admiration: "The *Criterion* has maintained a high level of artistic integrity and has proved itself to be contemporary literature's most distinguished and able medium of expression. In that review Mr. Eliot has not only erected a solid edifice of critical standards which have been influential in moulding modern philosophical criticism, but under his guidance a great part of the important creative thinking of the last five years has been reflected." [6]

At Harvard "*The Hound & Horn* and *The Criterion* were Gog

---

3   "Volume I, No. 1; September 1927: Volume VII, No. 4; July 1934", *H & H*, VII, 4 (Summer 1934), unnumbered page.
4   Williams, "The Advance Guard Magazine", *Contact*, I, 1 (February 1932), 89; Edward Titus, "The Flying Column", *This Quarter*, III, 4 (Spring 1931), 749. Cf., also, Austin Warren, "Some Periodicals of the American Intelligentsia", *The New English Weekly*, I, 25 (October 6, 1932), 595: "As for the range and point of view of the 'Hound and Horn': T. S. Eliot was (and doubtless remains) one of the chief gods in the founders' pantheon; and both poetry and criticism stem from Eliot."
5   "Periodical Reviews" (anon.), *H & H*, I, 1 (Autumn 1927), 69.
6   *H & H*, I, 3 (Spring 1928), 186.

and Magog",[7] but as the younger magazine grew away from Harvard, it also gradually asserted its independence of *The Criterion*, although its initial admiration never turned into rebellion and rejection. This revised attitude was indicative of increasing self-confidence; it was determined by the magazine's declaration of independence of Harvard in the autumn of 1929, its subsequent move to New York, and its alliance with Ezra Pound. *The Hound & Horn*'s coming of age was dramatically illustrated by the initial eagerness of its editors to secure from *The Criterion* an agreement for simultaneous publication of important contributions, and their subsequent change of heart. As late as 9 January 1930, Bernard Bandler had written to Eliot that the editors hoped that their "similarities of purpose, your interest in us, and your generosity, might bring about an exchange . . . nothing could gratify me more than a closer relationship with THE CRITERION; and nothing could strengthen THE HOUND & HORN and make it a less local and excentric and more general and responsible magazine than such an exchange with you." But when, in August of the following year, Eliot suggested simultaneous publication of Stuart Gilbert's essay on the later work of Joyce, Lincoln Kirstein answered that he considered it "inadvisable . . . to attempt simultaneous publication of any work however interesting, in this case, Mr. Gilbert's remarks about the WORK IN PROGRESS would be" (August 18, 1931). Whether this change of attitude was occasioned by Ezra Pound is impossible to establish, but the editors certainly acted in agreement with his view of the matter. Pound thought it "waste of space to print simultaneous with Criterion. It is against my interest (cash) not to sell same article to you both; but with only two quarterlies ready for serious stuff, it isn't right to hold up the traffic. The few hundred people who want FOOD can buy both."[8] The editors were sufficiently interested in Pound's opinion of *The Criterion* to publish his note on "Criterionism" in the autumn of 1930:

---

[7]   Francis Russell, *The Great Interlude* (New York, 1964), p. 155. After the suspension of *The Hound & Horn*, Kirstein wrote: "By the end of the second year the magazine was much less like a weak echo of *The Criterion*" (Kirstein [see note 2], p. 7).

[8]   Letter to *The Hound & Horn*, February 26, 1930.

"The danger of the *Criterion* policy", Pound wrote, "is that one can not indulge continually in a diet of dead crow without its tainting the breath. You can not spend *so much* of your time analysing the inperfections of dead and moribund writing without some odour of the undertaker's establishment penetrating the pages of the review." [9]

Although they admired its high standard of intellectual discussion, the editors felt indeed that *The Criterion* was not topical enough. Another point of divergence was their ambition to make *The Hound & Horn* an American magazine. On 27 July 1932, Bernard Bandler wrote to Edward J. O'Brien that the editors had been forced to adopt a very definite policy in respect to short stories: "We are so limited in space and can publish so few in each issue that we have decided to bring [in print] only those written by Americans." Half a year later Lincoln Kirstein informed the same correspondent that his interest was limited "almost entirely to essays which have a general reference to this country" (February 8, 1933). But although *The Hound & Horn* chose to develop independently of *The Criterion*, it always remained loyal to T. S. Eliot, and its advertisements proudly displayed *The Criterion*'s estimate of it as the "best magazine from the literary and philosophic-literary point of view of any in America".[10]

The Americanism of *The Hound & Horn* was a feature that distinguished it very sharply also from *The Dial*. Its physical appearance, however, was strongly reminiscent of the elegant lay-out of that magazine. Varian Fry has related how the prospective editors of *The Hound & Horn* initially merely thought of a "*multigraphed* publication", but how "that notion was soon abandoned in favor of laid paper, Caslon Old Style type, and deckle-edged cover stock". [11] But it is symbolic of the differences between the two magazines that the format of *The Hound &*

[9] "Correspondence: Criterionism", *H & H*, IV, 1 (Autumn 1930), 114.
[10] B[onamy] D[obree], "American Periodicals", *The Criterion*, IX, 35 (January 1930), 372.
[11] Note to Kirstein, p. 93. Kirstein himself wrote: "Fry and I were very much interested in fine printing ... Presentation was a big worry with us always" (p. 6).

Horn was changed five times during the seven years of its life. The magazine shows all the advantages and disadvantages of the youthfulness of its editors. Whereas the editorial taste of *The Dial* was wide but remarkably consistent through the nine years of its existence, the files of *The Hound & Horn* and, more especially, the editorial correspondence now in the Beinecke Library at Yale are an index to the phases of the intellectual development of its editors.

Lincoln Kirstein was the only editor who was associated with the magazine from beginning to end. It was the generosity of his parents which made the magazine possible and it was his "capacity for being on the spot", as his co-editor Hyatt Mayor characterized it,[12] that made it as exciting and "contemporary" as it was. Kirstein's early interest and accomplishment in different arts are concisely depicted in Bernhard Taper's recent book on George Balanchine:

As a young man, Kirstein essayed various arts, showing some talent in all of them. He won a prize at Harvard for freehand drawing, he had a book of poems published, he wrote and published a novel, he played the piano better than competently, he collected art work and wrote articles on painting and photograhpy, he was one of the co-founders of the Harvard Society for Contemporary Art, which is generally credited with being the germinal source out of which grew New York's Museum of Modern Art, and, while still in college, he helped establish the highly regarded literary quarterly *Hound & Horn*, which he later edited.[13]

Kirstein's main interest, the ballet, resulted in the founding of the School of American Ballet which opened in January 1934 and with which he has been connected ever since. Although Kirstein did not excel in any one art he possessed sufficient knowledgeable enthusiasm for most of them to recognize and sponsor some of the major talents of his day. It was his talent for organization and his capacity for hero-worship which transformed the early miscellaneous undergraduate magazine into the most inspired critical review of its day in America. The history

---

[12] Undated letter [1930] to Kirstein.
[13] *Balanchine* (New York, 1963), pp. 159-160.

of *The Hound & Horn* is the record of Kirstein's admiring loyalty to a number of important literary figures of the time.[14] These men, in turn or simultaneously, influenced editorial decisions, and in some instances virtually ran the magazine. Kirstein's susceptibility to contemporary intellectual and artistic movements made *The Hound & Horn* a forum of intense and often heated debate, very different from the aloofness and self-sufficiency of the later *Dial*. This editorial alertness was, of course, complemented by the intellectual adventurousness and earnestness of the time, which had been instigated by the economic depression. The magazine's intellectual rather than prophetic attitude towards the problems of the time saved it from the pitfalls of an exclusive adherence to one ready-made solution. Such a solution for many contemporary magazines was Marxism. *The Hound & Horn* rather took an interest in a number of contemporary movements. Although some of its contributors showed Marxian sympathies, the magazine was best known for its discussions of such conservative causes as humanism and agrarianism. Its intellectual vigilance was indeed partly the direct result of pressures from outside: it put a number of contemporary panaceas to the test of intellectual discussion. Whereas *The Dial,* with decreasing justification, had urbanely taken its function and its audience for granted, an aesthetic review of the early 'Thirties like *The Hound & Horn* had to justify its existence all along.

The attitude of *The Hound & Horn* towards *The Dial* was never one of unquestioning admiration. Already in its second issue, it joined the chorus of fault-finders: "The *Dial* used to be exciting: it is now – not exactly dull or dreary – but quiet,

---

14 Bernhard Taper has written that "it has been one of Kirstein's sadnesses all his life to feel himself a mere cultivated amateur in the midst of professionals whose professionalism he admires beyond words" (*Balanchine*, p. 161). Kirstein's friend, W. H. Auden, however, in his review of *Rhymes of a Pfc*, a recent volume of poetry by Kirstein, attacked "our modern passion for labelling people", according to which Kirstein has always been stigmatized as a mere impresario who is, "by definition, someone who does not himself 'create'" ("Private Poet", *The New York Review of Books*, III, 7 [November 5, 1964], 8). It was in the capacity of impresario, however, that Kirstein's importance for *The Hound & Horn* primarily lay.

careful; its ardor is very thin. It has its own variety of 100% reputation to maintain." [15] There was, however, never any doubt that it was up to *The Hound & Horn* to take the place of *The Dial,* but it was also generally held that it must improve upon it. "We have been labled 'successor of the Dial' ", wrote Ezra Pound to Lincoln Kirstein, "but we certainly do not mean to carry on any sort of Dialish conservatism"; and James W. Lane was glad to think that *The Hound & Horn* "should be able to fill the niche lately vacated by The Dial", but he warned against "such heights of preciousness as, in my opinion, undid The Dial!" [16]

The course of *The Hound & Horn* was close enough to *The Dial's* for the latter's demise to have a noticeable effect. In a letter, dated 8 June 1929, R. P. Blackmur wrote: "in a way we ought to benefit a little from *The Dial's* death, I mean we ought to get a few of their contributors and a few subscribers", and a few months later, on 2 October, he could indeed announce that "the death of The Dial did do us considerable good (plus all the harm that comes of having to read the bunk that would have been submitted to it). I mean we have Burke, Cowley, Williams, and possibly a few others." [17]

In the matter of payment for contributions *The Hound & Horn* continued the *Dial* tradition, although its rates were considerably lower and its financial worries often acute. It paid $7 a page for poetry, $3,50 a page for prose, $10 for a long review and nothing for a shorter mention. Although these rates could not vie with *The Dial's* remuneration, a considerable number of letters to the editors testify to the importance of these payments in the lives of several writers during the depression. They could,

[15] "Periodical Reviews" (anon.), *H & H*, I, 2 (Winter 1928), 177.
[16] Pound to Kirstein, October 26 [?1930]; Lane to Kirstein, October 25, 1929. On 8 February 1930 Pound told Kirstein: "I don't believe the Dial gained a damn thing by its excess of caution."
[17] Letters to Jorge Manach and Ezra Pound. The possibility of a special connection of Cowley and Burke with *The Hound & Horn* seems to have been considered. When, in late 1929, Blackmur had to give up his post as managing editor of the magazine, he reassured Cowley that "as far as I know nothing has been changed with regard to the tentative arrangements between the Hound and you and Burke" (November 12, 1929, Malcolm Cowley papers, Newberry Library).

however, not be maintained till the end. In the autumn of 1932 the editors reluctantly decided to reduce them, although, in the words of Bernard Bandler, "it's hell that the writers should have to suffer, but we have reduced expenses in every possible way and find that a further saving is still necessary".[18] Although the editors had hoped that the reduction would only take effect with the Winter 1933 issue, they finally had to apply it to the preceding number, "in order to be able to take care of all its contributors".[19] The new rates were $5 a page for poetry, $2.50 a page for prose and $10 for a long review.

The financial problem became increasingly acute and was partly responsible for the magazine's discontinuance. Initially, however, there were hopes that *The Hound & Horn* would prosper, and ideas for its expansion were considerably kindled by its association with Ezra Pound. The latter's life-long interest in little magazines as well as in *avant-garde* printing presses is well known. Already in 1916, he had praised "the sporting endeavor of *The Egoist* to do in this dark isle [England] what the *Mercure* has so long done in France, i.e., publish books as well as a magazine".[20] This idea had stayed with Pound throughout the years. In Paris he had been connected with the Three Mountains Press, and in 1927 he had suggested to Harriet Monroe that *Poetry,* as it could not print books, would at least distribute them.[21] He was still advocating this notion in *Hound & Horn*

---

[18] Letter to Yvor Winters, October 6, 1932.

[19] Doris Levine (Kirstein's secretary) to Caroline Gordon, November 2, 1932.

[20] "The Reader Critic", *The Little Review*, III, 2 (April 1916), 36. Pound thought that reprints were "one of the things the Dial neglected" (Letter to *The Hound & Horn*, January 7, 1930). Among the publications of The Egoist Ltd. were T. S. Eliot's *Prufrock and Other Observations*, James Joyce's *Portrait of the Artist*, Wyndham Lewis's *Tarr* and Pound's own *Quia Pauper Amavi*. It was at Pound's instigation that Eliot, Joyce, and Lewis, "the men of 1914" in Lewis's phrase, regularly appeared in both *The Egoist* and *The Little Review*. (See, e.g., Geoffrey Wagner, *Wyndham Lewis: A Portrait of the Artist as the Enemy* [London, 1957], p. 16; and Noel Stock, *Poet in Exile: Ezra Pound* [Manchester, 1964], pp. 69-83).

[21] Cf. Eustace Mullins, *This Difficult Individual, Ezra Pound* (New York, 1961), p. 147; Pound to Harriet Monroe, March 23, 1927, *Poetry* papers, Chicago University Library.

days: "Have written to Johns [of *Pagany*]", he told Louis Zukofsky, "and Bill Wms [William Carlos Williams] (as being in
communic with Wheelwright [of *The Symposium*]) suggesting
Pagany, Symp. and Bitch & B. [Bitch & Bugle, i.e. *The Hound
& Horn*] shd each agree to handle 150 copies of whatever I print
cheaper here [in Italy]." [22] In the pages of *The Hound & Horn*
itself he wrote: ". . . less than a million dollars wd. purchase an
uptodate printing press and pay the annual salaries of three or
four printers; and this press cd. be used to further communication
between the intelligent or at least between the mentally alert
citizens of the republic, IF the selection of matter to be printed
were confided to a dozen men who had each, apart from personal
talent, shown a capacity for discovery of, and interest in, some
notable contemporary work save his own." [23]

In *The Hound & Horn* business manager, Alan Stroock, Pound
met with a gratifying optimism: "We should like . . . gradually
to become a monthly and go into publishing", Stroock wrote to
Pound on 11 March 1930; "the books that we publish would
more or less be articles which might appear in THE HOUND &
HORN except for their length." He announced that at that time
the circulation of the magazine was only about 2500 and the
subscription list under 500, but he saw no reason, "if things
continue as they now seem to be going, why, at the end of this
year, we should not have a circulation of between five and seven
thousand, and a subscription list of at least 1500". Stroock called

---

[22] Letter of February 21 [?1931], Zukofsky papers, Texas University
Library at Austin. Another person who Pound thought might possibly
be interested in such a project was Nancy Cunard: "I am writing her by
this post to say that if she will handle the stuff I shall start printing some
booklets at 10 fr. . . ." (Pound to Samuel Putnam, November 5, 1930, Putnam papers, Princeton University Library; see also Nancy Cunard, "The
Hours Press", *The Book Collector*, XIII, 4 [Winter 1964], 488-496).
[23] "Correspondence: And the Remainder", *H & H*, III, 3 (Spring 1930),
419. Pound apparently also considered the possibility of operating a press
himself. "I shd like to see the advertisement of one of those latest smallest
lightest printing presses again. The kind advertised fer bizniz houses: 'Do
your own printing'." Pound sent this request to William Carlos Williams
on 2 December 1929 asking him for "FULL and bloated particulars" (*The
Letters of Ezra Pound, 1917-1941*, pp. 225-226). Cf. also Charles Norman,
Ezra Pound (New York, 1960), p. 308.

this "a conservative estimate" but conservative estimates in the early 'Thirties were as liable as not to turn out to be extravagant, and three months later, on 20 June 1930, Stroock had to inform Pound that *The Hound & Horn* would certainly not be able "to consider expanding until late in the Fall and perhaps not until after the Winter". Pound's scheme was not to materialize; financial straits proved a persistent handicap.[24] "Lack of funds necessitated our cutting down the issue considerably and we had to omit two whole articles", Kirstein wrote to Kenneth White on 13 January 1931, and, as we have seen, in the autumn of the following year contributor rates had to be reduced. In 1935, after the magazine had expired, Kirstein figured the annual loss at "approximately $10.500".[25] Pound could only repeat his malediction: "God eternally damblast a country that spends billions interfering with people's diet and that can not support a single printing press which will print stuff that people like me want to read; i.e., regardless of immediate fiscal profit." [26]

Whether *The Hound & Horn* ever seriously considered the possibility of appearing as a monthly is doubtful, but the fact that it remained a quarterly posed problems very different from the ones *The Dial* had faced. When, for instance, Katherine Anne Porter proposed to review two new novels, Kirstein declined apologetically: "It may be bad of me, but I cannot afford to review more than one batch of novels a year . . ." (March 31, 1933). Also, whereas *The Dial* had presented its readers with a tasteful, leisurely, sometimes esoteric monthly fare, the contributions to the later *Hound & Horn* appear pruned and compressed to justify every line of the quarterly space they took up. This impression is undoubtedly strengthened by the fact that the magazine tended to carry more criticism than fiction and poetry.

---

[24] Although Pound had been trying to persuade the editors of *The Hound & Horn* with unabating energy, he was never completely sanguine about the results: "there are various things that they wdnt print", he wrote to Samuel Putnam, "even IF they arranged the series" (November 10, 1930, Putnam papers, Princeton University Library).

[25] Letter to Robert Linscott, December 30, 1935.

[26] "Correspondence: 'Costa Piu Della Divina Commedia' ", *H & H*, IV, 4 (Summer 1931), 571. Pound summed up the outcome of his campaign in "Terra Italica" (*The New Review*, I, 4 [Winter 1932], 386).

This was partly due to its interest in aesthetic criticism and in the cultural and intellectual problems of its day, but also to the force of circumstances. When the Summer 1929 issue appeared with no short story, the editorial "Comment" admitted to a sad truth: "Whether from shyness on the part of writers or from a positive dearth of material, the fact is that no stories came to hand that we cared to publish".[27] At about the time this Summer issue was made up, Blackmur wrote to Pound: "I quote your paragraph – 'I take it The Hound & Horn exists for licherchoor only', and say I think so. That is why we publish almost nothing but criticism, there not being much of the other available" (May 20, 1929). The usual quota of creative writing per issue was one third; the remaining space was taken up by essays, reviews and chronicles.

The magazine's taste in stories is well characterized by Alan Stroock: "To us a melodramatic plot means very little, compared to the manner of handling, the means of expression, the delicacy of diction, and the artistry of presenting the whole." [28] To be entirely acceptable, a story which met these technical requirements would also be from the pen of an American who would appear in the magazine for the first time, and it would, preferably, have an American setting. The files of the magazine prove that these were no hard and fast rules but directives subject to the rules of supply and demand. "I suppose it is a good thing to print nothing but American things", Mayor wrote to Kirstein in 1930. "Of course the difficulty is getting something good – a difficulty that did much to ruin the Dial." But when Kirstein proposed to publish a story by one of his new discoveries, the Irish writer Sean O'Faolain, Mayor objected to its length, "and besides, I don't want to be chauvinistic, but the H & H is an *American* magazine. Its criticism may legitimately look abroad, indeed ought to, but not its poems and stories." [29]

It was actually Kirstein, more than any other editorial associate, who was responsible for the American tone of the maga-

[27]   *H & H*, II, 4 (Summer 1929), 338.
[28]   Letter to Clifford Near, August 14, 1930.
[29]   Letter to Kirstein, n.d. [?October 1931].

zine. When in 1933 Albert Guerard won the *Hound & Horn* Undergraduate Competition for the short story, Kirstein wished that his winning entry had been "a story definitely with an indigenous scene, although this may seem frightfully NRA of me".[30] After having spent the summer of 1933 "avidly following the ballet in Europe", Kirstein decided that he did not want "to go abroad again for years and years and years".[31] His faith in indigenous qualities for the purposes of art was also frequently voiced in the pages of his magazine. He complained that American artists had failed to record their own country, especially their own cities, on canvas: "New York persists in its pale, disinterested impermanence, under as intense skies as Tiepolo ever knew, charged with the round action Rubens loved, generally ignored by those eyes which should see it best." [32] Kirstein cherished the film as a native American achievement; although there was hardly an American play that could compete with even the second best of Europe, the film industry "is our creation, and its worldwide expansion is due to our ingenuity". James Cagney, with whom Kirstein was personally acquainted, was featured as the all-American hero: "No one expresses more clearly in terms of pictorial action the delights of violence, the overtones of a semi-conscious sadism, the tendency towards destruction, towards anarchy which is the basis of American sex-appeal." [33]

The Hound & Horn, then, set great store by the American qualities of its stories; it was also eager to print young and unknown authors. On 19 October 1931, Kirstein wrote to one of the magazine's favourite story writers, Janet Lewis [Mrs. Yvor

---

[30] Letter to Yvor Winters, August 31, 1933.
[31] Doris Levine to George Tichenor, June 27, 1933. Cf. letter, Kirstein to Winters, August 31, 1933: "After three concentrated months in the midst of the so-called culture capitals, I am convinced more than ever that this country is the one place to do something." Talking of this summer in his reminiscences of *Hound & Horn* days, Kirstein wrote: "I realized then there was little of interest either on the continent or in England for an American. Any ideas of an extended stay abroad, with the exception of Russia, seemed pointless for an American artist or writer" (Kirstein, p. 10).
[32] "Philip Reisman", *H & H*, VI, 3 (Spring 1933), 441-442.
[33] Kirstein, "Film Chronicle: James Cagney and the American Hero", *H & H*, V, 3 (Spring 1932), 467.

Winters]: "I feel very strongly that our policy in relation to fiction should be this: we want to print work of writers who either have not been published before at all or who have not been published in THE HOUND & HORN, and to enable us to do this continuously we must make it a rule not to publish the same fictioneer twice."

There are, then, a number of striking differences between *The Hound & Horn* and *The Dial*. Particularly relevant to the present discussion is *The Hound & Horn*'s exclusive interest in straightforward technical criticism. It was against personal or biographical criticism. "Our critical attitude", Kirstein wrote in 1929, "must depend on an impersonal consideration of the artists and authors isolated without reference to the personal minutiae which in many people's mind create the character".[34] We have seen that a number of contributors to *The Dial* would readily have agreed to this opinion but that the cause of aesthetic criticism had by no means been victorious in that magazine. With *The Hound & Horn* it virtually became an editorial criterion for acceptance or rejection. On 8 June 1931, Kirstein wrote to Roger Sessions, the composer: "I feel THE HOUND & HORN has a definite function to fill which, generally speaking, is to provide as good technical criticism for intelligent laymen as possible, the minimum of rhetoric and rhapsody." Apart from its being technical, the criticism in the magazine was also to have specific bearing on the present. When George Williamson, in 1929, submitted "John Donne and his Shroud", the first chapter of his book on *The Donne Tradition,* Blackmur had to point out that as space was "really limited" about the only sort of essay on John Donne that the magazine could use would be an essay "not about John Donne himself alone, but about, say, the relation of Donne's sensibility to that of Baudelaire, Corbière and eventually to certain American poets" (March 25, 1929).

These critical ideas figure all the larger in the history of *The Hound & Horn*, because in the later years virtually all criticism was assigned. The core of the magazine's critics and reviewers was much smaller and much more consolidated than that of *The*

---

[34] Letter to Edward J. O'Brien, April 8, 1929.

Dial. Whereas issues of *The Dial* had at times conveyed the suggestion of a tasteful miscellany, *The Hound & Horn* bore the stamp of a very particular group of critics. Some of these and other like-minded critics would continue their work in *The Southern Review*. Indeed both *The Hound & Horn* and *The Southern Review* were primarily influential as critical magazines although the stories and the poems in *The Southern Review* were in general perhaps superior to those in *The Hound & Horn*. The latter magazine did publish occasional poems of such *Dial* regulars as T. S. Eliot, William Carlos Williams, Wallace Stevens, E. E. Cummings, Ezra Pound and Marianne Moore, but the editorial taste in poetry was very uneven and changed with the different editorial alliances. Of both *The Hound & Horn* and *The Southern Review* it may be observed that their critics also contributed a considerable number of the poems. As these poems were judged by the same technical standards as the printed poetry which was reviewed in their pages, it was sometimes not entirely clear whether the methods of criticism had been developed to elucidate the poetry or the poetry written to confirm the methods of criticism. This, however, is a venerable point of debate in any discussion of formalist criticism.

II

In the preceding remarks we have tried to sketch *The Hound & Horn*'s relation to *The Dial* and *The Criterion* and have consequently touched upon various aspects of its editorial policy and upon different episodes of its career. We shall now proceed to a more detailed chronological account of the magazine's fortunes which, it is hoped, will throw additional light on its place in the tradition of the literary review in the United States.[35] The varying

---

[35] The reader will find a virtual issue to issue account in Leonard Greenbaum, "*The Hound & Horn*: Episodes in American Literary History, 1927-1934" (doctoral dissertation, University of Michigan, 1963); the quotations from the editorial correspondence are very extensive. Greenbaum has published his thesis as *The Hound & Horn: The History of a Literary Quarterly* (The Hague, 1966).

services and opinions of the different editorial associates would seem to provide a solid framework to support an account of the variegated history of the magazine.

We have mentioned earlier that *The Hound & Horn* was established by Lincoln Kirstein and Varian Fry as "A Harvard Miscellany". This is a perfectly acceptable definition of the magazine during its first two years. The interest in Harvard affairs was all-pervasive. The second issue contained a spirited defence of football spiced with many anecdotes, and "Notes on Sport" in the fourth issue had a good many things to say about rowing at Harvard, concluding that it was "in splendid condition".[36] There were also a number of editorials dealing with Harvard affairs. More representative, however, of the magazine's aspirations was the editorial "Comment' of the third issue which drew its readers' attention to the first half of R. P. Blackmur's essay on T. S. Eliot in the same issue; it was to be the first in a Harvard Series which had been briefly announced in the previous number: "The plan involves the publication of contemporary studies and collated bibliographies of the works of certain Harvard men who have achieved distinction in the field of letters during the last half-century." [37] Other studies were announced of George Santayana, Henry James, Irving Babbitt, and Henry Adams, but when in later years studies of the latter three did happen to appear, the original plan had long been abandoned if not forgotten. Blackmur's essay in two parts, on Eliot's poetry and criticism, was, however, of crucial importance in the history of the magazine. It established a pattern of critical presuppositions and high critical standards which was to guide the editors till the end. The essay on Eliot proved the first in a series by Blackmur, not on Harvard alumni, but on modern American poets. This series was to be one of the main distinctions of *The Hound & Horn*.

Blackmur's influence on the magazine lasted throughout its

---

[36] Huntingdon R. Hardwick, "The Old Days", *H & H*, I, 2 (Winter 1928), 135-139; Carl H. Pforzheimer, Jr., "Notes on Sport", *H & H*, I, 4 (Summer 1928), 353.
[37] *H & H*, I, 3 (Spring 1928), 185.

existence but was of central importance only during the first two formative years. Blackmur at that time was working in the Dunster House Bookshop in Cambridge, Mass. where "his influence on the boys of his time who bought books suggested by him [was] inestimable".[38] His first contribution to *The Hound & Horn* appeared in the first issue; it was a review of Wyndham Lewis's *The Lion and the Fox* – "Mr. Lewis' essays are violent notebooks for masterpieces" – and he found occasion to consolidate his criticism of Lewis in the third issue when he reviewed *Time and Western Man* and remarked that Lewis had "superlatively the talent for starting hares in the reader's mind; and some of them run in otherwise trackless warrens".[39] In the third and fourth issues appeared his essay on T. S. Eliot; the second part, published in the summer of 1928, deals with Eliot's criticism and is especially relevant to our discussion because it shows how Eliot's critical ideas were assimilated. The editors were well aware of the importance of the essay. Bernard Bandler, even before he decided to accept a co-editorship of the magazine proposed to Kirstein: "If you haven't already done so, why don't you write five or six people such as Oppenheim and Fergusson, requesting general comments on Dick's Eliot article. They could run for twenty-five pages or so, stir up discussion, permit Dick to rejoin with his more clarified ideas, and possibly suggest further topics" (July 8, [1928]).

What made Eliot, in Blackmur's eyes, almost unique as a critic was the purity of his interest in literature as literature and the fact that his approach to literature was invariably technical: "I mean the matters touched on are always to some degree generalized characteristics of the work in hand. No overt attack is made on the 'contents' of the work directly; the marvel and permanent value of the technical method is that, when prudently and fully applied, it results in a criticism which, if its implications are taken up, provides a real and often immaculate judgement on those 'contents'." This method had the merit of being alto-

---

[38]   Kirstein, p. 7.
[39]   "Hubris", *H & H*, I, 1 (Autumn 1927), 43; "The Enemy", *H & H*, I, 3 (Spring 1928), 270.

gether literary; we are interested in the intensity with which a poet expresses his emotions, Blackmur argued virtually paraphrasing Eliot, "not the intensity of the emotions, which matters only to the individual, but the intensity of the artistic process". This interest in expression does away with a great deal of loose "self-expression". It results in a technical judgement which will also be seen to be a moral judgement, as long as we do not confuse moral values in the arts with the preoccupations of professional moralists; they "concern, first, a technique of language, and, second, a technique of feelings which combine in a sensibility adequate to a view of life".[40] Blackmur, then, was interested in technical criticism which would result in a moral judgement. This is in accord with the editorial "Comment" preceding Blackmur's article. Looking back on the achievement of the first volume and looking ahead to future issues, the editors stated that *The Hound & Horn* was working towards a definite end. "That end is the establishment of a sound criterion of values in a time when there is a great confusion of values." [41]

The relevance of these ideas to Blackmur's own criticism will not need insisting upon. His essays will be sufficiently familiar and a detailed exploration would be outside the scope of this chapter. One example will have to suffice. In his controversial essay, "Notes on E. E. Cummings' Language", Blackmur commented on the sentimentality of many of Cummings's poems due to the fact that "we are admitted to the bare emotion. . . . What is most striking, in every instance, about this emotion is the fact that, in so far as it exists at all, it is Mr. Cummings' emotion, so that our best knowledge of it must be, finally, our best guess. It is not an emotion resulting from the poem; it existed before the poem began and is a result of the poet's private life." [42] This reportage of private emotions in poetry may be condemned in words taken from Blackmur's Eliot essay: "Emotions in art are never reproductions of experience, but its result. Art judges as well as expresses its field" (p. 313). If the emotions in Cummings's

[40] "T. S. Eliot II", *H & H*, I, 4 (Summer 1928), 294, 301, 311-312.
[41] *H & H*, I, 4 (Summer 1928), 289.
[42] *H & H*, IV, 2 (Winter 1931), 165-166.

poetry were often private and meaningless, so was the distortion practised upon the language: "merely because his private fancy furnishes his liveliest images, is the worst reason for assuming that this private fancy will be approximately experienced by the reader or even indicated on the printed page." [43] The impact of Blackmur's specific criticisms of individual writers on the magazine's contributors may well have been as powerful as was that of his interpretation of Eliot's general critical methods. When, for instance, Francis Fergusson reviewed Cummings's *Eimi*, he censured his use of language, which, he wrote, was "slammed together out of whatever odds and ends come to hand, and is as ramshackle as a house in Hooverville".[44]

Two other important essays by Blackmur in *The Hound & Horn* were "Examples of Wallace Stevens" and "Masks of Ezra Pound". Both were again concerned with the poet's use of language, and it was in Stevens that Blackmur discovered what he had found lacking in Cummings. "Both Mr. Stevens and Cummings issue in ambiguity – as any good poet does; but the ambiguity of Cummings is that of the absence of known content, the ambiguity of a phantom which no words could give being; while Mr. Stevens' ambiguity is that of a substance so dense with being, that it resists paraphrase and can be truly perceived only in the form of words in which it was given." Indeed, one of the most interesting observations of the essay is that the way in which Stevens combines words is so skilful and unique that it results in the perception of something previously unknown, "something which is literally an access of knowledge".[45] This argument in a sense anticipates the discussion of literature as knowledge in the pages of *The Southern Review*. Stevens was one of the few modern poets who was unreservedly esteemed by the *Hound & Horn* contributors and whose poetry the editors were most anxious to secure for the magazine. "There is no American poetry we

---

[43] *Ibid.*, 174.
[44] "The Individualists", *H & H*, VII, 1 (Autumn 1933), 155. Fergusson's judgment is very possibly indebted to Blackmur's criticism, but it must of course be understood that it is next to impossible to trace direct influences unless one has access to unequivocal personal statements or documents.
[45] "Examples of Wallace Stevens", *H & H*, V, 2 (Winter 1932), 224, 225.

would rather publish the best of than yours", Blackmur wrote to Stevens on 13 April 1929, and some months later Kirstein reaffirmed this when he wrote: "we should always feel honored to include work of one of America's first poets." [46] Stevens was asked for contributions twice again but he could only reply that "nothing short of a coup d'état would make it possible for me to write poetry now".[47] The only poem of Stevens published in *The Hound & Horn* was "Academic Discourse at Havana".[48]

Blackmur's criticism of Pound was much less favourable than his estimate of Stevens. Blackmur thought of Pound as a great maker of verse rather than as a great poet; "he is all surface and articulation", which, according to Blackmur, explained why his best poems were his best translations. Blackmur's description of *The Cantos* registered a similar sense of confusion such as the *Dial* critics had formerly evinced. *The Cantos* were not complex, he wrote, but complicated. "They are not arrayed by logic or driven by pursuing emotion, they are connected because they follow one another, are set side by side, and because an anecdote, an allusion, or a sentence, begun in one Canto may be continued in another and may never be completed at all. . . . The Cantos are what Mr. Pound himself called them in a passage now excised from the canon, a rag-bag." [49] Most contributors agreed with this judgement. Yvor Winters maintained that "in fact, some of his recent Cantos are scarcely more coherent than his correspondence", and Allen Tate felt that the simple historical contrast in the *Cantos* between ancient civilization and modern vulgarity was "a static feat of abstraction that cannot hold the work together".[50] But apart from the criticism of *The Cantos,* the magazine's association with Pound testified to his acknowl-

---

[46]   Letter to Stevens, December 17, 1929.
[47]   Letter to Kirstein, April 10, 1931.
[48]   *H & H*, III, 1 (Autumn 1929), 53-56.
[49]   "Masks of Ezra Pound", *H & H*, VII, 2 (Winter 1934), 178, 192.
[50]   Winters, "Traditional Mastery", *H & H*, V, 2 (Winter 1932), 323; Tate, "The Whole Image of Man", *H & H*, VI, 2 (Winter 1933), 345. An exception to the chorus of objections was Dudley Fitts's review of *A Draft of XXX Cantos* which Pound, however, disliked ("Music Fit for the Odes" *H & H*, IV, 2 [Winter 1931], 278-289).

edged if waning importance as a man of letters and a literary force.

Blackmur's contributions, then, constituted one of the few distinctions of the early "Harvard Miscellany" and his close connection with the magazine was officially sealed on 1 January 1929, when he left Dunster House Bookshop to join the staff as managing editor. But this official association proved of short duration; it was terminated within that same year when *The Hound & Horn* planned to merge with *The Symposium,* a new magazine which was being projected in the second half of 1929. "You may have heard", Blackmur wrote to Malcolm Cowley on 12 November 1929, "that the Hound & Horn has merged with the New Symposium, and that I have thereby lost my job as m.e." [51] The story of the proposed merger with *The Symposium* belongs to the next chapter; negotiations to that end were shipwrecked within two months, but there are no indications that *The Hound & Horn* sought to engage Blackmur's services again afterwards. Although his official association had come to an end he remained an important contributor and still read manuscripts for the magazine.

The two remaining editors were Lincoln Kirstein and Bernard Bandler. Bandler had been invited to join the staff of the magazine in the summer of 1928 at the time of his graduation. After some initial indecision, he eventually wrote to Kirstein, on 20 July 1928: "the attractions of working on the 'Hound & Horn' with you have overcome me". He immediately suggested two changes in the magazine: "First, that in view of our rather grandiose hopes and future intentions we drop the subtitle 'a Harvard Miscellany'. It adds nothing, establishes neither national prestige nor local influence, and might limit unduly our prospective activity. Second, that the names of the editors be published in each issue. Until we decide on official anonymity we should come out responsibly under our own names. Facts of race are and should be irrelevant." Kirstein's reaction to the first proposition must have been negative, because in a letter, dated 25 August 1928, Bandler wrote: "you are convincingly right about

[51] Cowley papers, Newberry Library.

the Harvard Miscellany. The 'Hound & Horn' is strictly amateur, I am innocently inexperienced and serve to learn."

It was one year later that Bandler's suggestion was finally accepted; the Autumn issue of 1929 carried the following statement of policy:

The 'Harvard Miscellany' has been dropped from the title because it misrepresented our intention. However admirable it is to represent something definite, a university, a political movement, a program for art, we have no real connection with Harvard. The fact that Harvard men have hitherto been the principal contributors and the subjects of many of the articles is largely accidental, a matter of geography and accessibility. The word 'Miscellany' is also unfortunate as descriptive of THE HOUND & HORN. If a distinctive attitude, recognizable as common to the group writing for THE HOUND & HORN does not in time become increasingly approved, we have no reason for continued existence.[52]

The issue itself promised well for the future of the now unattached magazine. It opened with S. Foster Damon's "The Odyssey in Dublin", a detailed and careful interpretation of *Ulysses* which – reprinted as a special pamphlet as Blackmur's Eliot essay had been – circulated at Harvard;[53] it was followed

[52] "Comment", *H & H*, III, 1 (Autumn 1929), 5.
[53] Russell, *The Great Interlude*, p. 153. The history of Damon's appreciation of *Ulysses* is representative of the difficulties a number of intelligent readers in the 'Twenties experienced in their efforts to come to terms with the book. On 15 July 1922, he informed Malcolm Cowley that he had read the last chapter in great haste. "Can anyone seriously say that it is anything but disgusting?", he inquired; "Well, perhaps yes. I can think of several worse adjectives now. Perhaps it is a fault of this age that no one can be successfully Rabelaisean." Damon was hardly less antagonistic when he wrote to Cowley again a few months afterwards (September 21, 1922): "There seems to be neither humor, nor pathos, nor phantasy. It is Realism at its most painstaking worst. Such 'frankness' violates the fundamental principles of psychology. When one walks down the street one may notice that it is dirty; but Joyce counts every dog-turd. It is not True, it is merely Factual; it is not Art, it is Photography. ... I regret it is DISGUSTING." He admitted, however, that the literary method was interesting: "it is saved by its technique & also by one or two scenes, including the splendid Walpurgis Night". On 6 July 1929, he reminded Cowley of their correspondence about *Ulysses* seven years earlier: "You will laugh when you see the next *Hound & Horn*: it contains a eulogy and analysis of *Ulysses* by me. Do you remember once writing me 'Take off them skirts!' when I protested against its unattractiveness?" (Cowley papers).

by a short story by Dale Warren, Wallace Stevens's "Academic Discourse at Havana", two photographs and two reproductions, Bernard Bandler's "The Individualism of Irving Babbitt", Kenneth Burke's "Seventh Declamation", a poem by William Carlos Williams ("Rain"), and Norman Foerster's essay "Historian and Critic of Letters: A Diagnosis", a rather pedestrian exposition of the fallacies of historical approaches to literature. Among the book-reviewers were Lawrence Leighton, Yvor Winters and R. P. Blackmur.

This issue also carried an extensive roster of four editors: Kirstein, Bandler, Blackmur and Fry, but in the following number – Winter 1930 – the names of Blackmur and Fry were dropped. We have touched upon Blackmur's short career as managing editor. Fry was a strong advocate of the magazine's ties with Harvard; he "felt vaguely" that *The Hound & Horn* was going off the track when it "was floundering between Harvard and the 'national (if not international) scope', and that it suffered for it". In other words, his idea of the magazine was directly opposed to Bandler's. When Bandler joined the staff Fry left after "a family quarrel".[54] Bandler, however, was not the only editor who objected to the denomination "Harvard Miscellany". The following passage from a letter which Blackmur wrote to Pound on 16 March 1929 indicates a similar editorial embarrassment at the magazine's subtitle: "In the first place, both 'Harvard' and 'Miscellany' were unwise words to have chosen and really, I think mean nothing except to advertisers. As soon as we can manage it we will drop the 'Harvard Miscellany' part of the title altogether." Blackmur's letter was, however, clearly not so much concerned about the implications of the "Harvard Miscellany" subtitle as about the impression it would make on Pound whose

---

[54] Fry, Note to Kirstein, p. 93. That editorial disagreements were not unusual is illustrated by a letter of Alan Stroock to Hyatt Mayor (August 9, 1930): "So now the Pope [Bandler?] and Henry VIII [Kirstein?] are having another fight, and I hardly know where to apply my subordination. ... I agree with you that *one* head should direct and have the final say, but just try asking both Lincoln and Bernie at the same time, which that should be!" Stroock may refer to a disagreement between Kirstein and Bandler about the choice of a story by Erskine Caldwell.

contributions the editors would "very, very much like to have". Bandler's association with the magazine proved a very considerable intellectual stimulus. His early interests were more strongly philosophical than literary, and his enthusiasm for intellectual discussion was instrumental in consolidating a closer homogeneity among like-minded contributors, especially editor-contributors. Bandler was always bristling with ideas; in Kirstein's words, he "had a mind that was so fluent, so much the master of intellectual and philosophical abstractions, so deeply involved with the real business of the spirit, that when he first talked to me at any length I was exhausted for two days".[55] We have already mentioned Bandler's proposition to invite several comments on Blackmur's Eliot essay in the hope of eliciting a wider discussion of critical principles and of crystallizing a common point of view. A letter written six weeks later indicates that the new editor was considering a general statement on criticism: "I haven't forgotten the pronunciamento. It will be necessary to read all the literature of serious criticism written in recent years in the States, and an analysis of the miscellaneous material should yield an article less pompous and more serviceable than the . . . [illegible word] pronunciamento." [56]

In the same letter Bandler suggested doing an article on Paul Elmer More if "it harmonizes with your general program for the 'Hound & Horn' ". The idea for such an article had come from Irving Babbitt and to Bandler it seemed "a perfect subject . . . to think my way through to a program".[57] Indeed, the magazine's involvement in humanism was mainly inspired by Bandler, but his coordinating influence reached much farther. He was always strongly aware of the possibilities of the magazine as the organ

---

[55] Kirstein, p. 7.
[56] Bandler to Kirstein, August 25, 1928.
[57] Bandler had been a pupil of Babbitt's at Harvard and admired him greatly. In early 1930 he proposed getting out a Festschrift in honour of Babbitt: "I think a tribute from his former students or those greatly influenced by him and those contemporaries of his who are in sympathy with his thought would be a very graceful testimony of our affection and admiration. I can think of no man who is more deserving of such a volume" (Letter to Robert Shafer, February 4, 1930).

of communication of a specific group with a specific programme, and he was continually concerned with strengthening the inter-relations between different members of the group. His intentions are represented, with characteristic enthusiasm, in a letter to Allen Tate written in early 1932, just after Tate had become officially associated with the magazine as regional editor: "I think we can do enormous things with it [*The Hound & Horn*]. Each year we should have a number devoted to one special man, not necessarily living or American. Each of us should contribute to it. We plan to commence next fall with a Henry James number. ... Writing on a common subject should help immensely the working out a common attitude." [58] In this letter he also sug-gested a series of articles on American statesmen and political thinkers from Jefferson to the present day, in order to analyse the American political tradition and to test its applicability to contemporary problems: "I think if we chose our men carefully, both subjects and contributors, we could run a series of interest. ... Do you think each of us (the hypothetical H. & H. group) might take a man and work him up? That would secure at least the point of view." Bandler's active editorial connection with *The Hound & Horn* came to an end in October 1932 when his medical studies began to demand his full attention: "Bernard has told me", Kirstein wrote, "that he can no longer spend any time on the magazine, inasmuch as he is fitting himself to be a phy-sician and psychiatrist. This will of course preclude any work by him for ten years." [59] He did, however, like Blackmur although not as frequently continue to read occasional manuscripts for the magazine.

We have noted above that Bandler was the main inspiration behind *The Hound & Horn*'s preoccupation with humanism. On 20 March 1929, Blackmur wrote to T. S. Eliot that "the way that things look now, no amount of Humanism would be too much" and two weeks later Kirstein confirmed this when he told Edward O'Brien: "The Hound and Horn has undergone a meta-

[58] January 19, 1932, Allen Tate papers, Princeton University Library.
[59] Letter to Tate, October 31, 1932.

morphosis in so much as the critical articles must be related in some way to the problems of Humanism, either in relation to the gospels of Professor Babbitt or Eliot or Plato as more or less outlined in the essay on W. C. Brownell in our last issue" (April 8, 1929). This essay on Brownell had been written by Bandler. He had argued that Brownell's failure sprang from his incapacity to order his isolated insights into a philosophy, although they implied "a doctrine which is the only personal solution of subjectivism. That doctrine is humanism." [60]

Humanism had been preached, mainly by Babbitt and More, from the beginning of the century, but it was only in the later 1920's that it attracted a wider audience. Its demand for "decorum" and its campaign against moral laxness put as much emphasis on the ethical as on the aesthetic aspects of literature and were, at the same time, as easily and as vaguely applicable to the problems of society as of literature. Its earnestness brought order in the moral confusion attendant on the new prosperity of the 1920's. Its vogue was both intense and short-lived. In late 1929, such a reliable barometer of contemporary literary and intellectual fashions as Gorham Munson pronounced humanism "the only movement . . . in contemporary American thought that is of international importance." [61] This statement appeared in *Pagany*. Exactly one year later, the same magazine published the following remark of Sherry Mangan: " 'humanism' (query: does Erasmus shake Basel minster at impudent misuse of term?), beyond being merely moderation carried to excess, involved invocation of outgrown ethical criteria, and vulgarization which makes Eliot-cult look like select gentleman's club beside Ku-Klux-Klan." [62] Humanism was doubly attractive to *The Hound & Horn* because it also engaged the interest of T. S. Eliot's *Criterion*; and Eliot's growing exasperation with humanism was closely paralleled by that of the editors of *The Hound & Horn*. "I am trying to work up Humanism in the Criterion", Eliot had

---

[60]   "The Humanism of W. C. Brownell", *H & H*, II, 3 (Spring 1929), 219.
[61]   "The Artist's Stone", *Pagany*, I, 1 (Winter 1930), 3.
[62]   S[herry] M[angan], "Final Remarks on Criticism", *Pagany*, II, 1 (Winter 1931), 101-102.

written to Tate on 11 February 1929, but, on 8 August of the
following year, he confessed to Tate that he was "so sickened
by the kind of publicity which these philosophical discussions
have obtained in America, and by the reciprocal violence of
vituperation, that I never want to hear the word *humanism*
again".[63]

Eliot himself contributed to the discussion of humanism in the
pages of *The Hound & Horn*. When the editors solicited an
article on Henry James – an early indication of a persistent
interest – Eliot suggested instead an article on Babbitt and the
new humanism which was published simultaneously in *The Hound
& Horn* and in Middleton Murry's *New Adelphi* as "Second
Thoughts about Humanism".[64] The editors were so pleased with
a contribution from Eliot that they offered a special rate for it,
"the only exception that we have made", and the article itself
received their full approval: "We all think it is a very fine paper",
wrote Blackmur, "and feel that it fits in amazingly well with what
little we have of a 'programme' ".[65] In his essay Eliot questioned
a humanism without religion, and emphasized that humanism
was not a doctrine but that it operated "by taste, by sensibility
trained by culture;" that it was not its business to refute but "to
persuade, according to its unformulable axioms of culture and
good sense." [66] This lack of any fixed dogmas in humanism was
a recurrent theme of the different discussions in the magazine.
In his descriptive article on "The Individualism of Irving Babbitt", Bernard Bandler remarked that Babbitt's message was not
new: "It is an amalgam of all orthodoxies. He has annexed them
as they afforded him a vocabulary, a methodology, and a discipline, without accepting their dogmas, and often without committing himself as to their literal truth." His humanism was in-

---

[63]   Tate papers.
[64]   Actually publication was not quite simultaneous; the essay appeared
one month earlier in the *New Adelphi* (its title: "Second Thoughts on
Humanism") than in *The Hound & Horn* (cf. Donald Gallup, *T. S. Eliot:
A Bibliography* [London, 1952], p. 97).
[65]   Blackmur to Eliot, February 13, 1929 and March 20, 1929.
[66]   "Second Thoughts About Humanism", *H & H*, II, 4 (Summer 1929),
347.

deed "not so much a subject matter, or a system of ideals, as a way of life".[67]

Bandler's article in explanation of Babbitt's views was followed in the next issue (Winter 1930) by a much more critical contribution from Allen Tate. This essay, "The Fallacy of Humanism", – "a corrected copy of the Criterion version" of his essay [68] – was perhaps the most interesting contribution to the discussion in *The Hound & Horn*. "The Humanists", Tate wrote, "have no technique. How, under the special complexities and distractions of the modern world, they intend to validate their values they do not say; they simply urge them." [69] His basic criticism was, like Eliot's, that humanism as an ethical system lacked authority because it rejected the dogma of organized religion. Although the essay was, in a Socratic manner, critical of both Babbitt and More, Tate assured Bandler that he was not anti-humanist at all; "I differ with the Humanists on the question of method" (February 7, 1930). And when Tate offered a third version of the original *Criterion* essay to C. Hartley Grattan, who was getting up an anti-humanist symposium, he pointed out that his essay was not "in 'opposition' but rather in 'clarification' ".[70] The confusion attendant on the humanist discussion was the source of all subsequent complaints in the pages of the magazine. "The humanism of today has too many rules", stated the reviewer of Norman Foerster's *The American Scholar*; "a certain mental paralysis attends the reading of more than twenty pages of its tenets".[71]

[67]   *H & H*, III, 1 (Autumn 1929), 60, 64.
[68]   Tate to Blackmur, November 17, 1929.
[69]   *H & H*, III, 2 (Winter 1930), 235.
[70]   Letter to Grattan, February 19, 1930.
[71]   James W. Lane, "The Raising of Literary Critics", *H & H*, III, 2 (Winter 1930), 289. The vagueness of humanism as a programme is nowhere better illustrated than in the following notorious passage from Norman Foerster's introduction to his symposium in explanation and defence of humanism which provoked Grattan's counter volume: "In one way or another, its doctrine and discipline have been clarified by persons as various as Homer, Phideas, Plato, Aristotle, Confucius, Buddha, Jesus, Paul, Virgil, Horace, Dante, Shakespeare, Milton, Goethe; and more recently, by Matthew Arnold in England and Emerson and Lowell in America: a

The editors' disillusionment finally led them to abjure the humanist issue in the Summer number of 1930:

Now that everyone has uttered his 'second thoughts' and 'last words' on Humanism, it is possible to seek grounds for its failure. The most general is the lack of precision, of localization, of the ideas involved; verbally exact, they have been vague in reference, so that summary is almost impossible ... when they [ideas] spring from general reflections and embody no imagination, as is the case with Humanism, they may be acute, they may be indisputable, they may be true, but they solve no dilemmas, because they faced none concretely; they lead nowhere because they never started for a definite destination.[72]

It proved, however, impossible to break off the discussion so abruptly. The same number contained a long article by Robert Shafer, entitled "The Definition of Humanism", which sought to discredit the essays of both Eliot and Tate. This blatant contradiction of editorial intentions had been unavoidable.[73] The effect of Shafer's article was, however, to some extent neutralized by Francis Fergusson who in the same issue, in a review of the two rival symposiums on humanism edited by Norman Foerster and C. Hartley Grattan, upheld the point of view of the editors. The magazine's humanist adventure was perhaps most characteristically epitomized by the spiritual progress of Babbitt's disciple and the instigator of *The Hound & Horn*'s initial interest in humanism, Bernard Bandler, who contributed both to the "pro"-

---

strange assortment of names, no doubt, but also an indication of the inner diversity as well as the central unity of the humanistic ideal" (*Humanism and America* [New York, 1930], p. x).

[72] "Comment", *H & H*, III, 4 (Summer 1930), 467.

[73] Shafer's article had been accepted in December 1929. When the editors decided not to allot any more space to the humanist discussion they asked Shafer to withdraw it, which he refused to do. The editors keenly felt the anomaly of the juxtaposition of the editorial "Comment" and Shafer's article; as the magazine's business manager Alan Stroock wrote to Shafer: "A magazine which attempts in each issue to present aspects of a policy, cannot afford to be quite as ambiguous as the publication of your article made us seem, and, as I pointed out in my last letter, you, too, were considerably hurt by appearing in an unfavorable light" (Letter of July 14, 1930).

humanist manifesto of Norman Foerster and the "anti"-humanist symposium of Hartley Grattan.[74]

The ideas of humanism were not marked out for a very satisfactory explanation of the position of the writer in a society in crisis. In their manifesto *I'll Take My Stand* "Twelve Southerners" protested that the humanists shunned their responsibility to give guidance in social and economic affairs as well as in literary affairs:

Humanism, properly speaking, is not an abstract system, but a culture, the whole way in which we live, act, think, and feel. It is a kind of imaginatively balanced life lived out in a definite social tradition. And, in the concrete, we believe that this, the genuine humanism, was rooted in the agrarian life of the older South and of other parts of the country that shared in such a tradition. ... We cannot recover our native humanism by adopting some standard of taste that is critical enough to question the contemporary arts but not critical enough to question the social and economic life which is their ground.[75]

I'll Take My Stand propagated the theory of agrarianism which was to stimulate wide-spread discussion throughout the 'Thirties. It left a marked imprint on the later issues of *The Hound & Horn*, mainly through its association with Allen Tate, but before investigating the magazine's part in this new debate, we shall consider the earlier influence of that unfailing guide of little magazines, Ezra Pound.

Pound's association started concurrently with the magazine's discussion of humanism, which it outlasted by a year. It was a typically Poundian editorial venture with a good deal of sound

---

[74] On 6 February 1930, Bandler informed Tate that he had been indirectly approached about contributing to the Grattan volume "and if it were not for the fact that I am rather dubious about the ethics of appearing on both sides of a controversy, I should be delighted to contribute". His changeableness astounded the editors of *The Bookman*, at that time the bulwark of humanism, who thought it "questionable not merely how much in sympathy with them [Babbitt and More] he is, but how well he has understood them" ("Chronicle and Comment", *The Bookman*, LXXI, 1 [March 1930], 76).

[75] *I'll Take My Stand* (New York, 1930), p. xvi. The sudden and virtually universal eclipse of humanism was sadly reported in *The Bookman*. (See "Chronicle and Comment", *The Bookman*, LXXIV, 3 [November 1931], 253).

advice but also with a violent energy in the service of a limited
stable of hobby-horses which took no consideration of practical
difficulties or of the opinion of others. If this association did not
leave such a noticeable mark on the printed issues of *The Hound
& Horn* as humanism did, it constituted a much more lively and
important episode in its history. Contact with Pound had been
established by the early months of 1929, and on 20 May of that
year the editors offered him a "free perennial subscription".[76]
In September Pound apparently offered his services in some sort
of editorial capacity. Although the editors felt very flattered by
this proposition, they detected too clearly potential causes for
irritation and dissent to enter blindly into such an association.
Blackmur's answer showed guarded enthusiasm: "It is very hard
for me to answer your very gracious letter without an appearance
of ingratitude and ungraciousness. When you suggest an overt
alliance between us, we can only, on the face of it, eagerly accept; but when we begin to consider the probable terms of such
an alliance, it is difficult not to be immediately aware of much
that might happen to irritate, even exacerbate, in a truly political
fashion, that alliance" (October 2, 1929). The editors foresaw
that their tastes would differ from Pound's in many instances
and that this could only result in unpleasantness. They were
aware of the distinction *The Little Review* and *The Egoist* had
reaped in earlier days from his tireless search for manuscripts,
but they must also have realized that since then he had been
rather repetitious, and that his new flock of protégés would hardly
grace their magazine as T. S. Eliot, James Joyce, and Wyndham
Lewis had graced *The Little Review*. Only two years previously Pound had started a magazine of his own, *The Exile*, in
which he had intended "to present, or at least to examine the
possibility of presenting an equally interesting line-up" of authors
as he had presented in 1917: "if the job bores me I shall stop
at the end of Vol. I." [77] *The Exile* had only appeared four times.
Its contributors included Louis Zukofsky, Robert McAlmon,
John Rodker and Carl Rakosi. Pound may well have been bored

---

[76]   Blackmur to Pound.
[77]   E. P., "The Exile", *The Exile*, I, 1 (Spring 1927), 88.

by the drudgery of bringing it out single-handed, but he did not discontinue it because of any disillusionment with its contributors. He was still enthusiastic about them when he offered his services to *The Hound & Horn*, but he cannot have been surprised at Blackmur's ambivalent reaction. Two years earlier, when the first issue of *The Exile* had appeared, *The Hound & Horn* had been severely critical of both its contributors and its tone: "This magazine issues circulars about the promotion of new talent and the publication of new and unusual works. It is Mr. Pound with his old tricks in a new bag. It is one form of seriousness in letters, the public form." The anti-American attitude of *The Exile* had been characterized as "a sickening apotheosis of its title." [78] Although not all contributors were so critical of Pound and *The Exile*, the best proposition Blackmur could make to Pound was for *The Hound & Horn* to "take everything you send us (especially poems and stories), do our best to agree with you, and publish so much as we can of it" (October 2, 1929).

Pound in other words would be a contributing adviser. His abilities as a correspondent were immediately apparent; his letters were full of advice and full of prejudices, and so numerous that they outnumbered by two to one the letters of his main American correspondents, Blackmur, Stroock and Kirstein. And *The Hound & Horn* was not the only magazine in which Pound took an interest during these years. He was in regular contact with *Pagany* and on 20 October 1930 he accepted a contributing editorship of *The New Review*. "I have had three invitations in three days to be a member of editorial boards", he wrote to Samuel Putnam, the editor of *The New Review,* on that day; "I doubt the wisdom of accepting all the invites." He was, however, willing to lend his services to the *Review*, "if you are convinced that it wd. help you *sell* the mag. rather than merely concentrate hostility".[79] The inevitable quarrel with *The New Review* came in 1932, a year after the break with *The Hound &*

[78] "Periodical Reviews" (anon.), *H & H*, I, 1 (Autumn 1927), 68, 69.
[79] Putnam papers, Princeton University Library.

Horn.[80] In 1932 also, Pound made unsuccessful advances to William Carlos Williams's *Contact* and, soon afterwards, to F. R. Leavis's *Scrutiny.*[81] Towards the end of that same year Harriet Monroe contemplated asking Pound to become foreign correspondent of *Poetry,*[82] although in late 1930 she had written an angry letter to the editor of *The English Journal,* who had published Pound's essay "Small Magazines", saying that Pound "wearied of POETRY, of *The Little Review,* of *Blast,* of *The Dial,* even of his own *Exile.* The wrecks of his wild runs strew the path of progress." [83] Pound actually exerted some influence over *Poetry* during his years with *The Hound & Horn,* be it through his disciples Louis Zukofsky and Basil Bunting. In early 1931 Zukofsky edited the Objectivist Number of *Poetry* – Miss Monroe objected to "The Arrogance of Youth" in the next issue (March 1931) – and on 22 January 1931, Pound wrote to Zukofsky that Bunting had informed him "that our sportin' frien' Miss Monroe has axd him to do a Bri'sh number. This is goin' one be'r than I had suggested (?, or did I)." [84]

[80]   Putnam, in his autobiography, had very little to say for Pound's editorship: "As a literary adviser, Pound was not a great help. In fact, he was practically no help at all. It was not that he was not willing enough to be; it was, rather, that his range of interests was too narrowly personal. Pound and the half-dozen writers whom he approved – that was present-day literature" (*Paris was Our Mistress* [New York, 1947], p. 151).

[81]   In 1932 Williams wrote that Pound had "more or less objectionably" asked him if he was editing *Contact* to offer him a mouthpiece but that he had told him "to go to hell" (*The Selected Letters of William Carlos Williams,* ed. Thirlwall, p. 126). Pound's overtures to *Scrutiny* met with a similar reception. "I see no point in giving him space in *Scrutiny*", its editor F. R. Leavis wrote to Ronald Bottrall on March 19, 1933. "You see, he isn't what one feels he ought to be. I'm just going to write a curt reply" (Bottrall papers, Texas University Library at Austin).

[82]   Draft of letter, Harriet Monroe to Pound, December 17, 1932, *Poetry* papers, Chicago University Library.

[83]   Harriet Monroe to Wilbur Hatfield, November 22, 1930, *Poetry* papers. Margaret Widdemer wrote recently: "Harriet believed in Ezra Pound as completely as she did in avant-garde poetry." Miss Widdemer maintained that Pound's "technique of insult enslaved her completely, as it had, to quote Amy Lowell, other literary spinsters. ... She would take, and believe, anything he gave or told her, as he said, laughing about her" (*Golden Friends I Had* [New York, 1964], p. 42).

[84]   Zukofsky papers, Texas University Library. "Spurred however to still higher flights of fawncy", Pound continued, "I wonder if Harriet wd

The Hound & Horn was, indeed, by no means Pound's only iron in the fire, although he kept it hotter than any of the others. Both the comparative wealth and the youthful inexperience of the editors must have appeared attractive tools for the advancement of his literary schemes. It soon became evident, however, that the magazine's courtesy to Pound did not necessarily extend to his protégés. Pound was sanguine at first: "Hound & H. want you", he wrote to Louis Zukofsky on 31 October 1929, "but are still unconscious of the fact",[85] but Alan Stroock soon acquainted Zukofsky with "the sad fact ... that Lincoln Kirstein is not enthusiastic about your poetry, and at the same time, has been given almost free hand in the selection for that department of THE HOUND & HORN" (June 15, 1930). And as strongly as Pound might feel that "the magazine needs Mr. [Robert] McAlmon", Kirstein had "yet to see anything of his in the last three years that I would like to print".[86]

Pound took, of course, very little interest in the humanist debate; he felt that "one ought to devote *one* obituary to each of these winds ... and then move out into criticism".[87] It will therefore not be surprising that he resented the fact that "Mr. B. B. III [Bernard Bandler II] etc. may want their space for their own elucubrations on Babbitt, Elmer and co. MerrrDDDRReeh!"[88] Pound was indeed hampered by this utilization of *The Hound & Horn*'s space, for if all his suggestions had been followed up they would have given him the virtual monopoly of the magazine.

---

stand fer a french number edited by your elderly friend?" Incidentally, Bunting had not been invited by Miss Monroe to prepare a British number, but had invited himself: "I might be able to collect samples of a number of young poets, mostly English, at present very little known, at least in America, who have serious merits" (Bunting to Miss Monroe, December 1930, *Poetry* papers).

[85] Zukofsky papers, Texas University Library.

[86] Pound to Zukofsky, October 22, 1930, Louis Zukofsky papers; Kirstein to Pound, February 27, 1930. McAlmon himself wrote to Kirstein that "the live stuff" in *The Hound & Horn* was "almost lost in the litter of highly intellectual meanderings to conceal lack of life-sense or thought" (September 28, 1930).

[87] Letter to *The Hound & Horn*, January 7, 1930.

[88] Letter to Zukofsky, October 31, 1929, Zukofsky papers.

Quite a number of his contributions were printed, however. In the Winter 1930 issue appeared a short poem of Robert McAlmon, "The Crow Becomes Discursive", but the association really started to bear fruit in the Spring issue which contained the first part of Zukofsky's study of Henry Adams – which was to run on for two more instalments and a postscript and which *The Dial,* incidentally, had rejected in the face of Pound's strong recommendation – and *Cantos* XXVIII, XXIX, and XXX. These three *Cantos* actually were Pound's only substantial contribution; his prose piece, "Terra Italica", was rejected by *The Hound & Horn* which suggested he submit it to *Pagany.* Pound, however, sent it to *The New Review.* "Bitch and Bugle has been sittin' on it", he wrote to its editor, "but didn't understand it ANYhow. It is about the only important prose I have written for some time, but so goes it. The minute one really says something, the obstruction begins." [89] *The Hound & Horn's* rejection, however, was hardly a matter of "obstruction" because "Terra Italica" repeated essentially what Pound had already been saying in the magazine's "Correspondence" section from issue to issue. His letters were, indeed, his most characteristic contributions and Kirstein was particularly grateful for them. When Pound in a moment of irritation with the lack of "action" of the magazine threatened to leave, Kirstein wrote an alarmed letter to the effect that "we'd hate to lose you in any way in connection with the magazine, particularly to have you stop writing us critical letters" (January 8, 1931).

The final break-up, however, was not to be prevented. Pound wanted the editors "to go hell for leather and much more the Little Rev. pace than the Dial or Criterion pace", [90] but the direction in which he tried to steer them suited them less and less. Mutual discontent finally exploded over an instance of editorial carelessness. Pound had sent *The Hound & Horn* a translation of Cocteau's *Le Mystère Laïc* which Kirstein did not like and mistakenly thought he had returned. Pound, however, expected

---

[89]   Letter to Samuel Putnam, May 12 [?1931], Putnam papers at Princeton.
[90]   Letter to Stroock, March 24, 1930.

that the manuscript had been "mislaid in transferring your offices from one palatial office to another". In the same letter of 8 July 1931, he expressed "sincere regret for the time wasted by me in correspondence with H & H", and indicated that "taken as a whole our relations have been thoroughly unsatisfactory to me". When the manuscript turned up almost a month later, Kirstein apologized for his inefficiency but saw no reason for the sentiments which it had provoked from Pound. He did not entirely discard the possibility of a reconciliation but Pound was too "fed up at working fer 2 years fer a pair of rich fahrts & *not* getting paid" [91] to prolong the association.

Kirstein did not mind his departure much: "Pound has finally broken with us for good I guess", he wrote to Hyatt Mayor, "and so much the better or worse" (August 3, 1931). But he did change his mind about the translation. In the same letter he had still maintained that "it was a poor translation", but when he found *Le Mystère Laïc* three days later he "was overwhelmed with a sense of guilt" that they had not published it. "It seems to me it's so very good really. So few of the things we publish have anywhere nearly its distinction and lucidity." [92] It finally appeared in *Pagany* in early 1932 and Pound was "pleezd to see that damn good trans/" printed there.[93]

So ended the magazine's alliance with Pound but not the efforts of the editors to secure contributions from his pen. His demands, however, were high; "we can't possibly promise him fifty dollars an article for each quarter", Bandler wrote from Paris in September 1932; "I don't want to publish that much of him or any man." Bandler asked Tate to serve as middleman, "and when I get back to New York I will ask Mayor to communicate with you and Pound. Leave Kirstein and me out of it. I mention Mayor only in case he wants to hear from one of the New York editors." [94] This letter indicates that Bandler was not ignorant of Pound's personal preferences. The only editor of *The*

91   Pound to Louis Zukofsky, September 8, 1931, Zukofsky papers.
92   Letter to Mayor, August 6, 1931.
93   Pound to Zukofsky, March 1932, Zukofsky papers.
94   Letter to Tate, September 15, 1932, Tate papers.

Hound & Horn whom Pound thought highly of was Hyatt Mayor; he singled out Mayor's criticism of painting together with Zukofsky's essay on Henry Adams as examples of the advance in critical writing he detected in *The Hound & Horn*.[95] The admiration seems to have been mutual because Mayor dedicated his article on "Translation," which appeared in the Autumn of 1931, after the *Mystère Laïc* affair, to "Ezra Pound: *il santo atleta, benigno ai suoi, ed ai nemici crudo*".[96]

Mayor had graduated from Princeton in 1922 and had received a B.Litt. from Oxford as a Rhodes Scholar in 1926. During the early years of *The Hound & Horn* he taught at the school of the American Laboratory Theater. He joined the editorial staff in 1931 and then only with some reluctance. In an undated letter to Kirstein (presumably written in August 1930), Mayor had remarked: "I of all things study to avoid becoming an *editor* of the H & H, however close I want to grapple to it in all other ways." Mayor had been close to the magazine some time previously. Already on 20 June 1929, he had reminded Bandler of "your once saying that you would not object to my suggesting books worthy of revue", and it was Mayor who, together with Francis Fergusson, had arranged for Bandler and Kirstein to meet with the prospective editors of *The Symposium*. As an adviser and a reader of manuscripts Mayor was indeed an important force in the history of *The Hound & Horn* although his modesty – which was not a striking characteristic of his fellow editors – kept him back from the limelight. Art was his special department. His article on Picasso, which traced the painter's development through the successive periods, drew the admiration of both Pound and Kirstein.[97] "It is absolutely brilliant", the

---

[95] "Small Magazines", 702. In early 1931 Pound wrote: " 'Hound & Horn' is printing good critical work (Stokes, Zukofsky, Hyatt Mayor). They are hereby declared *d'utilité publique*" ("After Election", *The New Review*, I, 1 [Jan.-Feb. 1931], 55).

[96] Morton Zabel wrote about this article: "We have been too great an admirer of Hyatt Mayor's art criticism not to regret the unstudied Ezraic violences which seriously wrench the persuasive logic of his paper on *Translation*" (M.D.Z., "Recent Magazines", *Poetry*, XXXIX, 6 [March 1932], 347).

[97] "Picasso's Method", *H & H*, III, 2 (Winter 1930), 176-188.

latter wrote, "and I have never seen a more illuminating and profound analysis of any painter's work".[98] Mayor gave up his editorial duties late in 1932 to accept a position in the Metropolitan Museum of Art in New York, where he is at present the curator of prints.

The magazine's "Art Chronicle" became Mayor's special province. Chronicles of Music, Drama and the Fine Arts had been announced in the Spring issue of 1930. They were to be "conducted by thoroughly good men", would bring the magazine "closer to the actual American scene than we have been heretofore", and would, it was hoped, "be more than running commentaries or Dialish appreciations".[99] Art, Drama and Music were, however, not the only quarterly departments; the Spring 1932 issue carried the most impressive array of chronicles, seven in number, of Architecture, Theatre, Jewish Art Theatre, Art, Dance, Film, and Music, and in the Winter 1934 issue six chronicles and four foreign letters took up more space than the reviewing section. The average number per issue, however, was three. "Notes" on architecture, the cinema and printing, among others, had already appeared in the magazine before the official announcement of the chronicles, but not as systematically or as frequently.

The Hound & Horn, then, was not a one-man magazine; different editors influenced it at different times and left their personal imprint on it. The effect was one of exciting contemporaneity and cumulative distinction. The last two years were, in Kirstein's words, "by far the most interesting from every point of view",[100] the climax of the magazine's existence. Those were the years when Allen Tate and Yvor Winters were regional editors.

Already some years before their official recognition in an editorial capacity, Tate and Winters had been frequent contributors and counsellors. In the autumn of 1929 Blackmur had been eager to secure regular contributions from Tate: "I wonder

[98]   Letter to Mayor, October 31, 1929.
[99]   Bandler to Robert Shafer, December 11, 1929.
[100] Kirstein, p. 9.

if you would care to write reviews for us more or less regularly
– poetry and criticism", he wrote on 5 October of that year; "If
so I should be glad to exchange suggestions." [101] Three months
later, Bernard Bandler wrote to Tate: "if you have any essays
on hand or that you are planning to write, I hope you will give
us the opportunity to publish them" (January 23, 1930). Winters's
first contribution to *The Hound & Horn* was his review of
Malcolm Cowley's *Blue Juaniata,* a careful, discriminating discussion of the individual poems. Winters had told Cowley that
he would send it to *The Nation,* and, if that failed, *The Hound
& Horn.*[102] After a disagreement with *The Nation,* he decided
to try *The Hound & Horn*; he surmised that the editors were
duly impressed by the fact that he had contributed to *The Dial,*
because they always addressed their magazine to him as an
Esq.[103] Bandler, before he left the magazine, was Tate's regular
correspondent whereas Winters addressed most of his letters to
Kirstein.[104]

The idea of regional editors seems to have originated from
Tate. On 11 January 1932, Bandler told Tate that Kirstein was
"delighted with the idea and nothing could give me greater
pleasure than that you should be the first person to be asked to
join us in that capacity". A similar invitation was sent, some two
weeks later, to Yvor Winters. Tate was to be regional editor for
the South, and Wmters for the Pacific seaboard. The New York
editors hoped their regional representatives would be able to
send them some manuscripts which, in Kirstein's words, "we
would not otherwise know about and [about] which you would

[101]   Tate papers.
[102]   August 13, 1929, Cowley papers, Newberry Library.
[103]   Different letter also dated August 13, 1929, Cowley papers. Blackmur
was very pleased with Winters's review: "I had been trying to get out an
accurate review of the book myself and failing; so that the receipt of your
review was a distinct personal relief" (September 7, 1929).
[104]   When Bandler left the magazine in the autumn of 1932, Kirstein
wrote to Tate expressing the hope that Bandler's "separation from the
magazine will not influence your own, and that you will be willing to
serve still in your capacity of regional editor and general help. . . . I think
Winters and myself are in a little closer cooperation" (October 31, 1932).

probably be in a position to instruct us".[105] The preferences of
the two new editors were very pronounced: Tate sponsored the
Southern agrarians, mainly his friends from the days of *The
Fugitive* (1922-1925) and some new recruits to that group, and
Winters campaigned for a group of writers on the West Coast,
mostly his own students at Stanford University where he was
then an instructor.

Winters especially proved a disturbing associate. His comments were perhaps even more outspoken than Pound's, but
they were also more precise and useful. His reaction to Kirstein's
invitation to become a regional editor was fair indication of what
was to come; he wrote that he would be glad to accept the invitation, but he thought it a trifle rash because he could count
the stories and poems in *The Hound & Horn* of which he did
not actively disapprove, on ten fingers.[106] Winters's letters were
often violently critical and prejudiced, but his honesty was beyond
doubt. A few months after their appointment as regional editors,
he wrote to Tate that he would as soon have his name posted
as manager of a bawdy house as editor of the last few issues of
The Hound & Horn. But he felt that it would be too inconsid-
erate of too many people to turn down the position of regional
editor at the outset. He threatened, however, that he would pose
an ultimatum if the contributions which he had selected and
submitted were rejected; he would ask that he be allowed to edit
a definite allotment of space or that his name be withdrawn.[107]
He had decided not to deliver that ultimatum until two more
issues had come out. But his exasperation must soon have got
the better of this decision because, within a fortnight, he informed
Tate that he had asked Kirstein to scratch out his name unless
he could edit twenty pages a year. He expected, however, that
Kirstein would not agree. Although he was sorry to leave Tate,
he could not go on.[108] But Winters was to stay with the magazine
till the end. The following proposition of Bandler's took the sting
out of his ultimatum:

[105]   Letter to Winters, January 27, 1932.
[106]   Letter to Kirstein, February 1, 1932.
[107]   April 22, 1932, Tate papers.
[108]   May 5, 1932, Tate papers.

Does this arrangement seem feasible to you? That no story or poem be published which has not been seen and commented on by all the editors, namely you, Tate, Kirstein, Mayor and myself. All stories and poems that are recommended for publication by any of us must be accompanied by an analysis that states our main reasons for desiring publication. All stories and poems which are favored by some and yet rejected by others must be accompanied by the reasons for rejection. If we disagree each of us is to have one vote in the matter. (May 9, 1932)

This arrangement appealed to Bandler's predilection for *Hound & Horn* discussions. It pacified Winters although he warned the New York editors that they had taken an adder to their bosom.[109]

Winters now started his campaign to mould the magazine after his own tastes. A week after Bandler had sent off his proposal for the new editorial arrangement, Winters answered with a general criticism of *The Hound & Horn*; in his opinion, the simple fact of the matter was that nearly all of the verse and fiction in the magazine was atrociously written and at bottom without meaning. Winters thought that in the matter of verse *The New Republic* scored higher than *The Hound & Horn*, and that in the matter of fiction, *This Quarter, Pagany,* and *Scribner's* were quite as good if not better. Criticism was the only field in which *The Hound & Horn* was probably ahead, though *The New Republic* and *The Symposium* were not far behind. But then, Winters wrote, it was as much easier to find a good critical article than a good poem, as it was easier to memorize the ten commandments than to observe them. It required relatively little judgement.[110] This general criticism of the magazine was followed by more detailed criticism of individual contributions.

Three months later, on 6 August 1932, he wrote to Kirstein that he would gladly sacrifice his reputation to civilize *The Hound & Horn*; he returned a batch of manuscripts and voted against all of them unreservedly and regardless of whatever other material might become available. Two weeks later Winters could inform Tate that his relations with *The Hound & Horn* were improving. He had insulted everybody minutely and carefully, and the result

---

[109] Letter to Bandler, May 16, 1932.
[110] *Ibid.*

was gratifying. He said he was glad that he had not taken Tate's advice to write politely and to Bandler only; he preferred to write insultingly and to Kirstein.[111] His progress was soon reflected in the magazine. During 1933 the names of his protégés, Howard Baker, Don Stanford, Achilles Holt, J. V. Cunningham, and Clayton Stafford graduated from his letters to the pages of the magazine itself. Incidentally, the *Hound & Horn* Undergraduate Competition was won by two of his students, J. V. Cunningham for verse and Albert J. Guerard, Jr. for the short story.[112]

It was to be expected that there would be frequent clashes between the two regional editors. Their tastes differed on a number of subjects.[113] Eliot's poetry was a case in point. When some time before the regional editors were appointed, Winters was asked to review Eliot's *Ash Wednesday*, he replied that he had taken so many pot shots at Eliot that he would be embarrassed to take more. It is true, *Ash Wednesday* did seem better than *The Hollow Men* or *The Waste Land,* but then those poems seemed to him excessively bad.[114] Tate's estimate of Eliot was quite the reverse and it was Tate who reviewed *Ash Wednesday* for *The Hound & Horn*. When the editors read his review they had to admit that they had hoped that he "would give more attention to the intrinsic merit of the poem"; but Tate felt that

---

[111]   August 22, 1932, Tate papers. Two months later, on October 23, 1932, Tate advised Kirstein that the only way to get along with Winters was "to be as rude as he is; but of course he doesn't know that he is rude and so he doesn't know that you are".

[112]   The official announcement of the prizes in the magazine stated that Dudley Fitts, one of the judges of the contest, "dissented in the fiction award, voting for BREAK-DAY, a story by J. Allan Conley of the University of California". In July 1933, Fitts had written to Kirstein: "I *hope* my taste doesn't coincide with yr Western Editor's."

[113]   A letter from Tate to the staff of *The Hound & Horn* is instructive; Tate is at a loss to explain "how it is that both he and I agree that the poetry has improved, but agree on different evidence? In my opinion, the poems by Blackmur [*Sea Island Miscellany*], which win Mr. Winters' almost unqualified praise, are worthless pastiche; while those by Eliot [*Difficulties of a Statesman*] and Bishop [*Perspectives are Precipices*] are among the best ever printed in the magazine."

[114]   Letter to Kirstein, June 4, 1930.

because of the "atmosphere of opinion that has been gathering about his work in the last three years, it was not safe to assume that the poetry could be properly analyzed to good effect", and that "the defense of Eliot required all the space" he gave it.[115] But whatever their disagreements, the regional editors respected each other as writers. They had been exchanging frank critical comments on each other's works for some years past, and they were now pleased to see each other's writings in *The Hound & Horn*; they repeatedly commended the New York editors for printing them. Tate, for instance, considered Winters's eleven page review of René Taupin, *L'Influence du Symbolisme Français sur la Poésie Américaine* "a highly distinguished piece of criticism which, long as it is, should have been much longer", and Winters praised Tate's story "The Immortal Woman" – of which he had been rather critical initially – as probably the highest point reached by the magazine in fiction since the publication of Katherine Anne Porter's "Flowering Judas".[116]

---

[115] Stroock to Tate, September 5, 1930; Tate to Stroock, September 8, 1930. When Eliot's *Selected Essays* came out in England, Tate inquired whether it was also scheduled to appear in the United States. "I should very much like to do a long piece on it, incidentally clearing away some of the rubbish that the recent attacks on Eliot have dropped around him" (Letter to Kirstein, October 17, 1932). *Selected Essays* was actually reviewed by Henry Bamford Parkes for the Winter 1933 issue.

[116] Tate to Kirstein, July 9, 1931; Winters to the Editors, July 23, 1933. Cf. also Yvor Winters, "The Critiad: A Poetical Survey of Recent Criticism", *This Quarter*, III, 4 (Spring 1931), 738-739:

> I turn to that fine poet, Allen Tate,
> Dimly fuliginous against the State
> (When all the landscape darkens to the south
> One waits for distant mutterings from his mouth),
> Who writes an essay on the poetic scene
> Explaining chiefly what I really mean,
> Then drops a footnote from a teeming head,
> Saying I meant exactly what I said.
> Yet if one penetrates the smoke one finds
> A critic, sound . . .

"The Immortal Woman" was Tate's first published story. Tate and Winters had had a heated debate about it. When Tate sent in the revised version, he told Kirstein: "I know it is vastly improved, and I fear after my counter-attack on Winters I have really taken a good deal of his advice" (December 23, 1932). "Flowering Judas" was perhaps *Hound & Horn's* most famous story.

But admiration and cooperation proved two entirely different matters. Their joint editorship provided numerous causes for irritation and friction. On 30 April 1933, Tate complained to Kirstein that "those fine people in California" made a habit of doing one another's washing in public. "I admire Winters enormously but I've got so I'm afraid to mention him in print lest I be mistaken for a partner in the laundry", and on 8 December of that year he stated: "I could not get along with him in an editorial relationship. ... I've got so that I can't write to him; he will no longer discuss, he shouts and delivers his bull." This editorial friction led to a final quarrel over John Crowe Ransom's essay "Poetry: A Note in Ontology" which Tate submitted and which he described as "the only piece of writing I have ever insisted upon for the Hound & Horn".[117] The essay, however, was rejected by both Winters and Blackmur and although, as it turned out later, this was not yet the final editorial decision, Tate asked to have his name removed from the magazine's masthead. "You have lost the best essay that has come your way in your whole career", he wrote to Kirstein. "How under heaven you can turn this essay down, and yet print MacLeish's absurd outburst ... is more than I can ever understand. But so be it" (December 18, 1933). Archibald MacLeish was a subject on which both regional editors agreed. The 'outburst' to which Tate referred was MacLeish's laudatory review of *Poems* by Stephen Spender in which he attacked "the young amateurs in writing, with a few of the regulation slim volumes of the period to their credit (or the opposite), [who] emit godlike judgements which a Dante would hesitate to sign". "I am merely a spectator", MacLeish wrote, "I am not a judge. As a spectator I am profoundly moved by Mr. Spender's poems ... I do not know how different he may be or may not be from other poets. I am bored by all the talk about difference, about 'new voices', about originality." [118] Kirstein was a friend and admirer of both MacLeish and Spender

---

[117] Letter to Kirstein, December 18, 1933. Ransom's essay appeared eventually in *The American Review* in 1934.
[118] "Stephen Spender and the Critics", *H & H*, VII, 1 (Autumn 1933), 146.

but he must have realized that MacLeish's review went against everything *The Hound & Horn* stood for. Yvor Winters, like Tate, denounced MacLeish's review as a disgrace to the magazine. In his opinion it was a criticism neither of Spender nor of criticism; if MacLeish disliked criticism, he should refrain from reading or writing it; if he wished to write it, he should write like a gentleman.[119]

Tate was the spokesman for the South on the editorial board and in this capacity he sponsored both Southern literature and agrarianism. For Tate the advocacy of agrarianism was, certainly in the early 'Thirties, primarily an act of faith in the Southern tradition and in the Southern way of life rather than an economic program, as it was for the more naive supporters of the South. Tate was interested in the Southern scene as a background for the artist; the Southern past existed for him as a usable myth, which he could oppose to a contemporary materialistic and mechanized society. It provided a frame of reference for his own poetry — some of the best of which, he was to admit later, was written during the agrarian phase [120] — and a heightened sense of tradition and of the importance of the cultural environment for the poet. Reminiscing in 1956 about this period of his life, Tate remembered that for him agrarianism had meant "religious humanism; that was my label for it".[121] When *I'll Take My Stand* appeared in 1930 — Robert Penn Warren, significantly, felt that it ought to have been called *Tracts Against Communism* [122] — Tate wrote to Malcolm Cowley: "the agitation behind our symposium is a sheer act of faith not clearly supported by history . . . by defending the agrarian order, we defend the oldest economy in the country . . . even though it has little chance to survive." [123] Although Tate believed in agrarian-

[119] Letter to Kirstein, October 23, 1933. *Partisan Review* also felt that the review "remarkably demonstrated. ... MacLeish's abject intellectual surrender" (Obed Brooks, review of MacLeish's *Poems, 1924-1933*, *PR*, I, 1 [Feb.-March 1934], 54).
[120] Rob Roy Purdy (ed.), *Fugitives' Reunion* (Nashville, Tenn., 1959), p. 180.
[121] *Ibid.*, p. 207.
[122] *Ibid.*, p. 207.
[123] December 19, 1930, Cowley papers, Newberry Library.

ism and adapted some of its concepts to his own literary purposes, he was more sceptical about the possibilities of its economic
implications than some of the Southerners whose work he submitted to *The Hound & Horn.*

Interest in the agrarian cause was first properly kindled in the
New York editors when Bandler, Fergusson and Mayor got
together in the summer of 1931 to do their "type of New Republic
editorial" on *I'll Take My Stand,* but were so fired by its contents
that "instead of doing you in an editorial, we all but bought
tickets for Nashville".[124] In the early months of 1932 Bandler
offered several suggestions to the new regional editor for contributions pertaining to the South. These included articles by
Robert Penn Warren on John Crowe Ransom, by John Crowe
Ransom on Henry James, and by Donald Davidson on sectionalism. Warren's article on Ransom became a source of friction;
it was advertised but never published because none of its different
versions met with unanimous editorial approval. Ransom's article
on Henry James was probably cancelled when the magazine's
Henry James issue was delayed. Indeed, of the three essays,
Davidson's on sectionalism was the only one to appear in *The
Hound & Horn* although Tate had initially counselled against it;
in his opinion Davidson would not do "a good article on sectionalism in general, but he would surely write a paper in which the
philosophy of Southern sectionalism received a stirring defense".[125] Davidson's essay appeared in the Summer issue of
1933 and only confirmed Tate's doubts. He characteristically
insisted that Davidson ought to have made "a sharp distinction
between his economic and aesthetic arguments". He felt that the
provincial economy could be urged for its own sake because it
offered certain qualities of stability to social life, "but it is another
matter to argue that we must have a provincial society for the
sake of literature". Tate maintained that the farthest "we are
allowed to go in that direction is this, that a self-sufficient society
tends to give the writer certain continuities of experience and

---

[124] Bandler to Tate, November 10, 1931.
[125] Letter to Bandler, February 24, 1932.

fixed references, that he may make the most of *provided* he has access to a source of high culture. This source may be identical with the provincial tradition; or again, as in the case of Gopher Prairie, it may not." [126]

Bandler's most important proposal to Tate concerned the series of articles on American statesmen and political thinkers which we have described earlier in this chapter. Tate evidently interpreted this suggestion as referring to Southern statesmen and political thinkers, and he urged that the editors would not spread the contributions too thin but would rather concentrate different issues on different political figures. Bandler agreed in principle but would not seriously consider Tate's suggestion of an issue concentrated on Calhoun because he feared it might "affect seriously the circulation of The HOUND & HORN".[127] On 24 February 1932, Tate suggested that Andrew Lytle should review biographies of Robert Barnewell Rhett and Edmund Ruffin, as "the first step towards the political program we've outlined", and after that he kept up a steady flow of propositions for assignments, a number of which were accepted though not all of them were published. These assignments were as often literary as sectional and the only propagandistic agrarian contributions to *The Hound & Horn* were Davidson's article, and reviews by Andrew Lytle and Frank Owsley.[128]

The economic and political side of agrarianism became the province of *The American Review* which was edited from 1933 to 1937 by Seward Collins, one-time editor of the by then defunct *Bookman*, to sponsor "the writings of four groups of traditionalists or conservatives: the Humanists of the North, the Neo-Thomists of France and America, the Distributists of England,

---

[126]   Letter to Kirstein, February 6, 1933. In his reminiscences of *The Hound & Horn*, however, Kirstein was to write: "Donald Davidson's important analysis of 'Sectionalism in the United States' appeared and provided subjects for our political conversations for a year" (Kirstein, p. 9).

[127]   Letter to Tate, February 8, 1932.

[128]   Davidson, "Sectionalism in the United States", *H & H*, VI, 4 (Summer 1933), 561-589; Lytle, "Principles of Secession", *H & H*, V, 4 (Summer 1932), 687-693; Owsley, "Two Agrarian Philosophers: Jefferson and Dupont de Nemours", *H & H*, VI, 1 (Autumn 1932), 166-172.

and the Agrarians of the South." [129] Collins came down to the South in early 1933, in Tate's words, "to get us lined up. We intend to write for him, mostly on the economic side." [130] Indeed, virtually all Southerners who took an interest in agrarianism appeared in the pages of *The American Review* during its relatively short span of life: Tate, Davidson, Owsley, Lytle, Ransom, Warren, John Donald Wade, Cleanth Brooks, Herbert Agar, Lyle Lanier and Stark Young.[131] In *The Hound & Horn* agrarianism was approached in the same manner as Marxism, humanism and T. S. Eliot's Anglo-Catholicism. The following words written by Henry Bamford Parkes could ultimately be applied to any of these causes:

The intellectual can become a partisan only by doing violence to his own nature. The true intellectual aspires to be 'a free spirit'; he achieves greatness to the extent that he frees himself from the ideas peculiar to a particular class or race or period. Contemporary literature must necessarily take account of the class struggle, but if it is written with the purpose not of understanding it but of idealizing one side or the other, falsifying or sentimentalizing the crude realities, it ceases to be literature and becomes propaganda.[132]

Parkes was of course writing about the influence of Marxism on literature. Most contributors to *The Hound & Horn* took a similar stand towards Marxism but not all. Lincoln Kirstein for one, was more susceptible to the contemporary excitement it caused. "I realize now", he wrote in 1934, "that had the magazine continued it would have been definitely left". He related how his contact with Max Nomad, the "ex-anarchist", Harry Potamkin, the magazine's film critic, and the painters Philip Reisman and Ben Shahn made him increasingly aware of the "great rich-

---

[129]   Donald Davidson, *Southern Writers in the Modern World* (Athens, Ga., 1958), p. 61.
[130]   Letter to Kirstein, April 17, 1933.
[131]   See Albert E. Stone, Jr., "Seward Collins and the *American Review*: Experiment in Pro-Fascism, 1933-37", *The American Quarterly*, XII, 1 (Spring 1960), 3-19.
[132]   "The Limitations of Marxism", *H & H*, VII, 4 (Summer 1934), 580.

ness in revolutionary subject matter".[133] On August 11, 1932, Max Nomad was informed that the editors of *The Hound & Horn* were "extremely anxious to publish some articles dealing with the outstanding figures in the revolutionary movement today". This expressed Kirstein's wish rather than that of the other editors, who, however, did not object very strongly as long as enough space in the magazine was allotted to their preferences. It was not till the Spring issue of 1933 that Kirstein's new interest became very noticeable in the magazine. That issue opened with a chapter from a biography of Karl Marx which Nomad was then preparing and was followed by three photographs by Walker Evans – a gifted photographer sponsored by Kirstein – illustrating the misery of the depression. The issue further contained a eulogy on Philip Reisman by Kirstein, and the "Art Chronicle" was a talk given by Leon Kroll for the John Reed Club art class in January of that year.[134] Harry Potamkin's thirteen page "Film Chronicle" treated Pudovkin and the revolutionary film. Both regional editors praised the issue although their comments rather concerned the non-Marxian contributions. Tate called the issue "one of the best, certainly the most solid and concentrated for over a year", and Winters admitted that he had not had time to

[133]   Kirstein, p. 10. Kirstein's admiration for Reisman and Shahn led him to organize the special exhibition of mural painting at the Museum of Modern Art in New York in the summer of 1932 (cf. Selden Rodman, *Portrait of the Artist as an American. Ben Shahn: A Biography with Pictures* [New York, 1956], p. 99). In his recent reminiscences of the 1930's, David Cornel DeJong wrote: "During the Thirties I moved to New York, soon after the publication of my second novel. Just about that time Lincoln Kirstein found it expedient to mark me as a true specimen of the proletariat, to give some sort of social significance to my appearing off and on in the Hound & Horn" ("Money and Rue", *The Carleton Miscellany*, VI, 1 [Winter 1965], 51).

[134]   John Reed's adventurous revolutionary career will be familiar. His name was given to a communist club in New York founded by *The New Masses* as part of its programme "to develop promising artists of the proletariat". New York's example was soon followed by Chicago and other cities. The Clubs were dissolved when the Popular Front policy was adopted in 1935. For further information, see Daniel Aaron, *Writers on the Left* (New York, 1961), pp. 213, 280-282, and Rudolf Sühnel, "The Marxist Trend in Literary Criticism in the USA in the Thirties", *Jahrbuch für Amerikastudien*, Band 7 (Heidelberg, 1962), 53-66.

read the complete issue, but that it looked very good.[135] Tate found special praise for the reviewing section, Winters for the poetry and story. The Summer issue of 1933 contained a note on Ben Shahn by Jean Charlot, a "Film Chronicle" by Potamkin dealing with Eisenstein and the theory of cinema, and a review by M. R. Werner of three books on Russia. That summer Harry Potamkin died, and with him died the magazine's short-lived interest in "the Revolution". The Autumn issue, apart from a touching "Comment" in memory of Potamkin, only contained Max No-mad's study of the Russian revolutionary Sergei Nechayev.

The disappearance of Marxism from *The Hound & Horn* was a result of an editorial decision to put a stop to all extra-literary discussion. This decision pertained as much to agrarian as to Marxist subject-matter and was taken in the autumn of 1933 on the advice of Bernard Bandler. Already on 13 March of that year, Bandler, although he had no editorial voice, had written a general criticism of the magazine. He felt that the recent issues had not paid sufficient attention to literature. "The real importance of the Hound and Horn lies in its genuine interest in letters and not in its excursions into politics, into philosophy, or informative essays on Russian political thinkers, on Christian Science, or on Judaism. Much more important would be a study on any man, dead or living, who happens to have written well." [136] But it took a personal interview in the autumn of 1933 to win Kirstein over to the purely literary point of view. "Bernard came in here and we had a terrifying half hour's talk", he wrote to Tate on 17 October 1933. He informed Tate that he had decided "to eliminate all articles for the magazine not of a distinctly literary nature" and that by literary he meant "really technical: that all critical articles must have something to do with questions

[135]   Tate to Kirstein, April 17, 1933; Winters to Kirstein, April 18, 1933. A *Hound & Horn* circular letter which was sent out to potential patrons in September 1933 is illustrative of the new political commitment, although parts of it were evidently mere tactics to attract material support: "The early aestheticism is gone. More European writers of importance, such as DuBos and Gilson are being introduced; more foreign books are being noticed in our reviews. The future will see an increase in our political scope."
[136]   Letter to Kirstein.

directly involving the materials of writing". Two weeks earlier, he had informed Yvor Winters of the same decision: "I am cancelling all the contracted Russian articles and I am prepared to quarrel with Tate about the old South." He had come to realize that "if the magazine has any function at all, that is, any real special function, it is of a literary quarterly" (October 4, 1933).

The direction of the magazine's evaluation of a Marxist approach to literary criticism was exemplified in Blackmur's important review of Granville Hicks's Marxian interpretation of American literature, *The Great Tradition*. The review appeared in the Winter 1934 issue. Blackmur considered Hicks's treatment of John Dos Passos representative. In his opinion, Hicks's endorsement of Dos Passos's politics had caused him to pass over "the weakness and sentimentality with which, for example, Dos Passos' proletariat is conceived, and ... the barbarous inadequacy of Dos Passos' general expression of the quality of life. I do not think that in either instance Mr. Hicks is dishonest. It is merely that in his mind he has subordinated literature to a single interpretation of a single one of the many interests that condition it to-day – the Marxian analysis. That is heresy within heresy; and it would be nothing but privation to follow him." [137] The "Limitations of Marxism" were again examined by Henry Bamford Parkes in an essay of that title in the last number of *The Hound & Horn* (Summer 1934), which also contained Blackmur's joint review of Cowley's *Exile's Return* and Eliot's *After Strange Gods*. Both Parkes and Blackmur denied the validity of any orthodoxy, be it Marxian, humanist, Anglo-Catholic, or agrarian, as an exclusive approach to literature. Blackmur emphasized that neither Eliot nor Cowley was an absolutist, but he questioned "the tacit assumption of both men that any particular frame of faith, political, moral, or religious, can fit any large body of men at any one time, or even, what is more important, the abler minds among it".[138] This was the magazine's final

---

[137] "Heresy within Heresy", *H & H*, VII, 2 (Winter 1934), 354-355.
[138] "The Dangers of Authorship", *H & H*, VII, 4 (Summer 1934), 719. At the time he was writing this review, Blackmur wrote to Malcolm

assertion of its belief in the autonomy of art without limiting and simplifying orthodoxies.

The climax of the career of *The Hound & Horn* was the Spring issue of 1934 which was entirely devoted to Henry James. Such an issue had been an ambition of the editors for some years past. On 21 August 1931, Kirstein had written to Edna Kenton that *The Hound & Horn* was planning "an international tribute to Henry James for its spring 1932 issue", but the uncertainty of the whole venture is nowhere better illustrated than in Kirstein's correspondence with William Troy. On 7 December 1932 Kirstein told Troy that he planned to entrust the issue to his editorship, only to inform him on 27 February of the following year that he had "decided definitely to abandon any idea of the Henry James number". Definite editorial decisions of *The Hound & Horn* were, however, often not as definite as the editorial decisions of *The Dial* had been, and two weeks later Bandler urged Kirstein to go on with "your splendid idea of the Henry James number".[139]

When "Homage to Henry James, 1843-1916" finally appeared, it opened characteristically with the editorial statement that there was no American artist who could "serve as such an admirable

Cowley: "My reading, thinking, and observation, have increasingly compelled me to see myself as a political outsider; for the simple reason that I cannot see any radical leadership to which I can submit" (April 27, 1934, Cowley papers, Newberry Library).

[139] March 13, 1933. The organization of *The Hound & Horn* was much less efficient than that of *The Dial*. The loss of the *Mystère Laïc* manuscript is only one example. Another instance is described in a letter from Tate to Kirstein (February 22, 1931), which refers to the former's earliest association with the magazine. "It would be useless for me to conceal the fact that I am annoyed at the editorial manners of The Hound & Horn. I have never yet received the slightest token of regret for the cavalier treatment I received two or three years ago: I was invited to contribute some poems; I sent them and they were accepted; and three or four months later they were returned without the least explanation." There were frequent complaints from subscribers who failed to receive their copies of the magazine. Kirstein was also bothered about his "incredible faculty of hurting people's feelings through the mails" (letter to Tate, May 2, 1933), and on September 28, 1932, he told Winters that letters "are never received in the spirit in which they are sent, and never can be. I know from talking with the editors of the DIAL what they went through in exactly the same kind of thing."

point of departure for an inquest into the present condition of our literature".[140] This editorial also drew attention to an earlier James memorial in *The Egoist* of January 1918, followed by *The Little Review*'s homage in August of the same year.[141] The final roster of the contributors to *The Hound & Horn*'s Homage listed Marianne Moore, Lawrence Leighton, Edmund Wilson, Francis Fergusson, Stephen Spender, Newton Arvin, R. P. Blackmur, John Wheelwright, Robert Cantwell, Edna Kenton, H. R. Hays, and Glenway Wescott.[142] The issue also contained two unpublished letters, three photographs and one wood-engraving of James, and the hitherto unpublished scenario of *The Ambassadors* which had been a wedding-present from Bandler to Mayor. The issue was rather uncoordinated and very uneven in quality, ranging from such excellent and controversial essays as Blackmur's on "The Critical Prefaces" and Wilson's on "The Ambiguity of Henry James" to Wescott's "A Sentimental Contribution", which was just that. But it certainly deserved the praise which it received in a number of newspapers and periodicals. No American magazine had yet published a special issue on such a scale and of such excellence. William Rose Benét predicted that it was "sure to become a collector's item." [143] Much of its success was due to the labours of Edna Kenton who had been in charge of the organization of the issue. "I want to say privately, as I have publicly," Kirstein told her, "how grateful I am to you for everything you have done for us. Without you, the issue could never have been possible." [144]

140 "Homage to Henry James, 1843-1916", *H & H*, VII, 3 (Spring 1934), 361.
141 Morton Dauwen Zabel felt that *The Hound & Horn*'s Homage "lacked the liveliness as well as the direct personal interest of the *Little Review*'s tribute in 1918, where Pound, Eliot, Ford and the Misses Mayne and Bosanquet wrote with the stroke of an older, more immediate generation" ("Recent Magazines", *Poetry*, XLIV, 3 [June 1934], 170).
142 Manuscripts had been solicited in vain from other critics including Ezra Pound, T. S. Eliot, Gertrude Stein, William Troy and Peter Quennell.
143 "Phoenix Nest", *Saturday Review of Literature*, X, 45 (May 26, 1934), 720.
144 March 26, 1934. *The Hound & Horn* had planned other annual symposia on Melville and Whitman to follow the James number. Kirstein's interest in Melville had prompted him already in 1931 to arrange for an

III

The end of *The Hound & Horn* came with the Summer issue of 1934. On 23 January 1933, Kirstein had still been in a position to tell Tate that the magazine was "continuing indefinitely", but on 11 September of that year he informed his Southern editor that he thought it "extremely unlikely that the magazine will go on after next June". Although by 1934 Kirstein's attention was focussing more and more exclusively on the ballet, he supported several attempts to keep the magazine alive. He remembered that there were "at least four schemes on hand to resurrect it, one of which had a kind of advanced insanity which attracted me strongly. I knew it was nuts, but I loved that scheme. It all blew up when some (I was never quite sure what, how, or why) British bonds depreciated in value between Arizona and New York." [145] None of these schemes worked, and on 1 July 1934, *The Hound & Horn* sent out a circular to announce its discontinuance to its subscribers. The editors felt that this step was "a little less deplorable, now that THE MAGAZINE has come into existence as the only periodical, in our estimation, that could in any way replace HOUND & HORN." The editors offered to refer their readers' unexpired subscriptions to *The Magazine*. This new periodical, a monthly literary journal of poetry and fiction, was started on the West Coast in December 1933. From June 1934 onwards it appeared bi-monthly. Its most regular contributors during its half year as a monthly included Albert Guerard, Achilles Holt, Howard Baker, J. V. Cunningham, Barbara Gibbs, Janet Lewis, Henry Ramsey, Don Stanford, and Yvor Winters; in other words virtually the complete list of Winters's Stanford poets. Winters's association with *The Magazine* appears soon to have led to disagreements because the July-August issue of 1934 announced very plainly that "from now onwards selection will be made from

---

edition of *Billy Budd* to be published in Paris "with illustrations by William Littlefield", and together with Jere Abbot he had "prepared a libretto from the text of MOBY DICK for three danced scenes for orchestra, male chorus and ballet" (Kirstein to John Birss, December 17, 1931).
[145]   Kirstein, p. 92.

all present-day literary groups, playing no favorites. ... 'The Magazine' in entering upon Volume II refuses to promote the interest of any special group."[146] Volume II included several new names such as Allen Tate, Robert Penn Warren and Kenneth Patchen, but carried no more contributions from Winters. "Winters and myself have both ceased to care much for *The Magazine*", Kirstein wrote in the autumn of 1934; "It's too scrappy and salad-like".[147] *The Hound & Horn* had advertised in *The Magazine* and had still offered its subscription, at $2.00 for one year and $3.50 for two years, as late as April 1934, although by that time chances of its continuance were very low indeed. *The Magazine* did not last long; on 19 June 1935, one of its editors, Richard W. Perry, informed Kirstein's secretary, Doris Levine: "we are suspending publication . . . until Jan.-Feb., 1936", but the May-June 1935 issue was the last that ever appeared.

The history of *The Hound & Horn* was perhaps more exciting than that of any of its successors save *Partisan Review*, although it never indulged in little magazine histrionics, as had for instance, *The Little Review, Blast,* and *Secession.* It attracted some attention during its life-time, but never to the extent *The Dial* did. "We hoped", Kirstein has written, "it was going to take the place of *The Dial,* which after its long and valuable existence had recently died, but it didn't".[148]

It will not be surprising that many of the comments *The Hound & Horn* drew during its life-time were from the militant left, and that they were by no means favourable. Certainly, magazines like *The Criterion, Poetry,* and *The Nation* praised the high quality of its contents, especially its essays and reviews, as they had praised *The Dial,* but the Marxian critics were quite as vocal. *The Modern Monthly* maintained that *The Hound &*

---

[146] "Editorial Note", *The Magazine*, II, 1 (July-August 1934), inside front cover. On 23 July 1934, Winters had written to Kirstein that he had broken with *The Magazine* and that, if he could scrape together the money, he would repurchase his unpublished poems.
[147] Kirstein, p. 92.
[148] *Ibid.*, p. 7.

Horn was "certainly not unaware of the present crisis, although behind the cover of these attacks on communism it presents it not in terms of war and starvation but of a sense of inadequacy and isolation in the individual"; and *Partisan Review* traced one of the "dominant bourgeois theories of criticism . . . [to] a group, Yvor Winters, Allen Tate, R. P. Blackmur, etc., who have fused Eliot with Imagism and regionalism".[149] A critic of *The New Masses* attacked Kirstein's highly favourable review of Archibald MacLeish's *Conquistador*; in that same magazine, one year earlier in February 1933, Granville Hicks had investigated "The Crisis in American Criticism" and had asserted that MacLeish, "an associate of the *Hound & Horners,* has attempted in the New Republic . . . to create an up-to-date rationale of the leisure class". In that same article Hicks remembered how the editors of *The Hound & Horn,* when they were accused of trying to create a leisure class culture, "began scurrying around to defend themselves".[150] This accusation had been levelled by Hicks himself in the pages of *The New Republic* almost a year earlier, in a review of Kirstein's novel *Flesh is Heir*. Hicks had been as much concerned with Kirstein's magazine as with his novel:

Mr. Kirstein, his fellow editors and most of their contributors have leisure, the means to publish a magazine and enough intelligence to master the ideas of others. Belonging to the leisure class, they have desired a leisure-class culture to sustain them, and they have tried to patch one together out of whatever odds and ends lay at hand – Eliot's royalism, Maritain's neo-Thomism, tags of classical learning, and an acquaintance with the names and often, indeed, the works of various recondite authors. That such a hodgepodge could be, and in a sense deserved to be taken seriously is a commentary on the state of American criticism. But there are signs that the structure is already cracking. The depression which has blown down so many pretty castles, is remote enough from the young men of the Hound & Horn to have had little immediate effect on their thought. By this time, however,

---

[149] Obed Brooks, "The Literary Front", *Modern Monthly*, VII, 2 (March 1933), 117; Wallace Phelps, "The Anatomy of Liberalism", *PR*, I, 1 (February-March 1934), 47.
[150] Margaret Wright Mather's review of *Poems* of MacLeish, *New Masses*, X, 3 (January 1934), 26; Hicks, "The Crisis in American Criticism", *New Masses*, VIII, 7 (February 1933), 3.

it is clear even to them that the men of power, whom they had expected to make the patrons of this leisure-class culture, are concerned with much more urgent problems. There is, in short, no real basis for all their efforts. In what direction will they now turn? [151]

Hicks and *The New Republic* were too important and the attack too near the truth to leave the editors of *The Hound & Horn* unruffled. Bandler had to admit that "Hicks made some good points" although, he told Tate, "I have taken advantage of his carelessness of expression to write a letter protesting to the New Republic" (April 29, 1932). The controversy was indeed continued in the correspondence columns of *The New Republic*. Its acrimony, especially of Hicks's attacks on the "leisure class", was resented by a number of readers. It prompted John Wheelwright to join the controversy in support of *The Hound & Horn*. Allen Tate had reason to write that "Hicks gave his whole case away in the controversy, and behaved very badly besides".[152]

In the course of the tumult it became apparent that Hicks's wrath was partly aimed at the editors' "preference for the more difficult of contemporary poets and novelists".[153] Hicks was not

---

[151] "Inheritance Tax", *The New Republic*, LXX (April 20, 1932), 278-279. In the course of the ensuing controversy Hicks pointed out that "since it was clear to me that Mr. Kirstein's 'Flesh is Heir' was scarcely worth reviewing except insofar as it threw some light upon The Hound & Horn, I tried to bring out the relations between the novel and the magazine" ("Hounds and Horns", *The New Republic*, LXXI [May 25, 1932], 49).

[152] Letter to Bandler, June 17, 1932. The relations of *The New Republic* with *The Hound & Horn* remained cool till the end. When C. Hartley Grattan reviewed the Henry James number he had to admit that it was "not only worth looking through but actually worth reading", but he significantly found praise mainly for the Marxian contributors to the issue ("Composite Photograph", *The New Republic*, LXXIX [June 13, 1934], 133). The literary editor of *The New Republic*, Malcolm Cowley, wrote after the demise of the magazine: "I didn't have to choke back great sobs when I heard that The Hound and Horn was suspending publication, but none the less I was sorry to see it go" ("Midsummer Medley", *The New Republic*, LXXX [August 15, 1934], 24).

[153] "Hounds and Horns", 49. Edward Dahlberg referred to the *Hound & Horn* writers as "the Fastidious Movement in American literature today. Though their achievements are still slender and tenuous, their aesthetic program is not to be dismissed" ("The Fastidious Movement", *The Nation*, CXXXIV [April 6, 1932], 402).

the only critic to find fault with the literary taste of *The Hound & Horn* and with its severe criticism of such contemporary literature as did not come up to its high standards of aesthetic perfection. Hicks's attitude was shared, for instance, by Archibald MacLeish in his attack on literary criticism which we have described earlier, and by Thomas Wolfe who, in his letters, spoke of "Hound & Horners" and "young precious boys".[154] These may be seen as examples of the incessant fight of the middlebrow mentality against the highbrow literary reviews, but they also testify to the occasional pedantry of editors and contributors.

The Hound & Horn had a different kind of controversy with *This Quarter,* which was set off by the latter magazine's question: "what could be a plainer sign of the decline of the review than that the publication run by a group of youths, however talented, should occupy today a place once the place of the North American?" [155] This question was prompted by *This Quarter*'s dissatisfaction with Blackmur's severe "Notes on E. E. Cummings' Language". The reason for its defence of Cummings became evident in the next issue when its editor, E. W. Titus, announced the magazine's decision to award the Richard Aldington Poetry Prize to Cummings, thus rejecting Aldington's own choice of Walter Lowenfels. The same issue published an angry letter from Kirstein and a rather long-winded but good-natured reply by Titus.

Although the magazine stopped publication in the summer of 1934, the Hound & Horn Corporation was continued in existence for possible publication of pamphlets and booklets on the dance. By the end of 1938 the last assets of the corporation were sold. *The Hound & Horn* was definitely a thing of the past.

---

[154] *The Letters of Thomas Wolfe*, ed. Elizabeth Nowell (New York, 1956), p. 633. Wolfe had taken a similar attitude to *The Dial* (p. 175).
[155] Edward Titus, "The Flying Column", *This Quarter*, III, 4 (Spring 1931), 748.

4

THE SYMPOSIUM (1930-1933)*

I

The Symposium was edited by two young teachers of philosophy at New York University, Philip Wheelwright and James Burnham. Their acquaintanceship dated back to the time when they had both been at Princeton, Wheelwright as an instructor in philosophy and Burnham as a student majoring in English. Burnham had worked under Wheelwright for one year; he graduated in 1927. He subsequently spent two years at Oxford in England and in 1929 joined Wheelwright at Washington Square College, New York University, when the latter invited him to come and teach in the philosophy department and help edit a magazine. James Buell Munn, the millionaire Dean of Washington Square College, was to sponsor this magazine in a private capacity. Munn, who was already supporting an art magazine, put up the money, provided a room in New York University at 100 Washington Square, and left the editors to the job of running the review as they thought fit. His generosity made it possible to pay one cent a word for contributions.[1]

The Symposium ran for exactly four years with sixteen quarterly

* I have based my account of *The Symposium* to some extent on conversations both with Philip Wheelwright (on April 2, 1965 at Riverside, Cal.) and with James Burnham (on May 25, 1965 in New York, N.Y.). The editorial correspondence of *The Symposium* cannot be traced; it was most probably destroyed.

[1] Frederick Hoffman, Charles Allen, and Caroline Ulrich (*The Little Magazine: A History and a Bibliography*, 2nd ed. [Princeton, N.J., 1947], p. 209) mistakenly state that *The Symposium* "never found enough money to pay its contributors".

instalments. Before its first issue appeared in January 1930, the editors had gone through rather strenuous negotiations with their contemporary, *The Hound & Horn*. Lincoln Kirstein had been much impressed by a circular which the forthcoming magazine had put out to announce its programme, and had his friends Hyatt Mayor and Francis Fergusson introduce himself and Bernard Bandler to the prospective editors.[2] A merger of the two magazines was agreed upon, which, as we have already noted in the preceding chapter, resulted for one thing in the dismissal of R. P. Blackmur as managing editor of *The Hound & Horn*. Wheelwright and Burnham felt that the salary paid to Blackmur was rather a recognition of his genius as a literary critic than remuneration for actual services rendered. Blackmur himself described the situation as follows in a letter to Malcolm Cowley: "For your information the New Symposium was not a magazine de facto as it was never published, but was composed in uneven proportions of money and intentions and a good deal of manuscript material on hand, including among the last a hymn upon his 70th birthday by John Dewey. The composition of money and hagiology was too great to resist." [3] The "hymn" Blackmur referred to was very probably Dewey's article "Qualitative Thought". Dewey offered it to *The Symposium* and refused payment for it because he had an exaggerated impression of the poverty of the young editors.[4] They could only graciously accept it, but not without misgivings as to its appropriateness for their magazine. The essay proved one of the points of friction between the editors of *The Hound & Horn* and of *The Symposium*.

For the time being, however, they were seriously planning "the line up" of a December 1929 number which was more or less agreed upon by the middle of November. "It is a good issue", Burnham told Bandler on 19 November 1929; but on the same

[2]   Both Mayor and Fergusson were ex-Rhodes scholars and at the time connected with the American Laboratory Theater.

[3]   November 12, 1929, Malcolm Cowley papers, Newberry Library.

[4]   Wheelwright remembers that the editors, in their turn, offered Dewey a free subscription, but as the publisher failed to remove the payment blank from Dewey's free copy of the magazine, Dewey sent a cheque for the regular two dollars fifty for a year's subscription.

day Burnham reminded Kirstein that Wheelwright and himself would "naturally expect to extend our criticisms whenever there is any doubt about a manuscript".[5] Contributions in hand for the first issues included essays by Paul Valéry, Julien Benda, David Garnett, Kenneth White, and Franklin Gary, and two poems by Allen Tate, "Mother and Son" and "Thoughts for a Friend". I. A. Richards was asked to write under the general title "Art and Experience", and the Rev. M. C. D'Arcy S.J. was to expound "Contemporary Definitions of Philosophy".

Other contributions were described in *The New York Times* on 24 November 1929, in a notice announcing the merger of the two magazines:

A new magazine, with the ambitious aim of 'attempting to bring some order and direction into the perplexed tangle of American intellectual and artistic activity' will make its appearance on December 10. The publication which is to be known as *The Hound & Horn: An American Symposium*, will print in its first number an article by Professor John Dewey of Columbia University, entitled 'Qualitative Thinking', which is to be a summation of the key chapter of the noted philosopher's yet unpublished definitive work on logic . . .

Among the contributions to the first issue of the magazine, which is to be a quarterly, are Francis Fergusson, director of the American Laboratory Theater, who has written an article on Eugene O'Neill; Hyatt Mayor, with an illustrated article on Picasso; Herbert Read who contributes a critical essay on Nathaniel Hawthorne; Kenneth Burke, making 'The Eighth Declamation', a series begun in *The Dial*: Ramon Fernandez on classicism and Montgomery Belgion on 'Gold and Mammon', an examination of certain American critics, with a refutation of certain portions of Walter Lippman's 'A Preface to Morals'.[6]

The Fergusson, Mayor, Burke, Belgion, and Read items were eventually published in *The Hound & Horn*, and Dewey and Fernandez in *The Symposium*. It is ironic that at about the time of this announcement in *The New York Times*, the negotiations between *The Hound & Horn* and the as yet unpublished *Symposium* shipwrecked because Kirstein's lawyer insisted that *The Hound & Horn* get fifty-one percent of the shares. Wheelwright and Burnham then threatened to sue, but tempers were soothed at a

---

5   *Hound & Horn* papers, Yale University Library.
6   *The New York Times* (November 24, 1929), Part II, 4.

dramatic meeting of both parties when Kirstein agreed to pay six hundred dollars to *The Symposium* as compensation for loss of time. Friction between the two magazines, however, was not eliminated for some time to come. Both sides complained that the other retained manuscripts. "Our relations during the last few weeks have been most unpleasant", Kirstein told Louis Zukofsky on 23 January 1930, "and despite repeated requests that they return to us this [Zukofsky's] and other manuscripts, which they of course have no right to retain, the manuscript has not been forthcoming".[7] The proposed merger had been an exasperating affair particularly because *The Hound & Horn* felt that it would lose more than it would gain and acted accordingly. "It seemed to Kirstein and myself", Bernard Bandler wrote, "that we were giving far more to two practically unknown men than we were receiving".[8] For better or for worse the two magazines were now set on their own separate courses, but the following editorial notice published in *The Nation* towards the end of January 1930, is an indication of the public confusion concerning their relative positions: "We regret to announce that the excellent *Symposium* has expired with its first issue; it has been taken over by the *Hound & Horn*."[9]

The Symposium has attracted less attention from contemporaries as well as from later scholars than any comparable twentieth-century literary review. If it has been mentioned at all it has been, with few exceptions, in one breath with *The Hound & Horn*, and most of the exceptions took issue with the magazine's political position. When in October 1932, *The Symposium* published its first poem, *The Criterion* remarked: "It is rather hard lines that just as the *Symposium* makes its first venture in publishing creative work, the *Hound & Horn* should manage to produce such a good

[7]　*Hound & Horn* papers. In his reminiscences of *The Hound & Horn* Kirstein wrote: "Largely through misunderstanding, but not without stupidity, I had almost involved myself in a lawsuit with the editors of *The Symposium*, with whom we thought we'd like to merge. The matter was settled amicably however. *The Symposium* and *The Hound & Horn* were on excellent terms, exchanged material, and the editors Burnham and Wheelwright became our good friends" (Kirstein, p. 8).
[8]　Letter to Robert Shafer, December 11, 1929, *Hound & Horn* papers.
[9]　"Editorial: The New Magazines", *The Nation*, CXXX (January 29, 1930), 116.

number as the October-December one." [10] This early comparison of the two magazines typifies the conception of *The Symposium* as a slightly inferior contemporary of *The Hound & Horn*. This conception was current from the start and was given additional weight by the authors of the standard history of the little magazine, who considered *The Symposium* "on the whole . . . a more conservative, less stimulating periodical than *The Hound & Horn*." [11] In their context words like "conservative" and "stimulating" are emotive rather than precise. They were probably evoked by certain editorial characteristics of *The Symposium*, such as its lack of interest in contemporary subjects of debate like humanism and agrarianism, its refusal to pay attention only to contemporary literature to the exclusion of the literature of the past, its interest in general ideas rather than events, and the almost complete absence of chronicles on the contemporary arts. These characteristics constitute some of the most striking differences from *The Hound & Horn* and they will be discussed in greater detail presently. They gave *The Symposium* an air of detachment from its surroundings which might easily be confused with staidness. A more than superficial inspection of its pages, however, reveals an intellectual maturity and disinterestedness which was not always matched by *The Hound & Horn*. Any account of the development of the American literary review in the twentieth century will have to pay attention to the peculiar qualities of *The Symposium*. They were understood by Allen Tate, who was probably the most important force in shaping the history of the critical review in the United

---

[10]   H.S.D. [Hugh Sykes Davies], "American Periodicals", *The Criterion*, XI, 48 (April 1933), 543. It must be pointed out, however, that *The Criterion* was genuinely appreciative of *The Symposium*. In April 1931 it stated that the two magazines which came "most obviously within the circle of the *Criterion*" were *The Hound & Horn* and *The Symposium*. "If it were necessary to choose one American magazine only, for reading on this side of the water, it would be hard to decide" between them (X, 587, 588). Similarly, another English magazine, *The Adelphi*, described *The Symposium* as "a quarterly which shares with the *Hound & Horn* the distinction of being the most interesting and intellectually alive of American magazines" ("Some Periodicals", *The Adelphi*, II, 5 [August 1931], inside front cover).
[11]   See *The Little Magazine*, p. 209.

States. Tate called *The Symposium* "the best critical quarterly ever published in America", and the context of this remark is as significant as the remark itself. It occurs in the blueprint for a critical quarterly which Tate, although not an editor himself, was asked to write for *The Southern Review*.[12] Indeed we can only arrive at a satisfactory understanding of *The Southern Review* after we have investigated the significant ways in which *The Symposium* differed from *The Hound & Horn*. Our first approach to *The Symposium*, therefore, ought to be in terms of a comparison with *The Hound & Horn* in the light of the tradition of the literary review. This approach will acquaint us with some of the salient features of the magazine's history.

II

The physical make-up of *The Symposium*, like that of *The Dial* and *The Hound & Horn*, gave the impression of solid financial backing. Its cover was sober, almost stern. A woodcut of Socrates and his disciples had been commissioned to serve as cover design, but the result had proved disappointing and unacceptable. When the first issue appeared in January 1930, it displayed on its cover the table of contents in black lettering on a light grey background underneath the title *The Symposium* in red capitals followed by the subtitle "A Critical Review" in black capitals. In contrast to the typographical experiments of *The Hound & Horn*, and much like *The Dial*, it did not change its sober exterior during its short existence. It does, indeed, not seem too far-fetched to suspect some correlation between the magazine's appearance and its reputation.

The Symposium's subtitle "A Critical Review" has to be taken quite literally as a review which only published criticism in its widest sense. This description applies to the greater part of the career of the magazine. In July 1932, however, it published two selfconsciously experimental fragments of a novel by David Burnham, a brother of the editor; this was an inauspicious first choice

[12] "The Function of the Critical Quarterly", *SoR*, I, 3 (Winter 1936), 551-559.

which Morton Dauwen Zabel set down as "perhaps purely a family matter".[13] The following issue, that of October 1932, featured a long poem, *Red Decision*, by Ben Maddow preceded by an interesting editorial "Comment" explaining the change of the magazine's policy:

It was at no time the fixed intention of the editors to restrict the magazine exclusively to criticism, but this restriction was, actually, until July, operative. The reasons for it were various, some of them of merely biographical interest. Chief among them, of course, is the difficulty of discovering really first rate 'creative' writing, poetry or prose. We live at a time when, as has been more than once pointed out, criticism seems to be more readily possible than creation. And criticism of a high order: perhaps lacking in direction, even, most of it, verging towards sterility; but of a precision and analytic acuteness that has seldom been surpassed. THE SYMPOSIUM has tried to represent a level of this criticism for which there was no other medium, and to group it together in an at least partly coherent manner.

The change to publishing creative work was inspired partly by a feeling of growing monotony of tone but it did not affect the essentially critical nature of the magazine. Creative work would occupy only a small number of its pages and would be presented "not simply as a possibly enjoyable interlude, but consciously in the context of the magazine as a whole, to be referred to the magazine's critical discussions, to be, specifically, the subject of criticism".[14] It is significant of the attitude of the editors that they explicitly referred to the faults of *Red Decision* as interesting illustrations of a critical thesis; Ben Maddow was a communist and the editors announced that some of the problems raised by his poem would be the starting point for a discussion of proletarian and revolutionary aesthetics in the January 1933 issue. This is an instance of the unique "symposial" character of the magazine which we shall discuss in some detail later on. Although the editors insisted that they were not publishing the poem merely as "a carcase for dissection", one of its functions was unmistakably that of a provocative of critical and ideological discussion. The creative writing featured in the subsequent issues of the magazine,

[13] M.D.Z., "Recent Magazines", *Poetry*, XLIII, 4 (January 1934), 172.
[14] "Comment", *Symposium*, III, 4 (October 1932), 419, 420.

the poetry and fiction of Alfred Young Fisher, Walter Donnelly, Paul Goodman, Louis Zukofsky, Bernard Raymund, and Myra Marini, marks the least distinguished aspect of its history. It reminds one of the career of another review whose function was mainly critical, the English *Scrutiny*. The resemblance, however, is no more than superficial. *The Symposium*'s life span was only one fifth of *Scrutiny*'s. Moreover, its less regimented critical programme, due partly to the much wider and more variegated circle of its contributors, its concern for "ideas rather than events", and its lack of uncompromising cultural pessimism, distinguish it from the English magazine, and in part account for the fact that *The Symposium* never even approached the degree of influence which *Scrutiny* exerted.

The Symposium's subtitle, then, was no empty slogan, but the editors must have decided to adopt it only shortly before the first issue appeared: while they were still negotiating the merger with *The Hound & Horn* their notepaper head carried a different subtitle, namely, "A Quarterly Journal for Philosophical Discussion". Why this subtitle was changed at the last minute is impossible to establish, but it is not far-fetched to impute the change at least partly to the editors' close contact with *The Hound & Horn* during the crucial first months of editorial planning. The initial subtitle is of more than occasional interest in a discussion of the history of the magazine. Both editors, as we have seen, were teachers of philosophy although one of them had majored in English, and the first issue of their magazine might with as much justice have been called "philosophical" as "literary".

The issue opened with the conventional editorial statement that *The Symposium* was not to be "the organ of any group or sect or cause" but that of necessity the point of view of the editors would form to some extent the point of view of the magazine. With considerable aplomb, the editors stated that there was "no critical tradition in America, nor can one be created by the mere enunciation of an editorial policy".[15] This editorial was followed by John Dewey's "Qualitative Thought", Ramon Fernandez's "On Classicism", Morris Cohen's "The Faith of a Logician", Franklin

[15] "Comment", *Symposium*, I, 1 (January 1930), 3, 4.

Gary's "Galsworthy and the *Poetics*" and a symposium "Remarks on the Novel". Most of the book reviews concerned books of philosophy. The issue was indeed top-heavily philosophical and had evidently been put together from whatever material the editors had in hand. In contrast to *The Hound & Horn*, most of the contributors were academics, a number of them clearly colleagues who could not very well be disappointed before the magazine had publicly established its own character. This it was not long in doing and signs of its academic foundations were soon all but obliterated.

What remained was a strong interest in ideas for their own sake. "The first task", the editors wrote in their important "Comment" for the second issue, "is to know what we are talking about, and what we *can* talk about; and to know this we must be concerned with ideas rather than events, with analysis rather than consequences".[16] It was possible, the editors felt, to be contemporary without getting down to rigidly practical matters. Even when they became susceptible to the increasing influence of Marxism, they kept defending, however weakly, an interest in ideas for their own sake; and Marxism, it must be added, was the only contemporary "system" which was more than mentioned in passing in the magazine. "There is in ideas, in the most general ideas removed from immediate relations with contemporary events and in that sense limitedly timeless, an intrinsic interest that does not need defending." [17] This unequivocal editorial statement of James Burnham marks what is perhaps the crucial difference between *The Symposium* and *The Hound & Horn*. In comparison with *The Hound & Horn*, which was excitedly contemporary and which virtually from issue to issue bore the marks of the power-struggle of personal idealisms and ambitions, *The Symposium* seems disinterestedly and solidly intellectual. The issues of *The Symposium* consisted almost solely of articles and reviews; they carried no notes on contributors, no advertising, and very few chronicles of the contemporary arts. The magazine published two "Paris Letters", the first by Stanislas Fumet on contemporary French poetry,

---

[16]   *Symposium*, I, 2 (April 1930), 148.
[17]   J.B., "Comment", *Symposium*, III, 2 (April 1932), 133.

the second by Philip Wheelwright on Paul Valéry and Stendhaliana. It had an excellent art-critic in C. R. Morse who was on the Princeton faculty and who contributed articles on Corot and Daumier, Matisse, and Picasso, but the only chronicle explicitly concerned with the contemporary world of art was "Art Notes" in the April 1932 issue in which Herbert Read commented on "French Art in London" and Laurence Buermeyer on "Matisse at the Museum of Modern Art". There were no chronicles of the theatre, of music (except for A. Lehman Engel's "Music Notes" on the Yaddo Festival of American Music in the October 1932 issue), of architecture, or of the cinema (although Dwight Macdonald contributed two very informative instalments of "Notes on Hollywood Directors" to the April and July 1933 numbers).

A short inspection of *The Symposium*'s attitude to contemporary movements and writers will illuminate the relevance of its editorial detachment. Humanism, which had been so thoroughly and often so emotionally discussed in *The Hound & Horn*, was treated as an issue concerned rather with personalities than with ideas. In the second issue the editors turned their attention to the humanists, perhaps because, in the words of James Burnham, their "mass production these days is stimulated by a large and eager demand".[18] The joint editorial remarks in "Comment" of that issue formulated *The Symposium*'s position concisely and unequivocally. The editors pointed out that they did not pretend to judge an article solely with an eye on its "excellence": "An essay on Humanism or Fundamentalism, judged by its own standards, might be of considerable merit; yet we should not for that reason publish it. It is, of course, conceivable that from subjects of current debate so publicly sterile and confused there might arise an essay we should want to consider; but this would be only when the writer showed through his treatment of the subject a recognition of issues which lie back of any intelligent discussion."[19] As the same issue contained Felix Morrow's essay on Paul Elmer More, this essay may be taken as meeting the qualifications laid down by the editors. Morrow was severely critical of the new humanism and

---

[18] "On Defining Poetry", *Symposium*, I, 2 (April 1930), 221.
[19] "Comment", *Symposium*, I, 2 (April 1930), 147-148.

related forms of reactionary thought, especially the intellectual position of T. S. Eliot. But More was his main target. For More literature had been "only a springboard from which to proclaim his theories", and in the dozen or more volumes he had written he had proposed "scarcely one estimate which could be called literary". According to Morrow, More might as well have written essays on morals, religion, and economics without a literary varnish. As to More's followers, the New Humanists, they, Morrow wrote, were "fighting old battles which never had any meaning".[20]

Morrow's article was the magazine's only full-scale contribution to the humanist debate and it did not fail to rouse the anger of humanism's bastion *The Bookman*; its editor, Seward Collins, accused Morrow of combining "the usual socialist arguments with unusually vicious misrepresentation".[21] Humanism made another appearance in *The Symposium* in Charles Ruthven's dispassionate review of Grattan's symposium *The Critique of Humanism*. Ruthven's general feeling about the controversy was that it "served to obscure the issues as much as to clarify them. Interest was focussed upon personalities instead of ideas, and critical detachment was submerged in partisanship and wounded feelings".[22] Ruthven was interested in the fundamental principles involved in the controversy and he explained the general confusion of both Foerster's and Grattan's symposium from the fact that none of the participants was primarily a philosopher. Ruthven's review in the magazine's fourth issue was the last contribution directly concerned with humanism.

Humanism, it may be objected, was already getting threadbare when *The Symposium* was first issued and consequently cannot be considered illustrative of the magazine's determination only to discuss contemporary ideas if they were of more than contemporary interest. But another cause, agrarianism, which created a considerable stir in the pages of *The Hound & Horn* and which

---

[20] "The Serpent's Enemy: Mr. More as Social Thinker", *Symposium*, I, 2 (April 1930), 171-172, 182.
[21] "Criticism in America", *The Bookman*, LXXII, 2 (October 1930), 228.
[22] *Symposium*, I, 4 (October 1930), 550.

might have furnished an attractive point of departure, *pro* or *contra*, for any critical magazine of the early 1930's, attracted even less attention than humanism. The agrarian symposium *I'll Take My Stand* was reviewed by James Southall Wilson in a characteristically non-partisan fashion. Wilson did not think it likely that "by taking thought or by writing symposia the march of industrialism can be halted before its time". But the agrarian symposium was not less important because it lacked economic constructiveness: "a wide reading of these able discussions throughout the Southern states will be provocative of the kind of thinking needed by an old country in the process of violent economic and social change".[23]

Apart from a review of *I'll Take My Stand* – and a review was accorded to most of the interesting books which came within the wide scope of the magazine's interest – agrarianism was not directly discussed. However, the kind of perceptiveness which at its best it inspired, was in evidence in one of the most interesting essays published in *The Symposium*, Allen Tate's "New England Culture and Emily Dickinson". This was Tate's only contribution to *The Symposium*. When he sent it in, the editors doubted if they could publish it because just over a year ago, a short span of time for a quarterly of 130 to 160 pages, Morris Schappes had contributed a sizeable review of Genevieve Taggard's *The Life and Mind of Emily Dickinson*. Furthermore, Burnham informed Tate on 13 January 1932, the editors had already some time ago "arranged to publish an essay on Emily Dickinson" in the April issue.[24] Wheelwright was away at the time but when, on his return, the editors went over the essay together, they decided "that in spite of the editorial unbalance resulting, it is too good not to publish".[25]

The essay opened with some remarks on the contemporary state of criticism. Although he would be concerned with the poet's historical setting, Tate did not turn to the scholars for valuable insights. "We have an institutionalized scholarship, but that is no

[23] *Symposium*, II, 1 (January 1931), 148.
[24] Allen Tate papers, Princeton University Library. The essay referred to was Morris Schappes's review of *Letters of Emily Dickinson* which appeared together with Tate's essay in the April 1932 issue.
[25] Burnham to Tate, February 8, 1932, Tate papers.

substitute for a critical tradition. Miss Dickinson's value to the research scholar, who likes historical difficulty for its own sake, is slight; she is too near to possess the remoteness of literature." Both the content and the tone of this passage anticipate the battle of critics against scholars which was to be waged a few years later in *The Southern Review* and in *The Kenyon Review*. But the primary importance of the essay lay in Tate's interpretation of the development of New England puritanism in the nineteenth century and its effect on Emily Dickinson's poetry.[26] Tate felt that though the New England idea was perhaps not very attractive socially, it had in the nineteenth century "an immense, incalculable value for literature: it dramatized the human soul. It created the perfect 'literary situation' – a situation that the Southern culture did not, or never had enough time, to produce". But soon this homogeneous culture declined; after 1830 "the great fortunes were made ... and New England became a museum". At this juncture Emerson arrived on the scene, "the Lucifer of Concord", Tate called him, "for he was the lightbearer who could see nothing but light, and was fearfully blind. ... He destroyed more than any other man the puritan drama of the soul." After Emerson came Emily Dickinson. She deliberately lived in seclusion and in her poetry strove for personal revelation which Tate interprets as the "unconscious effort of the individual to live apart from a cultural tradition that no longer sustains him". As this tradition was disintegrating the poet had to probe it consciously and to put it to the test of experience. It was the advantage of Emily Dickinson to live in a world with a system of ideas that did not stifle her sense of the natural world nor gave her "purely personal quality" a chance to get out of control. Her poetry showed those "metaphysical" qualities which would become the touchstones for good

---

[26] Tate was to reject historical determinism in later years. In 1965 he wrote: "we must not fall into the historical trap where, immobilized, we apply a doctrine of historical determinism to poets, and pretend that after a certain date a certain kind of poetry could not be written. I fell into the trap thirty-five years ago when I said that after Emerson had done his work, the tragic vision was henceforth impossible in America. I am glad to have been proved wrong" ("The Unliteral Imagination; Or, I, Too, Dislike It", *The Southern Review*, I, 3 [Summer 1965], 542).

poetry in *The Southern Review*. It exhibited "the perfect literary situation – the fusion of feeling and thinking. Unlike her contemporaries, she never succumbed to her ideas, to easy solutions, to her private desires." [27]

One of the most lively chapters in the history of *The Hound & Horn* was, as we have seen, its association with Ezra Pound. Pound's influence on *The Symposium* was also considerable although he stood in no official relation to it. The editors underwent the Pound treatment somewhat more dispassionately than their colleagues of *The Hound & Horn*, and they incurred Pound's anger when they refused to publish and pay for the customary barrage of letters and postcards. Wheelwright was enthusiastic about Pound's earlier poetry, but when he offered three times the contributor's rate for a poem as good as *The Seafarer* or *The Return*, Pound's answer was a rude postcard. Pound himself in his letters to contemporaries of *The Symposium* was not complimentary about it, but then, there had been no magazine since *The Exile* of which he had been very tolerant. "Symposium sounds more Bloomsbuggard than H. & H", he told Louis Zukofsky towards the end of 1930, and his exasperation was again apparent in a letter to the same correspondent which he wrote at the beginning of the following year: "Does Mr. Wellwright [*sic*] insist on ALL his contributors except YOU carrying on in the verbose and indef. manner and always drifting out of concrete statement of an idea into the question of Hegel and the infinite?" [28] When he

---

[27] "New England Culture and Emily Dickinson", *Symposium*, III, 2 (April 1932), 206-226. Tate's reactionary social ideas were another manifestation of his search for the perfect "literary situation"; they were intelligently evaluated by R. P. Blackmur in a letter to Malcolm Cowley (April 27, 1934, Cowley papers):

"I had a letter from Tate about my attack on the sectionalists in which occurs the statement that social problems 'were not only insoluble but really ought to be insoluble forever if we are to maintain the social tensions which give to a culture its vitality'. ... I think it is a bad and defeatist sentiment to entertain politically, in the field of political action, but I think it is a sound sentiment for the artist to make use of in relation to his view of his material; it will help him both to feel and to represent the drama and conflict that confront him."

[28] November 24-25, 1930, and January 29, 1931, Zukofsky papers, Texas University Library. "I began Tuesday a note DE DUOBUS IMPOSITORIBUS

wrote this second letter, however, the Winter 1931 issue had come out and Pound had to agree that it was "better than the others, less taint of Bloomsbury snailsmear"; and on 12 February, in a letter to Samuel Putnam, he praised Zukofsky's article "American Poetry 1920-1930", which was published in the Winter issue with the significant subtitle "A Sequel to M. Taupin's Book, 1910-1920". Pound admired René Taupin's *L'Influence du Symbolisme Français sur la Poésie Américaine*[29] and in January 1932 *The Symposium* published Zukofsky's translation of Taupin's "The Classicism of T. S. Eliot".

Zukofsky's article on "American Poetry 1920-1930" was the first indication that Pound was exerting an influence on the magazine. The essay was Poundian in tone and sentiment. Although the editors did not agree with some of the literary judgments,[30] they rightly considered it of sufficient interest for publication in their magazine. The essay pivoted on the following orthodox Poundian "portmanteau bibliography of poetry after 1920": Pound's *Cantos*; Eliot's *The Waste Land*; Marianne Moore's *Observations*; Williams's *Spring and All* and *Primavera*; Cummings's *Is 5* and some earlier poems; Stevens's *Harmonium*; the poems of Charles Reznikoff and Robert McAlmon; and *Exile* 3 and 4. The essay closed, "by way of finale", with a special note in praise of the work of William Carlos Williams.[31] Williams himself contributed two reviews to *The Symposium*, one on Pound's *A Draft of XXX Cantos* and the other on Zukofsky's *An "Objective" Anthology*,[32] and in the final issue of *The Symposium* Williams was the subject of an article by Carl Rakosi who had been one of Pound's protégés in the pages of *The Exile*. Pound himself

---

(meaning Marx and Thos. Aquinas tho I think rather better of Marx than of Tommy) . . . If Wheelwright wanted the article I shd. remove the *Duobus* so as to include some of his contributors" (January 29, 1931).

[29] See Pound's long letter of advice to Taupin in *The Letters of Ezra Pound, 1907-1941*, ed. D. D. Paige (New York, 1950), pp. 216-218.

[30] Wheelwright especially objected to Zukofsky's dismissal of Robert Frost ("He is just too cutely pastoral, too cutely rampant to be alive, to be true" [p. 70]).

[31] *Symposium*, II, 1 (January 1931), 72, 79.

[32] *Symposium*, II, 2 (April 1931), 257-263; IV, 1 (January 1933), 114-117.

only wrote two reviews for *The Symposium* of books evidently of his own choosing. In the October 1932 issue he defended, "of set purpose", Adrian Stokes's *The Quattro Cento* against "a few people who have considerable intelligence but who are afflicted by fixed ideas"; it was to Pound "almost incomprehensible that any man can have as great a concern for the shapes and meanings of stone beauty as Stokes has, without its forcing him to take the tools in his hands." [33] In his second review, Pound waxed lyrical about the economic theories of Major C. H. Douglas; he could not see "how anyone wishing to understand contemporary life" could dispense with them. [34]

The publication of these various articles and reviews in *The Symposium* was undoubtedly to a great extent the fruit of Pound's tactics for the advancement of his old friends and of his new disciples, but there is no indication that the publication of these contributions was due to anything but independent and discriminating editorial choice. The editors were in no way dependent on Pound's goodwill, and Pound's own publications were by no means sacrosanct; his edition of Guido Cavalcanti, for instance, was severely criticized by Jefferson B. Fletcher who objected to the "militant" tone of the editor's comments and who stated indignantly at the end of his review: "I do not understand Mr. Pound. I even make bold to say that he is not understandable – by others." [35]

In the course of this chapter it has become clear that *The Symposium* was not as topical as *The Hound & Horn*; it published hardly any chronicles, it did not take a more than casual interest in humanism and agrarianism, and it steered clear of an explicit commitment to its contemporary Ezra Pound. Nor did it demand that its articles be explicitly linked with present problems or conditions as *The Hound & Horn* did. *The Hound & Horn* had felt that, whatever its intrinsic merits, the publication of George Williamson's "John Donne and His Shroud" would have been a contradiction of its editorial policy. *The Symposium*, however,

---

[33] *Symposium*, III, 4 (October 1932), 519.
[34] *Symposium*, IV, 2 (April 1933), 256.
[35] *Symposium*, III, 3 (July 1932), 392.

published such articles as Austin Warren's "The Mysticism of Richard Crashaw" (which had been unsuccessfully submitted to *The Hound & Horn*) and Franklin Gary's "In Search of George Eliot", both of which appeared in the April 1933 issue.

The Symposium was also much less nationalistically American than *The Hound & Horn*, but the scope of its interest in the literary and cultural life of Europe was by no means as wide as *The Dial*'s. Demands on its quarterly space were pressing, and apart from occasional articles on French writers and artists, such as Justin O'Brien's excellent discussion of Valéry Larbaud, William Troy's and Justin O'Brien's notes on Proust, Philip Blair Rice's essay on Guillaume Apollinaire,[36] and C. R. Morse's discussions of French painters, the interest of *The Symposium* was divided between England and America. The interest in England must be mainly accounted for by Burnham's recent experience of that country, but, for at least part of the time, *The Symposium* also had an important eye-witness on the scene in the person of Franklin Gary, a student of English and a personal friend of the editors. Gary was a promising young critic who, however, after the *Symposium* days turned to other pursuits and only very recently has returned to literature. Gary was responsible for steering a number of English contributions to the magazine. He was personally acquainted with T. S. Eliot and shared with Philip Wheelwright a great admiration for Eliot's poetry,[37] but the magazine never managed to get Eliot to contribute to its pages. When the editors had been discussing the merger with *The Hound & Horn*, Burnham had informed Bernard Bandler that Eliot had promised an article and had given "as his *subject* 'On the Place of Belief in the Appreciation of Poetry' ";[38] but it was actually I. A. Richards who broached this subject in the pages of *The Symposium*.[39] Wheelwright remembers that Eliot promised an

---

[36] *Symposium*, III, 3 (July 1932), 315-334; II, 3 (July 1931), 385-400; II, 4 (October 1931), 468-483.
[37] On Eliot's death the two friends got together for an evening to listen to a gramophone recording of Eliot reading from his own poetry.
[38] Letter of November 19, 1929, *Hound & Horn* papers.
[39] "Belief", *Symposium*, I, 4 (October 1930), 423-439. It was Burnham who was acquainted with Richards and who arranged for him to contrib-

essay on poetry and music to *The Symposium* but that after Wheelwright mentioned this to Seward Collins, the latter persuaded Eliot that the essay would appear more appropriately and to better advantage in *The Bookman*.[40]

But although Eliot did not personally appear in *The Symposium*, his work was often discussed in its pages. Like most of its contemporaries, it found more to praise in Eliot's poetry than in his thought.[41] Felix Morrow, in his attack on Paul Elmer More singled out Eliot as "the foremost of the younger reactionaries" and considered it "one of the curiosities of our literary generation" that Eliot's prestige as a poet had given him standing as a philosopher.[42] Eliot's thought was often considered in the light of the poetry rather than in its own right; thus Wheelwright, for instance, observed that Eliot's Anglo-Catholicism seemed "to act as catalyst for the most rare lyric utterances".[43] But Wheelwright's sympathetic assessment of the influence of the thought on the poetry cannot be taken as representing the "official" point of view of *The Symposium*. As with so many topics discussed by different critics in the magazine, there was no absolute agreement among the contributors, not even among the editors. For Burnham Eliot was "poetically least successful in his infrequent attempts to incorporate this logic [of his religious beliefs] in his poetry: he remains the *poet* of the waste land, though as human being he has found his way out of the waste land";[44] but, three months earlier, Philip Blair Rice had stated that it was not Eliot's "last

---

ute to *The Symposium*. Burnham also reviewed Richards's *Practical Criticism* (*Symposium*, I, 1 [January 1930], 115-124).

[40] Two articles by Eliot appeared in *The Bookman* during the lifetime of *The Symposium*: "Poetry and Propaganda", (LXX, 6 [February 1930], 595-602) and "Arnold and Pater" (LXXII, 1 [September 1930], 1-7).

[41] Eliot himself commented on this practice in *After Strange Gods* (New York, 1934), p. 30: "I am not of course interested by those critics who praise my criticism in order to discredit my verse, or those who praise my verse in order to discredit my opinions in religious or social affairs. ... I should say that in one's prose reflections one may be legitimately occupied with ideals, whereas in the writing of verse one can only deal with actuality."

[42] "The Serpent's Enemy: Mr. More as Social Thinker", 168.

[43] "Poetry and Logic", *Symposium*, I, 4 (October 1930), 443.

[44] "Marxism and Aesthetics", *Symposium*, IV, 1 (January 1933), 28.

word on the subject even in *The Waste Land*" that we are hollow men in a desolate country, and that between his earlier and his later poetry "there is not, indeed, so wide a gulf as some critics have found there." [45]

But however different the emphases in the critical manoeuvering around the enigmatic figure of Eliot the poet and Eliot the thinker, there was no further specification required when the editors in their "Comment" of October 1932 stated that "the post-war disillusion made possible at least one first-rate poem in English".[46] Indeed, whatever qualifications different critics might adduce, there was never any doubt that Eliot was the greatest living poet; and however reactionary *The Criterion* might be, there was never any doubt that *The Symposium* and *The Criterion* were critical reviews in the same tradition. This notion was furthered by the frequent notices of *The Symposium* in *The Criterion* and by the fact that a number of characteristic *Criterion* writers, such as Herbert Read, Ramon Fernandez, and I. A. Richards, also contributed to *The Symposium*. They did not write much for *The Hound & Horn*. Indeed with a view both to contributors and to interests *The Symposium* was nearer to *The Criterion* than was *The Hound & Horn*. Whereas *The Criterion* and *The Dial* were acknowledged progenitors of *The Hound & Horn*, *The Symposium* had its roots in *The Criterion* and *The Hound & Horn*. The editors never discussed its parentage to the extent *The Hound & Horn* did, but they were well aware of what company they were keeping. The following note by Wheelwright in the penultimate issue of the magazine speaks for itself: "American readers who find nourishment in *The Symposium*, *The Hound & Horn*, and *The Criterion* would do well to glance at *Scrutiny*. . . . Its articles and reviews are generally excellent." [47]

[45] "Out of the Waste Land", *Symposium*, III, 4 (October 1932), 424.
[46] *Symposium*, III, 4 (October 1932), 420.
[47] P.W., "In Passing", *Symposium*, IV, 3 (July 1933), 400. F. R. Leavis, however, wrote to Ronald Bottrall: "We are *not* merely [?] a Cambridge *Symposium*" (November 4, 1932: Leavis especially emphasized *Scrutiny*'s educational function), and a few months later: "We had neither room nor time to talk up the *Symposium* as you suggested" (May 25, 1933, Bottrall papers, University of Texas).

Not only did *The Symposium* bring a new English magazine with a new group of critics to the attention of its readers, it also heralded the first signs of a new generation of English poets. The appearance of W. H. Auden, Stephen Spender, and Cecil Day Lewis was "perhaps the first convincing indication that the epoch of *The Waste Land* in England is near its end", wrote H. B. Parkes. Discussing Auden's *The Orators*, Parkes noticed obvious signs of immaturity nor did Auden's technique rival that displayed in *The Waste Land,* but "it may prove to be of similar importance in helping to formulate the spiritual tone of an epoch".[48] In Wheelwright's opinion, the new young English poets promised "as convincingly as anyone . . . to become the legitimate successors . . . of Pound, Eliot, and Crane".[49]

The excellent, detailed and technical reviews which appeared in *The Symposium* rivalled those in *The Hound & Horn.* They ranged in length approximately from one thousand to six thousand words. Admittedly, *The Symposium* could not equal the accomplishment of *The Hound & Horn*'s staff of poetry reviewers, such as Tate, Winters and Blackmur, but it took a wider, less narrowly aesthetic interest in the novel. This interest was manifested already in the first issue in the symposium "Remarks on the Novel" under which general heading the editors grouped together "articles written independently of each other, but related in a manner which we feel justifies considering them as contributions to a single discussion." These introductory editorial remarks were followed by an extract from a letter from "Stephen Hudson" stating reasons why he could not write about the novel for *The Symposium*; by F. Cudworth Flint's "Fiction and Form", a discussion of six books on the novel singling out Edwin Muir's *The Structure of the Novel* as "the subtlest and best-written" of them; and by David Garnett's chatty remarks in "Some Tendencies of the Novel". The fourth and by far the most important item of this symposium was Lionel Trilling's joint review of Hemingway's *A Farewell to Arms,* Faulkner's *The Sound & the Fury* and Edward Dahlberg's *Bottom*

[48]   *Symposium,* IV, 2 (April 1933), 245-247.
[49]   *Symposium,* IV, 3 (July 1933), 400.

Dogs under the general title "Tragedy and Three Novels". Trilling's highest praise went to Hemingway who "continues as probably our most skilful writer of tragedy" and in comparison to whose *Farewell* "Mr. Faulkner's *The Sound & the Fury* seems a little far away". Trilling went on to say that there was so much art in *The Sound & the Fury* that, "with the best will in the world toward art, it is inevitable to feel that a little less of it would have allowed the human situation to appear – not more easily . . . but more distinctly". The story, in his opinion, was "bent by the weight of technique".[50]

That there was no *Symposium* orthodoxy with regard to Hemingway and Faulkner is apparent from James Burnham's comments on the two novelists in subsequent issues. In his review of *A True Story* by "Stephen Hudson" he made a remark in passing about Hemingway which was not an attempt at a critical evaluation, but which borrowed a note of censure from its context. Burnham suggested that Hemingway was read widely because it was so easy to feel for and with his characters: "Through his method of understatement, of marking a soul-stirring by another demi of beer, he leaves his readers the job of creating the emotions of his characters (consider the last part of *A Farewell to Arms* in this connection), and readers quite naturally revel in the opportunity." [51] The editorial "Comment" of the issue in which this remark appeared lent added significance to it. The editors, discussing "dollar novels" stated that there were no sufficient grounds to suppose that an art is any better or any worse for appealing to few people or to many, but there was no doubt in their minds that "in writing a book for larger groups of people, the novelist . . . has less he can make use of".[52] Burnham's subsequent article on Faulkner, a critique of *Soldier's Pay*, *The Sound & the Fury*, and *As I Lay Dying*, contained an explicit defence of that novelist's technique which was admittedly still experimental; "yet I cannot believe, as has been charged against him, that he is interested in

50 "Editors' Symposium: Remarks on the Novel", *Symposium*, I, 1 (January 1930), 82-114.
51 *Symposium*, I, 3 (July 1930), 400.
52 *Symposium*, I, 3 (July 1930), 292.

technique for its own sake or that he is obscure that he may appear profound. There is no reason why literature shouldn't be difficult; but the truth is many of the difficulties in Faulkner come from a refusal to read carefully what is there." [53] At the beginning of the article Burnham had stated that if all significant American novelists would simultaneously bring out a new novel and if he could only have one, he would choose Faulkner's.

Complexity and simplicity of technique and their effect on the reader also preoccupied William Troy when he reviewed some leftist novelists, Edward Dahlberg, Erskine Caldwell, J. T. Farrell, and Albert Halper. Troy noticed in these novelists a movement towards objectivity and towards the impersonal, away from the intense subjectivism of their predecessors, and he asked the vexing contemporary question in how far committing themselves to a dogma "would give to their work a consistency of meaning which it at present lacks ... [and] how much of what is now effective in their writing would be lost by the possible limitations of that dogma operating in their work". Troy found much to praise in these novelists but realized that the mood created by them would appear "strangely simplified ... perhaps *too* simplified" to a great many readers. [54] It needs to be emphasized, however, that Troy was genuinely appreciative of these novelists and that Troy was perhaps the most important critic of the novel writing for *The Symposium*. His point of view like Trilling's, another important contributor, was undogmatically social and moral and it is ultimately this approach which accounts for the excellence of *The Symposium*'s criticism of the novel. The prevailing aestheticism of many of the *Hound & Horn* critics found a more suitable subject for criticism in poetry, and a few years later the *Southern Review* critics would take a definite stand against naturalism in the novel and in favour of aesthetic and imaginative complexity.

The disinterestedness of Troy's perspective, which always focussed on the specific intellectual and emotional provocation offered by the work under discussion was apparent in all his critiques. The manner in which Troy could subscribe to a critical

[53] "Trying To Say", *Symposium*, II, 1 (January 1931), 56.
[54] *Symposium*, IV, 2 (April 1933), 235, 228.

point of view and adapt it to the exigencies of a particular situation is exemplified in the following quotation from his review of Proust's *Time Regained*:

The view of literature taken by Proust, which is first and last the subjective view, is the narrower of the two possible views that may be taken, but as it seems to be the only one which writers in our time are capable of adopting with sincerity we must judge his work according to its own standards. It will then be recognized that its force and beauty derive from nothing else but the absoluteness with which Proust has adhered to these standards, from the intensity and completeness with which he has worked out his limited personal vision within the conditions of his perspective.[55]

Troy's most important contribution to *The Symposium* was a long essay on Virginia Woolf which was published in two instalments. Especially the second half, on "The Poetic Style", is of great interest. Troy noticed that the "facile traditionalism" of Virginia Woolf's style, which depended on mastery of the traditional resources of language, was eminently suitable for burlesque as in *Orlando*, but that as a vehicle for serious thoughts and emotions it often degenerated into mere cleverness. Language was made its own object; it was not used "to realize emotion by evoking particular objects of concrete experience".[56]

For the majority of the *Symposium* critics it was no longer Joyce who was the most significant British novelist, as he had been categorically for the *Dial* and less categorically for the *Hound & Horn* critics, but D. H. Lawrence. According to Burnham, Joyce in *Work in Progress* had "isolated himself from any accessible tradition",[57] and *The Symposium* in general concerned itself very little with his work. A novel had to be something beyond technical virtuosity, and technique ought not to be the only access

---

[55] *Symposium*, II, 3 (July 1931), 392.
[56] "Virginia Woolf, 2. The Poetic Style", *Symposium*, III, 2 (April 1932), 164, 161.
[57] "Progress and Tradition", *Symposium*, I, 3 (July 1930), 358. The only contribution directly concerned with Joyce was Michael Stuart's "Mr. Joyce's Word-Creature" (*Symposium*, II, 4 [October 1931], 459-467), which indicated "possibilities of word-meanings" in an analysis of "The Ondt and the Gracehoper" and which was a scholarly exercise rather than a critical evaluation.

to it. In the third issue of the magazine, Lionel Trilling set the tone of the discussion of Lawrence in his essay "D. H. Lawrence, a Neglected Aspect". Lawrence's work, Trilling wrote, was inaccessible to the new ideas and techniques which modern criticism had developed to deal with literary experiments. "The form of his work cannot profitably be discussed, for both the poems and the novels generally have about as much form as a completed emotion – which is considerable – but no more. The qualities of his prose, the intensity of his poetic insight are entirely personal, the result of a personal manipulation of traditional means." For the modern reader Lawrence's deepest significance must be as "a poet of rebellious social theory", although Trilling warned that the truth about him could not be reached by "systematizing his insights". Lawrence's central distinction which set him apart from the dehumanization of modern art even in such works of considerable human significance as the novels of James Joyce and Thomas Mann and Hart Crane's *The Bridge,* was his "excited, angry, loving interest in humanness" and "his refusal of the abstract in any manifestation".[58] William Troy considered the *Letters* Lawrence's masterpiece; his poems and novels were "attempts at finding himself". Taking his cue from Lawrence's famous words: "One sheds one's sicknesses in books – repeats and presents again one's emotions to be master of them", Troy noticed how different was Lawrence's approach to his art from that of the modern artist as we have come to think of him, "the artist consumed by the passion of *making* and by the desire of achieving perfection in the *thing made*". Troy viewed Lawrence, in the last analysis, as "a religious prophet, one of the few really sincere and impressive examples of the type in our time". Like Trilling, he warned against a dismissal on purely aesthetic grounds: "To interpret him as an artist, even as a certain kind of artist, as Mr. Huxley does, is to expose him to a too facile application of literary standards, ending perhaps with ultimate dismissal. The other error is to attempt to reconstruct the ideological structure of his works in strictly intellectual terms." Troy praised Lawrence significantly

---

[58]   "D. H. Lawrence: A Neglected Aspect", *Symposium*, I, 3 (July 1930), 361, 363, 365.

as "easily the most *living* of contemporary English writers" although he had been dead for almost three years.[59] It was indeed Lawrence's vitality rather than accomplished artistic craftsmanship or systematized teaching that struck the *Symposium* critics as timely and important, but this vitality provided no ultimate answers; like Trilling and Troy, Philip Blair Rice only found "the seeds of a healing philosophy" in Lawrence, not a way out of the waste land.[60]

III

In the preceding section we have discussed some aspects of *The Symposium* in the light of the history of *The Hound & Horn*. We shall now discuss the magazine in the light of its editorial intentions with regard to a number of characteristic preoccupations. In *The Symposium*, more than in any earlier or contemporary American critical review, we sense a pervasive editorial concern with the interrelations of the different contributions both in the individual and the successive numbers. This is a concern not, as we have seen, for a critical orthodoxy but for a "symposial structure". The magazine's title was indeed well chosen and the editors were very successful in their effort to live up to its implications. They understood very well that this was no easy task, that it was "even more dependent on the material which becomes available" than finding "impersonal", "disinterested" criticism was. They frankly admitted that the fact that the second issue exhibited "a symposial structure in a variety of aspects" was as much "good luck as careful planning".[61] But however lucky the

---

[59] Review of *Letters of D. H. Lawrence*, ed. Huxley, *Symposium*, IV, 1 (January 1933), 93, 85.
[60] "Out of the Waste Land", *Symposium*, III, 4 (October 1932), 439. In his review of Lawrence's *The Man Who Died* and Middleton Murry's *Son of Woman*, T. O. Beachcroft emphasized Lawrence's distinction as a writer: "In fact in contrast with Mr. Murry's book a very different construction of Lawrence's position is likely to come to mind. In this view Lawrence is first and last a great writer, and his 'teaching' is of no great account. That is to say that he has that intuition that one is accustomed to say belongs to the artist" (*Symposium*, II, 4 [October 1931], 543).
[61] "Comment", *Symposium*, I, 2 (April 1930), 147.

editors may have been, the success of their symposial policy in subsequent issues shows that they knew how to protect their good luck by careful planning.

To widen our acquaintance with the interests and attitudes of *The Symposium*, we shall investigate a number of instances of its symposial structure. We have already discussed a good example when we examined the symposium "Remarks on the Novel" which appeared in the first issue. The magazine's concern with the novel provides another interesting example which also illustrates its tolerance of divergent opinions. When John Dos Passos' *1919* was published the editors originally planned to have it reviewed by Frederick Dupee and, on second thoughts, they considered the novel of sufficient interest to suggest that Dupee expand his review into an article. Eventually, however, it was not Dupee who wrote on *1919* but Morris Schappes, whose highly laudatory review appeared in the July 1932 issue and was followed by extracts from a letter from Dupee which stated his reasons for declining to write the review. "The book is loathsome to me", Dupee wrote, "– bogus modernism in technique – stale incidents – stale attitudes – hundreds of pages of dreary literal writing about lyric brawls and college friendships, Bohemia, Toughtown, and The Big Parade. ... Not a spark anywhere that I can find." [62] Schappes's judgments were in direct opposition to Dupee's. Whereas Dupee complained of "hundreds of pages of dreary literal writing", Schappes praised the "hurrying, matter of fact style, which admits of no lingering, no emphasis, except such as involuntarily exudes from the incidents themselves". Schappes did not discover any "bogus modernism in technique"; on the contrary: "the plain dynamic writing would make the characters appear silhouettes did not Dos Passos confer a depth dimension upon them by an elaborate, ingenious, and rhythmically interspersed reminder of the world background against which the activity occurs. There are three devices, taking up about one-fifth of the book, by which this fullness is achieved." Schappes found the novel deficient in form but it did have structure, "and a very skilful one". In contrast to Dupee, who could not use the book

[62]   Letter, Dupee to Editors, *Symposium*, III, 3 (July 1932), 387.

for a text, as the editors had suggested, "without too much pussy-footing and evasion", Schappes, who held decidedly Marxian opinions, thought *1919* "not only of great intrinsic worth but also of seminal historical significance" as a novel with social impli-cations.[63]

The disagreement between Dupee and Schappes concerned an instance of applied criticism. *The Symposium* contained a number of critical articles on individual works and authors, mostly of fiction, but it also took a theoretical interest in the nature and meaning of poetry. This may indeed be considered the central concern of the magazine and it is here that we find the clearest traces of the philosophical training of the editors. It was this theoretical concern also which mainly accounts for the success of the editorial attempts to increase the symposial structure of the magazine. The unifying effect of a pervasive interest of this nature will be obvious. Although the discussion would in turn concentrate on different aspects of it – from the more general attempt at a definition of poetry to a discussion of belief in poetry and the uses of psychology to elucidate the making of poetry – there was a basic continuity of interest which establishes the character of the magazine. We have described earlier that the interest in general ideas differentiated *The Symposium* from *The Hound & Horn,* which was repeatedly caught up in contemporary movements. This interest was mainly focussed on the nature of literature and the function of criticism.

The magazine's second issue, whose symposial structure was, according to the editors, as much a result of luck as of planning, featured James Burnham's "On Defining Poetry" and Louis Gru-din's "A Definition of Poetry". Burnham first pointed out that no poet or critic had yet offered a completely satisfactory definition of poetry, that such a definition would indeed render any further dis-cussion pointless. He then investigated the theories of those critics who seemed to him most relevant to contemporary critical discus-sions: Coleridge, Eliot, Richards and Grudin. He could not entirely agree with the views of any of them, but Grudin's article seemed to

---

[63] *Symposium*, III, 3 (July 1932), 383, 384-385.

him at least to suggest "a fresh approach not only to an isolated question of defining poetry, but to a way of considering a great many other questions in general criticism".[64] Grudin's article "A Definition of Poetry" followed Burnham's exploratory remarks. It dealt in generalizations and abstractions which made sense at their own level of discourse but which offered little practical help to the literary critic. Indeed, in a consecutive account of the development of *The Symposium*'s interests, Burnham's essay is mainly important in so far as it foreshadowed the discussion of the place of belief in the appreciation of poetry, rather than as an introduction to Grudin's argument. The reviewing section of this same second issue contained a review by and of Curt Ducasse – a favourite editorial policy – and F. Cudworth Flint's review of Herbert Read's *The Sense of Glory*. Flint's remarks were on the whole favourable, but he objected to a certain vagueness and to changing definitions in Read's argument. Some of Flint's critical points were taken up by Read in the following issue in his article "The Form of Modern Poetry", which in its turn was followed by Flint's rejoinder "Metaphor in Contemporary Poetry". Read thought Flint's conception of poetry "too democratic; for poetry is a rare and aristocratic mode of communication ... It is foolish to ask what the poet 'means'. Poetry 'means' nothing. It *is*".[65] Flint accepted what he took to be the substance of Read's description of a poem, but he felt that if nothing whatever could be done by way of explaining poetry, "final disaster seems to await the Muses' already distressed estate".[66]

Read was involved in another controversy in the pages of *The Symposium*, this time concerning his psychographic explanation of Wordsworth's career as a poet in terms of his love for Annette Vallon. Morris Schappes had written a review critical of Read's thesis for the April 1931 number and Read answered in the following issue with "Personality in Literature", an essay, as the subtitle indicated "in defense of psychography". Read realised that he was taking a stand "even against my best friends in criti-

---

[64]   *Symposium*, I, 2 (April 1930), 230.
[65]   *Symposium*, I, 3 (July 1930), 307, 308.
[66]   *Symposium*, I, 3 (July 1930), 310.

cism, such as Mr. Eliot himself", but persisted in his belief that "criticism must concern itself, not only with the work of art in itself, but also with the process of writing, and the writer's state of mind when inspired".[67] Read's essay was followed by Schappes's "Notes on the Concrete as a Method in Criticism", which implicitly opposed Read's argument. Criticism, according to Schappes, had a dual function: to guide the reading public and to point out deficiencies and excellences to the artist. The only kind of criticism which could serve these two purposes was "a precise, specific analysis, line by line, word by word if need be, of a particular work of art". "All poetry is contemporary", Schappes stated, which means that each generation has to rewrite its history of poetry to determine anew "the aesthetic validity of its past." [68]

Schappes's essay attracted favourable attention from William Carlos Williams; when Williams discussed the contemporary magazine situation he wrote: "Of the purely critical quarterlies The Symposium seems the least biased and has to its credit at least one essay, Notes on the Concrete as Method of Criticism, by Morris U. Schappes, meriting wide attention." [69] If Schappes had no use for Read's approach, another Symposium contributor, Franklin Gary, had. In his discussion of Buxton Forman's edition of Keats's Letters in January 1932, Gary described how Read's "Personality in Literature" appeared just after he had read the Letters. "I was immediately struck by the light which Mr. Read's distinctions threw on the development of Keats's mind and work", Gary wrote. "It occurred to me, also, that to apply some of these distinctions to the Letters would be to approach in a fresh way what have already been approached from various

[67] Symposium, II, 3 (July 1931), 293. The uses of psychology for literary criticism were examined by Harold Rosenberg in his essay Myth and Poem. His conclusions may be considered representative. He discussed both the Freudian conception of the artist as a neurotic and Jung's theory of the Collective Unconscious, or the poet as the creator of a personal myth and the poet as the creator of a human or racial myth. Rosenberg opined that psychology "deals very well with the emerging myth but its apparatus is insufficient to describe the made poem" (Symposium, II, 2 [April 1931], 187).

[68] Symposium, II, 3 (July 1931), 315-316.

[69] "The Advance Guard Magazine", Contact, I, 1 (February 1932), 89.

angles".[70] The "Etiology of the Wordsworth Case", which had set off the dispute between Read and Schappes, was eventually exhaustively discussed by Hi Simons in an essay of that title in the July 1933 issue.

A subject which intrigued a number of the more philosophically orientated contributors to *The Symposium* was the relation of poetry and belief. Eliot, we have seen, had agreed to write on the place of belief in the appreciation of poetry, but his discussion appeared elsewhere.[71] It was I. A. Richards who initiated the discussion in *The Symposium* in October 1930 with his essay "Belief", and it was Richards's theories, worked out both in this essay and in his earlier criticism, which provided the points of issue of the subsequent contributions. Richards may have been led to write his essay in response to Burnham's review of his *Practical Criticism* in the first issue of *The Symposium*. Burnham had rejected Richards's solution of "this puzzling and too little studied problem" of belief in poetry. He had again shown his dissatisfaction with Richards's position in the second issue in his essay "On Defining Poetry" which partly concerned itself with this problem. Another probable, though less direct challenge for Richards was Philip Wheelwright's "Notes on Meaning" which appeared in the third issue and which referred back to the Burnham-Grudin discussion of a definition of poetry. Although this essay did not deal explicitly with Richards's ideas it was concerned with the multiple meanings of art, especially of poetry; it ended with a plea for a willingness to analyse, "to distinguish between the several sorts of meaning that an aesthetic object can have, and thereby to make way for a more intelligible formulation of aesthetic criteria".[71a]

Richards began his article on the problem of belief in poetry with a philosophical exploration of the implications and uses of the word "belief", but as the general situation had arisen for him "out of a definite literary problem" he soon posed the more

[70]   *Symposium*, III, 1 (January 1932), 83.
[71]   In *The Use of Poetry* (1933); with Eliot's interpretation, Robert W. Stallman wrote in 1947, "all later critics concur" ("The New Criticism and the Southern Critics", *A Southern Vanguard*, ed. Allen Tate [New York, 1947], p. 43).
[71a] *Symposium*, I, 3 (July 1930), 371-386.

specific question of whether we can understand the many great poems, which have arisen from beliefs, and which embody them, without ourselves accepting and holding such beliefs: "The presence of the belief in the poet seems to have been a condition of the poem. Is its presence in the reader equally a condition for successful reading – for full understanding?" There were several ways out of the problem which were for different reasons unsatisfactory, but finally Richards sought, if not to solve it, at least to get nearer to a solution by making a distinction between two kinds of belief which he called "verifiable belief" and "imaginative assent". "Imaginative assent" is asked of anyone who wants to understand good poetry; if "verifiable belief" is expected, "then clearly we can understand very little poetry".[72]

Richards's essay was followed by Philip Wheelwright's "Poetry and Logic", which dealt with the same problem. Wheelwright praised both Eliot and Richards for having "in their different ways directed attention to the important problem of how far poetic appreciation depends on the acceptance of particular beliefs", but he quarrelled with them about the appropriateness of words like "believe" and "disbelieve" which, in his opinion, gave undue emphasis to "the poem's prose equivalent". He felt, however, that Richards's new distinction was "of great importance", because it recognized that imaginative assents and verifiable beliefs differed "not merely in respect to their objects but as types of mental occurrence". Richards had moved from his earlier differentiation of "belief-objects" to a differentiation of "belief-states". "The suggested distinction", Wheelwright wrote, "is no longer between what is poetically true and what is factually true but between what is poetically intelligible and what is logically intelligible". Wheelwright's preoccupation with the intelligibility of a poem led him to consider the possibility of objective critical standards. He realized that "a poem may be greater in one age than in another",

---

[72] "Belief", *Symposium*, I, 4 (October 1930), 423-439. This distinction echoes Richards's earlier distinction between "intellectual belief" and "emotional belief" in *Practical Criticism* (London, 1929), pp. 274-275. But see also Wheelwright's "Poetry and Logic" in the same issue.

but he maintained that objective standards within one's own age and cultural environment are possible and necessary.[73]

The symposial structure of the fourth issue of *The Symposium* extended beyond Richards's and Wheelwright's essays. In a footnote to his article, Wheelwright referred his readers to "an interesting commentary on the problem" in a Note appended to John Middleton Murry's "Beauty is Truth" published in the same number. Murry took issue with Richards's use of the term "pseudostatement", which, if not in intention, was in effect often used derogatorily as a synonym of "false statement". Murry wrote: "Statements concerning the intimate nature of man are neither true nor false; they correspond to experience (not 'fact') or they do not." For the sake of giving an accurate description of a fact of human experience – which is by its very nature a unique fact – we often have to resort to pseudo-statements which are consciously recognized as such but which are in a very real sense "true" in the total statement. In terms of "belief" this means that the modern reader aware of the necessity and the imaginative value of pseudo-statements will be able to accept the true total statement without accepting the truth, in isolation, of the pseudo-statements which are the necessary terms of the total statement.[74] Richards answered Murry's note in an essay "Between Truth and Truth" which was published two issues later in April 1931. It was an essay mainly in definition and did not add substantially to Richards's earlier argument. Richards felt that most of Murry's disagreements could be reduced to a different, more emotional habit of prose.

Some threads of Richards's earlier "Belief" were taken up again in October 1931 by F. Cudworth Flint who was concerned with religious belief proper rather than with belief as a condition for

[73] "Poetry and Logic", 440-457.
[74] "Beauty is Truth", 466-501. Morton Zabel described Murry's article as "a particularly boresome and futile kind of conjecture", but praised a number of other articles which made *The Symposium* "a valuable record of critical thought. Reputable opinion, however biassed or specialized, has become so thoroughly debased in America by journalistic pressure, that we hope *The Symposium*'s career will be a long one" (M.D.Z., "Recent Magazines", *Poetry*, XXXVIII, 3 [June 1931], 171).

the appreciation of religious poetry; his topic was "The Predicament of Religious Belief" in an age of science. Flint concluded that the progress of the different sciences had discredited religious belief based on the bible or dogma. We do not need religion primarily for intellectual satisfaction but for redemption; "Mysticism alone can nourish the religious attitude." [75] Flint's opinions were debated in the next issue by Philip Wheelwright and T. Lawrason Riggs. Wheelwright began his article, "A Defense of Orthodoxy", by saying that Flint's advocacy of mysticism would strike many readers as too anarchical, and proposed to supplement Flint's argument with a search for a justification of a more orthodox type of religion. This seemed all the more profitable in view of the fact that "both Roman Catholicism and Anglicanism have lately gained some extremely able adherents and have become more articulate and of greater secular interest in consequence". Wheelwright then proceeded to define religious certitude, if not to establish it.[76] Riggs followed suit in a more direct attack on Flint's position in his article "Is Mysticism Enough?". Riggs as a Roman Catholic did not find Flint's argument "consistent or even ultimately intelligible".[77]

The "Correspondence" section of the magazine sometimes provided welcome opportunities for enhancing the symposial structure. One instance of debate again concerned T. S. Eliot's position as poet and thinker. In the magazine's second issue Franklin Gary had discussed Eliot's *Dante* and *Animula,* and although the review had thrown some doubt on Eliot's position as a philosopher, it had on the whole been a veritable panegyric. The following issue contained a letter from Bernard C. Heyl, who warned that "if Messrs. Eliot and Gary are not careful, they will soon be transformed from excellent literary critics into 'specialists in devotion' ".[78] A more interesting instance of the use to which the Correspondence section was put was a letter from Leon Trotsky in the

---

[75] "The Predicament of Religious Belief", *Symposium*, II, 4 (October 1931), 427-458.
[76] *Symposium*, III, 1 (January 1932), 3-24.
[77] *Symposium*, III, 1 (January 1932), 28.
[78] "Correspondence", *Symposium*, I, 3 (July 1930), 388.

October 1932 issue which took up some points raised by James Burnham in his favourable review of the first volume of Trotsky's *History of the Russian Revolution.* As Burnham's interest in Marxism was growing rapidly at the time, the editors invited their readers to join the discussion: "If important and authenticated attacks on the accuracy of the *History* are forthcoming, they will be published together with Mr. Trotsky's reply to them in our next issue." [79] There appear, however, to have been no interesting reactions to this challenge.

The search for symposial structure, illustrated in the preceding selected instances, was a pervasive editorial concern, and the more successful the editors were in strategically arranging the contents of their magazine, the more confidently the present-day reader may point to specific editorial concerns and attitudes. How dangerous it can be to distil editorial attitudes from a single essay or review is illustrated by the reception of Joseph Wood Krutch's *The Modern Temper* in the pages of *The Symposium.* Krutch's sombre estimate of the contemporary state of affairs was widely reviewed, and it was the sort of book which might inspire a critical journal to make an editorial or semi-editorial statement. The general reader was therefore liable to pay special attention to a magazine's treatment of the book. *The Symposium*'s review appeared in the first issue and was written by one Norman Warren, a student of New York University, who felt that the reasons for Krutch's gloom were "almost all without ground". He called the book "a shadowy structure of empty dilemmas and false alarms". [80] The review had initially been assigned to Eliseo Vivas, but when Vivas's review was late the editors asked Warren at the last moment to help out. The editors thought Warren's treatment very unfair and for a moment Wheelwright considered publishing Vivas's and

---

[79] "Correspondence", *Symposium*, III, 4 (October 1932), 505.
[80] *Symposium*, I, 1 (January 1930), 132, 133. In *Partisan Review*, for example, one of the editors, Philip Rahv, attacked *The Modern Temper* in order to defend Marxist literature. ("How the Waste Land Became a Flower Garden", *PR*, I, 4 [Sept.-Oct. 1934], 37-42). A second attack on Krutch's position in *Partisan Review* was Harold Rosenberg's review of Krutch's "Was Europe a Success?" ("A Specter Haunts Mr. Krutch", *PR*, II, 7 [April-May 1935], 82-84).

Warren's estimates side by side in true *Symposium* fashion, but that proved impracticable.

The search for symposial structure was also frequently in evidence in the discussion of two topics which were of special interest to *The Symposium* and to which we shall turn our attention next: the new Shakespearean criticism and Marxism. James Burnham's discussion of George Wilson Knight's *The Wheel of Fire* was the leading review of the October 1930 issue. Although the book was not without "extravagance both of content and of language", Burnham was enthusiastic about Knight's approach and found "among the excellences" of the book two deserving particular mention: firstly, that Knight had kept his attention fixed on the plays themselves and had thus avoided "the irrelevancies of misplaced scholarship, inept comparisons, and ethical meanderings", and, secondly, that Knight had been strikingly successful in "revealing something of the general vision uniting the plays".[81] Knight's position was further illuminated in the April 1931 issue. Although reviews were normally printed without titles, two reviews in this April issue were given special prominence by their annoucement on the front cover under the general title "Towards the Integration of Shakespeare". This title comprehended Franklin Gary on Caroline Spurgeon's *Leading Motives in the Imagery of Shakespeare's Tragedies* and F. C. Kolbe's *Shakespeare's Way*, and George Wilson Knight on E. K. Chambers's *William Shakespeare*. Gary noticed that different critics seemed independently to have adopted the new approach which had been inaugurated by *The Wheel of Fire*, and praised Knight's pioneering work. Knight himself detected "signs that the tide is turning in Shakespearian criticism" but indicated that he did not want all-out rebellion: "It would be the extremity of ingratitude and ignorance if those of us who look ahead to new lines of approach and new kinds of Shakespearian 'truth', regarded the older school of 'realistic' criticism as inept." [82]

The main advocate of the new approach in *The Symposium* was James Burnham who had first discussed *The Wheel of Fire*.

[81] *Symposium*, I, 4 (October 1930), 537-541.
[82] *Symposium*, II, 2 (April 1931), 242-257.

The extent of Burnham's interest is illustrated by the following quotation from an essay which had no direct connection with Shakespearean criticism at all – the modern approach to Hamlet is adduced to illuminate a discussion of "Marxism and Aesthetics": "If Hamlet gets angry", Burnham wrote, "we 'explain' this by something else in the play; not by going back to a chronicle that might say that on such and such an occasion a historical prince of Denmark got angry".[83] In the penultimate issue, Burnham looked back on *The Symposium*'s contribution to the Shakespearean debate and noted that, to the best of his knowledge, it had been the only periodical in the United States "to take seriously the new development in Shakespearian criticism and interpretation inaugurated about four years ago with the publication of G. Wilson Knight's *The Wheel of Fire*". He also pointed out, as Gary had done before him, that the number of books exhibiting the new method which were in no way directly influenced by Knight's interpretation, suggested that Knight's methods were not idiosyncratic, "but rather offered in their due time". Although *The Wheel of Fire* had been a pioneering study, Knight's subsequent books, *The Imperial Theme* and *The Shakespearean Tempest* (Knight had contributed an essay under that title to the October 1931 *Symposium*) had somewhat modified Burnham's enthusiasm: "It is true that Mr. Knight is an extremist, and that we must be reserved in the acceptance of his methods and his conclusions." The best introduction to the new approach was, in Burnham's opinion, L. C. Knights's *How Many Children Had Lady Macbeth?*. To read this pamphlet was "probably the easiest way for the American reader to decide whether this whole movement is worth his serious attention".[84]

If Shakespearean criticism was one of the more prominent issues discussed in the pages of *The Symposium*, no topic was so tenaciously debated as Marxism. The debate grew in intensity from one number to the next, and whatever symposial structure is to be found in the last few issues revolves around it. It was the

---

[83] *Symposium*, IV, 1 (January 1933), 7.
[84] Review of *The Imperial Theme, The Shakespearean Tempest*, and *How Many Children Had Lady Macbeth?*, *Symposium*, IV, 3 (July 1933), 397-399.

subject of a formal editorial pronouncement signed by both editors but it finally led to editorial dissent which, in its turn, was one of the reasons for the magazine's expiration with the October issue of 1933. Most contributors agreed in differentiating between the virtues of Marxism as an economic programme and Marxism as a critical methodology. The articles which are strictly concerned with the economic and ideological aspects and which are not direct pronouncements of editorial sentiments – such as Arthur Wubnig's "Economic Rationalization" and Sidney Hook's "Towards the Understanding of Karl Marx" [85] – are of less importance to the present discussion than those articles and remarks which move in the borderland of Marxism and aesthetics.

It is always hazardous to generalize about the attitude of a magazine towards a particular topic, but when we say that in political matters *The Symposium* moved from the right to the left we are nearer the truth than is customary with most generalizations. In October 1933, *The Symposium* folded with a vote of confidence in Marxism on the part of at least one editor; but in its discussion of the Summer 1931 issue, *The Criterion* had found *The Symposium* to the right of *The Hound & Horn*, which it described as "Left Inside".[86] Indeed both as regards contributors and subject-matter, *The Symposium* moved from a position akin to that of *The Criterion* to one akin to *Partisan Review*. We may underline this shift in a negative manner by saying that some of Burnham's later essays would have looked odd in earlier issues. Conversely, an essay like Ramon Fernandez's "Thought and Revolution" was more in tune with the contents of the January 1931 issue in which it appeared than it would have been with the contents of a later issue. Fernandez stated unequivocally that a victory of communism would mean the death of the individual and the loss of democratic humanitarian beliefs.

After we have taken note of this turn to the left we must differentiate between *The Symposium*'s attitude to the economic and to the aesthetic implications of Marxism. Whereas a number

---

[85]   *Symposium*, II, 1 (January 1931), 26-50; II, 3 (July 1931), 325-364.
[86]   H.S.D., "American Periodicals", *The Criterion*, XI, 43 (January 1932), 362.

of contributors were sympathetic towards the economic implications, they were very wary of Marxist arguments and methods when applied to or woven into works of literature. Philip Blair Rice for instance, spoke of "the hysterical thrill of mob emotions" which, in his opinion, was substituted for genuine vitality in American Communist *belles lettres.* Although the result of the Communist experiment was uncertain, one certainty there was: "that a satisfactory solution of our aesthetic and moral difficulties would by no means flow from a solution of the economic problem as a simple consequence." [87] Even a critic as sympathetic towards Marxism as Robert Cantwell complained that most proletarian writers assumed that "a strong belief in a cause excuses any amount of careless writing about it".[88] Frederick Dupee noticed the adverse effects of Marxist convictions on the literary criticism of Edmund Wilson. In his review of *Axel's Castle* Dupee sought the reason for some "uncertain judgments" in the fact that Wilson was "by temper in sympathy with the Symbolists while by profession he is a Communist".[89]

As in *The Hound & Horn,* an important commentator on the relation of Marxism and literature was Henry Bamford Parkes. In the April 1933 issue, Parkes made a strict distinction between the contemporary economic and aesthetic uses of Marxism – a position which he was to maintain throughout the 'Thirties – when he wrote: "Communism, perhaps, if it is accepted as a technique for making the necessary changes and not as a dogmatic religion, is the best available method of regeneration; it does, at least, aim at prohibiting individual acquisitiveness. But it remains to be seen whether artistic honesty and the organic growth of the individual ... can be reconciled with its present intolerance." [90] When Parkes discussed "Jeffersonian Democracy" in the following issue, he

---

[87] "Out of the Waste Land", *Symposium,* III, 4 (October 1932), 442.
[88] "No Landmarks", *Symposium,* IV, 1 (January 1933), 81. Morton Dauwen Zabel called this investigation of the direction of contemporary American fiction "one of the most spirited contributions to *The Symposium*" ("Recent Magazines", *Poetry,* XLIII, 4 [January 1934], 172).
[89] *Symposium,* II, 2 (April 1931), 266.
[90] Review of W. H. Auden's *The Orators, Symposium,* IV, 2 (April 1933), 248.

emphasized the peculiar contemporary significance of Jefferson's political ideas which in the eighteenth century brought him on the side of the small farmers, and which in the twentieth century might in logical consequence have resulted in communism.[91]

In general outline, therefore, the attitude towards Marxism of *The Symposium*'s contributors was very similar to that of *The Hound & Horn*'s. It was primarily concerned with the relation of Marxism and aesthetics and most contributors were sceptical about a final reconciliation of the two. But whereas *The Hound & Horn*'s editor, Lincoln Kirstein, the only one on the editorial board who had Marxian sympathies, was soon persuaded that his was a literary magazine which would best avoid all political discussion, the political awareness of at least one of the editors of *The Symposium*, James Burnham, grew apace. Before the expiration of the magazine Burnham had moved from a liberal or perhaps rather a politically undefined position to one which a few years later would be stamped as Trotskyist. Philip Wheelwright's interests remained primarily literary and philosophical and he was only able to follow Burnham part of the way.

Burnham's approach to Marxism, especially in the early stages, was entirely intellectual and he refused to be carried away by slogans and battle cries. He admired Trotsky because he was a man who had "done much more than adopt at second hand a convenient methodology for filing his ideas".[92] His initial attitude towards Marxism was mildly adverse. He felt that any discussion of the whole economic machine from a social point of view was likely to lead the critic to "some form of economic fatalism". He doubted whether the mind could greatly influence the social order. Less doubtful was the efficacy of the mind in the life of the individual. "And it is even now not too preposterous to suppose that the latter is legitimately the first center of interest." [93]

In their October 1932 "Comment", when the editors clarified their position in the matter of publishing creative writing, they

[91]   *Symposium*, IV, 3 (July 1933), 302-323.
[92]   Review of Vol. I of Trotsky's *History of the Russian Revolution*, *Symposium*, III, 3 (July 1932), 379-380.
[93]   J.B., "Comment", *Symposium*, III, 2 (April 1932), 151, 152.

went on to discuss some problems arising from Ben Maddow's poem *Red Decision* which was featured in that issue. They described how the staleness of the nineteenth-century attitude to poetry had become apparent at about the time of the first World War, and how the too negative vision of the writers of the 'Twenties could only form a temporary basis for art, and they concluded that "the sensitivity of the present generation is being sharpened more and more directly toward the problems of our social and economic environment". This development was illustrated in *Red Decision* in which the individual's isolation was redeemed by his acceptance of the proletarian cause. The directly propagandistic conclusion of the poem had been "an initial obstacle" for the editors and remained a hindrance, but they realized that their reaction might be merely a stock response. However, stock responses "cannot be tossed away by a mere declaration of critical detachment; they are part of the critic's native equipment, and his function is to become progressively critical toward the vision of life that they give".[94] The editors closed their "Comment" with the promise of a partial clarification in the following issue. It is significant that this clarification was not in the form of a joint statement of both editors but in the form of a leading article by James Burnham, "Marxism and Aesthetics". Other contributions to the same issue of January 1933 bearing on the question were William Phillips' "Categories for Criticism" and Robert Cantwell's "No Landmarks"; as a matter of fact the only essay in the issue which did not apply itself to the question was C. R. Morse's discussion of Matisse.

Burnham, in his discussion of Marxism and aesthetics, showed more sympathy for the Marxian position than most other contributors, but he could not give final assent to all its implications. His essay was one more investigation into the nature of poetry and of criticism. Burnham's main objection was that the Marxists in their concern for the paraphrasable content of a work of art, neglected the unique logic of the medium, aesthetic form, which contributes to the meaning of the work. Reacting against pure art theories, Marxism had fallen into the other extreme and had

[94]   *Symposium*, III, 4 (October 1932), 419-421.

denied "the autonomy of art, the validity of an aesthetic category, altogether". For the artist, the Marxian insistence on "social awareness" might be a valuable antidote against the "spiritual waste" of modern life. Indeed, if "social awareness" only were insisted upon, many critics would be sympathetic, but an acceptance of the more extreme forms of Marxism implied an acceptance of the revolutionary principle and, consequently, in the writings of Marxists "the revolutionary optimism of the intellectually accepted program is in conflict with the demands of the medium". Ben Maddow's *Red Decision*, published in the preceding issue, furnished a good example. Burnham decided that Marxism as a system was, in the last analysis, false, because it was "inhuman" and offered "an order of values not acceptable to man nor in keeping with man's nature"; it could therefore not form the basis of a satisfactory theory of art.[95]

In the following number the editors issued jointly "Thirteen Propositions" in answer to some reproaches by readers and critics that the editors had failed to take "an unequivocal position toward those matters about which it is nowadays customary to expect a position to be taken". In the "Thirteen Propositions" the editors intended to restate certain of the previously formulated policies of the magazine and to make explicit certain other policies that had up to then remained implicit only. As these Propositions are of crucial importance for an understanding of the history of *The Symposium*, some of the latter category may be briefly stated here; they were mainly concerned with the economic and political aspects of Marxism. The sixth Proposition stated that "the natural end of the industry of any society is the providing of material goods to the individuals of the society in question, in proper subordination to moral and spiritual goods", but, according to the seventh Proposition, capitalist methods could no longer sufficiently fulfil this natural end. Proposition eight emphasized the necessity of a "revolutionary change" in these methods which according

---

[95] *Symposium*, IV, 1 (January 1933), 3-30. Granville Hicks called Burnham's article the "only one reasonably intelligent criticism of the Marxist position" he had seen ("The Crisis in American Criticism", *The New Masses*, VIII, 7 [February 1933], 3).

to Proposition nine would involve "collectivization of naturally social property". This economic change, the tenth Proposition stated, could be accomplished only after those interested in bringing about the change had seized political power; reformist attempts, according to the eleventh Proposition, were inadequate; mass pressure "under the leadership of a militant and organized party" was necessary. The nearest approach to such a party in the United States, the Communist Party, was, in the words of Proposition twelve, "not acceptable", because at a level of social practice it failed "to adjust its methods to the specific character of the United States", and because, in theory, it related "the politico-economic program to inacceptable moral and spiritual goods". According to Proposition thirteen, the contemporary situation was such that criticism had to break its rightful isolation to recognize also the issues at the level of social practice. In a final paragraph the editors maintained that the moral and spiritual goods which must be the ultimate justification of all action were, for them, given by "the tradition of western civilization, generally, and, further, by the American cultural tradition." This "western tradition" lay at the root of *The Symposium*, and as it had become clear that revolutionary action was necessary to conserve that tradition, revolution was justified.[96]

The "Comment" of the following issue, which was only signed by James Burnham, rang with the rhetoric of class-warfare. The New Deal, according to Burnham was "a fascist program: the final consolidation of monopoly capitalism bringing a pseudo-order out of the dissolving competitive chaos, under the open and active leadership of the state, in a last stand against the claims of the masses". Burnham insisted on the need for revolution in order to bring about the collectivization of "the instruments of production and distribution"; this seems to go beyond Proposition nine which had more vaguely advocated "the collectivization of *naturally social* property" (italics added).[97]

The next and last issue, that of October 1933, started off with

[96]   J.B. and P.W., "Comment: Thirteen Propositions", *Symposium*, IV, 2 (April 1933), 127-134.
[97]   J.B., "Comment", *Symposium*, IV, 3 (July 1933), 271, 277.

a separate "Comment" by each of the two editors, who went divergent political ways. The "Thirteen Propositions" had drawn a number of comments from different sources and had "been accused, or praised ... for every position from anarchy to fascism". To Burnham, consequently, it was clear that they had been undesirably ambiguous, but he considered the different readings equally illustrative of the positions held by the different commentators. The two most interesting of these were T. S. Eliot in *The Criterion* and one Paul Salter in *The New Masses*.[98] The former took the Propositions to be a manifesto of the "coming type of liberal Reformer", the latter a fascist manifesto. Burnham answered both of them from an unmistakably communist point of view. He regretted the attitude of the Propositions towards the Communist Party: "I still believe that most of the charges are substantially correct but I believe also that they should be offered in such a way that the Party will be supported, not hindered; and I now understand better the objective difficulties against which the leaders strive". Burnham believed that the possible attitudes towards society were rapidly sharpening down to three: communism, fascism, or complete breakdown. "My choice of the first of these is unequivocal. My objections to 'the communist party in this country' are not to communism, but to the shortcomings of the official Party as representative of the cause of communism." He also accepted the dictatorship of the proletariat as "the indispensable instrument of the revolution". Burnham's final unequivocal assent to communism had been accelerated by his experiences during the preceding summer in the car factories of Detroit and

[98]   T. S. Eliot, "A Commentary", *The Criterion*, XII, 49 (July 1933), 642-647; Paul Salter, "Fascist Philosophers", *The New Masses*, VIII, 11 (July 1933), 13-14. Eliot, although he misunderstood *The Symposium*'s position, made a very interesting distinction between "two types of reformer or revolutionist: the coming type of liberal Reformer ... and the Reactionary, who at this point feels a stronger sympathy with the communist". Whatever the ultimate truth of this distinction, it had prophetic significance in view of Burnham's later career. In 1936 Burnham ran for President on the Trotskyist ticket, was a frequent contributor to the early *Partisan Review* and, in the words of Julian Symons, "may now be glimpsed occasionally far, far out on the Right, editing the *National Review*" ("Woofers and Tweeters", *The Spectator* [February 22, 1963], 232).

the coal mines of Illinois. As a result he had joined the American Worker's Party, better known in later years as the Trotskyist Party. But although these experiences had taught him the need for action, he was not yet willing to believe that "ideas, however minor may be their rôle, are in the end trivial", a very weak reminder, in other words, of the magazine's earlier defence of ideas for their own sake.[99]

Wheelwright in his separate "Comment" did not follow his co-editor all the way into the communist camp. He reckoned himself among those malcontents who would not accept communism or support the Communist Party as a *pis aller*, but who saw clearly enough "the necessity for some revolutionary change that will bring about a more just distribution of goods and a more workable distribution of purchasing power". Wheelwright agreed with Burnham in repudiating any fascist implications which the "Thirteen Propositions" might have suggested. He emphasized the essential difference between theory and practice and felt that communism, and certainly the Communist Party in the United States, had simplified theory in order to provide slogans for the action of the masses. Even if a simplified ideology could be made to serve a salutary practical end, there remained the problem of supplying an acceptable ideology for the intellectual leaders of the movement: "Individuals with much power of discernment must always be non-conformist in thought, and a communist party that establishes its ideology on too narrowly sectarian lines wastes its strength by alienating many of those who could perhaps serve it best." [100] This remark formulated a more widespread discontent among the intellectuals of the early 'Thirties which, in 1935, led the American Communist Party to adopt a less doctrinaire Popular Front policy.

The Marxian debate which had been such a prominent issue especially in the later numbers of *The Symposium*, and which had brought it some measure of public attention, had finally caused editorial dissent. The editors did not only differ in intellectual matters, they also disagreed about the place the debate

[99]   *Symposium*, IV, 4 (October 1933), 403-413.
[100] *Symposium*, IV, 4 (October 1933), 413-419.

ought to occupy in the pages of their review. Wheelwright had never shared the intensity of Burnham's interest. As the magazine's benefactor, James Buell Munn, moved to Harvard at about the same time, it seemed natural that the magazine should expire with the issue of October 1933 which had contained the two disagreeing "Comments". *The Symposium* had never occupied a very conspicuous place among contemporary periodicals. It never attracted even the slight degree of contemporary notoriety *The Hound & Horn* attracted. When Pound drew Samuel Putnam's attention to the magazine, Putnam asked: "Where in the hell does one buy the Symposium? I never see it." [101] This chapter, it is hoped, will serve to illustrate, not only the importance of *The Symposium* as a link in the chain of American critical reviews of this century, but also its interest as a magazine in its own right.

[101]   Putnam to Pound, February 12, 1931, Putnam papers, Princeton University Library.

5

THE SOUTHERN REVIEW (1935-1942)

I

"Congratulations on the announcement of the first *Southern Review*. From the typographical dress, prospectus, and table of contents it looks as if the *Hound & Horn* has moved south of the Mason and Dixon line." [1] This reaction of B. A. Botkin, the editor of the regional magazine *Space,* foreshadowed the more considered opinion of most literary genealogists in later years. The first issue of *The Southern Review* appeared in July 1935. *The Hound & Horn* had then been gone for over a year and no other magazine had appeared since which had approximated to its general direction or excellence.[2] The announcement of the new magazine augured

---

[1] B. A. Botkin to Cleanth Brooks, July 21, 1935, *Southern Review* papers, Yale University Library.

[2] At the time when the first issue of *The Southern Review* was published *The Criterion* complained: "the recent discontinuance of *Hound & Horn* leaves a want in American literary journalism which it could very well be without. It finds itself at the moment, in fact, with no important journal in which left and right, humanistic and humanitarian, can rub shoulders in creation of literature valuable as one or another form of art ... it is desirable that some successor to *Hound & Horn* be found ..." (D. G. Bridson, "American Periodicals", *The Criterion*, XIV, 57 [July 1935], 729). A year later there appeared in *Poetry* the following description of the situation of the literary review: "The end of *The Dial* forecast the early doom of its successors, *The Symposium* and *The Hound & Horn*, whose abrupt disappearance completed the havoc which had for a decade been marked by the rapid deaths of many smaller and more obviously ephemeral magazines. For two or three years now it has seemed doubtful if America would again see a regular critical journal, or anything approaching the importance in England of *The Criterion*. It is a matter for general congratulation that this gloom has been relieved by *The Southern Review* ..." (Morton Dauwen Zabel, "Recent Magazines", *Poetry*, XLVIII, 1 [April 1936], 51).

another episode in the history of the American literary review. Like *The Symposium, The Southern Review* had its domicile in a university, the Louisiana State University at Baton Rouge, but, in contrast to the position of *The Symposium*, there was nothing accidental about its academic connection. *The Southern Review* was paid for by the Louisiana State University; the funds it could draw on were more lavish than those of its predecessors, except *The Dial*, and each quarterly issue numbered over two hundred large pages. It was the largest critical quarterly of its kind ever published in the United States and the distinction of its typography, paper and general make-up has rarely been rivalled. No ordinary State University would have been prepared in 1935 to put up money for such an elaborate, mainly literary magazine. But L.S.U. was no ordinary State University; it was the show-piece of Louisiana's autocratic governor Huey Long. During his time in office he spent $ 15.000.000 on it and increased the student body from 1500 to 4000; by 1938 this number is reported to have increased to 8500.[3] Such progressive management would not shrink from a mere $ 10.000 as a minimum guarantee for a literary review which would enhance the university's reputation beyond State borders.

It was L.S.U.'s President, James Monroe Smith who, on a Sunday afternoon around the middle of March 1935, asked Robert Penn Warren of the University's English Department "if a literary quarterly could be edited here [at L.S.U.] if he could get the jack in large quantities".[4] On the following morning Warren got together with Cleanth Brooks, also of the English Department, and Charles W. Pipkin, Dean of the Graduate

---

[3] Stan Opotowsky, *The Longs of Louisiana* (New York, 1960), p. 117; Albert J. Montesi, "*The Southern Review* (1935-1942): A History and an Evaluation" (unpublished doctoral dissertation, State University of Pennsylvania, 1955), p. 61.

[4] Robert Penn Warren to Allen Tate, March 20, 1935, Tate papers, Princeton University Library. Warren's letter, dated March 20, stated that Smith's visit had taken place on "Sunday afternoon". In 1953, however, Brooks and Warren remembered that the meeting between Warren and President Smith occurred on "a bright Sunday afternoon in late February" (*Stories from the Southern Review*, ed. Cleanth Brooks and Robert Penn Warren [Baton Rouge, 1953], p. xi).

School, and by half past three in the afternoon the whole matter had been approved. Pipkin was to be editor, Warren and Brooks managing editors, and Albert E. Erskine business manager. The literary side of the review would be the concern of Brooks, Warren and Erskine. Apart from the earliest issues, there are few references to Pipkin's activities; "we have seen Pip very little", Brooks wrote to Tate in the autumn of 1937; "he sulks a little, but in general he has been friendly and cordial and very affable".[5] Pipkin, who had appointed Brooks and Warren, was a social scientist and probably managed the political side of the *Review*. This may very well have led to disagreements with Brooks, Erskine and Warren whose interests were mainly literary. A remark in a letter of Andrew Lytle to Allen Tate in 1944, when Tate took over the editorship of *The Sewanee Review*, seems to indicate as much; Lytle told Tate that he was glad that "with no sociology to mar it, the [Sewanee] Review will not be embarrassed as was the Southern by Pipkin".[6] Warren and Brooks were, however, invariably courteous in their references to Pipkin. When Pipkin died in August 1941 there was no substitute appointment; from then on Brooks and Warren were the only editors. An earlier change in the editorial staff had been the appointment, towards the end of 1940, of a new business manager, John E. Palmer. *The American Oxonian* commented on it as follows:

Mr. Albert Erskine, business manager of the *Southern Review*, having left to join the New Directions press, J. E. Palmer (Louisiana and Exeter, '37) has been elected to succeed him. The *Review* thus becomes an all Rhodes Scholar quarterly, staffed, in addition to Palmer by C. W. Pipkin (Arkansas and Exeter, '22), Cleanth Brooks, Jr. (Louisiana and Exeter, '29) and R. P. Warren (Kentucky and New College, '28).[7]

The announcement of *The Southern Review* was one of the features of the Diamond Jubilee celebration of the Louisiana State University; it was made at the Conference on Literature and

---

[5]   Tate papers.
[6]   October 16, 1944, Tate papers.
[7]   *The American Oxonian*, XXVIII, 1 (January 1941), 35. After Erskine's departure, Pipkin, Brooks, and Warren were all called editors and Palmer managing editor.

Reading in the South and South-West which was held at L.S.U. on 10 and 11 April 1935. The editors had approximately three months to prepare the first issue, but in practical matters they were given all the assistance they needed. As Warren told Tate in a postscript to his letter of 20 March 1935: "I forgot to say that the scale of the Review's ambitions is large. We are aiming at a national distribution and have a considerable sum for promotion. Hold that in mind for your suggestions. The iron is hot here, and I feel that we can get whatever we ask for." The *Review*'s promotion fund proved a considerable advantage over its predecessors. Before the appearance of the second issue Warren could announce that the "paying circulation was over 900".[8] The *Review* was off to a promising start; its paid circulation increased to an average of some 1500 copies (which still meant a deficit of about $ 7000 a year) and its development was not endangered, as some friends had feared, by the assassination of Governor Long soon after the first issue had appeared. The *Review* managed to steer clear of State or University interference.[9]

In contrast to *The Hound & Horn* and *The Symposium* which had had to compete with a number of influential if somewhat different magazines, there was no contemporary magazine to challenge the achievement of *The Southern Review* during the first years of its existence. Its only American rivals in later days were John Crowe Ransom's *Kenyon Review* and *Partisan Review*. *The Southern Review* showed some kinship to the English *Criterion* and *Scrutiny*, but a number of characteristic preoccupations gave it a decidedly individual flavour. Most of its characteristics, however, may be profitably discussed in the light of the accomplishment of both *The Hound & Horn* and *The Symposium*. It will then be seen that *The Southern Review* followed a number of trails started by these predecessors, with an editorial consistency and

---

[8]   R. P. Warren to Howard Baker, November 9, 1935, *Southern Review* papers.
[9]   "It must be granted that when the editors began the magazine they did so with some fear of political interference. In the atmosphere of the Louisiana of that time, the apprehension was real. The editors agreed that if any interference came they would resign. Their resolution was not put to the test" (*Stories from the Southern Review*, p. xiii).

efficiency which could only be achieved by a prosperous, intelligently edited magazine aware of an established tradition. B. A. Botkin, as we have seen at the beginning of this chapter, was struck by the similarity of appearance and purpose between *The Hound & Horn* and *The Southern Review*, and the editors of *The Southern Review* themselves realized that they appealed to much the same audience as the earlier magazine; they hoped that R. P. Blackmur might be able to tell them "whether we could get the Hound & Horn list, or how to go about getting it".[10] *The Southern Review* was also aware of the distinguished career of *The Symposium*. Allen Tate, who was perhaps the first person outside Baton Rouge to be informed of the project for a new quarterly, mentioned *The Symposium* as the nearest approximation to his ideal image of such a new quarterly.[11] Tate was the most important adviser of *The Southern Review* as he was to be of the early *Kenyon Review*. The editors repeatedly solicited his advice and, at his suggestion, invited a number of writers, such as Leonie Adams, Phelps Putnam and William Troy, to contribute to their magazine. They took his contributions to *The Southern Review* so much for granted that they announced an essay of his for their special Yeats issue without having inquired beforehand whether he would be willing to write such an essay.

[10]   Editor to Blackmur, January 21, 1937, *Southern Review* papers. Like *The Hound & Horn, The Southern Review* had an early ambition to publish books. In a letter to Tate, probably written in the autumn of 1935, Warren announced a "series of critical books and anthologies – the SOUTHERN REVIEW SERIES, nicely printed (we hope to get Paul Johnson to design them uniformly with the magazine), numbered in series, etc.". Warren, however, warned Tate that the scheme was only a probability: "for I cried 'wolf!' once before. But I am even more confident now." The series might also contain "one anthology of poetry a year from the REVIEW, with the accompanying critical notes and an introduction. We might even get around to bringing out a collection of our best fiction at the end of a period of several years" (Tate papers). On 13 October 1936 Warren referred to the series – which would be published by the L.S.U. Press – as a "strong probability" (Letter to Blackmur, *Southern Review* papers). The candidates for the critical series included Brooks, Warren, Ransom, Tate, Blackmur, Davidson, Frank Owsley, John Wade, F. Cudworth Flint, and Howard Baker.
[11]   "The Function of the Critical Review", *SoR*, I, 3 (Winter 1936), 552.

The first task of the editors was to spread the news among possible contributors. As the *Review* would be able to pay one and a half cents a word for prose and thirty-five cents a line for verse, they could fairly confidently solicit contributions from such distinguished literary contemporaries as Sherwood Anderson, Conrad Aiken, William Empson, T. S. Eliot, William Faulkner, Dudley Fitts, F. Scott Fitzgerald, Horace Gregory, F. R. Leavis, Archibald MacLeish, Marianne Moore, Herbert Read, Thomas Wolfe, and W. B. Yeats. The outcome of these solicitations, however, was not very impressive: none of these writers became a very regular contributor. It was rather the editors' friends in criticism such as Allen Tate, R. P. Blackmur, Kenneth Burke, J. C. Ransom, Howard Baker, F. O. Matthiessen, Delmore Schwartz, Morton Zabel, and Arthur Mizener who set the tone of the magazine.

The editors were indeed trying "to make THE SOUTHERN REVIEW a clearing house for literary criticism." [12] The *Review*, like *The Hound & Horn* and *The Symposium,* paid special attention to its reviewing section; the editors hoped theirs would be "one quarterly in this country that really gives attention to the critical review".[13] They tried to make reviewing, "once more, a department of criticism, rather than a department of sales promotion." [14] Since the magazine was a quarterly they decided that they would be most effective in realizing this aim "by a concentration on a relatively small number of topics, ... on long studies of a closely selected list." [15] They were eager to build up a pretty consistent staff of reviewers and critics whose reputations would be "to a degree associated with THE SOUTHERN REVIEW" [16] and whose reputations would, in turn, support the reputation of the magazine

[12] Brooks to William Empson, August 2, 1938, *Southern Review* papers.
[13] Editor to Crane Brinton, February 24, 1936, *Southern Review* papers.
[14] Warren to Catherine Wilds, May 25, 1936, now among the Allen Tate papers.
[15] Warren to Marianne Moore, April 26, 1937, *Southern Review* papers; Warren to Ronald Latimer, May 10, 1935, Latimer papers, Chicago University Library.
[16] Warren to Howard Baker, November 9, 1935, *Southern Review* papers.

itself. These critics would be able, in so far as space permitted, "to develop their programs" in the magazine.[17]

The book reviews in *The Southern Review* were often even longer than those in *The Hound & Horn* and in *The Symposium*, and the *Review* also featured a larger number of review articles. The editors liked the reviews to be "as nearly like independent articles as possible"; when, for instance, they sent Mortimer Adler a book on education to review they wished he would use it "merely as an occasion for whatever you would like to say on the subject".[18] Although the reviews were as critical as those which appeared in *The Hound & Horn* and *The Symposium*, they perhaps lacked a note of unnecessary harshness which was occasionally heard in *The Hound & Horn*. Although objective standards were never tampered with, the *Review* preserved a certain sense of decorum which it is impossible to define very closely. The following instance may be considered representative. In 1941 Donald Davidson wrote a long review essay on W. Cash's *The Mind of the South* which treated the book rather adversely from a partisan regional point of view and which was given the lead space of the Summer 1941 issue. But before the issue appeared the author of the book died. Consequently, the editors appended a note saying that "although no change could have been contemplated in the nature of the judgment passed upon Mr. Cash's work, the editors (and they speak, they believe, for Mr. Davidson as well) feel that the reader should be assured that the light raillery which the article admits at certain points is to be read with the reservations which the author himself would undoubtedly have observed in the light of this event." [19]

The most impressive outcome of the editorial emphasis on critical reviewing was the group book review of fiction and poetry and, occasionally, of criticism. These reviews presented a thorough examination and a critical evaluation of the fiction and poetry of each quarter. They appeared in all of the first nine issues until the

[17]   Warren to R. P. Blackmur, December 17, 1935, *Southern Review* papers. Warren told Blackmur that the editors should like to feel that they could count on him "for, say, a minimum of two essays a year".
[18]   March 3, 1939, *Southern Review* papers.
[19]   "An Editorial Note", *SoR*, VII, 1 (Summer 1941).

Autumn issue of 1937. The names of the reviewers constitute a roll-call of some of the most accomplished critics of the time, who were, with few exceptions, regular contributors to *The Southern Review*. The poetry reviewers in those first nine issues were Burke, Baker, Ransom, Davidson, Zabel, Brooks, Blackmur, Matthiessen, and Tate; the fiction was discussed by Baker (twice), Randall Jarrell, Warren, Blackmur, Ransom, Henry Nash Smith (then on the editorial board of *Southwest Review* with which Brooks, Warren and Pipkin had been associated before they edited *The Southern Review*), F. Cudworth Flint, and Mark Van Doren. But it proved impossible to continue these high-powered, exacting reviews through the years. From the Autumn 1937 issue onwards, the chronicles appeared with irregular intervals. That Autumn issue only carried a poetry chronicle by Matthiessen. The Winter 1938 issue contained a discussion of the short story by Baker, and the Spring number of that year featured another poetry chronicle by Zabel which was accompanied by an Editor's Note to the effect that Zabel had not been able to finish his review in time for publication but that he would review other recent poetry in a later issue. A much later issue, as it turned out, because it was not until the Winter of 1940 that Zabel's "Two Years of Poetry: 1937-1939" appeared. Although this chronicle covered forty pages, a Note explained that the books discussed or mentioned formed a "*selection* of the volumes of verse published during the past two years", and the review itself was mainly concerned with "selected or collected evidences of mature achievement".[20]

If the poetry chronicle was an editorial headache, the fiction chronicle was even more so. In June 1937, Brooks had to admit that the fiction chronicle was "a tough assignment ... which we may have to revise", and some months later Warren wrote to John Peale Bishop: "The burden of doing the general chronicle was too much for our reviewers." [21] A change of policy in the reviewing of fiction proved indeed necessary and in the autumn of 1937 Warren, in a letter to James T. Farrell, announced that the

[20]   *SoR*, V, 3 (Winter 1940), 568, 569.
[21]   Brooks to Tate, June 28, 1937, Tate papers; Warren to Bishop, January 12, 1938, *Southern Review* papers.

editors had decided to "run a very long annual fiction chronicle in the fall and in the other issues run shorter reviews of individual novels".[22] Three of the four annual chronicles under the new arrangement were written by the *Review*'s most important fiction reviewer, Howard Baker. In the spring of 1939 Baker discussed no less than forty-five novels, but this feat paled beside his review of fifty novels exactly one year later. In Baker the editors had found the ideal critic to "make some general comments about the season as a whole and to point out any real discoveries that ought to be pointed out, and, if necessary, puncture reputations that have been inflated by enterprising blurb writers".[23]

Another editorial innovation of *The Southern Review* was the publication of groups of poems rather than miscellaneous pieces. As Warren told James Agee: "We try to publish long groups of poems by a single author, so that the reader may be able to get a real sample of the poet's work." [24] The original intention was to accompany such a group of poems (or one long poem) with a critical note on the work of the poet represented, with special reference to the poems published in the *Review*. It will be remembered that *The Symposium* had adopted a rather similar attitude to the poems published in its later issues. Brooks and Warren were only able to realize their critical ambition in three issues, all in the first volume. The second issue featured a group of poems by John Peale Bishop with a Note by Allen Tate, and the subsequent two issues carried poems by Mark Van Doren and George Marion O'Donnell with Notes by Baker and Ransom. From the *Review*'s second year onward the poetry was published without comments although the editors did try to continue their practice of publishing selections of poems of one poet. This proved no easy matter as the manuscripts submitted by a promising poet were often uneven. In some cases it took months for the editors to make up a satisfactory selection from the batches of poems which the poet was asked to submit regularly. Cases in point were the poetry of John Berryman and David Cornel DeJong. Berryman

[22]   October 6, 1937, *Southern Review* papers.
[23]   Brooks to Baker, July 26, 1938, *Southern Review* papers.
[24]   March 3, 1936, *Southern Review* papers.

was published twice but in both cases he had to share the quarterly poetry space with another poet. This was sometimes, especially in later issues, necessary if the editors failed to gather a group of poems of sufficient length by one poet.

By far the most popular poet in the pages of the *Review* was Randall Jarrell, a student of John Ransom. He was published four times and the first group of his poems to appear was the selection which Jarrell had submitted in the competition for the *Southern Review* Poetry Prize. The editors had had such a Prize in mind from the beginning. Already at their first meeting when they had discussed plans for a new magazine, they had decided to post "prizes of $ 100 for poetry, not to exceed 150 lines, and $ 150 for a story, plus the usual rate on publication".[25] Although this plan did not materialize in the proposed form, the second issue announced a Poetry Prize of $ 250 for the best long poem or group of poems to be submitted before 15 May 1936; some time later the closing date was moved to 1 August 1936. The entries, which included work of Howard Baker, John Peale Bishop and John Berryman, were judged by Allen Tate and Mark Van Doren, and from the 478 unsigned manuscripts they chose Jarrell's for the Prize. Other poets whose work was published in *The Southern Review* included R. P. Blackmur, Wallace Stevens (twice), Howard Baker, Josephine Miles (twice), W. H. Auden (twice) and Oscar Williams.

"Poetry is as hard as hell to get", Brooks wrote to Tate in January 1940; "we can get any amount of goodish stuff – but practically none that is really good." [26] This dearth of good poetry was painfully evident in the last two volumes. Of the last eight issues two were special issues on Hardy and Yeats which did not carry creative writing, one appeared without poetry, one featured the Spanish poet Frederico García Lorca, and the last number presented a ragbag of eleven poets, evidently bits and pieces which the editors were committed to print. One also, the Autumn 1940 issue, featured seven young poets, including John Malcolm Brinnin,

[25]   Warren to Tate, March 20, 1935, Tate papers.
[26]   Tate papers.

Rolfe Humphries and Richard Eberhart; the issue carried the following explanatory editorial note:

In this issue *The Southern Review* departs from its practice of publishing groups of poems (or long poems) by individual authors, and presents instead a miscellany by a number of young poets. The editors have felt that this departure is, at least in part, justified by the state of poetry at present. The period is characterized by the emergence of a number of young poets of promise, most of whom have not yet produced any considerable body of work.

It is interesting to note that five of the seven young poets were connected with universities, one as a student and four as teachers.

With regard to fiction, *The Southern Review* published on average four stories per issue, but especially towards the end this average number was not always reached.[27] Occasionally the *Review* published one novelette instead of a number of stories, such as Kay Boyle's "The Bridegroom's Body" and P. M. Pasinetti's "Family History", and twice when the novelette was from the pen of the *Review*'s most distinguished story writer, Katherine Anne Porter, it was granted the lead space of the issue.[28] Otherwise, the stories were published as a group in between the political and regional essays and the literary essays. There were fewer "names" among the story writers in the magazine than among the poets, and the editors tried to judge the contributions which came to hand as objectively as possible. "Our attitude toward the publication of new writers has been consistently the same", Cleanth Brooks wrote in October 1939: "Red [Warren] and I turned down for the first number a story by a Nobel Prize winner, because we felt that to accept an unworthy story – it was poor – merely to have a name, would be the very worst way to start out. I don't think that we have consciously varied from that policy

[27]   There was some discontent about some of the later stories in the magazine; Andrew Lytle, for example, wrote to Tate, on February 17, 1941: "I told Cleanth when he was here how bad I thought some of the recent fiction was they printed, the Albrizio, for example . . ." (Tate papers). Incidentally, the story of which Lytle disapproved particularly, Gene Albrizio's "The Bereft", was reprinted by Brooks and Warren in their anthology of *Stories from the Southern Review*.

[28]   "Pale Horse, Pale Rider", *SoR*, III, 3 (Winter 1938), 417-466; "The Leaning Tower", *SoR*, VII, 2 (Autumn 1941), 219-279.

one iota." [29] The editors were similarly critical in their judgment of new work by writers they admired. For instance, they rejected as often as accepted the stories of Caroline Gordon, then Allen Tate's wife, who was among their favourite writers of fiction. They published a considerable number of younger, relatively unknown storywriters, two of whom, Eudora Welty and Peter Taylor, have gained wide recognition since. Other contributors of note included Robert Penn Warren, Nelson Algren, Mary McCarthy, Andrew Lytle, Jesse Stuart, George Milburn, and Michael Seide.

The poetry and fiction were distinguished features of the *Review*'s accomplishment but its primary importance rested in its critical attitudes towards literature and society. These attitudes can be reduced to a number of related antitheses which were recognised by virtually all regular contributors and which gave *The Southern Review* a stronger sense of critical direction than any of the earlier magazines. Some of these antitheses were: the opposition of small town culture to urban civilization, of agrarianism to industrialism, of regionalism to federalism, of religion and myth to rationalism and pragmatism, and cumulatively and most importantly, of poetry to science, or, in the parlance of the day, of the imagination to positivism. These antitheses which had, with differing degrees of emphasis and commitment, been recognized by the earlier magazines, provided *The Southern Review* with a unified point of view which was brought to bear on each of its three major interests, the South, contemporary politics, and literature.

There had been two earlier *Southern Reviews*, both published in the nineteenth century, and they had both taken their Southern allegiance very seriously. The first *Southern Review* was published in Charleston from 1828 to 1832. One paragraph of its prospectus read: "It shall be among our first objects to vindicate the rights and privileges, the character of the Southern States, to arrest, if possible, that current which has been directed so steadily against our country generally, and the South in particular; and so offer to our fellow citizens one Journal which they may read without finding themselves the objects of perpetual sarcasm, or of affected

<hr>

[29]   Letter to Donald Davidson, October 23, 1939, *Southern Review* papers.

commiseration."[30] The second *Southern Review* was founded at Baltimore in 1867 by the former assistant secretary of war in the Confederacy and "for the next decade lauded everything about the Old South without seeing anything good in the New".[31]

The new *Southern Review* interpreted its allegiance to the South much more loosely than its earlier namesakes. When, shortly after the founding of the *Review*, the editors sent out a number of letters to solicit contributions for the first issues, they stated emphatically that the new magazine would not aim, "especially in its literary aspect, at a sectional program". They hoped to provide a large quarterly which would be "a real index to the most vital contemporary activities in fiction, poetry, criticism, and social-political thought, with an adequate representation in each of these departments".[32] Although the social-political thought would often be focussed on Southern problems the editors aimed at "a national distribution".[33] This aim was realized with a vengeance; when, in 1939, Tate asked the *Review*'s business manager, Albert Erskine, for figures regarding the sale of the magazine in the South, Erskine replied that the answers were "appalling". Against an average of ten copies in the State of Georgia, the sale of the magazine in New York City averaged eighty. "Incidentally we have as many subscribers in Massachusetts (20) as in Georgia, Alabama, Mississippi, and Florida put together. I could go on like this for a long time. We sell more copies in Tokyo than we do in Atlanta. A bookshop in Melbourne, Australia takes two copies for sale, but none in Birmingham, Alabama. It is too depressing to go on."[34]

The Southern tag was, however, by no means meaningless. The *Review* was genuinely interested in Southern history, and agrarianism and Southern regionalism had their firm advocates in its

[30] Quoted in W. T. Couch (ed.), *Culture in the South* (Chapel Hill, 1934), p. 162.
[31] John Samuel Ezell, *The South Since 1865* (New York, 1963), p. 279.
[32] Cleanth Brooks to Conrad Aiken, March 24, 1935, *Southern Review* papers.
[33] Charles Pipkin [?] to Herbert Agar, March 23, 1935, *Southern Review* papers.
[34] Letter to Tate, March 29, 1939, Tate papers.

pages. In this respect, the magazine was in direct line of succession from *The Hound & Horn* and *The American Review*. Its attitude towards agrarianism was rather similar to that of *The Hound & Horn* although its influence was felt much more pervasively. But *The Southern Review* had drawn a lesson particularly from the Utopian extravagances of *The American Review* and its concern was with regionalism rather than with agrarianism, or with agrarianism rather as a way of life than as an economic programme. This is of course a generalization which does not cover a number of exceptions. In the first issue of the *Review* Rupert B. Vance, who himself held more progressive views about the management of the South, noted that agrarianism was in a stage of transition from "a literary movement to agricultural economics. Nor should this come as a surprise to those who have followed the pages of the *American Review*". More representative of the magazine's direction, however, was the leading article of the first issue from the pen of the "most notable" convert to agrarianism, Herbert Agar.[35] Agar defended the way of life, the culture, of the small American town against the "judgment, the ambitions, the interests, the conditions and habits of life, represented by Chicago and New York".[36] The distrust of urban civilization was an integral part of the *Review*'s defence of regionalism. John Donald Wade, for instance, felt that Erskine Caldwell would have been a more impressive novelist if he had not affiliated himself with "the detached, nervous, thrill-goaded metrocosmopolitans of his own day".[37]

In the Spring 1936 issue, Allen Tate stated characteristically that agrarianism was not "*a legitimate object of belief, nor can it be*". Tate defended a traditional community, however, in which "making a living" and a "way of life" were not different pursuits. "In societies dominated by the moral and religious view, the life of men and their livelihood approximate a unity in which to speak

[35] W. J. Cash, *The Mind of the South* (New York, 1941), p. 383.
[36] "Culture Versus Colonialism in America", *SoR*, I, 1 (July 1935), 17. Solomon Fishman discussed Agar's article as "a representative exposition of the regionalist-agrarian argument against metropolitan culture" (*The Disinherited of Art* [Berkeley and Los Angeles, 1953], p. 104).
[37] "Sweet are the Uses of Degeneracy", *SoR*, I, 3 (Winter 1936), 466.

of the one is to speak of the other." [38] The *Review*'s emphasis, then, was on the quality of a society rather than on an economic programme. As Donald Davidson put it: "The agrarians want to cut the economic system to fit the society rather than the society to fit the economic system." [39] But if most contributors did not consider agrarianism a realistic economic programme, they certainly considered it of more than academic interest. "If vigorous discussion is a measure of well-being in the body politic", Donald Davidson wrote in the Spring issue of 1937, "the South is the healthiest region in the nation today". [40] Indeed, contributors to the early issues were decidedly optimistic about the ultimate fruitfulness of the debate. Crane Brinton was representative of this optimism when, in the Summer of 1936, he wrote that the agrarians seemed to have "many of the essential characteristics of the kind of 'school' that leaves a mark on intellectual history, that influences men's behavior". [41]

The more intransigent regionalists, however, wanted their readers never to lose sight of the fact that the South was "in the position of poor white and the North in the position of absentee landlord". [42] The debate on the practical level of the opposition North-South tended to be acrid rather than productive and it could only lead to defeat. And as practical considerations and cultural abstractions were inextricably interwoven, the debate lost its *raison d'être* before the expiration of the *Review*. The note of hope gradually changed to disillusion until, in 1941, Donald Davidson had to admit that the various rebellions against "the cultural lordship of New York over the Hinterland . . . including the regional rebellions", had availed nothing. [43] Davidson, in other words, admitted to defeat on a cultural as well as on an economic level,

[38] "A Traditionalist Looks at Liberalism", *SoR*, I, 4 (Spring 1936), 734, 740.
[39] "The Class Approach to Southern Problems", *SoR*, V, 2 (Autumn 1939), 270.
[40] "Expedients vs. Principles – Cross-Purposes in the South", *SoR*, II, 4 (Spring 1937), 647.
[41] "Who Owns America", *SoR*, II, 1 (Summer 1936), 15.
[42] Frank Owsley, "A Key to Southern Literature", *SoR*, III, 1 (Summer 1937), 37.
[43] "Mr. Babbitt at Philadelphia", *SoR*, VI, 4 (Spring 1941), 700.

although just four years earlier he had hailed "the rise of a new Southern literature which is of no negligible importance in the American scene", and the emergence of "a brilliant and powerful school of Southern historians whose work is already modifying the course of Southern, if not of national, thought", and along with them "an able group of economists, sociologists, and political scientists who are organizing data and drawing up programs of reform".[44]

The agrarian debate encouraged conservative ways of thought and nostalgic tendencies which manifested themselves in many different contexts. The reviewer of the Lynds' *Middletown in Transition,* for instance, recalled nostalgically how in their earlier investigation, *Middletown,* in the Twenties, "we saw a little community of 36.000 Americans, all free and the captains of their souls, all going about their innocent affairs with never a hint of covert cruelty, all wholly unaware of the existence of any iron hand within a velvet glove".[45] In the mid-Thirties the agrarians tried to form a united front with another conservative group, the English distributists, and an occasional article by a distributist found its way into the magazine. The main American representative of this English group was Herbert Agar, who was highly esteemed by the editors and a particular friend of Allen Tate, together with whom he edited the joint agrarian-distributist symposium *Who Owns America?* in 1936. Among the English distributists whose work was published and discussed in the magazine was Douglas Jerrold. The *Review* also gave the leading space of its third issue to Hilaire Belloc's discussion of "The Modern Man", which advocated "a change of philosophy; that is, of religion" and the "reinstitution of private property", and Herbert Agar praised G. K. Chesterton as "one of the truest democrats of modern history".[46]

---

[44] "Expedients vs. Principles – Cross-Purposes in the South", 655.
[45] C. E. Ayres, "Middletown Comes Clean", *SoR*, III, 1 (Summer 1937), 40.
[46] "The Modern Man", *SoR*, I, 3 (Winter 1936), 435; "A Great Democrat", *SoR*, III, 1 (Summer 1937), 96. For a more elaborate discussion of the cooperation of agrarians and distributists, cf. Albert J. Montesi, "*The Southern Review* (1935-1942): A History and an Evaluation", pp. 40-44, and

The editors did not object to the adverse view of agrarianism in the pages of their review, perhaps because the "cause" was so ably defended by others. A rising young Southern historian, for instance, C. Vann Woodward, reacted to "the romanticism of the type that envisions a charming agrarian past of a golden age", but he was soon taken to task by Donald Davidson for obscuring "the exploitation of the South as a colonial dependency of the North".[47] Davidson, the inveterate defender of Southern traditional ways, was agrarianism's warmest advocate in the *Review*, but he caused the editors occasional embarrassment. Their genuine interest in the South was no match for Davidson's zeal; "the S.R. in general puzzles me", the latter wrote in October 1939, "and my feelings towards it have received some decided shocks in the past year". He insinuated that the editors were not interested in "discovering" able young Southern writers, but preferred to see them "establish, or prove themselves elsewhere" before taking them up.[48] Brooks, however, pointed out that the *Review* had published very few established writers and "of the young writers which we have run I imagine that a good 75% have been from the South and Southwest".[49] Once, "after the magazine had been operating for several years", Brooks and Warren checked on the local origins of their contributors and estimated that 51% of them were Southern and of the remaining 49% "a great many were not even American." [50]

The South was only one interest of the *Review*; politics was another, and here also the articles dealing with practical politics have less significance for the modern reader than the discussions of political ideas and their relation to literature. Commentaries on the contemporary political situation are in the tradition of the

Alexander Karanikas, *Tillers of a Myth: Southern Agrarians as Social and Literary Critics* (Madison, Wis., 1966), pp. 55-58.

[47] Woodward, "Hillbilly Realism", *SoR*, IV, 4 (Spring 1939), 680; Davidson, "The Class Approach to Southern Problems", *SoR*, V, 2 (Autumn 1939), 262.

[48] Letter to Brooks, October 15, 1939, *Southern Review* papers.

[49] Letter to Davidson, October 23, 1939, *Southern Review* papers.

[50] *Stories from The Southern Review*, pp. xiii-xiv.

general review, such as *The Yale Review* and *The Virginia Quarterly Review*, rather than in the tradition of the literary review, and consequently need not detain us long. But we cannot altogether disregard them, because it was during the years of *The Southern Review* that the discussion of Marxism, fascism and democracy became increasingly a matter of practical politics rather than a subject of intellectual debate, especially after the Hitler-Stalin Pact and the invasion of Poland in 1939. Like the earlier literary magazines, *The Southern Review* was consistently averse to fascism and, as the international situation worsened, its attitude to communism also hardened. The *Review* was no longer faced, as James Burnham had been in *The Symposium*, with the possibilities of communism, fascism and complete breakdown but rather with the threat of fascism and, less urgently, of communism against democracy.

One of the most acute problems the magazine sought to solve was the ideological differentiation between fascism and democracy. The problem was tackled by R. M. MacIver in the Summer issue of 1939 when the campaign against fascism reached its climax. MacIver first pointed to the ambiguity of the concept of democracy: "There must be some universal appeal in the name of democracy, for even its destroyers proudly claim possession of its soul. Fascist writers announce that theirs is the genuine democracy and that so-called democracy is only a sham. Soviet spokesmen assert that they have now the most democratic constitution on earth, and Stalin himself declared that the 1937 elections in Russia were 'the most democratic the world has seen'." It was therefore highly important to clear up this notion of democracy and to discover the salient features which differentiated it from fascism and communism. There were, according to MacIver, two criteria by which democracy could be identified: "(1) *Democracy puts into effect the distinction between the state and the community*. ... (2) *Democracy depends on the free operation of conflicting opinions*." [51] In that same summer 1939 issue, at a time when it seemed likely that Europe would "be plunged to-

---

[51] "The Genius of Democracy", *SoR*, V, 1 (Summer 1939), 22, 26, 27.

morrow into another conflict",[52] other contributors were facing the same problem. C. J. Friedrich, for instance, detected the danger of the tendency in a democracy to equate an electoral majority with unlimited power, a tendency which he had found exemplified in an earlier article in *The Southern Review*.[53] Friedrich emphasized that "Hitler rose to power upon a huge wave of popular support. ... In the last parliamentary elections his party and that of his Nationalist allies together polled fifty-one percent of the votes. Just the one percent that the outright majoritarian insists justifies everything." [54]

The most interesting anti-fascist contribution to the issue was Kenneth Burke's analysis of *Mein Kampf*. Burke stressed the importance of a close reading of the book and of accepting the inescapable conclusions. Hitler's book was "exasperating, even nauseating". Yet Burke felt that if "the reviewer but knocks off a few adverse attitudinizings and calls it a day, with a guaranty, in advance, that his article will have a favorable reception among the decent members of our population, he is contributing more to our gratification than to our enlightenment". Burke sought the reason for Hitler's appeal primarily in his reliance on "a bastardization of fundamentally religious patterns of thought". "Our job, then, our Anti-Hitler Battle, is to find all available ways of making the Hitlerite distortions of religion apparent, in order that politicians of his kind in America be unable to perform a similar swindle." [55] At this juncture in world affairs most contributors would have agreed with MacIver that the United States had taken on "a new and more decisive rôle in the drama of democracy" (V, 38).

The next issue, the Autumn number of 1939, was more concerned with an analysis and a prognosis of the political situation

[52] Dixon Wecter, "Hulme and the Tragic View", *SoR*, V, 1 (Summer 1939), 141.
[53] Friedrich referred to Willmoore Kendall's "The Majority Principle and the Scientific Elite", *SoR*, IV, 3 (Winter 1939), 463-472.
[54] "One Majority against Another: *Populus Sempervirens*", *SoR*, V, 1 (Summer 1939), 48.
[55] "The Rhetoric of Hitler's 'Battle'", *SoR*, V, 1 (Summer 1939), 1, 20, 21.

than with ideas proper. Lindsay Rogers, for instance, in an article written before the invasion of Poland, gave an estimate of the preparedness for war of England and France, and William Gilman discussed the availability of oil in the different western countries.[56] From the Winter 1940 issue onward, apart from an occasional article mostly concerned with the ideological and literary aspects of Marxism, politics gradually disappeared from the pages of the *Review*. The political interest of the intellectuals which had been so intense during the 'Thirties, and which had to some extent influenced the tradition of the literary review, had turned into a sense of defeat and apathy. The disillusion attendant upon the breakdown of political ideals was movingly described by Robert Penn Warren at a meeting of the Fugitives seventeen years later: "Before we got in the last war, just before it and several years after, there was a period of unmasking of blank power everywhere. And you felt that all your work was irrelevant to this unmasking of this brute force in the world – that the de-humanizing forces had won. And you had no more relevance in such discussions as we used to have, or are having this morning, except a sort of quarrelling with people over the third highball." The only function left for the artist and the critic was that of a fifth column. "We couldn't step out and take over the powers of the state. Poetry is a fifth column." [57]

Whereas fascism posed the greater political threat, Marxism like agrarianism had a literary dimension the interest of which was affected, but not completely obliterated, by the facts of practical politics. Marxism as a political doctrine was discredited: communism or socialism, Henry Bamford Parkes wrote in the Winter 1939 issue, had nowhere been able "to convert a majority of the population or to achieve power by legal and democratic methods", and was therefore not likely to do so by force. Dixon Wecter, in the same issue, drew attention to the anti-intellectualism of both

---

[56]   Rogers, "England and France at 'White War' ", *SoR*, V, 2 (Autumn 1939), 211-227; Gilman, "Oiling the War Machines", *SoR*, V, 2 (Autumn 1939), 228-241.
[57]   Rob Roy Purdy (ed.), *Fugitives' Reunion – Conversations at Vanderbilt, May 3-5, 1956* (Nashville, 1959), pp. 208, 216.

fascism and Marxism.[58] In the Autumn of 1940, when the eclipse of Marxist movements throughout the world was "almost complete", Sidney Hook set out "to inquire into those doctrinal aspects of contemporary Marxist movements which seem definitely invalidated, and those aspects of the Marxist tradition, broadly conceived, which may still be integrated into a sound synthesis".[59] The débâcle of Marxism had, according to Joseph Frank, imposed a new responsibility on the liberals. After the attack on Finland a defence of communism was no longer possible and it was now imperative for the liberals to attempt to "work out an economic program which would translate liberal ideals into feasible political alternatives".[60] Indeed, as agrarianism gradually lost its appeal as a political and economic programme, and as the defence of democracy and the American way of life became increasingly important, the tone of the political essays inclined more and more to liberalism, and became less and less relevant to the other interests of the *Review*. By January 1941, *The Nation* considered it "rather piquant ... that both contributors and subjects often veer to the left".[61] By then the political section of the *Review* had been waning for some time and was soon to be discontinued altogether.

The Southern Review could be more self-assured than its predecessors in its rejection of the Marxist approach to literature. Literature was securely pigeonholed as an autonomous activity which did not need any social or political justification. In their insistence on art as propaganda, Cleanth Brooks wrote in the third issue of the magazine, the "Marxists have merely revived and restated the oldest and stubbornest heresy of criticism – the didactic theory", and some years later, Herbert J. Muller stated that Marxian literary criticism had "as yet offered little but five-

[58] Parkes, "Some Marxist Fallacies", *SoR*, IV, 3 (Winter 1939), 476; Wecter, "Planned Economies of Truth", *SoR*, IV, 3 (Winter 1939), 493.
[59] "What is Living and What is Dead in Marxism", *SoR*, VI, 2 (Autumn 1940), 293, 294.
[60] "An Economic Basis for Liberal Values", *SoR*, VII, 1 (Summer 1941), 22.
[61] *Nation*, CLII, 1 (January 4, 1941), 22.

finger exercises in dialectical materialism".[62] In much the same way as Sidney Hook tried to give a final estimate of the durable virtues of Marxism as a political ideology, Philip Rahv, in the Winter 1939 issue, performed a "political autopsy" on proletarian literature. Rahv, an editor of *Partisan Review*, which had publicly broken its allegiance to the Communist Party two years earlier without relinquishing its Marxist bias, emphasized that it was impossible to understand the development of proletarian literature, "its rise and fall", without understanding its relation to the Party. In the early 'Thirties, according to Rahv, there had been plausible enough reasons for assuming that the left-wing in American literature would triumph. Its defeat within a decade was due to a confusion of party and class. Whatever "elaborate and often weirdly sectarian theories" the individual members might claim, the programme of the Marxist movement was quite simple and "so broad in its appeal as to attract hundreds of writers in all countries". Rahv reduced this programme to the following formula: *"the writer should ally himself with the working class and recognize the class struggle as the central fact of modern life."* Alliance with the working class, however, meant in fact surrendering one's independence to the Communist Party. A work of literature was acceptable and praiseworthy only if its political ideas corresponded to those of the Party. "Within the brief space of a few years the term 'proletarian literature' was transformed into a euphemism for a Communist Party literature which tenaciously upheld a fanatical faith identifying the party with the working class, Stalinism with Marxism, and the Soviet Union with socialism." [63]

There was one critic whose intelligent, idiosyncratic use of Marxist criteria drew reluctant praise from a number of contributors: Kenneth Burke. Burke as a critic ranked high in the opinion of the editors. On 2 August 1938, Cleanth Brooks wrote to William Empson: "We have published rather frequently the

---

[62]   Brooks, "Three Revolutions in Poetry", *SoR*, I, 3 (Winter 1936), 572; Muller, "Pathways in Recent Criticism", *SoR*, IV, 1 (Summer 1938), 197.
[63]   "Proletarian Literature: A Political Autopsy", *SoR*, IV, 3 (Winter 1939), 616, 618, 620.

critics in this country whom we think the best – Kenneth Burke, R. P. Blackmur, Allen Tate, Delmore Schwartz, etc." [64] Burke's critical position was first, and most severely, questioned by Allen Tate *à propos* of Burke's essay "Symbolic War", a discussion in the Summer 1936 issue of an anthology of *Proletarian Literature in the United States*. In the following number Tate commented on "Mr. Burke and the Historical Environment." He began by emphasizing his admiration for Burke's critical talent: "Mr. Burke alone of the extreme left-wing critics seems to me to possess the historical and philosophical learning necessary to the serious treatment of the literary problems of Marxism." But Burke was hampered by Marxism all the same; although he was embarrassed by the propagandistic excesses of other Marxian critics, he only issued to them "an appeal for moderation; he asks them *not to go too far*". But what was, according to Tate, more urgently needed was "some fundamental aesthetic thinking", for the artist, under Burke's theory, was cut off from "the exercise of the critical intellect". Burke had stated that the novelist or poet must be preoccupied, directly or indirectly, with the historical environment, but this theory, Tate wrote, was a relapse into the "standard eighteenth-century belief in the inherent dignity of the subject".[65] Burke elaborated his position in the following issue (Winter 1937) with his essay "Acceptance and Rejection" in which he maintained that the didactic which "today is usually called propaganda" really ought to *coach* the imagination "in obedience to critical postulates". In so far as that was impossible "the attempt to coerce the imagination leads to the problems of 'will' that are bothering such contemporary critics as Allen Tate".[66]

II

The Southern Review was primarily and increasingly a literary magazine although the extra-literary interests often contributed

[64] *Southern Review* papers.
[65] "Mr. Burke and the Historical Environment", *SoR*, II, 2 (Autumn 1936), 363, 368, 369.
[66] *SoR*, II, 3 (Winter 1937), 621, 625-626.

to the integration of its contents. We have noted earlier that the trend of the different contributions was against "positivism" and that the more specific antithesis of the literary discussions was the opposition of poetry to science. Cleanth Brooks, for instance, argued for an absolute division of the two. In a discussion of Yeats's *A Vision* he maintained that the scientific method is valid and relevant when it is applied to subjects which demand a scientific approach, but that "there is nothing 'escapist' about a hostility to science which orders science off the premises as a trespasser when science has taken up a position where it has no business to be".[67] It is not surprising that the use of the word science in the *Review* was sometimes more emotive than precise. Some contributors failed to make an adequate distinction between science and technology and often used the word science to elicit a mere stock response. But it is characteristic of *The Southern Review* that this simplistic usage could be criticized in its own pages. The most consequential attack on the narrow conception of science among a number of regular contributors was Herbert J. Muller's discussion of "Humanism in the World of Einstein". Muller described the effect of Einstein's relativism on Newton's absolutes in contemporary terms as "the overthrow of the totalitarian state in the world of thought, and the establishment of a democracy in which all hypotheses are freely elected". He summarized this revolution as "the triumph of the postulate over the axiom", and stated that it was an antiquated seventeenth-century notion to look upon science as organized common sense.[68] In later issues, the radical opposition of poetry and science would occasionally lead to somewhat extravagant claims for the unique knowledge which poetry provides, but this notion also was to be challenged in *The Southern Review* itself.

[67] "The Vision of W. B. Yeats", *SoR*, IV, 1 (Summer 1938), 116.
[68] *SoR*, V, 1 (Summer 1939), 122, 123. Soon after the publication of this article, Muller was awarded a Guggenheim Fellowship "in order to write a book on the principles of criticism in the light of the philosophy of modern science" ("Notes on Contributors", *KR*, II, 3 [Summer 1940]). See also Muller's "The New Criticism in Poetry", *SoR*, VI, 4 (Spring 1941), 811-839, and his book written as a Guggenheim Fellow, *Science and Criticism: The Humanistic Tradition in Contemporary Thought* (New Haven, Conn., 1943).

The wider campaign against the pervasive influence of science and technology, and the attitudes which they inspired, culminated in the Spring issue of 1941 in a symposium on the discussion of American culture which had been conducted by the American Philosophical Society at its meeting in Philadelphia in April 1940. The editors agreed that the papers published in the *Proceedings* of the society were "interesting enough to provide a jumping off for a little symposium of our own". The discussions at Philadelphia had dealt with characteristics of American culture and its place in general culture. "I shan't undertake to review in this note the various papers", Cleanth Brooks wrote to Mortimer Adler, "but two or three of them seem to be pretty far in error in their statements and in their underlying assumptions. I think that these errors are so widely held that they deserved the right sort of attack." [69] The editors solicited contributions to their symposium from Mortimer Adler, Howard Roelofs, Allen Tate, Donald Davidson, and Kenneth Burke. Adler, who was invited to contribute to the magazine on a number of occasions, could not make the deadline; his place was taken by R. P. Blackmur. Although Allen Tate did not contribute to the symposium proper, his article "Literature as Knowledge: Comment and Comparison" preceded the symposium as the leading article of the Spring 1941 issue, and was the most elaborate exposition of the literature as knowledge theory to appear in *The Southern Review*. John Crowe Ransom was impressed by the high intellectual level of the symposium. "Have been reading intensively and intensely in the new number of So. Review", he wrote to Tate on April 14, 1941; "It is certainly a headache of dialectic; the most ambitious number I've seen yet; an astonishing piece of independence in a literary journal. Nearly everything in it revolves around our science-poetry issue." [70] A short examination of the number will give us an insight into several characteristic preoccupations of the magazine.

The four contributors to the symposium had in common that they were more pessimistic about the state of American culture and the uses of science and technology than the participants of the original discussion. Especially the optimism of Frederick Lewis Allen was severely criticized. His analysis, according to Davidson, broke "all records, surely, for impudent complacency",[71] and Roelofs detected in it the voice of the promotor of the popularization of culture. Blackmur pointed to the dangers of this popularization. As Allen was avowedly "bent on selling American art and letters in quantity" rather than with regard to quality or significance, and as the American public had not been educated to intelligent discrimination, it was necessarily "only the popularizeable aspect of the art" which was "actually sold and consumed".[72] Both Blackmur and Roelofs noticed that religion had been conspicuously absent from the discussion of the Philosophical Society. Blackmur contended that the future would have to do without religion because there was no access to a supernatural order, but he warned against the sole use of reason excluding the imagination: "a frankly provisional, avowedly conventional imagination is the only superrational authority we can muster" (VI, 664). Roelofs felt that religion had been left out of the discussion because the favourite adjectives of the participants, "thrilling" and "exciting", could not very well have been applied to religion. But he thought that if science was going to take the place of religion, as one of the participants had implied, a change of such magnitude would have merited "explicit consideration".[73] Kenneth Burke was puzzled because practically no one had discussed American culture "as a *business* culture, with its major trends directed by business motivations".[74] Both Davidson and Roelofs maintained that the discussion had been conducted by experts who had spoken about their specialities and who had hardly reached the general problem.

We have said earlier that the symposium was preceded by Allen Tate's "Literature as Knowledge: Comment and Comparison". In order to be able to appreciate the argument and the significance of this article it will be necessary to examine the approach to

---

[71] "Mr. Babbitt at Philadelphia", *SoR*, VI, 4 (Spring 1941), 697.
[72] "Chaos is Come Again", 661.
[73] "Thrill as a Standard", 706, 707.
[74] "Character of Our Culture", 676.

literature as it gradually took shape in the pages of *The Southern Review*. This approach was conditioned by two considerations. Firstly, the growing prestige of science led the hard core of the *Review*'s contributors to emphasize the uniqueness of literature, its complexity, and the special kind of „knowledge" it provided. Secondly, as more and more contributors found a living in the university, they became increasingly interested in the practice and the possibilities of teaching literature; here again, their primary aim was to defend literature as a self-justifying activity and the proper object of the literary critic. As, in the words of John Crowe Ransom, poetry "distinguishes itself by an act of the will from prose",[75] it could be expected to supply in a more concentrated fashion the kind of knowledge the contributors were seeking. Prose as such was not neglected, but essays which dealt with literary theory tended to draw their illustrations from poetry.

The most important critic to set the tone of the discussion of poetry in the early issues of the *Review* was Cleanth Brooks in a series of three essays under the general title "Three Revolutions in Poetry". These essays were strongly indebted to the criticism of T. S. Eliot and I. A. Richards. They presented an eminently clear if somewhat schematic synthesis of the literary revaluation which had been accomplished during the preceding decades. They were important for certain emphases; their publication in the first three issues of the magazine had a crucial influence on the formulation of its literary attitudes.

Brooks took certain characteristics of modern poetry, such as its complexity, its tension, its use of irony and paradox, its "employment of bizarre and undignified figures of speech", as touchstones for the evaluation of the poetry of the past. The metaphysical poets of the seventeenth century came closest to the modern ideal, so close that "an appreciation of our own radicals demands an ability to enjoy the metaphysicals". In the later seventeenth century the concept of poetry was overtaken by a "*simplification*". The romantic poets reacted against this simplification – the belief that subject-matter is inherently poetic or unpoetic, the belief in an appropriate poetic diction and the belief that

[75]   "The Tense of Poetry", *SoR*, I, 2 (Autumn 1935), 223.

the use of intellect in poetry is antithetical to the expression of emotion – but their reaction was not fundamental enough. Brooks's emphasis on the "metaphysical" aspects of good poetry led to far-reaching conclusions as the following quotation will show:

If metaphysical poetry is, as this essay maintains, 'the balance or reconciliation of opposite or discordant qualities' and the product of the synthetic imagination, and if it is true that the scientific spirit is antithetical to it, then the history of English literature will have to be rewritten. Obviously; for a change in the definition of poetry involves far more than an influence on the poets writing what happens to be at the time modern poetry. It has repercussions on all the poetry which has ever been written, since all poetry is ultimately to be measured against it. Our revaluation of metaphysical poetry is directly related, therefore, to a body of criticism.[76]

There is a radical quality about this statement which goes beyond the "rediscovery" of metaphysical poetry which had been going on for the past fifteen years. We detect this same quality in the criticism of John Crowe Ransom. In his essay "The Tense of Poetry", which appeared in the second number, Ransom supported Brooks's offensive in favour of the metaphysicals: "The poetry which makes the manliest effort to be contemporary, and to retreat as little as possible upon the road that has been travelled, is like that of the so-called metaphysical school of the Seventeenth Century. It is being tried today by poets who are the real outposts of the poetic movement" (I, 234). In the spring of 1937 Ransom confidently announced that the present age was "the age which has recovered the admirable John Donne; that is the way to identify its literary taste".[77]

But a too rigid identification of good poetry with "metaphysical" poetry might easily lead to questionable statements. Ransom's criticism provides an example: "I am led to the proposition that a little privacy, a little obscurity, is a grateful sign of authenticity in a poetry; and, conversely, that a poetry that is too easy will hardly do any longer, even if it is Shakespeare's poetry." [78] Ransom's

[76] "Three Revolutions in Poetry", *SoR*, I, 1 (Summer 1935), 151, 163; *SoR*, I, 2 (Autumn 1935), 332; *SoR*, I, 3 (Winter 1936), 576.
[77] "The Poet as Woman", *SoR*, II, 4 (Spring 1937), 784.
[78] "The Making of a Modern: the Poetry of George Marion O'Donnell", *SoR*, I, 4 (Spring 1936), 866. The dangers of "a little obscurity" had

evaluation of Shakespeare's sonnets became indeed an embarrassment to the magazine. When, in the autumn of 1937, he submitted
his essay "Shakespeare at Sonnets", the editors felt, "sad to relate,
that certain objections in the present form should be taken care
of" before they could publish it.[79] Both editors had read the essay
carefully and repeatedly and had singled out six points about
which they disagreed with Ransom; their criticisms covered four
closely typed pages. Ransom revised the article and it appeared in
the Winter 1938 issue, but the editors were far from happy about
it. "There is nothing to do but publish", Brooks wrote to Tate;
although he felt that it was "certainly publishable", he also
realized that it would probably rather harm than enhance Ransom's reputation.[80] Ransom felt that Shakespeare was so much of
an institution that "throwing a few stones at him" would do no
harm. He began his essay with some remarks about the lack of
correspondence between the metrical pattern and the logical pattern in a number of sonnets, and went on to say that although

---

dawned on Ransom when he wrote as editor of *The Kenyon Review* five
years later: "The gifted younger poets of our time are inclined to try to
make their brilliance the more wonderful by going in for a handsome
obscurity, by creating arbitrary difficulties in their text. They know, as a
generation of critics have now substantially shown, that obscurity, the
delayed communication, the teasing revelation, is a standard poetic device,
much employed for example in that famous 17th Century. They overdo
this effect . . ." ("Editorial", *KR*, III, 4 [Autumn 1941], 492-493).
[79] Letter, Brooks to Ransom, October 29, 1937, *Southern Review* papers.
R. P. Blackmur gave the following explanation of Ransom's criticism of
the *Sonnets*: "It is interesting to see that when he tackles Shakespeare's
Sonnets and Milton's 'Lycidas', the sonnets largely disappear because he
has not the means in *his* structure and texture to get at what Shakespeare's
structure and texture were *of*, while on the other hand 'Lycidas' comes
out, after a vast amount of argument, rather well" ("San Giovanni in
Venere: Allen Tate as Man of Letters", *SR*, LXVII, 4 [Oct.-Dec. 1959],
615. For a similar statement by Blackmur, see his *New Criticism in the
United States* [Tokyo, 1959], p. 14).
[80] [Autumn 1937], Tate papers. In a footnote to his article "Tension in
Poetry" (1938), Tate remarked: "Ransom's rejection of Shakespeare's sonnets seems to be a result of deductive necessity in his premises, or of the
courage of mere logic; but the essay contains valuable insights into the
operation of the metaphysical 'conceit' " (in *Collected Essays* [Denver,
1959], p. 79).

Shakespeare had not "ordinarily been credited with being one of the metaphysicals", many sonnets were "early examples of that style". He then professed surprise at the fact that he could find "no evidence anywhere that Shakespeare's imagination is equal to the peculiar and systematic exercises which Donne imposed habitually upon his." Ransom blamed this disability on the fact that "Shakespeare had no university discipline, and developed poetically along lines of least resistance." [81]

It was to be expected that such statements would not go unchallenged. Arthur Mizener replied, first in a side remark in a very laudatory review of Ransom's book of critical essays, *The World's Body*, and later, in the Spring 1940 issue, in an essay on "The Structure of Figurative Language in Shakespeare's Sonnets". Mizener argued that it was Ransom's strategy "to set Shakespeare up as a metaphysical poet and then to assail his metaphysical weaknesses", but that Shakespeare's method was "fundamentally different from the metaphysical method".[82] The editors were very pleased with Mizener's contribution; Brooks wrote to Tate that it was "excellent".[83] Their reception of the essay showed clearly that they shared *The Symposium*'s interest in Shakespearean criticism: "We are considering the preparation of an issue of THE SOUTHERN REVIEW devoted to essays on Shakespeare. We had, before your present essay came in, already decided to ask you to contribute to that issue. But this piece seems almost pat to the purpose." [84]

---

[81] "Shakespeare at Sonnets", *SoR*, III, 3 (Winter 1938), 531, 541.

[82] *SoR*, V, 4 (Spring 1940), 730, 732. Another regular contributor who disagreed with Ransom was Randall Jarrell: "Ransom and Jarrell had each separately spent the preceding summer studying Shakespeare's *Sonnets*, and had emerged with unorthodox and widely differing theories. Roughly, Ransom thought that Shakespeare was continually going off the rails into illogical incoherence. Jarrell believed that no one, not even William Empson, had done justice to the rich, significant ambiguity of Shakespeare's intelligence and images. I can see and hear Ransom and Jarrell now, seated on one sofa, as though on one love-seat, the sacred texts open on their laps, one fifty, the other just out of college, and each expounding to the other's deaf ears his own inspired and irreconcilable interpretation" (Robert Lowell, "Randall Jarrell, 1914-1965", *The New York Review of Books*, V, 8 [November 25, 1965], 3).

[83] January 1940, Tate papers.

[84] Editor to Mizener, January 17, 1939, *Southern Review* papers.

The editors hoped to have the Shakespeare issue ready for the winter of 1940, but nothing came of it and Mizener's article was published by itself in the following spring.

In *The Southern Review* criticism and critics became subjects of frequent debate. "Our knowledge is better than our performance", Allen Tate wrote in the second issue.[85] There was indeed a general feeling that the times produced a more distinguished criticism than poetry or fiction. This criticism became known as the "new criticism" during the lifetime of *The Southern Review*; the name became generally accepted after the publication of John Crowe Ransom's book *The New Criticism* (1941) although it had been used before. The history of *The Southern Review* may be viewed to some extent as a series of strategic moves in the cause of the new critical theory but especially in the cause of the new critical methodology. Whereas the new critical methodology was mainly directed at the practice of the scholars in the universities, the new critical theory was primarily developed to counteract the increasing prestige of science. The *Review*'s most important and most combative theorist was Allen Tate. His best essay, "Tension in Poetry", appeared in the Summer of 1938, but in subsequent articles his zeal too often betrayed him to rather extravagant claims for poetry. His interest in the cultural environment of the poet, which had been so prominent in the early 1930's, had waned, and in accordance with the new critical orthodoxy he now kept his attention focussed on the words on the page. "For good verse can bear the closest, literal examination of every phrase, and is its own safeguard against our jeers and irony." This remark is taken from "Tension in Poetry", which was essentially a defence of and plea for the recognition of complexity in poetry; in a well-known statement, Tate found the meaning of poetry in "its 'tension', the full organized body of all the extension and intension that we can find in it".[86]

In the autumn of 1940, *The Southern Review* published Tate's "The Present Function of Criticism", a very pessimistic, in places vitriolic, essay in defence of "the high forms of literature [which]

---

[85] "A Note on Bishop's Poetry", *SoR*, I, 2 (Autumn 1935), 358.
[86] *SoR*, IV, 1 (Summer 1938), 104.

offer us the only complete, and thus the most responsible, versions of our experience". This essay was a contribution to the symposium "Literature and the Professors", the *Review*'s most ambitious attempt to confront the teachers of literature in the universities with the new criticism. This symposium had been inspired by Tate himself who had "ignited a bomb when he read his paper, 'Miss Emily and the Bibliographer' before the English Club at Princeton in the spring of 1940".[87] Tate's essay was subsequently published in *The American Scholar*. Its title referred to an elaborate metaphor comparing the situation of the Miss Emily of Faulkner's story "A Rose for Emily" to that of the scholars. Both had bodies to hide and both their life stories were tales of horror; "I submit", Tate wrote, "that the greater horror, for me, is the scholar's insincerity. .... It is better to pretend with Miss Emily that something dead is living than to pretend with the bibliographer that something living is dead." Tate's argument was in close agreement with the principles of the *Southern* as well as the *Kenyon* reviews. He maintained, for instance, that "the formal qualities of a poem are the focus of the specifically critical judgment because they partake of an objectivity that the subject matter, abstracted from the form, wholly lacks", and he described the historical method as an approach to literature as "an imitation of scientific method." The past should always be approached through "the formed, objective experience of our own time. ... The scholar who tells us that he understands Dryden but makes nothing of Hopkins or Yeats is telling us that he does not understand Dryden. ... If we wait for history to judge there will be no judgment; for if we are not history then history is nobody. He is nobody when he has become the historical method." [88]

Tate's essay was enthusiastically received by John Crowe Ransom who published a summary of it in *The Kenyon Review* and invited comments. In fact, he received so many comments that he suggested a simultaneous symposium on the subject in *The*

[87]   John L. Stewart, *The Burden of Time: The Fugitives and Agrarians* (Princeton, 1965), p. 192.
[88]   "Miss Emily and the Bibliographer", *The American Scholar*, IX, 1 (Winter 1940), 450, 456, 457, 459, 460.

Kenyon Review and in *The Southern Review*. Brooks thought it a "splendid" scheme, but he suggested the following alternative: "we might get four or six people lined up to do a Symposium, and allocate two or three of the articles to THE SOUTHERN and two or three to THE KENYON. . . . This plan would actually get more writers enlisted – four to six instead of three – and might get heavier gunfire on the subject than the first plan." [89] Ransom then suggested that they get "two students from important places, graduate students if we can't get the right undergraduates"; the editors liked the idea although they feared that they might be asking some student "to jeopardize his career by asking him to put himself on record".[90] The following critics were asked to contribute: Allen Tate, Arthur Mizener, Joe Horrell (a L.S.U. graduate student), Willard Thorp, Morton Zabel, I. A. Richards, Harry Levin, and Lionel Trilling. Ransom and Brooks would send a contribution each to the other's review.

The Summer 1940 issue announced that six writers would be represented in "an interrelated discussion of the topic, 'English Professors and the Criticism of Literature'". The symposium appeared in the Autumn number and was introduced by a short explanatory note. "The lag between modern criticism and the current methods of teaching literature in most colleges and universities has from time to time occasioned comment." But such comments had rarely been systematic. "In the light of this situation, the editors of *The Kenyon Review* and *The Southern Review* have felt that a useful service might be rendered by providing a forum for an extended discussion of the question." [91] The discussion in *The Southern Review* opened with Ransom's "Strategy for English Studies". Ransom paid due homage to the older generation of literary scholars but he pointed out that they had done their work so thoroughly that there was hardly anything left for their successors. Also, now that most of the principal findings of

---

[89]   Letter to Ransom, April 13, 1940, *Southern Review* papers.
[90]   Ransom to Brooks (April 19, 1940) and Brooks to Ransom (April 24, 1940), *Southern Review* papers.
[91]   "Literature and the Professors: A Symposium" (editorial), *SoR*, VI, 2 (Autumn 1940), 225.

the scholars were readily accessible in handbooks, the existing "professor-and-student relation ... has become an anachronism, or a survival that is more nominal than functional". The professor who really wished to do worthwhile work would have to turn to a critical rather than historical study of literature (VI, 227). Both Joe Horrell and Wright Thomas felt that students were taught a great number of things except to read a poem critically.[92] Harry Levin's "Pseudodoxia Academica", the last contribution to the symposium, was harder on the literary scholars than Ransom had been, although it did not dismiss them altogether: "Literary scholars, in particular, have been performing prodigies of evasion all in the day's work. They, by rights, are the custodians of the collective experience of humanity. Yet, in their hands, 'the best that is known and thought in the world' smells of the stacks. It is no longer experience, it is merely memory" (VI, 265).

The symposium was a strategic move towards the recognition of the new criticism in the universities. Ransom, in particular, was alive to the possibilities it presented. He proposed to "circularize the whole membership of M.L.A. with the matter, with an idea not only to the circulation of the periodicals but to some uproar at the next-Christmas meeting of the scholars in Boston; the rift has been steadily widening right in that body".[93] We have indeed come a long way since the time of *The Dial*. By 1940, both the *Kenyon* and the *Southern* reviews were frankly addressing an academic audience rather than the legendary "common reader". "We are a soberer and more concentrated Dial", Ransom wrote to Tate at the time when he was preparing the first issue of *The Kenyon Review*.[94] Its sobriety, solidity and efficiency were very much part of the literary academicism of the 1940's, but the little magazine spirit, the excitement of being with the *avant-garde* which *The Dial* had exhibited to a limited extent, had been lost almost entirely. The same may be said of *The Southern Review*. There is much truth in William Barrett's statement written twenty years ago that

---

[92] Horrell, "The Graduate Approach", *SoR*, VI, 2 (Autumn 1940), 247-254; Thomas, "The Professors and Literature: Clinical Evidence", 255-262.
[93] Letter to Tate, April 19, 1940, Tate papers.
[94] May 28, 1938, Tate papers.

"The Southern Review was rapidly becoming a review written by English teachers for English teachers." [95] But then, so many writers were finding jobs in the English departments of the universities. It must also be observed that *The Southern Review* was representative of the literary trends most alive in its own time and that those trends were critical rather than creative. A new *Dial* on the old model would have been an anachronism in the time of *The Southern Review.*

The symposium about literature and the professors in the Autumn 1940 issue was of course not the last word on the teaching of literature in the universities, nor on the theories and methods of the new criticism. Leo Spitzer, for instance, found himself "so fullheartedly in agreement" with the symposium that he could not forbear to set down his experience "in more than twenty-five years of teaching in the Romance field, and to give actual examples which bear out your statements". [96] His essay "History of Ideas versus Reading of Poetry" appeared in the following issue (Winter 1941). It did not aim at depreciating the value of history, and particularly not history of ideas, but it attempted "to delimit the position which history should assume and the *dosis* and *timing* with which it should be administered in our teaching of literature". [97] The reading of poetry was autonomous just as history was autonomous. The last contribution to the discussion was also the best balanced and in many ways the most interesting. It was Robert Heilman's "Footnotes on Literary History" in the Spring 1941 number. Heilman agreed that there was no denying the bad teaching of literature and certain extravagances of the historical approach, but he believed that they had been sufficiently exposed in the symposium. He regretted the loose use of the terms history and historical study and emphasized that "history is critical; it can hardly be indicted for the laborious absurdities of library-dusting and cranny-probing". History was not only a valuable education to critical awareness, it also proved, in

[95]   "The Resistance", *PR*, XIII, 4 (Sept.-Oct. 1946), 486.
[96]   Letter to the editors, quoted in "Notes on Contributors", *SoR*, VI, 3 (Winter 1941).
[97]   *SoR*, VI, 3 (Winter 1941), 601-602.

practice, an indispensable part of the curriculum of literary studies. As teachers of literature had to deal with "unselected undergraduates in whose minds the past is in unbelievably gross disorder", they could not "easily toss off their responsibility for trying to introduce some order into that monstrous chaos. Otherwise, 'tradition' is nonsense and criticism remains pleasantly academic".[98]

The symposium on the teaching of literature and the subsequent discussion illustrate the *Review*'s lively interest in problems of education. This interest dated back to the first issue, to Aldous Huxley's "Literature and Examinations", which attacked the "feats of mere industry for industry's sake", and "an examination system that encourages the candidate for a degree to adorn his non-literary and non-artistic knowledge of literature and art with a veneer of 'appreciative' cant".[99] The most interesting contribution to the discussion of education prior to the symposium was L. C. Knights's "University Teaching of English and History: A Plea for Correlation" in the Winter 1940 issue. The title itself indicates how well this essay was attuned to the educational trend of the *Review*. Knights, however, had doubted whether the editors would be interested in it: "Very possibly you will feel that the background and implications are too 'English', without sufficient bearing on the practical problems of American universities." He indicated that Eliot would have taken it if *The Criterion* had not been closing down and that he could not publish it in *Scrutiny* "since I draw to some extent on papers of mine that have already appeared in *Scrutiny*".[100] Indeed the *Review*'s interest in education was one of the features that made it more like the English *Scrutiny* than like any contemporary American quarterly save *The Kenyon Review*. The editors pursued their interest in education also outside of the pages of their magazine; the Brooks and Warren of the literary textbooks, a number of which were first published during the years of *The Southern Review*, have been known to a generation of students

---

[98]   *SoR*, VI, 4 (Spring 1941), 763, 765. For another relevant comment on the symposium, see Yvor Winters, *In Defense of Reason* (Denver, 1947), pp. 564-568.
[99]   *SoR*, I, 1 (Summer 1935), 103.
[100]   Knights to Brooks, January 25, 1939, *Southern Review* papers.

who have never heard of *The Southern Review*. John L. Stewart has recently written that the collaborations of Brooks and Warren, in such textbooks as *An Approach to Literature* and *Understanding Poetry*, were to have "much more lasting importance" than the *Review*,[101] but it is also true that tracing the emergence of certain critical attitudes in *The Southern Review* is incomparably more interesting and fruitful than going through the cut and dried literary exercises in the textbooks, however useful they may be for the classroom.

The teaching of literature symposium, then, had been a concentrated discussion of one of the essential preoccupations of the magazine. It had called forth some additional comments concerning the practical problems of the teaching of literature, but it also stimulated a more vehement debate about the character of literature and of criticism. This debate was set off by Allen Tate's contribution to the teaching of literature symposium, "The Present Function of Criticism". It was in this essay that Tate first made an unequivocal claim for the "knowledge" which literature provides. "The scholars", Tate wrote, "have not maintained the tradition of literature as a form of knowledge; by looking at it as merely one among many forms of social and political expression, they will have no defence against the censors of the power state, or the hidden censors of the pressure group". [102]

Tate's essay was the most outspoken contribution to the symposium, and it is not surprising that it was the specific subject of two letters from irate readers. Nor is it surprising that one correspondent, Sidney Hook, matched Tate's irritability and violence of statement. Under the title "The Late Mr. Tate", Hook accused Tate of having the "bad manners of all belated reactionaries." By bad manners he did not mean "merely arrogance but intellectual bad manners — gross distortion and misstatement, evasion of fundamental issues, and blithe fabrication of facts wherever it seems convenient for his purposes". Tate had stated that the tradition of free ideas was as dead in the United States as in Nazi

---

[101] *The Burden of Time*, p. 453.
[102] *SoR*, VI, 2 (Autumn 1940), 240.

Germany, but Hook pointed out that the fact that there still existed a magazine in the United States in which Tate could make such a statement was "sufficient evidence of its falsity, and of its irresponsibility". Hook had less fear of the effect of positivism on the tradition of free ideas than of "the intellectual manners of Tate in discussing positivism".[103] The second communication was from David Daiches who had been attacked in Tate's article. Its language was much milder. Daiches countered Tate's charge that he was substituting history for evaluation by asserting that he was "merely trying to show that some historical understanding is necessary before the critic can be perfectly sure of seeing his data with sufficient clarity – of seeing them as literary data and not as any other kind". As men had written certain things under certain circumstances, moved by certain emotions, urged by certain purposes, he did not see what "in heaven's name is lost by admitting this".[104]

Tate's essay, however, had ended inconclusively. "Literature is the complete knowledge of man's experience", Tate had written. "By knowledge I mean that unique and formed intelligence of the world, of which man alone is capable. ... But", he had added, "that will have to be discussed at another time" (VI, 246). Tate elaborated his position in the Spring 1941 issue – which also contained the letters from Hook and Daiches – in the leading essay entitled "Literature as Knowledge: Comment and Comparison." The editors, in their "Notes on Contributors" of that issue, suggested that readers might be interested in comparing Hook's and Daiches's communications "not only with Mr. Tate's symposium essay, but also with the general position taken in his extended discussion of the relation of literature to 'knowledge' in the current issue". Ransom, who had seen Hook's letter before it was published, had urged Warren not to print it, but the latter "felt that he ought to ... though he resented it". "I imagine", Ransom wrote to Tate, "the boys thought that you could stand it, especially when they

[103] "Communications: The Late Mr. Tate", *SoR*, VI, 4 (Spring 1941), 841-843.
[104] "Communications: Notes for a Reply to Mr. Tate", *SoR*, VI, 4 (Spring 1941), 844-845.

could devote their lead space to a new essay of yours elaborating your same position".[105]

Tate's second essay was a milder, less aggressive and more philosophic version of the first. Although it did not show essential changes, it was a much more acceptable intellectual statement. The strident dogmatism of the first version had largely evaporated. The final sentence is representative: "However we may see the completeness of poetry, it is a problem less to be solved than, in its full import, to be preserved." [106] Tate's arguments in these two essays, together with Ransom's rather similar though less extreme remarks on the subject in *The New Criticism*, were the subject of an article by Francis X. Roellinger in the final issue of *The Southern Review*. Roellinger sympathized with Tate's and Ransom's concern about the growing influence of positivism, but he felt that in their reaction against the positivists they had exaggerated an opposite point of view. However healthy an effect this reaction might have after I. A. Richards's early description of poetry "as a kind of mental and emotional therapeutic", the probability was that we should eventually be "forced to find some other alternative".[107] Roellinger's article was the last discussion of the literature as knowledge theory in *The Southern Review*. One critic of Tate has observed that after its publication, "the terms 'cognitive' and 'complete knowledge' virtually disappear from Tate's vocabulary. This article on poetic theory seemed to have influenced him in his change in attitude." [108]

It is often said that the new critics were better practitioners than theorists. Indeed, the main critical achievement of *The Southern Review*, as of its predecessors, lies in the large numbers

---

[105]   April 14, 1941, Tate papers.
[106]   "Literature as Knowledge: Comment and Comparison", *SoR*, VI, 4 (Spring 1941), 657. This last sentence also illustrates, of course, the inconclusiveness of the argument. Quoting it, R. K. Meiners pointed out: "We have learned very little more than that we must steadfastly fix our attention on the poem itself, which offers 'full cognition' " (*The Last Alternatives: A Study of the Works of Allen Tate* [Denver, 1963], p. 70).
[107]   "Two Theories of Poetry as Knowledge", *SoR*, VII, 4 (Spring 1942), 691.
[108]   Willard B. Arnold, *The Social Ideas of Allen Tate* (Boston, 1955), p. 53.

of critical evaluations of particular authors and specific works. However, as the preceding discussion has shown, the practice of the new critics cannot be considered profitably without reference to their conception of literature. In *The Southern Review* itself, the achievement of the new criticism was critically reviewed by Herbert J. Muller in the Spring of 1941, in a long article entitled "The New Criticism in Poetry". Muller believed that it was time "for admirers of this group to mark the limits and dangers of their own practice. They are beginning to suffer from inbreeding and to become victims of their half-truth. They are tending toward a narrow aestheticism in which they not only distinguish but disparage the 'ulterior' bearings of literature, rule them out of literary criticism entirely. They bristle at mention of its intellectual, moral, or social values – values that literature plainly does have, and as plainly are important." Muller felt that Ransom, for instance, "now often sounds like an aesthete of the 'nineties". He was especially discontented with the criticism of Cleanth Brooks, whom he accused of considering only "technique, mechanism, outward show". He also objected to Brooks's "exclusiveness" which led him to disparage English poetry from the Restoration to modern times so that "even Coleridge, whom he admires, finally goes down because he is Coleridge and not Donne".[109]

The publication of Muller's adverse comments on the new criticism shows again a willingness on the part of the editors to publish occasional criticisms of their own ideas and attitudes, or of those which might be considered representative of their review. It is a tribute to the effectiveness of their editorial supervision that there could be little doubt as to which ideas and attitudes were to be considered representative. This was, indeed, the result of editorial planning and of essential agreement among the hard core of contributors whom the editors had gradually gathered, because there were very few occasions which prompted the editors to make a direct editorial statement. One such occasion was Howard Mumford Jones's evaluation, in *The Saturday Review,* of the achievement of literary criticism of the past twenty-five years.

---

[109]   *SoR*, VI, 4 (Spring 1941), 813, 822.

Jones had discovered two trends in that criticism, one political, the other aesthetic, but he had failed to find a treatment of literature as "an end in itself, not a means towards something else". This was, of course, what aesthetic or "new" criticism claimed to be doing and Jones's article could therefore serve as a convenient peg for a defence of the new criticism which Jones had found too "private". The editors availed themselves of this opportunity to write their first and only full-scale editorial which appeared in the Autumn 1941 issue. They detected a number of objectionable assumptions in Jones's article; for instance, the assumption that "reading *is* easy. That assumption rests in turn upon the further assumption that the 'meaning', the real content, of a piece of literature, as contrasted with the 'meaning' of scientific or other rigidly expository prose, can be abstracted in a paraphrase." In a later essay Brooks was to brand this assumption as "the heresy of paraphrase", because it condoned a separation of "meaning" and "form".[110] In their editorial the editors maintained that in "setting up the opposition between a concern with the 'mechanisms of literature' and a concern with its ethical and political relationships, Mr. Jones has, as it were, used the forensic trick of the false option: in the left hand he clutches 'form' and in the right he clutches 'content', and he has heeded the Biblical injunction not to let his right hand know what his left hand doeth." [111]

This editorial, Brooks wrote to Tate, had been a collaborative effort of Warren, Palmer and himself. "Incidentally, we are planning a long editorial on the subject of Van Wyck Brooks, MacLeish and company for the next number." [112] These critics took a nationalistic, utilitarian attitude towards literature which was antithetical not only to *The Southern Review* but also to its fellow quarterlies. They were most vigorously attacked in *Partisan Review* and, later on, in *The Sewanee Review*, and may be best discussed in connection with these magazines. The editorial in *The Southern Review* never appeared. It had been planned for the

---

[110]   *The Well Wrought Urn* (New York, 1947), pp. 192-214.
[111]   "Editorial", *SoR*, VII, 2 (Autumn 1941), iv, viii, xii.
[112]   December 20, 1941, *Southern Review* papers.

Spring 1942 issue which marked the last appearance of *The Southern Review*.

III

In the course of this chapter we have traced the more important ideas which run through *The Southern Review*, and we have noticed how most of these ideas gradually emerged from the discussions of a number of different critics. The editors were the relatively impartial moderators of the different debates and they tried to give to them, as indeed to the magazine as a whole, what the editors of *The Symposium* had called "symposial structure". The scope of *The Southern Review* was larger than that of *The Symposium* and the possibilities of symposial structure proportionally more numerous. We have described how the editors of *The Southern Review* organized symposia on subjects which they thought would be of particular interest to their readers, but their editorial discrimination is less spectacularly but pervasively felt throughout the issues of their magazine. A description of a few instances of this symposial structure will round out our image of the *Review*.

One of the most obvious means the editors availed themselves of to improve the unity of their magazine was to solicit contributions from critics whose own work they were reviewing. When, for instance, Herbert Agar reviewed Douglas Jerrold's *England* in the second issue, the third issue featured Jerrold's article "Whither Europe", and when in the Spring 1938 issue Kenneth Burke discussed "The Virtues and Limitations of Debunking", that same issue contained Henry Bamford Parkes's review of Burke's *Attitudes toward History*.[113] In the Autumn 1938 issue John Crowe Ransom's essay "Mr. Empson's Muddles" was published side by side with William Empson's "Sense in Measure for Measure." [114]

---

[113] Burke wrote a twenty-page answer to Parkes's review, dated March 16, 1938, *Southern Review* papers.

[114] Ransom told Tate that his Empson article furthered "a big argument I was having with Brooks orally during the summer" (October 1, 1938, Tate papers).

The editors had an additional means of making these connections the more explicit: their "Notes on Contributors", which *The Symposium* had dispensed with. In the second issue, for instance, the editors gave their lead space to William Yandell Elliott's discussion of Harold Laski's political position and also published a review article on Elliott's book *The Need for Constitutional Reform* by Norman Thomas. In their 'Notes on Contributors" in that issue they pointed out that "Thomas was as critical of Elliott's opinion of constitutional change as Elliott was of Laski's reflections on democracy in crisis." To give another example: when they published L. C. Knights's "Henry James and the Trapped Spectator" in the winter of 1939, they drew their readers' attention to F. O. Matthiessen's review of Knights's *Drama and Society in the Age of Jonson* in the preceding number. Or when in the Winter 1941 issue, James T. Farrell attacked Lewis Mumford's political ideas, the editors wrote in their "Notes on Contributors": "One aspect of Mr. Farrell's article, his critique of the conception of American culture and civilization, will be dealt with more generally in a series of articles to appear in the Spring issue of *The Southern Review*." They referred, of course, to the symposium on American culture.

Farrell's essay furnishes an interesting instance of yet another means of editorial planning. Because of its controversial nature the editors sent a copy of the proofs to Mumford to give him an opportunity to answer to Farrell's charges, and, at the request of Farrell himself, they also sent proofs to Charles Beard, John Dewey, and a number of newspaper editors. No reactions, however, were published; the correspondence section of the following issue was devoted to Sidney Hook's and David Daiches's disagreements with Tate's literary theories. The editorial procedure with respect to Farrell's essay was not unusual. The editors had, for instance, sent copies of O. W. Riegel's essay on Woodrow Wilson's Secretary of State, Robert Lansing, to the President, the Secretary of State, and to members of the Foreign Affairs Committee, and had in the following issue published their reactions, which, they believed, would "serve as valuable and interesting footnotes" to the article.[115] But the most successful editorial attempt to stir up a discussion concerned Frederick L. Schuman's article "Leon Trotsky: Martyr or Renegade?" which was published in the summer 1937 issue. This article was inspired by the Moscow trials and tended to take the official Russian documents at their face value. As these trials caused a great deal of controversy at the time, the editors decided to steer some of it to their magazine. "Because of the controversial nature of the subject, because of the definiteness of Mr. Schuman's point of view, and because of the fact that other people have drawn directly opposite conclusions from the same set of facts", the editors felt that certain persons should be given the opportunity of reading and commenting on the article before it was published.[116] Consequently, they sent proofs of it to five persons who were closely concerned with the controversy: Leon Trotsky, Max Eastman, Malcolm Cowley, John Dewey, and Carleton Beals. Dewey and Beals had been members of the committee set up "to inquire into Trotsky's guilt or innocence with regard to the charges that he has worked against the present government of Russia".[117] Trotsky himself did not react to the invitation to contribute, in contrast to the active part he had taken in the debate about his position in *The Symposium*. The others, however, did. Indeed, more than half of the letters that appeared in the *Review*'s correspondence section concerned the Trotsky controversy. The editors published the first five letters in the same issue which also contained Schuman's article; the fifth correspondent was James T. Farrell.

The quite divergent reactions to Schuman's article proved that the editors had sized up the situation very accurately. Cowley, for instance, thought that Schuman's article was "about the soundest of all written on the controversy that has spread so widely since the last Moscow trials"; Eastman, on the other hand, stated that Schuman was "such a greenhorn in matters both of fact and theory

[115] Riegel, "The Pattern of the Unneutral Diplomat: Robert Lansing and the World War", *SoR*, II, 1 (Summer 1936), 1-14; "Correspondence", *SoR*, II, 2 (Autumn 1936), 419.
[116] Editors to John Dewey, June 3, 1937, *Southern Review* papers.
[117] "Notes on Contributors", *SoR*, III, 1 (Summer 1937).

relative to the Russian revolution that I find it difficult to comment briefly upon his article".[118] The opinions of Beals and Farrell showed a similar opposition. Such violent disagreements were bound to call forth further debate. The participants did not believe, as Schuman himself had, that "no definitive and final judgment of Trotsky's recent rôle is at present possible." [119] In the following issue Sidney Hook directed a full-fledged article at Schuman's position. This number also contained a lively exchange of letters; indeed the Sidney Hook – Carleton Beals exchange became quite personal.[120]

The preceding pages have been concerned with the efforts of the editors towards the integration of the contents of their magazine. Their two most ambitious efforts were the special issues on Thomas Hardy and William Butler Yeats. The Winter 1940 number announced a "Thomas Hardy Centennial Issue, 1840-1940," in which Hardy's poetry and prose would be examined "from a variety of critical points of view". This issue was put out to celebrate the centenary of Hardy's birth and the completion of the fifth year of *The Southern Review*. It appeared in the summer of 1940 after a good deal of editorial organization. The editors told potential contributors quite clearly what they hoped the symposium would achieve: "Although the mere fact of devoting an issue to Hardy implies a belief in Hardy's importance, it does not imply that only eulogy is appropriate to the occasion; it is hoped, in fact, that the essays collected in this issue will do something toward making a precise definition of his status as an artist, his limitations as well as his achievements." [121] The editors invited

[118] "Correspondence", *SoR*, III, 1 (Summer 1937), 199-200. Dwight Macdonald accused Schuman of "actually endorsing the essentials of the prosecution's case and smearing Trotsky and the defendants" (*Memoirs of a Revolutionist* [New York, Meridian Books, 1958 (1957)], p. 10).

[119] "Leon Trotsky: Martyr or Renegade?", *SoR*, III, 1 (Summer 1937), 53.

[120] When the anti-Stalinist *Partisan Review*, a few years later, discussed Schuman's position it stated that "considered from any point of view", Schuman's Trotsky article marked "a new low in American scholarship. It was exposed and refuted point by point by Sidney Hook in the subsequent issue (Autumn) of the *Southern Review*" (Frank N. Trager, "F. L. Schuman: A Case History", *PR*, VII, 2 [March-April 1940], 148).

[121] Brooks to L. C. Knights, February 10, 1939, *Southern Review* papers.

a number of critics and writers to contribute to this revaluation, some of whom, such as T. S. Eliot, William Empson, Frederick Dupee, Philip Rahv, I. A. Richards, Louis MacNeice, Thomas Mann, and L. C. Knights had to decline for various reasons. The actual contributors to the issue were Ransom, Blackmur, Baker, Tate, Zabel, W. H. Auden, F. R. Leavis, Bonamy Dobrée, Delmore Schwartz, Katherine Anne Porter, Donald Davidson, Jacques Barzun, Arthur Mizener, and Herbert Muller.

The emphasis of the symposium was on Hardy's poetry rather than on his prose. Muller, for instance, felt that Hardy was not "in crying need of revaluation − at least as a novelist".[122] The critics of Hardy's poetry found it uneven and generally agreed that its accomplishment had been overestimated or at least too indiscriminately taken for granted. "After Thomas Hardy had become a great figure on the British model", Tate wrote, "− that is to say, a personage to whom one makes pilgrimages − criticism of his work languished ... nobody had very much to say, except that one admired him." [123] Although Ransom confessed that lapses in Hardy's poetry "have often seemed to endear the poet to me",[124] most participants of the symposium were searching for means of strict discrimination. As Blackmur wrote: "Both for those who enjoy the bulk of Thomas Hardy's poems and for those whose genuine enjoyment of a few poems is almost overcome by a combination of depression and dismay at the bulk, the great need is some sort of canon − a criterion more for exclusion than for judgment." [125] The element of taste, however, was not to be ruled out; although the general estimates of Hardy's poetry were pretty unanimous, the choice of individual instances was remarkably divergent. The essays of Leavis and Zabel provide a striking example. Leavis began by saying that he did not share "the generally accepted estimate of Hardy. I think, in fact, that it greatly overexalts him." He dismissed Hardy's novels and the bulk of the poetry and insisted that "any real claim he may have to

[122]   The Novels of Hardy Today", *SoR*, VI, 1 (Summer 1940), 215.
[123]   "Hardy's Philosophic Metaphors", 99.
[124]   "Honey and Gall", 14.
[125]   "The Shorter Poems of Thomas Hardy", 20.

major status rests upon half-a-dozen poems alone".[126] He then gave the titles of six poems. Zabel was also aware of flaws in Hardy's poetry and, less assertively than Leavis, chose the seven poems he liked best. None of Zabel's seven titles corresponded to Leavis's half-a-dozen.

Most contributors were in agreement about the pernicious effect of Hardy's "philosophy" on his poetry, about the fact that Hardy's ideas were too often superimposed on the poetry. "To his ideas as such, then", Blackmur wrote, "there is no primary objection. The objection is to his failure to absorb them by craft into the representative effect of his verse" (VI, 29). There was also a general feeling that Hardy's technique, particularly his handling of the language, was inadequate, which was partly made to explain his incapacity to integrate his ideas into his poetry. Leavis, for instance, wrote: "There is something extremely personal about the gauche unshrinking mismarriages – group-mismarriages – of his diction, in which, with naif aplomb, he takes as they come the romantic-poetical, the prosaic banal, the stilted literary, the colloquial, the archaistic, the erudite, the technical, the dialect word, the brand-new Hardy coinage" (VI, 88). Some contributors related this surface quality to the uncertainty of Hardy's intellectual position. Blackmur, for instance, thought that Hardy "dispensed with tradition in most of his ambitious verse", which resulted in a "substitution of the authoritarian for the authoritative, of violence for emotion, frenzy for passion, calamity by chance for tragedy by fate" (VI, 27-28), and Schwartz saw Hardy as a victim of the influence of science on the modern poet.

The interest in the uses of Hardy's "philosophy", his "system", was very prominent, and several critics compared it to Yeats's set of symbols. Baker thought that Yeats had succeeded where Hardy had failed: "W. B. Yeats has proved that what may even be a ludicrous system of belief can also be fruitful." [127] Blackmur was more sceptical about the uses of any such system of belief:

---

[126]   "Hardy the Poet", 92.
[127]   "Hardy's Poetic Certitude", 55.

Yeats was addicted to magic, to a private symbolism, in much the same way, and for similar reasons, that Hardy was addicted to his set of ideas. Each had been deprived by his education, or the lack of it, of an authoritative faith, and each hastened to set up a scaffold out of the nearest congenial materials strong enough and rigid enough to support the structure imagination meant to rear. It was, and remains, a desperate occupation for each; for the risk was that the scaffold might become so much more important than the poetry as to replace it, and the mere preliminary labor come to be the sum of the work done. (VI, 31-32)

Another poet who had used a "scaffold" was T. S. Eliot, and in an earlier article on "The Later Poetry of W. B. Yeats" (Autumn 1936), Blackmur had compared the relative achievement of Hardy, Yeats and Eliot and the relevance of their systems in an ultimate evaluation of their poetry. "If it happens", Blackmur had written, "that we discard more of Hardy than we do of Yeats and more of Yeats than we do of Eliot, it is not because Christianity provides better machinery for the movement of poetry than fatalism or magic, but simply because Eliot is a more cautious craftsman".[128]

Like its predecessors, *The Southern Review* admired Eliot's poetic achievement. Apart from numerous references in passing, it published a number of independent articles on Eliot from the pen of Mario Praz, Cleanth Brooks, C. L. Barber, James Johnson Sweeney, and Leonard Unger. Although Eliot's plays were, on the whole, considered failures, his poetry was held in high esteem. Sweeney described *East Coker* as his "most considerable poetic achievement since *The Waste Land*", but in the same issue, Andrew Wanning thought it inferior to *Burnt Norton*.[129] Eliot's preeminence, however, was not as unchallenged in the pages of *The Southern Review* as it had been in the earlier magazines. Already in the first issue, John Gould Fletcher had written that it was Yeats who was, "by universal consent, the most eminent poet

[128]   *SoR*, II, 2 (Autumn 1936), 340.
[129]   Sweeney, "East Coker: A Reading", *SoR*, VI, 4 (Spring 1941), 771; Wanning, "Criticism and Principles: Poetry of the Quarter", *SoR*, VI, 4 (Spring 1941), 797.

now writing in the English language".[130] The consent was not as universal as Fletcher made it out to be, but it was certainly shared by a number of contributors. To Randall Jarrell, for instance, Yeats's poetry seemed "far and away the best of our time", and even Blackmur was to write in a later essay that Yeats "made himself into the greatest poet in English since the seventeenth century ... because ... he learned how to create fragments of the actual, not of his own time to which he was unequal, but of all time of which he was a product." [131]

Consequently, the special Yeats Memorial Issue which was published in the winter of 1942 – and from which the Jarrell and Blackmur quotations above are taken – was the culmination of the *Review*'s interest in and admiration for the poet. Among the contributors were virtually all the important *Southern Review* critics; Blackmur, Knights, Eliot, Matthiessen, Schwartz, Horace Gregory, Davidson, Ransom, Burke, Zabel, Tate, Mizener, Austin Warren, Baker, and Jarrell. Other critics who were invited but who did not contribute included William Empson, Edmund Wilson, I. A. Richards, Ezra Pound, and Oliver St. John Gogarty. As Yeats was considered a much superior poet to Hardy, his poetry stood in less need of rigorous selection and exclusion than Hardy's. The Yeats issue was primarily an evaluative investigation of Yeats's remarkable development as a poet, and of the relevance of the prose writings, as a reflection of his life and his ideas, to his poetry. Some critics were severer than others. Knights, for instance, wrote his essay in close agreement with the evaluation of Yeats as it has been elaborated in *Scrutiny*. He spoke of the "impotence and frustration that mark many of the latest poems", and also compared Yeats to Eliot. "Perhaps the best way of defining the disappointment that one feels on returning to so many of Yeats's poems that had previously seemed deeply moving is to say that they fail to 'gather strength of life, with being', to grow, that

---

[130]   Review of Yeats's *Wheels and Butterflies, SoR*, I, 1 (Summer 1935), 199.
[131]   Jarrell, "The Development of Yeats's Sense of Reality", *SoR*, VII, 3 (Winter 1942), 654; Blackmur, "Between Myth and Philosophy: Fragments of W. B. Yeats", *SoR*, VII, 3 (Winter 1942), 424.

is, with one's own developing experience – unlike so much of Eliot's poetry where each fresh reading brings fresh discovery." [132] Eliot himself described Yeats as "pre-eminently the poet of middle age"; he praised "a kind of moral, as well as intellectual, excellence", but could not feel complete agreement: "The questions of difference, objection and protest arise in the field of doctrine. ... I have been concerned only with the poet and dramatist, so far as these can be isolated. In the long run they cannot be wholly isolated." [133]

An unresolved question concerned Yeats's romanticism. It had been touched upon already before the Memorial Issue. In the summer of 1938, Cleanth Brooks had published an extensive examination of "The Vision of William Butler Yeats", because "to regard the magical system as merely a piece of romantic furniture is to miss completely the function which it has performed for Yeats".[134] Brooks evidently did not regard Yeats as a romantic poet although he did not state as explicitly as Howard Baker did in the Yeats symposium, that "the egregious romantic became in the end the champion of a regenerate classicism".[135] The question was discussed at length in the symposium in Allen Tate's "Yeats's Romanticism: Notes and Suggestions" and Arthur Mizener's "The Romanticism of W. B. Yeats". These two critics reached very different conclusions. Tate believed that Yeats began with a romantic use of language in the early poems but that "he ended up very differently, and ... is no more to be fixed as a romantic than Shakespeare as a Senecan". He believed Yeats's poetry to be "nearer the center of our main traditions of sensibility and thought than the poetry of Eliot or of Pound", but he feared that "Yeats's romanticism will be created by his [future] critics" (VII, 592, 600). Mizener, on the other hand, could only detect "a technical change rather than a substantial one" in the development of

---

[132] "W. B. Yeats: The Assertion of Values", 440, 434.
[133] "The Poetry of W. B. Yeats", 448, 453-454. The essay was reprinted from *Purpose*, XII, 3/4 (July-Dec. 1940), 115-127. Its original use had been as the first Annual Yeats Lecture delivered at the Abbey Theatre in Dublin in June 1940.
[134] *SoR*, IV, 1 (Summer 1938), 116.
[135] "Domes of Byzantium", 644.

Yeats's poetry. He agreed that the later poetry was "far finer" than the poetry Yeats wrote in the 1890's, but he insisted that it was "a romantic poetry". He imputed to contemporary literary fashions the refusal of the critics to admit this: "we are today almost pathologically sensitive about our romanticism, as up-to-date critics must, in Wordsworth's day, have been about their neo-classicism". Mizener found Brooks's treatment of Yeats unsatisfactory: it "seems to me to be devised to free him from the horrid charge of being a romantic" (VII, 622, 614). Knights agreed with Mizener that Yeats "in some important ways" remained a romantic to the end (VII, 431), and Delmore Schwartz wrote that even when Yeats "sees and understands much more than the romantic poet, the lurid glow of romanticism nevertheless hangs over the scene".[136]

Like *The Hound & Horn*'s Henry James issue, the special issues of the *Southern Review* were published towards the end of its career when the editors could count on the cooperation of an impressive number of regular contributors. These issues are a tribute to the intellectual resources which the *Review* could draw on and to the efficiency of the editorial staff. They were, of course, not faultless – the Hardy issue especially suffered from overlapping and repetition – but they were the most elaborate and most successful special issues of an American review to date. In the later 'Forties, John Palmer, the editor of *The Sewanee Review* and formerly managing editor of *The Southern Review*, called special issues "real editorial headaches. I've had to do with three – in the *Southern*'s on Hardy and Yeats, and now *Sewanee*'s on Ransom and after each one I've pretty well decided, never again".[137]

The preceding discussion has been mainly concerned with some of the *Review*'s characteristic attitudes to poetry, because poetry was much more frequently discussed than fiction. The *Review*'s treatment of fiction, apart from the fiction chronicles, was not very extensive for a magazine of its size, but it is possible to formulate a *Southern Review* approach to fiction which basically

---

[136] "An Unwritten Book", 483.
[137] Undated letter to Joseph W. Angell, *Sewanee Review* papers, Sewanee, Tenn.

resembles its approach to poetry, although, again, a number of exceptions may be pointed to. *The Southern Review* admired complex novels with complex characters and psychological situations, and with a fine moral discrimination matched by a corresponding complexity and appropriateness of style. Howard Baker, for instance, admired the long stories of Katherine Anne Porter and Allen Tate's novel, *The Fathers*; he especially liked Miss Porter's "Old Mortality" because it was "especially complicated, formidable to the analytical eye" and praised Tate for his "creation of a stylistic medium appropriate" to his concerns.[138]

The *Review*'s attitude to fiction may perhaps be more clearly defined by the negative statement that it had no use for naturalism; it was more interested to trace in what ways naturalism was transcended by the powers of the imagination. Naturalism was, characteristically, looked upon as a manifestation of the evil influence of science and industrialism. An explicit statement to that effect occurred in Delmore Schwartz's essay, "John Dos Passos and the Whole Truth" (Autumn 1938): "the physical sciences and industrialism changed the conception of the nature of literature and truth in literature, and made writers of great genius attempt to compete with the scientist by adopting something of his special method". Schwartz objected to the looseness of the structure of Dos Passos's trilogy *U.S.A.* but he found a more disastrous shortcoming in his approach to his subject-matter; Dos Passos, Schwartz wrote, exhibited "a beautiful imaginative sympathy which permits him to get under the skin of his characters, but there is no imagination." He characterized *U.S.A.* as "the greatest monument of naturalism", but its author as "the gifted victim" of that method.[139] Dos Passos had been much more sympathetically treated by Henry Nash Smith who had highly praised the third

---

[138] "The Contemporary Short Story", *SoR*, III, 3 (Winter 1938), 596; "Grand Tour of Fiction", *SoR*, IV, 4 (Spring 1939), 823. Baker also reviewed *The Fathers* for *The Kenyon Review*: "only a few modern novels, and of these few only the greatest, have been so symbolic, so full of implications, so organically significant as is this one. These are the aspects of *The Fathers* to which I want particularly to direct attention" (*KR*, I, 1 [Winter 1939], 90).
[139] *SoR*, IV, 2 (Autumn 1938), 366, 364, 367.

part of *U.S.A.*, *The Big Money*.[140] Howard Baker, on the other hand, expressed admiration for Schwartz's examination of "Dos Passos' self-destructive naturalism".[141]

Schwartz contributed two other important evaluations, of Hemingway and of Faulkner. He maintained that Hemingway's characteristic preoccupations "have to do with sensation rather than with a more complex human experience" and that the morality "which seems so much the substance of Hemingway's writing is a fairly limited one". The most admirable aspect of Hemingway's method was the fusion of his style and his values particularly through "his modification and extension of the rhetorical possibilities of speech".[142] The unifying theme of Faulkner's work was, according to Schwartz, his "obsession with the endless horror and irrationality of life", and the primary cause for his successes and failures lay in the uses and abuses of his style:

When Faulkner has a subject extreme enough in its horror and abnormality, his style is measured, under control, and directed at the specific description of specific things. . . . The reader is left to respond to the subject without the author's obsessive coaching. When the subject does not justify the author's horror, the devices of style become clumsiness and tricks, the writing is a stale version of the Swinburnian high poetic, and worst of all the style becomes purple, empty of specific objects, and sometimes insufferably periodic.[143]

Schwartz's moderate view of Faulkner was not shared by all contributors. Half a year previously, Don Stanford had savagely attacked *The Hamlet*: "The creatures of Faulkner's world are completely phony, but even if we believe them, they are so insensitive and stupid that their actions have no meaning for us." [144] The only other important critic of American fiction in *The Southern Review* was John Donald Wade, who contributed essays

140 Smith, "Notes on Recent Novels", *SoR*, II, 3 (Winter 1937), 577-593.
141 Baker, "Grand Tour of Fiction", 802.
142 "Ernest Hemingway's Literary Situation", *SoR*, III, 4 (Spring 1938), 771, 777, 775.
143 "The Fiction of William Faulkner", *SoR*, VII, 1 (Summer 1941), 151.
144 "The Beloved Returns and Other Recent Fiction", *SoR*, VI, 3 (Winter 1941), 619.

on Thomas Wolfe and Erskine Caldwell,[145] both of whom he considered important writers but with considerable shortcomings.

The *Review*'s coverage of foreign fiction was intermittent and haphazard. John Peale Bishop contributed a technical article in explanation of *Finnegan's Wake,* Theodore Spencer wrote on *Stephen Hero,* Philip Rahv, John Kelly and Austin Warren on Kafka, Wallace Fowlie on Jules Romains and Carlos Lynes on André Gide. Indeed, the cosmopolitanism and international coverage of *The Dial* had almost completely disappeared. But *The Southern Review* on the whole lacked the touch of nativism we found in *The Hound & Horn,* although Herbert Agar in the leading article of the first issue had admonished Americans to be nationally self-conscious.[146] It had the allure of a specialist magazine addressed to writers and to teachers of English, and its interest in things American was inherent in its very nature, rather than a thing to be insisted upon. Like *The Symposium* it showed an interest in England, especially in English criticism. This interest was undoubtedly related to the personal acquaintance of the editors with England as Rhodes Scholars. They published, for instance, three articles by Bonamy Dobrée, on "The Plays of Eugene O'Neill", on "Poetic Drama in England Today", and on Hardy's "The Dynasts".[147] They had also "made overtures to the *Scrutiny* crowd," Brooks told William Empson on 2 August 1938 "– so far, those letters have been friendly but have got no material – and we have been trying unsuccessfully to get in touch with I. A. Richards." [148] Richards proved indeed unapproachable, but, as we have seen earlier, the editors published three essays of a regular contributor to *Scrutiny*, L. C. Knights. When *The Southern Review* was started in 1935, the editors had immediately solicited an essay from F. R. Leavis on W. H. Auden perhaps, or on "the question

[145] "Prodigal", *SoR*, I, 1 (Summer 1935), 192-198; "Sweet Are the Uses of Degeneracy", *SoR*, I, 3 (Winter 1936), 449-466.
[146] "Culture versus Colonialism in America", *SoR*, I, 1 (Summer 1935), 1-19.
[147] *SoR*, II, 3 (Winter 1937), 435-446; *SoR*, IV, 3 (Winter 1939), 581-599; *SoR*, VI, 1 (Summer 1940), 109-124.
[148] *Southern Review* papers.

of belief in poetry, with particular reference to the positions of Mr. Eliot and Mr. Richards", but Leavis had been altogether too busy: "keeping *Scrutiny* going (the main burden falls on me) is something of a miracle".[149] Later on, however, on the advice of L. C. Knights, they persuaded him to contribute to the Hardy issue. They turned down essays by two other *Scrutiny* regulars, D. W. Harding on Jane Austen – which Leavis was only too happy to publish in *Scrutiny* – and Martin Turnell on "Racine's Phèdre" and on "The Criticism of Jacques Rivière" because they "were a little too far off our usual beat".[150] *Scrutiny* itself, which was anything but lenient to contemporary literary magazines, was particularly sympathetic to the work *The Southern Review* was doing. One of its most combative critics, Q. D. Leavis, wrote a perceptive and very laudatory review of the Hardy issue:

What really warms one's heart is the complete absence of the belletristic approach or of any aesthetic posturing, in this collective enterprise. Could one believe that any similar undertaking on this side of the Atlantic, even before the War, would have been so profitable or even harmless? It is certainly the most helpful critical work on Hardy I know, and since the best essays in it are by tough minded critics with a corresponding tightness of argument and idiom, who raise many debatable critical problems, it could be recommended for teething purposes at the university.[151]

Another English magazine with which the editors of *The Southern Review* entertained friendly relations was Desmond Hawkins's *Purpose*. In the autumn of 1938, they published Michael Roberts's essay "The Critic and the Public", which was an attack, rather in the *Scrutiny* vein, on a number of lamentable features of the literary life in England such as the Book Clubs, *The Sunday Times*, *The Observer*, and, to a lesser extent, *The Times Literary Supplement*. Roberts's contribution was one of the essays of a symposium by various poets and critics, which appeared "currently" in *Purpose*. The editors announced that "several of these essays"

---

[149]   Editors to Leavis, March 26, 1935, and Leavis to Brooks, April 7, 1935, *Southern Review* papers.
[150]   Brooks to Turnell, September 25, 1941, *Southern Review* papers.
[151]   "Hardy and Criticism", *Scrutiny*, XI, 3 (Spring 1943), 237.

were to appear in *The Southern Review*.[152] As a matter of fact, only one more was published: George Every's "The Task of Concentration" in the Summer 1939 issue.

In the winter of 1942 the editors of *The Southern Review* announced that their magazine faced "suspension of publication with the spring issue of 1942 unless arrangements now not foreseen can be made before".[153] Such arrangements were not made, but that does not mean that the editors did not try their very best. Their struggle to keep the *Review* alive, however, is so intricately related to the fortunes of other magazines which were to carry on the tradition of the literary review, that it is best discussed in connection with the careers of those magazines in the following chapter.

[152] "Notes on Contributors", *SoR*, IV, 2 (Autumn 1938). *The Southern Review* was described in *Purpose* as "one of the best periodicals in America, politics aside" (H[ugh] G[ordon] P[orteus], "Significant Journals", *Purpose*, X, 4 [Oct.-Dec. 1938], 242).
[153] "Announcement", *SoR*, VII, 3 (Winter 1941), inside front cover.

6

THE FORTIES AND AFTER

I

In late 1947 the Rockefeller Foundation made a substantial grant to *The Kenyon Review* for five years starting in 1948 to increase payments to contributors. At about the same time *Partisan Review* found a private patron. These benefactions worried a third literary magazine, *The Sewanee Review*. Its editor, John Palmer, wrote an anxious letter to the Rockefeller Foundation: "we have constituted a publishing triumvirate, dissimilar in certain respects but roughly equal in prestige, engaged in a friendly and about equal competition for the best writing and the best criticism"; the improved financial status of the *Kenyon* and *Partisan* reviews, however, had destroyed "the equality of bargaining power which we have heretofore enjoyed".[1] The Rockefeller Foundation quickly restored this equality by granting $27.600 to *The Sewanee Review* for increased remuneration of its contributors. At the time this grant was running out, in the latter half of 1952, we

[1] Draft of letter, Palmer to David H. Stevens, Director, Division of Humanities, Rockefeller Foundation, n.d., *Sewanee Review* correspondence, Sewanee, Tenn. As early as 29 November 1943, Allen Tate reported a visit of Stevens to John Crowe Ransom offering "to provide funds for 'overhead' for the Kenyon Review. John took the liberty of suggesting the Sewanee Review as the best possible investment in the country for the funds of a great foundation" (Letter to Alexander Guerry, Vice-Chancellor, University of the South, *Sewanee Review* papers). In the spring of 1944, the editors of *The Kenyon Review* announced that their magazine had received "a considerable three-year benefaction from a new source, greatly relieving the strain of financing in war time" ("Editorial Notes", *KR*, VI, 2 [Spring 1944], 275). The Rockefeller Foundation may well have been the benefactor.

find *The Sewanee Review*'s new editor Monroe Spears "deeply involved . . . in trying to get another subsidy".[2] In the following year the Rockefeller Foundation called a meeting of the *Kenyon, Sewanee* and *Partisan* reviews and of a newcomer, *The Hudson Review*, to discuss ways to promote sales so that these quarterlies might become financially independent. Suggestions to this end included advertisements in the *New York Times Book Review* and circulars to individuals from well selected lists. The results of such a promotion campaign seemed too uncertain to warrant new grants. The Foundation did, however, make a three year grant to these four magazines to award fellowships. This was "renewed and expanded" in 1956 for another three years.[3]

This information about the financial management of the most important quarterlies of the 1940's suggests some obvious conclusions. Firstly, the position on the literary scene of these magazines was very different from that of their predecessors. They were no longer supported by wealthy individuals only but also came within the compass of the activities of foundations and universities. In the 'Fifties they were able to award fellowships and already in 1948 the Rockefeller Foundation had endowed Kenyon College with $40.000 towards the operation of the Kenyon School of English during three summer sessions, in close connection with the *Review*. This new patronage was undoubtedly in some measure the result of the lively interest of the quarterlies in the educational possibilities of literature. In the preceding chapter we have already described how the emphasis on literary scholarship rather than on literary criticism in the American English departments had prompted *The Southern Review* and *The Kenyon Review* to devote their Autumn 1940 issues to a joint symposium "Literature and the Professors". It must be borne in mind that this symposium was not a surprise attack but rather an organized indication of growing discontent within the universities. Due largely to the exertions of the quarterlies, the

---

[2] Spears to Philip Wheelwright, November 19, 1952, *Sewanee Review* papers.

[3] Reed Whittemore (quoting from statement by Monroe K. Spears, *Sewanee Review*'s editor during the 'Fifties), "Foundations and Magazines: A Symposium", *Carleton Miscellany*, IV, 2 (Spring 1963), 46.

critical study of modern literature would soon figure prominently in the curricula of many English departments.

The position of the literary reviews in the cultural framework after World War II has indeed no precedent in magazine history. In 1963, Allen Tate wrote: "If we grant that the literary magazine is an institution necessary to the welfare of American intellectual life, we cannot go on thinking that it will survive on subscriptions and bookshop sales. This is like asking the university to live on tuition fees." [4] Tate's comparison of the position of the literary review to that of the university is significant. The identification of the two is the result of the organic development of both the literary review and the university. The second and third decade of this century produced a distinguished, often experimental literature and little magazines multiplied to publish their share of it. This was the main function of *The Dial*. The 1930's marked a noticeable decline in literary creativity which was often commented upon by the *Southern, Kenyon,* and *Partisan* reviews. These magazines devoted most of their pages to the elucidation of the experiments of earlier decades and, more sporadically, to a revaluation of the literature of past centuries. Because of the expansion of the English departments in the universities the critics who conducted this elucidation and revaluation were more and more often university teachers. Whereas most of the *Dial* critics had been professional men of letters, most of the later magazine critics were professional academics. The 'Forties were, in the words of John Crowe Ransom, an "Age of Criticism" [5] and its most characteristic and important

---

[4] "Foundations and Magazines: A Symposium", 74.
[5] Ransom made this statement in the first issue of *The Kenyon Review* (Winter 1939), 81. "An Age of Criticism" was also the title of an essay Ransom contributed to *The New Republic* thirteen years afterwards: "... in the half-century just finished we have witnessed a furious burst of creative activity, and many artists so far ahead of their public, yet causing such a passion of teased interest, that they employed critics for a whole generation before the public could have comfortable possession" (CXXVI [March 31, 1952], 18). One year earlier, Ransom had written: "one of the saving gifts of our age, against the many ways it has devised for being wretched, is its turn for literary criticism, and for a literary criticism evidently so enterprising and acute, and so grounded in good con-

outlet the critical reviews. They had taken the prominent place which the little magazines had held in the 'Twenties. As Eliseo Vivas wrote in 1951: "The function of the little mags of today is to carry on from where such reviews as *The Dial, The Hound & Horn, The Symposium,* and *The Southern Review* left off. What they do is to make available to a literate, and therefore, perforce exceedingly small, public, the products of the critical intelligence." [6]

If the patronage of universities and foundations points to the increasing institutionalization of the literary reviews, so does the attitude of commercial publishers. It is part of the tradition of the little magazine that it prints contributions which no commercial magazine or publisher would touch; indeed, during the 1920's publishers were the notorious whipping boys of little magazine editors. But when, in the autumn of 1937, John Crowe Ransom started to collect funds for a new magazine, he tried to interest Scribner's in backing it. *The Kenyon Review* eventually appeared without the assistance of Scribner's, but in 1944 it announced two short story prizes, of $500 and $250, which were sponsored jointly by Doubleday, Doran and Company, Inc. and the *Review,* and in the spring of the following year, *The Sewanee Review* announced the John Peale Bishop Memorial Literary Contest in collaboration with Prentice-Hall, Inc.

A second important conclusion to be derived from the support of the Rockefeller Foundation to the *Kenyon, Sewanee, Partisan,* and *Hudson* reviews is that there existed a strong feeling of solidarity among these magazines. This solidarity antedated the interest of the Rockefeller Foundation. It included *The Southern Review* during its later years. To give one example: when in 1938, Philip Rahv, an editor of *Partisan Review,* heard about the forthcoming first issue of *The Kenyon Review,* he told Allen Tate, "With the Southern Review, the Kenyon Review, and the

---

science, as can scarcely be predicated of the other periods of literary history" (ed., *The Kenyon Critics: Studies in Modern Literature from the Kenyon Review* [New York, 1951], p. viii).
[6] "Criticism and the Little Mags", *The Western Review,* XVI, 3 (Autumn 1951), 12.

Partisan all going at the same time, the critical atmosphere ought to improve in this country".[7] Tate answered with a proposal to make up a volume of criticism of the best contributions to the three quarterlies. Rahv welcomed the suggestion and promised to "write to Ransom and Warren and try to arrange such collaboration".[8] The feeling of solidarity and common purpose increased through the years. When in the autumn of 1961 the Association of Literary Magazines of America (ALMA) was founded it seemed natural, not only that Allen Tate should be honorary chairman, but that the four quarterlies should be differentiated from the other members by the special designation "the Council of Literary Magazines".

These quarterlies have indeed often been mentioned in one breath. Their common denominator was their invariably highbrow attitude to literary and intellectual matters. This attitude is rare enough at all times to ensure an at least superficial similarity. Furthermore, these quarterlies were primarily critical and it is for this that they were valued most highly. This was clearly illustrated by the results of a questionnaire which *Partisan Review* sent out to its subscribers in early 1941. Nine out of ten of those who answered the question: "What do PR readers want more of? What less of?" asked for more articles and book reviews. "Slightly more readers want less poetry than want more poetry, and slightly more readers want more stories than want less stories." [9] These quarterlies also insisted on the highest

---

[7]   October 24, 1938, Tate papers at Princeton. In 1960, *The Sewanee Review*'s editor Monroe Spears wrote that the quarterlies had in "some respects" come "uneasily to regard themselves as collaborators rather than competitors" ("The Present Function of the Literary Quarterlies", *Texas Quarterly*, III, 1 [Spring 1960], 34).

[8]   November 14, 1938, Tate papers. A few days later, on November 22, Tate wrote to Rahv: "I have read with great interest the current issue of the Partisan: it is a very fine number, the best issue of an American periodical that I've seen in a long time" (letter published in *Partisan Review*, VI, 2 [Winter 1939]).

[9]   Dwight Macdonald, "Results of the PR Questionnaire", *PR*, VIII, 4 (July-August 1941), 345. Malcolm Cowley commented rather scathingly on the effect of the all-important criticism on some novelists in the years after the war: "they are all 'serious' new writers, they are trying to produce works of art in accordance with the best literary standards and they

standards of criticism and it was therefore often impossible to predict whether an important piece of criticism would appear in one magazine or in another.

These are obvious similarities which have to be recognized before one can profitably mark out the characteristics of the individual magazines. One other point has to be made at the outset: three of these magazines, the *Southern, Kenyon* and *Sewanee* reviews, were directed by Southern "new critics", some of whom had collaborated in editing *The Fugitive* at Vanderbilt University in the early 'Twenties and in bringing out the agrarian manifesto *I'll Take My Stand* in 1930. They were Allen Tate, John Crowe Ransom, Robert Penn Warren, and their younger friends and associates Cleanth Brooks, Andrew Lytle and John Palmer. In 1944, when he took over the management of *The Sewanee Review,* Allen Tate thought it advisable, following Ransom's precedent with *The Kenyon Review,* to fire all associate editors. "There is a very specific reason for this", he told one associate editor, Cleanth Brooks, "and I am sure that you will understand and approve it. It is simply that most of our crowd have been on most of the magazines for the past ten or fifteen years, virtually taking in one another's washing, and I think it advisable to make our influence more effective by concealing it." [10] Brooks and Warren edited *The Southern Review,* Ransom *The Kenyon Review,* and Lytle and Tate successively reconstructed the old *Sewanee Review* and handed it over to John Palmer. The personal connections between these three magazines were indeed extremely close and so were their interests and activities. It will be the purpose of this chapter to investigate their origins, interrelations and editorial policies and to show in

---

would like to be admired by the critics who write for *Kenyon, Sewanee, Hudson,* and other quarterly reviews" (*The Literary Situation* [New York, 1954], p. 43). Some years earlier already Cowley had written: "The critical habit of mind has a recognizable effect on the fiction and poetry in the new little magazines: it gives them more polish and less daring" ("The Little Magazines Growing up", *The New York Times Book Review,* LII [September 14, 1947], 5).

[10]   July 31, 1944, *Sewanee Review* papers.

how far *Partisan Review*, which at its inception in 1934, was an important representative of the tradition of the Marxist little magazine, approached to the pattern they set and in how far it remained different. *The Hudson Review* is outside the scope of this study. It joined the *Sewanee, Partisan* and *Kenyon* reviews in the spring of 1948 after they had become firmly established. Although it approached closest to their ideal, it was one of a number of magazines which were inspired by their example and their success.

II

In early 1937 Gordon Keith Chalmers, the President of Kenyon College at Gambier, Ohio, came down to Nashville, Tennessee, to try and persuade John Crowe Ransom, who was teaching at Vanderbilt University, to accept an appointment at Kenyon. Ransom agreed and on 10 June 1937 *The Southern Review*, in conjunction with *The Virginia Quarterly Review*, organized in his honour a farewell dinner at Nashville with Ford Madox Ford as toastmaster.[11] On 29 October 1937, Ransom wrote to Tate from Gambier as follows: "A very interesting situation has come up. Our president called me in yesterday to talk in the greatest privacy about a project which he feels sure he can put through, beginning next year: a fine *Review* backed and financed by his Trustees." Aside from secretarial work, President Chalmers thought of its editing as a full-time one-man job, but as he did not want to withdraw Ransom from teaching altogether he proposed that Ransom share the editorship with another person to

[11] David Long and Michael Burr (eds.), "John Crowe Ransom: A Tribute from the Community of Letters", *The Kenyon Collegian* (Supplement to Vol. LXXXX, 7, Gambier 1964), p. 7. Ford's appearance as toastmaster has recently been described as follows: "Dressed in an ancient dinner jacket and white duck trousers bought especially for the occasion, Ford made it plain in the course of his remarks that Ransom should leave, if only to teach Tennessee a lesson, so that in future that state might give proper recognition to her writers. After this, as Mr. Ransom has remarked half-facetiously, he simply had to go to Ohio" (Frank MacShane, *The Life and Work of Ford Madox Ford* [London, 1965], p. 251).

be brought in from outside. Several names were mentioned; "I held my peace", Ransom wrote, "but instantly preoccupied my mind with the idea of: TATE. After Tate, Warren of course".

Ransom coveted Tate's presence at Kenyon both for the editing and the teaching: "I have an idea we could really found criticism if we got together on it." [12] Tate's reaction must have been prompt and positive because already on 4 November 1937 Ransom wrote to him enthusiastically: "Very greatly cheered over your acceptance of Kenyon and the Review project." [13] Tate's appointment, however, never came through, most probably because one of the interested Trustees suggested, to Ransom's dismay, that the magazine would be "a perfectly general Review, with all sorts of things, political and otherwise". The right co-editor of such a magazine would be "a political or round-about sort of man".[14] Eventually the appointment as "managing editor" went to Philip Blair Rice, of the University of Cincinnati, a philosopher and former Rhodes Scholar who had been a fairly regular contributor to *The Symposium* and *Partisan Review*. But Tate remained the closest associate of the early *Kenyon Review*. He was by far the most important of the Advisory Editors and Ransom consulted him continually on policy decisions.

The Advisory Editors had been chosen by Ransom and Tate together. Chalmers had wanted to include "a lot of Faculty editors" but Ransom, who felt that they would have been "either dummies or meddlers", managed to dissuade him.[15] When the *Review* appeared the list of Advisory Editors ran as follows: R. P. Blackmur, Paul Rosenfeld, Roberta Teale Swartz [Mrs. Chalmers], Allen Tate, Philip Timberlake [of Kenyon College], Mark Van Doren, and Eliseo Vivas [a friend of *Kenyon Review*'s managing editor Philip Blair Rice]. An earlier provisional list had included the names of Gilbert Seldes – "he represents Movie-art (if any)" [16] –, Paul Rosenfeld – "Rosenfeld doesn't write in

---

[12] Tate papers.
[13] Tate papers.
[14] Ransom to Tate, November 22, 1937, Tate papers.
[15] Ransom to Tate, June 22, 1938, Tate papers.
[16] *Ibid.*

our style, yet he's a fine gentleman, devoted to our success" [17] –, and Marianne Moore. If perhaps not a conscious act of homage to *The Dial,* these names are certainly symbolic of the tradition to which Ransom felt *The Kenyon Review* to be heir. When, in May 1938, the danger of a large comprehensive review had been killed off by lack of money, Ransom wrote enthusiastically to Merrill Moore: "It will be in fact what I wanted it to be in the first place, a periodical devoted to literature and the arts exclusively; like the old Seven Arts, which was followed by the reorganized Dial, which was followed by the Hound & Horn." [18] And to Tate he wrote: "We are a soberer and more concentrated Dial." [19]

But to find the right degree of sobriety and concentration was no easy matter. Ransom wanted to see his review "solid but not dull." [20] To keep it "from being too highbrow" he planned to have "a good deal of satirical and negative writing". That would perhaps be "a popularizing feature" but would not define the character of the magazine.[21] Particular attention would also be paid to the language and style of the critical contributions. According to a circular letter which they sent out on 28 September 1938, the editors hoped that *The Kenyon Review* would carry on "literary and aesthetic discussion in language of a rather severer economy than is usual, provided no sacrifice is

[17] Ransom to Tate, July 12, 1942, Tate papers. In the same letter Ransom wrote: "I've thought ... to leave music unrepresented in order not to seem to replace Rosenfeld", who had contributed a number of articles on music to earlier issues. The following passage from an essay by Edmund Wilson about Paul Rosenfeld evidently refers to the latter's connection with *The Kenyon Review:* "He was angry over his treatment at the hands of one of the highbrow quarterlies, the editor of which had first asked him to be a member of the advisory board and had then refused to print his articles, keeping them, however, for months without letting him know about them" ("Paul Rosenfeld: Three Phases", in *Paul Rosenfeld: Voyager in the Arts,* eds. Mellquist and Wiese [New York, 1948], p. 18).

[18] June 2, 1938, Merrill Moore papers, Library of Congress, Washington, D.C.

[19] May 28, 1938, Tate papers.

[20] *Ibid.*

[21] Ransom to Moore, June 2, 1938, Moore papers; Ransom to Tate, May 28, 1938, Tate papers.

required in the warmth of the style, or literary quality". At approximately the same time Ransom wrote to Tate complaining that the "biggest problem of a first number is not to fill up the space with rather good critical stuff, but to maintain a high standard of good *writing*. There are literally scores of willing and practised critics but as you know there are few literary men – men of letters, shall I say." [22]

The Kenyon Review appeared more than a year after Chalmers had first approached Ransom. At the spring meeting of the Board of Trustees of Kenyon College in 1938 the plan for a review was officially submitted by President Chalmers, although the Trustees had already shown an unofficial interest a few months earlier. The plan received their "eager approval".[23] At the end of April Ransom told Merrill Moore that he had been authorized to start "a full-sized, high-power general Review . . . provided certain initial funds are secured in subscription." [24] The figure aimed at for the subscriptions was $6000 and close to $5000 had already been subscribed at the time of writing. But before the end of May it was obvious that a general review would be too costly. The subscriptions did not exceed $5000 and the printing costs proved high. Therefore – as we have seen, to Ransom's relief – a quarterly of about a hundred pages, exclusively devoted to literature and the arts, was decided upon. Most of the subscriptions were pledges of $500 or $1000 a year for three years. In this way there would be "no great crowd of petty angels to make representations about the way we publish, only a small group of persons who are willing to turn the thing over to us".[25] The review would be able to pay "the highest rates, $5.00 per page" and would "go after the best stuff".[26]

Other urgent problems faced the new editor. Apart from physical details such as offices, cover design, stationery and equipment, a name had to be decided upon. Ransom had two

[22] October 1, 1938, Tate papers.
[23] Long and Burr, *op. cit.* (above, note 11 on page 254), p. 7.
[24] April 29, 1938, Moore papers.
[25] *Ibid.*
[26] Ransom to Moore, June 2, 1938, Moore papers.

rather colourless but telling suggestions: "The Quarterly" and "The Critic" (or "The American Critic"). He rather favoured the latter but as Chalmers was against it, Ransom waived his insistence "in view of more important concessions on his [Chalmers'] part".[27] Ransom therefore suggested the title *The Kenyon Review* with "some sort of sub-title, perhaps on the inside title page indicating that it will be devoted to the arts and letters and to critical ideas".[28] As had been understood from the outset, however, the magazine would have "no reference to the local setting whatever".[29]

The first issue came out in instalments from 9 to 12 January. Five thousand copies were printed in order to supply the 2700 alumni of Kenyon College in the hope of securing some subscriptions. This promotion campaign was successful: by the end of January there were five hundred paid annual subscriptions and two hundred copies had been sent on consignment to book stalls. As the first issue only counted 112 pages Ransom had decided against the publication of fiction, "this first year anyway. The best we hope for is an occasional fiction number."[30] The *Review* published its first story in August 1940 but poetry and criticism remained its most characteristic interests during the early years.

The Kenyon Review had made its first appearance, but in those early months it would have been impossible to predict that it would be one of the most distinguished literary publications for decades to come. As Allen Tate wrote twenty-five years afterwards: "not even his old friends were sure that he [Ransom] would become one of the great modern editors. He had not been

[27]   Ransom to Tate, June 22, 1938, Tate papers.
[28]   Chalmers to Moore, June 15, 1938, Moore papers.
[29]   Ransom to Tate, June 22, 1938, Tate papers.
[30]   Ransom to Robert Penn Warren, October 17, 1938, *Southern Review* papers, Yale University Library. In 1947 Malcolm Cowley stated mistakenly that *The Kenyon Review*, when it took over *Southern Review*'s subscription list, also took over "the custom of printing short stories – never more than three in an issue – to supplement the poems and critical essays that had filled its pages in the beginning" ("Ten Little Magazines", *The New Republic*, CXVI [March 31, 1947], 31).

very eager to know contemporary literature. . . . " [31] Nor was it certain that Ransom would remain at Kenyon College and if he had left, the future of the *Review* would have been doubtful. This threat was not imaginary. Immediately after the first issue was out, the Women's College of Greensboro, North Carolina, made an attractive offer to both Ransom and Tate. The prospect of working together was a strong incentive. On 22 February 1939, Ransom felt it was "pretty certain" he would accept the Greensboro position and on 22 April he figured the chances as "10 to 1".[32] But in the meantime President Chalmers was not idle. He secured a grant from the Carnegie Corporation which made it possible to increase Ransom's salary and to lighten his teaching load. By the middle of May Ransom had declined the Greensboro offer. Tate had done the same in favour of an appointment – also financed by the Carnegie Corporation – in charge of the Creative Arts Program at Princeton University.

A second major threat to the magazine's continuance was the American participation in World War II. In the months following Pearl Harbor its fortunes were intimately linked with those of *The Southern Review*. But the interrelations of the two magazines had been close from the very beginning. While preparing the first issue of *The Kenyon Review,* Ransom told Warren: "One of our embarrassments is in not too obviously following in the footsteps of The Southern Review. But we can't help it altogether, and shan't try." [33] The reviews decided to cooperate in "steering stuff to each other".[34] In print, Ransom praised *The Southern Review* several times. In the spring of 1940, the first sentence of his review of Cleanth Brooks's *Modern Poetry and the Tradition* read: "Consistently during its lifetime, the *Southern Review* has been the organ of the most powerful critical discussion in the language." [35] But in private statements Ransom was not uncritical. When he was planning his own magazine he de-

---

[31] Long and Burr, p. 18.
[32] Letters to Tate, Tate papers.
[33] October 17, 1938, *Southern Review* papers.
[34] Warren to Ransom, October 22, 1938, *Southern Review* papers.
[35] "Apologia for Modernism", *KR*, II, 2 (Spring 1940), 247.

scribed *The Southern Review* as a "brilliant example of what might be done, but which might itself be improved upon".[36] He felt that it had reached its high standard "by the pure accident that there are now a goodly number of fine critics who have not where to market their wares".[37] He was, however, genuinely distressed when he heard of its imminent demise; "a great loss to letters", he wrote to Tate.[38] In his editorial in *The Kenyon Review* in the spring of 1942, Ransom described *The Southern Review* as "a sumptuous publication in its physical aspect", which had been "almost jaunty in the bravery of its critical position". As no reasons for its suspension were given, "it may be supposed that its discontinuance is one of the early casualties of war".[39]

It was indeed the war which caused the demise of *The Southern Review*. Its existence had been endangered once before by the notorious L.S.U. scandals. President Monroe Smith had been deeply involved in them, but his successor, Paul M. Herbert, proved a sympathetic supporter of the *Review*. As a matter of fact, Cleanth Brooks thought that "under the new administration, THE SOUTHERN REVIEW should prosper".[40] It did until, after the United States had got into the war, Herbert was replaced by General Campbell Hodges. On 13 December 1941, *Southern Review*'s managing editor John Palmer was informed of the recommendation of the Budget Committee "that the University cease its financial support of the Southern Review as of June 30, 1942".[41] Before the end of the month the editors had approached the Rockefeller, Carnegie and Rosenwald funds to explore the

---

[36]   Ransom to Moore, May 13, 1938, Moore papers.
[37]   Ransom to Tate, November 4, 1937, Tate papers.
[38]   January 5, 1942, Tate papers.
[39]   "Editorial Notes: War and Publication", *KR*, IV, 2 (Spring 1942), 217.
[40]   Letter to Donald Davidson, August 9, 1939, *Southern Review* papers.
[41]   M. M. Wilkerson to John Palmer, December 13, 1941, *Southern Review* papers. "Says L.S.U.'s prexy, Major General Campbell Blackshear Hodges (ret.): 'They tell me the *Southern Review* is a fine publication, but I think its chances are damn poor' ... Said a military member of the faculty: 'I don't like the looks of anybody who reads it'. Said a student: 'What's the Southern Review? I never heard of it' " ("Books: Obit in Baton Rouge", *Time* [February 2, 1942], 74, 76).

possibility of help. "We got a polite no from each of them."
Brooks and Warren wanted to continue the *Review* but, if the
possibility arose, they would insist on the promise of "a reasonable continuance – 3 to 5 years. It's demoralizing to try to continue on a hand-to-mouth basis." [42] Ransom had taken the same
attitude towards editing *The Kenyon Review*; in 1938 he had
written to Merrill Moore: 'I don't want to edit another Fugitive,
or little magazine, which would be wondering if each issue might
be the last." [43]

In the early months of 1942 there were two plans afoot to save
The Southern Review. The first was variously referred to as "the
Georgia proposition" or "the Georgia business". *The Southern
Review* would hand over its name and subscription lists to Allen
Tate who would edit it from Georgia. "We know no better
news", the editors wrote to Tate on 18 February 1942, "than
that there is a good chance of your editing a critical review.
Somebody ought to have seen the light long, long back." [44] The
plan seems to have involved a merger but with which magazine
is uncertain. It was off by the beginning of March for lack of
money. The second plan concerned a merger of *The Southern
Review* and *The Kenyon Review*. Its great champion was John
Crowe Ransom who first proposed it on 21 January 1942. "I
do powerfully hope", he wrote to Warren, "that, if you discontinue there, you may go in with us in some fashion".[45] Ransom's proposal was prompted by the war situation which was
also endangering his own *Review*:

The crisis is not merely military, it's total, and it affects the K.R. In
other words, we will have to go on a reduced budget. There is in fact
a possibility that we will have to discontinue. . . . I am sure that presently we'll have a little card for use with our contributors – but not
with those whom we've accepted already, on our own terms – to the
effect that we'll pay just half what we formerly did. And we'll shorten
our office expenses, and after this spring go along on a student secretary rather than a graduate secretary. And I believe we'd better come

42   Brooks to Tate, December 31, 1941, Tate papers.
43   April 29, 1938, Moore papers.
44   Tate papers.
45   *Southern Review* papers.

down to an 'occasional' publication, which in fact would mean three times a year, rather than a quarterly. This last rather than the policy of keeping our regular dates but issuing in abridged and scrappy form.

Brooks and Warren reacted "very favorably" to Ransom's proposal but did not as yet commit themselves. They still had not given up hope of continuing on their own and had "postponed formal extinction, till March 1 anyhow".[46] In February Tate came up with the Georgia proposition. As Brooks and Warren did not expect L. S. U. to accept the Kenyon merger, they told Tate that they were "anxious to see your proposition at Georgia go through". They also felt that Ransom was "largely swayed by personal friendship" in making them the merger offer; L. S. U. would get far more out of it than Ransom.[47] To Ransom, however, the merger seemed the best way of saving *The Kenyon Review*. He made this clear to Tate when he described the crisis facing his *Review*; if the merger came off, "we'd be stronger here as a public organ and also as a College project, because of the great name of the other Review." [48]

Tate himself was intimately connected with the merger. It was probably he who, on hearing of the difficulties facing *The Kenyon Review* and of the merger, suggested that his friend Henry Church might help out. After spending some thirty years in France, where he edited and financed the magazine *Mesures*, Church had returned to the United States at the outbreak of the war and was connected with the comparative literature department at Prince-

[46] Letter, Ransom to Tate, January 28, 1942, Tate papers. At this time a third literary quarterly, *Partisan Review*, was also in financial straits: "Our financial situation is at present threatening but not desperate. Our angel can carry through the next two issues, but after that he'll be able to make up only half the annual deficit. Which means we must find somewhere about $1500. What's happening with 'Southern'? These are indeed trying times for literary magazines!" (Dwight Macdonald [?] to Tate, February 13, 1942, Tate papers).

[47] Brooks and Warren to Tate, February 18, 1942, Tate papers.

[48] January 28, 1942, Tate papers. As late as 22 April 1942, Ransom told Tate: "My opinion is that we could not easily put through the survival of the KR by itself, but could certainly put through a merger proposition; and that in fact there might be a good chance of becoming presently self-sustaining with a merger magazine and a consolidated subscription list to go on" (Tate papers).

ton University, where Tate was also teaching. He had already endowed Tate's "Creative Arts Program" with the Mesures Fund.[49] With the possibility of his support in mind, Ransom prepared two prospective budgets: "one to scheme a Kenyon Review partially subsidized by Church; the other a somewhat larger Kenyon-Review – Southern-Review partially subsidized by Church." [50]

The details of the merger were seriously considered after the Georgia project had fallen through. The starting sign was a telegram from the *Southern Review* editors to Ransom at the end of March: "Can proceed with merger negotiations if desired. Our full cooperation." [51] Ransom immediately answered with some practical suggestions. He expected that the merger would considerably increase the usual *Kenyon Review* sale of some 1200 copies per issue. He suggested as a name "THE REVIEW – formerly *The Southern Review* and *The Kenyon Review*". It seemed to him easiest to adapt the *Southern Review* cover and to keep the *Kenyon Review* printer. He also suggested that the first number of the merger would be the Summer number and that it would be edited by Brooks and Warren.[52] Ransom had to wait for almost one month for a reply to his proposals. It was negative. Although pleas for its continuance had been coming in since the news of its imminent demise had first been publicized, the Louisiana State University was determined to suspend *The Southern Review*.

The Kenyon Review survived thanks to the generosity of its friends and contributors. On 25 March 1942, Ransom and Rice sent out a circular letter to a selected number of their most valued contributors to acquaint them with the precarious financial state of the *Review* and to ask their advice: "This Review has lost its generous patrons who, as friends of Kenyon College, supported us up to the time of war. If they continue now to

[49] Cf. Allen Tate (ed.), *The Language of Poetry* (Princeton, 1942), viii.
[50] Ransom to Tate, February 6, 1942, Tate papers.
[51] No date, *Southern Review* papers.
[52] Ransom to Brooks and Warren, March 30, 1942, *Southern Review* papers.

make gifts, it is expected that these will be marked for the College war budget. As we are announcing in our Spring issue (to be mailed out April 7th), we must find $2.500.00 or so annually from new patrons in order to continue in something like our present size and style. This is after allowing for every possible economy in operation, including reduction in the page rate of payment to our contributors." [53] After an intensive campaign Ransom could announce, on 12 July 1942, that *The Kenyon Review* was "all safe now". The required funds had been raised; small gifts had totalled "better than $1000.00, and then there's Mr. Church ($500.00), another large donor, and the appropriation from the *Southern* to fill their unexpired subscriptions. We're not rich but we can manage all right".[54] The *Review* had not been able to make its regular appearance in the summer of 1942 but the Autumn issue appeared with a new cover, and the editors assured their readers that they felt "as secure in the prospect of entering upon and completing another volume, which will be Volume V, for 1943, as a merely literary enterprise has the right to feel in these times".[55] Nor did they expect to discontinue after that. The first crisis due to the war had been successfully overcome.

The Summer 1942 number was the only issue *The Kenyon Review* would miss in its long career. In early 1944 its financial situation was greatly improved by "a considerable three-year benefaction from a new source",[56] which enabled it to employ a full-time professional secretary and to introduce a revision of the scale of payments to contributors. Before the 1942 crisis *The Kenyon Review* had paid five dollars per page for prose and ten dollars per page for poetry but this rate had been halved when the magazine resumed publication in the autumn of 1942. In the Spring 1944 issue, the editors were able to announce that, "beginning with the contents of the present issue, we shall increase

---

[53] Tate papers.
[54] Ransom to Tate, July 12, 1942, Tate papers.
[55] "Editorial Notes: We Resume", *KR*, IV, 3 (Summer-Autumn 1942), 405.
[56] See note 1 on page 248.

the existing rate, though we cannot yet bring it up to the original figure".[57] The *Review*'s subsequent financial history has been touched upon at the beginning of this chapter.

The preceding description of the origins of *The Kenyon Review* shows how closely its early history was intertwined with *The Southern Review*. In the end it took over *The Southern Review*'s subscription lists and the Winter 1943 issue announced Brooks and Warren as advisory editors.[58] In subsequent years it gained a great prestige in literary and academic circles and it is probably true, as William Van O'Connor claimed in 1964, that it "dominated modern letters in America in the years after the War".[59] 1964 marked the twenty-fifth anniversary of *The Kenyon Review* and the seventy-fifth anniversary of John Crowe Ransom, its editor during the first twenty-one years. The London *Times Literary Supplement* celebrated the occasion with a rather extravagant claim: " . . . the *Sewanee*, since Mr. Allen Tate began editing it in 1944, the *Partisan Review*, since it switched its emphasis from left-wing politics to literary criticism, and the powerful baby of the quartet, the *Hudson Review*, since it began publication in 1948, have all broadened a tradition that is essentially the *Kenyon*'s creation." [60] This statement does not take account of the tremendous influence of *The Southern Review*. An examination of the contents of the early *Kenyon Review* will show the degree of its indebtedness.

There are two obvious ways in which *The Kenyon Review* differed from its predecessor. Firstly, it did not carry any political or regional discussion, and, secondly, its editor, John Crowe Ransom, figured large in its pages. These two factors caused a certain degree of intellectual simplification. We have described how the regional and literary contributions to *The Southern*

[57] "Editorial Notes: Announcement to Contributors", *KR*, VI, 2 (Spring 1944), 64.
[58] The Autumn 1943 issue was a Henry James number upon the occasion of the hundredth anniversary of his birth and was edited by Warren. Five of the nine contributors had also written for the James issue of *The Hound & Horn*.
[59] Long and Burr, p. 16.
[60] "Don't Bury the Hatchet", *TLS* (February 13, 1964), 127.

Review – its political articles were less predictable – tended to acknowledge a number of related antitheses which were in no need of regular editorial pronunciamentos. *The Kenyon Review,* on the other hand, was almost exclusively concerned with the opposition between poetry and science, and John Crowe Ransom kept up a running battle against what he considered to be presumptions and intrusions of science. Many of his early editorials were concerned with this problem; he organized symposia on the same theme; and occasionally published reactions of interested readers. His animosity towards science had a very noticeable influence on his literary criticism; it led him to emphasize exclusively aesthetic principles.

The first issue of *The Kenyon Review* was published in January 1939, and almost all its contributions could have been taken straight from *The Southern Review.* There were articles by John Peale Bishop, Delmore Schwartz, Paul Rosenfeld, Philip Rahv, and Ford Madox Ford, poems by Robert Lowell [61] and Randall Jarrell, and among the reviewers were Howard Baker, R. P. Blackmur, Herbert Muller, Yvor Winters, and Philip Blair Rice.[62] Ransom's "Editorial Notes" consisted of two parts; the first part, "Was Shakespeare a Philosopher", dealt with *Shakespeare's Philosophical Patterns,* a book published at the L. S. U. Press by his fellow-teacher at Vanderbilt University, Walter Clyde Curry. The second part has a direct bearing on our discussion. Entitled "The Teaching of Poetry", it was a discussion of the

[61] Lowell graduated from Kenyon College in the summer of 1940 and Ransom wanted him as secretary on the staff of *The Kenyon Review.* The appointment, however, went to David MacDowell, whom Charles Pipkin had tried to get as secretary for *The Southern Review.* In later years MacDowell went into publishing and has recently returned to the world of magazine publishing as the editorial adviser on the reprint of 27 little magazines, including *The Dial, The Hound & Horn* and *The Symposium* (1967).

[62] Note also, for instance, the reviewers of the second issue: Tate on Emily Dickinson, Ransom on Merrill Moore, Mark Van Doren on Delmore Schwartz, Randall Jarrell on Yvor Winters, Robert Penn Warren on Lionel Trilling, Gilbert Seldes on the American theatre, Lincoln Kirstein on the dance, F. Cudworth Flint on contemporary poetry, H. B. Parkes on a historical study; and reviews by Louis Kronenberger and Joseph Warren Beach.

state of scholarship and of criticism in the light of Brooks's and Warren's recently published *Understanding Poetry*. There was a high percentage of pedants among university professors, Ransom wrote, and it was "particularly high within the 'Departments of English' ". A pedant might be a very learned person but "discussing the poem, he is habitually off the point". But criticism was everywhere gaining a hold; the present age was to Ransom indeed the "Age of Criticism". He cited the names of Eliot, Richards, Empson, Tate, Winters, Blackmur − "a list of intensive critics the like of which has certainly not been furnished in literary history at one time before". Criticism had gained territory because poetry had become decadent; but a critical age had "its own passionate enjoyments". Brooks's and Warren's book was "one monument to this age". The fact that their analyses of old poems were as fresh, "or at least, nearly", as those of new poems, suggested to Ransom that "criticism as it is now practised is a new thing". This new criticism was probably even more important for the analysis of the classics of literature than "of the strange moderns".[63]

This editorial shows that Ransom shared the passion of the *Southern Review* editors for the close analysis of literary texts both in critical writing and in teaching. It will be remembered that it was Ransom who, on reading Tate's lecture "Miss Emily and the Bibliographer", had suggested that *The Southern Review* join the *Kenyon* in a symposium on the state of literature teaching in colleges and universities. In his official announcement of the symposium, Ransom described how Tate's observations had "helped to crystallize some editorial intentions".[64] *The Kenyon*

[63] J.C.R., "Editorial Notes: The Teaching of Poetry", *KR*, I, 1 (Winter 1939), 81, 82, 83.
[64] J.C.R., "Editorial: Mr. Tate and the Professors", *KR*, II, 3 (Summer 1940), 350. Recently Tate has described the outcome of the battle between critics and scholars: ". . . the old-line historical scholars have undergone a change of heart: the American English Department is no longer hostile to the practice of the art which, if it were sufficiently removed into the past, was the subject matter of its discipline. The English Department and the university are now among the necessary patrons of literature" ("What Is Creative Writing", *Wisconsin Studies in Contemporary Literature*, V, 2 [Autumn 1964], 183).

Review continued the battle for the recognition of new critical methods in the universities which Brooks and Warren had started and to some extent won in their *Review* and in their textbooks.

Ransom's idea of the function of contemporary criticism was coloured by his incessant fight against science, which at this point of the discussion ought to be investigated. The second issue of *The Kenyon Review* provides a convenient starting point. Ransom felt that this issue was more representative of his intentions than the first. "You will see", he wrote to Tate, "that this number is fairly rigorous in its standard, and I hope it will be in that respect an index to our general progress".[65] Featuring large in it was a symposium entitled "The New Encyclopedists", a discussion of *The International Encyclopedia of Unified Science* edited by Otto Neurath. Only a few parts of this encyclopedia had as yet appeared, but one of them was Charles W. Morris's controversial "Foundations of the Theory of Signs." The contributors to this symposium were professional philosophers who discussed the terms of the encyclopedia more or less dispassionately. Eliseo Vivas was "Pro", Howard Dykema Roelofs was "Contra" and Philip Blair Rice added some "Considerations". But the reader of this issue was left in no doubt as to which side the editor took. In "The Arts and the Philosophers" Ransom insisted on an absolute separation of art and science. The theory of the encyclopedists meant to him that the arts might be taken "as quasi-sciences". Ransom maintained that the cause of the arts had suffered at the hands of the philosophers who had often been likened to "a sort of court to which science and art, or other natural disputants, may resort for 'justice' for their claims. But this court is packed, and not with artists, or religionists, but with positivists and 'naturalists', who are the proper attorneys for science." Ransom maintained that the scientists were not equipped to discuss literature profitably. Looking at the past he recognized two major aesthetic systems, which equally regarded art "as a thing which is nearly science". The first regarded it as the "*decorative* or 'sensuous' version of science," the second –

---

[65] February 22, 1939, Tate papers.

as propagated, for instance, by I. A. Richards in his early criticism – as the "*emotional* version of science". Art in modern times
was gradually occupying the disreputable place religion had held
in the nineteenth century. But its cause was by no means lost:

The Encyclopedists are talking about the language of science. I imagine that now is a splendid time for the aestheticians, inside or outside the Encyclopedia, to make an assertion which would be round,
bold, metaphysical, just, and tactically perfect. To this effect: art has
a language of its own; it is not the same as the language of science;
its semantical meanings cannot be rendered in the language of science.
Art fixes a kind of knowledge of which science has no understanding,
and which gentlemen too confined within the scientific habit cannot
approach intelligently.[66]

Ransom's editorial clearly shows that the theory of the special
knowledge which literature provides was directly influenced by
the uncompromising division between art and science. This division also accounts for Ransom's refusal to discuss the "content"
of a work of art apart from the "form". He emphasized their
indivisible unity in the ensuing dispute with Charles Morris:

The paraphrase, schematization, or description of the work of art may
fairly be said to define its structural plan, or its 'value' as that term
is understood by those whose comment is exclusively upon this feature.
But the paraphrase is not the work of art. That is almost the elemen-
tary principle under which the able critics and interpreters of art now
practice, and perhaps that is almost enough to constitute the theoretical equipment of a critic. In paraphrasing the work of art we lose
the body, and though we keep a framework for it the omission is too
extravagant.[67]

Indeed, Ransom's theory of literature as it emerges from his
editorials and articles in the early *Kenyon Review* was not so

---

[66] J.C.R., "Editorial Notes: The Arts and the Philosophers", *KR*, I, 2
(Spring 1939), 194, 195, 197, 198.
[67] "The Pragmatics of Art", *KR*, II, 1 (Winter 1940), 87. This article
was attacked by Roellinger in *The Southern Review*; it was an answer to
Morris, "Science, Art and Technology", *KR*, I, 4 (Autumn 1939), 409-423.
It is interesting to note that a second article which prompted Roellinger's
attack, Tate's "Literature as Knowledge", was also mainly concerned with
Morris's ideas.

much a natural philosophical growth as a series of answers to scientific presumptions. This led to an unprecedented aestheticism which denied any moral dimension to literature. Anything that might verge on an ulterior use of literature, particularly of poetry, in the service of non-aesthetic interests, must be banned. Ransom recognized the necessity of a consistent literary theory; but it was here that critics, "and even new critics, who are the best yet known in our language", were weakest. This necessity, however, was imposed by extra-literary conditions, particularly the growing philosophic sophistication of science. The literary critics, according to Ransom, did not command "the technique of ultimate generalizations, which is the technique of philosophy". He pointed out that most scientists had similarly "lacked philosophy, and committed howlers on the speculative side, but that defect is being remedied in our time as rarely before. The philosophers have gone to the rescue of the scientists. The literary critics are still in the wilderness; their theories of poetry do not have philosophical standing. Nor have the philosophers interposed on their behalf." [68]

This statement is taken from an editorial which questioned the critical position of R. P. Blackmur. Although Blackmur's new critical practice was exemplary, his theoretical position, as Ransom distilled it from different statements in *The Expense of Greatness,* was that "criticism is moralism applied to the poem". This position, Ransom wrote, ought to be dismissed for the same reasons as the humanist and Marxist positions. Ransom here shows a lack of understanding of how morality got into Blackmur's criticism – which the reader of the early *Kenyon Review* is liable to blame on his embattled position. His objection was that poetry "is beyond passion, it is beyond even moral passion;" like any other kind of passion, moral passion was "inhibitive of the difficult poetic act". The best works of art were works of "pure" art; they would only provide an "aesthetic experience". Discussing, in a later issue, the editorial policy with reference to the selection of poetry for his magazine, Ransom stated that

<hr/>

[68] "Editorial Notes: Ubiquitous Moralists", *KR*, III, 1 (Winter 1941), 96.

he never interfered with the poet's freedom to choose the substance of his poems as long as he did not write "upon burning contemporary issues, moral or political. Poetry with this substance is hardly eligible whether with connoisseurs or with aestheticians, the reason being that it does not seem to them to be exactly the poetic substance." [69]

The literature-science opposition recurred in different guises also in non-editorial contributions. There was, for instance, Philip Wheelwright's philosophical discussion "On the Semantics of Poetry", in the Summer 1940 issue, which was a direct descendant of the dispute concerning the meaning of poetry in *The Symposium*. Wheelwright made a sharp distinction between the language of science and the language of poetry, or, to use his own terminology, between monosignificance and denotation and plurisignificance and connotation. His position was attacked by Josephine Miles who maintained that "all language is plurisignificant as all objects and words appear in context. . . . Science and poetry are kinds of selection from plurisignificance." But Miss Miles would gladly trade both her own and Wheelwright's terminology "and the equivalent terminology of his contemporaries . . . for ten pages of solid fact about the language of poetry not as it might be but as it has been writ".[70]

The Kenyon Review in its dispute with science, lacked the regional-cultural dimension of *The Southern Review*. On the philosophical level, however, it supervised a debate between metaphysical naturalism, the belief in the self-sufficiency of nature, and theism, the belief in the possibility of a supernatural

[69] "Editorial Notes", *KR*, III, 4 (Autumn 1941), 492. Since the early days of *The Kenyon Review* Ransom has of course modified his critical ideas. The first indications of this modification were recorded by Robert Wooster Stallman as early as 1948 in his bibliography of Ransom's writings to date (in the issue of *The Sewanee Review* celebrating Ransom's sixtieth birthday [LVI (1948)]). Ten years later, John Bradbury recorded that Ransom had "begun again to speak of 'substantive values' and 'moral Universals' in contradistinction to aesthetic values per se. He has even talked the heresy of a separable content . . ." (*The Fugitives: A Critical Account* [Chapel Hill, 1959], p. 128).
[70] "Correspondence: More Semantics of Poetry", *KR*, II, 4 (Autumn 1940), 505, 507.

principle. The debate was opened, in the autumn of 1941, by Eliseo Vivas with a favourable exposition of "The New Naturalism" which was followed by Philip Wheelwright's reply, "The Failure of Naturalism".[71] The "Editorial Notes" of the following issue were written by Philip Rice. They described the wide implications of the debate:

The topic is inescapable for a magazine with this Review's commitments. Not only does it have a profound if indirect bearing upon the standards of aesthetic criticism; it is of special moment to all who are concerned with the general reorientation of our culture which is being forced upon us by the tragic events of our time. More urgently than before, we are confronted by such questions as, how much can be preserved from the Christian and other religious traditions? must we resign ourselves to a primarily scientific and technological culture? is a new humanism possible and desirable?

The Kenyon Review, therefore, would continue the discussion and, what is more, this discussion would be conducted by professional philosophers. Rice pointed out that this had not often been the case in other magazines. In *The Criterion,* for instance, such issues had often been dealt with by men of letters or, in later years, "by theologians of a single religious order". *The Kenyon Review,* however, had chosen the philosophers Vivas and Wheelwright; they differed over the issue "whether that particular variety of 'private' or 'introspective' experience called mystical intuition is valid". Wheelwright thought it was; he emphasized the mystical experience rather than natural reason.[72] Rice's editorial was followed by Vivas's reply to Wheelwright with a note that Wheelwright would be invited to continue the dispute with Vivas in the next issue.[73] The only other professional

[71] William Barrett's "Christianity and Modern Man" – an anti-Naturalist review of Reinhold Niebuhr's *The Nature and Destiny of Man* in the same issue – also bore on the discussion of naturalism.
[72] P.B.R., "Editorial Notes: A Word about Naturalism", *KR*, IV, 1 (Winter 1942), 87, 90.
[73] Wheelwright, "Religion and Social Grammar", *KR*, IV, 2 (Spring 1942), 202-216. A good many years later, Vivas wrote an interesting, largely appreciative review of Wheelwright's *The Burning Fountain (Perspectives U.S.A.,* No. 14 [Winter 1956], 167-175).

philosopher who participated in the debate was Bertrand Russell with his anti-theistic "Non-Materialistic Naturalism".[74]

The preceding remarks upon some cardinal editorial concerns serve to show also that *The Kenyon Review* had inherited from its predecessors a concern for symposial structure. Apart from the group discussions of the new science encyclopedia, of naturalism, and of the teaching of literature, the editors conducted other debates which illustrate a wider range of interest. The fourth issue featured "The Present State of Poetry: A Symposium" which transcended national boundaries with a discussion of the state of poetry in England by Herbert Read, in France by Justin O'Brien – who had contributed valuable articles on French authors to *The Symposium* – and in the United States by Robert Penn Warren. The Spring 1940 issue gave an appraisal of "The Legacy of Sigmund Freud", a leading medical expert, Alexander Reid Martin, examining the therapeutic, Lionel Trilling the literary and aesthetic, and Eliseo Vivas the philosophical legacy. This symposium had been organized by *Kenyon Review*'s managing editor, Philip Blair Rice, who had noticed a renewed interest in the applications of Freudian methods and discoveries to different fields after the initial wave of popular interest in psychoanalysis in the early 'Twenties. Although "the work of many generations" would have to be done before Freud's principles could be "evaluated definitively", Rice felt that from time to time "inventories of such a movement must be made".[75] The preceding issue had featured a memorial poem on Freud's death by W. H. Auden.[76]

---

[74] *KR*, IV, 3 (Summer-Autumn 1942), 361-365. In the same issue Mark Schorer had defended the necessity of myths as controlling images to order chaotic and fragmentary experience ("Mythology for the Study of William Blake", 366-380). The juxtaposition of Russell's and Schorer's articles was deliberate because "they both bear on the controversy over naturalism". Commenting on these two articles Ransom maintained that myths are more useful to literary men than scientific universals ("Editorial Notes: Mr. Russell and Mr. Schorer", 406-407). He returned to the topic in the winter of 1946 with "Art Worries the Naturalists".

[75] "Editorial Notes: Psychoanalysis: The Second Wave", *KR*, II, 2 (Spring 1940), 226, 227.

[76] "For Sigmund Freud", *KR*, II, 1 (Winter 1940), 30-34.

The Kenyon Review, like *The Southern Review*, also conducted a symposium on "The American Culture", with Rushton Coulborn investigating "The Polity", Clyde Kluckholm "The Way of Life," and John Peale Bishop "The Arts". The symposium had been organized – in the spring of 1941 – "by way of tribute to the sense of a crisis imperilling all". Ransom characteristically apologized for introducing for the first time two papers "in expression purely of political and socio-anthropological views of our culture". But he argued that social and political conditions influence "the form and the prosperity of the arts as much as building, marrying, and baking do".[77] A purely literary symposium – on Gerard Manley Hopkins – was directed by Cleanth Brooks in the Summer issue of 1944. It celebrated the hundredth anniversary of the poet's birth with essays by Herbert Marshall McLuhan, Harold Whitehall, Josephine Miles, and Austin Warren. But, as Brooks pointed out, these papers were "not to be regarded as closing the discussion".[78] The next issue featured additional contributions by Robert Lowell, Austin Warren and Arthur Mizener under the general heading "The Hopkins Centennial (concluded)".[79]

In the winter of 1945 *The Kenyon Review* started a series of "Reconsiderations", reminiscent of *Scrutiny*'s "Revaluations" which, in their turn, had been inspired by the "Scrutinies" conducted by *The Calendar of Modern Letters*. It is perhaps no coincidence that "Reconsiderations VII" was an article by *Scrutiny*'s editor F. R. Leavis on Dr. Johnson. We have noted before that the English *Scrutiny* had a noticeable affinity to the tradition of the American literary review. It is not surprising that the reviewer of foreign periodicals in 1939 considered *Scrutiny* "perhaps . . . closest" to the ideal of the quarterlies although it still fell "wide of the mark:" its contributions lacked the "bril-

---

[77]   J.C.R., "Editorial Notes", *KR*, III, 2 (Spring 1941), 242.
[78]   "Gerard Manley Hopkins", *KR*, VI, 3 (Summer 1944).
[79]   A year after their publication in *The Kenyon Review*, the essays of the symposium, together with a biographical note by Austin Warren and an essay by F. R. Leavis ("Metaphysical Isolation", first published in *Scrutiny*) were published in book form by the New Directions Press (The Kenyon Critics, *Gerard Manley Hopkins* [Norfolk, Conn., 1945]).

liance and the philosophical incisiveness of *The Criterion* in its best days, the tone is often academic, and there is a more persistent concern with pedagogical than with larger aesthetic issues".[80] In the same number (autumn 1939) Delmore Schwartz appraised the achievement of Eliot's *Criterion* which had ceased publication early in the year. For all the occasional folly of some of its contributors – for instance, John Middleton Murry, Ezra Pound, and Montgomery Belgion – and the sometimes spuriously Socratic "Commentaries" of its editor, *The Criterion* remained an invaluable, variegated record of the crisis in Western civilization. Although its temper was attuned to the "supernaturalists" rather than the "naturalists", it was never used for the sake of a particular programme. Rather, Eliot's sense of the past and "of the whole of Western Literature as a living element in the present", and his responsible, "peculiarly intelligent" editorship had secured the widest possible circle of interests.[81] The American quarterlies of the 'Forties never attempted such a wide scope, which indeed the literary situation did not encourage.

III

The Southern Review ceased publication in the spring of 1942. *The Kenyon Review* missed its summer issue but appeared again

[80] "Foreign Periodicals", *KR*, I, 4 (Autumn 1939), 472. In the autumn of 1946, Eric Bentley – an Englishman who was then in the process of editing a *Scrutiny* anthology – claimed that there was more "new criticism" in the books of the *Scrutiny* group "than in all the other works of the 'new' school put together". But his estimate of the magazine as a magazine was more qualified: "Its offering of creative literature is negligible. Its coverage of foreign literature and of non-literary matters is haphazard and of uneven quality. The number of contributors to the magazine is very small, and of the happy few only three or four seem to have a character of their own; the others use the ideas of the editors as mechanical formulas. Obviously, then, we must credit the high achievement of *Scrutiny* (within its limits) to F. R. Leavis and his most intimate collaborators" ("This is the New Criticism", *KR*, VIII, 4 [Autumn 1946], 673). For Leavis's reaction, see " 'The Kenyon Review' and 'Scrutiny' ", *Scrutiny*, XIV, 2 (December 1946), 134-136.
[81] Delmore Schwartz, "*The Criterion*, 1922-1939", *Purpose*, XI, 4 (Oct.-Dec. 1939), 234, 226. This article was published simultaneously in *The Kenyon Review*.

in the autumn with a new cover and a new optimism. There was also a slight change in the autumn cover of its contemporary, *The Sewanee Review*: it was still crowded by the table of contents but the name of its editor, William S. Knickerbocker, which it had displayed throughout the 'Thirties, was missing. This was the first indication of the change of editorship which would completely refurbish *The Sewanee Review*.

During the 'Thirties the interests and taste of editor and magazine had virtually been identical; they were primarily focussed on the nineteenth century. The title of one of Knickerbocker's articles, "Suet with no Plums: Restoring Thomas Babington Macaulay", may be considered representative.[82] Rarely if ever did the name of a contributor to the *Southern* and *Kenyon* reviews appear on the contents page of *The Sewanee Review*. Knickerbocker was no friend of the Agrarians. Although he prided himself on having published Ransom's contribution to *I'll Take My Stand* prior to its publication in that collection, he told Merrill Moore in 1938: "As for the Nashville farmers, they have wantonly elected to label me as their 'enemy' because, in spite of their deserved following, nobody else regards them seriously enough to analyse their procedures and their achievements." He was not very eager to publish their essays because they had "their own log-rolling machines in *The American Review* and *The Southern Review*".[83] But the hostile attitude of the agrarians is not difficult to explain. Already in 1932, Knickerbocker had savagely attacked them in the magazine *Contempo*. He had written that the Southern way of life the agrarians advocated was "the most backward, least intelligent, most wasteful, most bitter and unrelenting of any pattern of life evoked in these States of America"; the agrarians, in Knickerbocker's opinion, thought that "by talk" they could resist the encroachments of industrialism; "but the Twelve [of *I'll Take My Stand*] are ignored because they chiefly have nothing to say, however beautifully they say it".[84]

[82] *SR*, XLVII, 2 (Spring 1939).
[83] August 14 [?17], 1938, Moore papers.
[84] "The Dilemma of the Fugitives", *Contempo*, II, 1 (May 25, 1932), 2.

At the time of the suspension of *The Southern Review*, Knickerbocker's position had become extremely difficult. His contract was running out and it was unlikely that it would be renewed. A number of observers thought him incapable of editing *The Sewanee Review*, among them Andrew Lytle. Already during the last months of 1941, Lytle had been in contact with Alexander Guerry, the energetic Vice Chancellor of the University of the South which sponsored *The Sewanee Review*. Guerry wanted to improve the standard of both the English department and the *Review*, and Lytle thought Allen Tate would be the best person to accomplish this. In January 1942, Lytle urged Tate to tell Guerry "that now is the time for the Sewanee Review to take the place of the Southern Review, and that you might take the Academy job until Knickerbocker's contract expired, when you would be made editor of that and do more or less what you have been doing at Princeton".[85] Lytle continued his efforts towards this end. In May 1942, he told Tate that Knickerbocker was "doomed" and that he would "almost bet that you are in the V.C.'s mind as his successor. I've made myself clear that I don't want it".[86] In the meantime Tate had been made an offer by the Louisiana State University but Lytle tried to persuade him to hold back on it as long as possible. Tate, however, wrote to Guerry saying that he had heard his name was being considered but that he "couldn't take a magazine that didn't pay". Guerry then approached Cleanth Brooks asking him to edit *The Sewanee Review* but Brooks declined.[87]

Finally, rather reluctantly, Lytle accepted the post of "Managing Editor", with T. S. Long of the English department as "Acting Editor". Their names and editorial titles appeared for

[85]   January 30, 1942, Tate papers. Guerry was held in high esteem by the different editors of *The Sewanee Review*. In 1945 Tate wrote: "The fact that Alexander Guerry, our President, renovated the Review in the midst of war and in face of the difficult future is nothing short of heroic. But he believes in what we are doing . . ." (letter to Huntingdon Cairns, February 13, 1945); and on Guerry's death in 1948, John Palmer wrote: "*The Sewanee Review* has certainly lost its kindest critic and best friend" (letter to J. C. Ransom, October 21, 1948, *Sewanee Review* papers).
[86]   Tate papers.
[87]   Cleanth Brooks to Tate, July 1942, Tate papers.

the first time in the Winter 1943 issue which looked very different from earlier numbers. Its cover was grey instead of yellow, carrying only the name of the magazine and the date of the issue in red letters. The contents also had changed significantly: there were poems by Wallace Stevens, George Marion O'Donnell, William Meredith, Arthur Mizener, Carlos Baker, and Louis Cox, and articles by Arthur Mizener and Cleanth Brooks. But the rest of the issue was not different from the earlier *Sewanee Review*. Lytle made an important start but it was Tate who made the magazine into the most distinguished companion magazine of *The Kenyon Review* and a worthy successor of *The Southern Review*. Lytle's achievement, however, was important, although he was not in sole charge of the magazine. In 1944, just before Tate took over the editorship, an admittedly somewhat partisan observer wrote: "Lytle transformed the old and once distinguished Sewanee Review from the condition into which it had sunk for more than a decade – a haphazard receptacle of second-rate academic-literary exercises – into a publication with character and difficult standards of excellence." [88]

Lytle's successive issues showed that *The Sewanee Review* was moving close to the editorial positions of the *Southern* and *Kenyon* reviews which it had still ridiculed in its Spring 1942 number. [89] Lytle's editorship was, however, of short duration. In the summer of 1943 he decided "to retire to his farm and write after the Autumn issue". [90] He was prevailed upon to edit the Winter 1944 issue but the Spring and Summer numbers of that year were edited by T. S. Long. By the autumn of 1943, however, *The Sewanee Review* had found a most important adviser, Allen Tate. In the summer of that year Guerry had discussed

[88]   Richard Croom Beatty, ed., *A Vanderbilt Miscellany 1919-1944* (Nashville, Tenn., 1944), 24-25.
[89]   "In a spirit of teamwork never before equalled in the history of criticism, the editor of the *Kenyon Review* writes for the *Southern Review* and *vice versa*, producing by this 'strategy' a curious effect of echo that sounds almost like public acclaim" (Joseph Baker, "The Philosopher and the 'New Critic' ", *SR*, L, 2 [Spring 1942], 167).
[90]   "Managing Editor No. 2" to J. D. Bennett, July 23, 1943, *Sewanee Review* papers.

the future of the *Review* with Tate. He had probably offered Tate the editorship but in August Tate left for Washington, D.C. to become Consultant in American Letters at the Library of Congress. But he told Guerry that, if he should wish to reopen the discussion "some time next summer" he would listen to him "with the greatest interest". In September he offered to help *The Sewanee Review* in any possible way but suggested that the most useful thing he could do would be to solicit manuscripts, since he was "advantageously located for that sort of thing".[91] Guerry accepted with alacrity and told Tate to "begin at once to see what you can do along this line".[92] On 13 October 1943 the Board of Directors of *The Sewanee Review* voted unanimously to extend an invitation to Tate to become editor. Tate accepted gladly and told Guerry that a friend of his wanted to increase the budget for the *Review*'s contributors by a gift of five hundred dollars a year for three years with the strong probability that the gift would be renewed indefinitely. A few days later Tate announced another gift, of three hundred dollars a year for three years, by his friend Henry Church who also made an occasional donation to *The Kenyon Review*.

Tate's editorship was announced in the Summer 1944 issue. For decades *The Sewanee Review* had carried the subtitle "A Quarterly of Life and Letters"; now it was simply called "A Quarterly". The inside front cover featured an eloquent announcement of the new editorial position. *The Sewanee Review,* it said, would favour "– while giving both sides a hearing – the humanities against the positivist spirit". This was exactly what the *Southern* and *Kenyon* reviews had been doing. Indeed, one specific editorial aim of the refurbished magazine would be "to continue in the South the recent service to letters performed by *The Southern Review* from 1935 to 1942". It finally proposed to join its "distinguished contemporaries in the quarterly field in bringing about a genuine collaboration in a great task which might otherwise remain undefined".

The change of editorship was given all possible publicity.

---

[91]   Tate to Guerry, September 21, 1943, Tate papers.
[92]   September 29, 1943, Tate papers.

Concurrently with this Summer 1944 issue, special announcements and subscription cards were sent out to university libraries and other potential subscribers. But Tate's first full-time editorial production was the Autumn issue. The Gotham Book Mart in New York City, famous for its support of little magazines and *avant-garde* literature, gave it a window display, and *The Sewanee Review* itself ran a very large number of exchange advertisements, "simply", Tate wrote, "because I wanted the announcement of the new regime here to get into circulation".[93] The issue contained poems by St-John Perse (translated by Denis Devlin), Denis Devlin, Robert Lowell, and Norman MacLeod, a story by Katherine Anne Porter, and essays by Jacques Maritain, John Peale Bishop, Marianne Moore, and Wallace Stevens. Hoyt Trowbridge wrote on "Aristotle and the 'New Criticism' ", in defence of the Chicago Aristotelians, only to be refuted by John Crowe Ransom, who distilled some dangerous heresies from the scanty publications of the Chicagoans. What these critics principally came to, Ransom wrote, were "elaborate versions of the *explication du texte* which French schoolboys learn to recite in their poetry classes. That is to say, they 'interpret' their poems or write out the prose 'arguments', or make 'paraphrases'." [94]

But by far the most important contribution to the Autumn 1944 issue, from the point of view of our discussion, was Tate's editorial, "The State of Letters". We shall discuss it at some length because it epitomizes not only the point of view of *The Sewanee Review* but also that of its fellow quarterlies. A serious difficulty facing the editor of a quarterly like *The Sewanee Review*, Tate wrote, was to reach a very small, scattered audience and offer it "good writing which has not yet got on the New York market (some of it does get there)" without high-pressure advertising. But no university could afford to advertise its publications, "even if propriety permitted it, because it would either lose its investment or achieve a financial success, either result being, from the university point of view, intolerable". The only literary magazine since the first World War – "in the tradition of which THE

93 Letter to Ransom, September 17, 1944, *Sewanee Review* papers.
94 "The Bases of Criticism", *SR*, LII, 4 (Autumn 1944), 556.

SEWANEE REVIEW will continue" – which had a large circulation, was *The Dial*, "and it was reputed to have lost money". The plight of the literary review was symbolic of the state of letters about which Tate was as gloomy as the editors of the *Kenyon* and *Partisan* reviews: "American literature and criticism have sunk since the war to predictable depths of confusion and vulgarity the menace of which could be matched by the inertia and smugness of the first decade of this century." The collapse of critical standards had already been prepared throughout the 'Thirties by "our popular critics who write books about literature which are more popular than the literature written about". The two most obvious offenders were Van Wyck Brooks and Bernard DeVoto. These two nationalistic, anti-highbrow critics – together with Archibald MacLeish – were looked upon as the Enemy by all the literary quarterlies in the early war years. Cleanth Brooks and R. P. Warren had planned to comment on their position in the final issue of *The Southern Review* and Ransom and Tate condemned them in their editorial capacities. But is was *Partisan Review* which devoted the closest attention to what it called the "Brooks-MacLeish Thesis", though, as we shall discuss presently, from a very different political perspective.

DeVoto was the latest offender. Tate took him to task primarily for his book *The Literary Fallacy* which had then just come out and which was adversely reviewed by Arthur Mizener in the same Autumn 1944 issue. Tate argued that the position of Van Wyck Brooks and DeVoto had been strengthened throughout the 'Thirties by the Marxists who had "done much to disorganize an entire generation" and whose Stalinist wing "is now talking very much like Mr. DeVoto about democracy and nationalism, the wonderful union of which will probably become the religion of the next age: I say this largely to reassure those of my readers who a few years ago liked to think that I was not only undemocratic but anti-democratic; I should not wish, on this of all occasions, to disappoint them. I am not a democrat if Mr. Bernard DeVoto is a democrat; but then I do not think that Mr. DeVoto is a democrat; I think he is a literary obscurantist. Critics of this kidney are likely to be for any successful political movement, if it can be called 'liberal' and if they are 'in on it'." When it would be "necessary for a literary review to consider politics", *The Sewanee Review* would oppose democracy if it made an all-engrossing demand for loyalty and thus became a national religion. "Then, regardless of what the state may call itself, it will be totalitarian." Tate warned against the official cultural activities which aimed at influencing the foreign image of America: "For when we deliberately undertake to export America we have got to feel a cause in it, and we succeed in sending out 'representative' writers, good and bad (the good to the bad in a ratio of about one to five), who after the social changes of ten years will cease to represent anything more than an historical document, unless being also good writers, they merely represent literature." The "great literary movement" of the first three decades of the century in Europe as well as in the United States, which because of the free exchange and non-political communication between the two continents had "produced for the first time in America a genuine literature" instead of a few great talents, had come to an end: "Whatever the new literature turns out to be it will be the privilege of THE SEWANEE REVIEW to print its share of it, to comment on it, and to try to understand it." [95]

Andrew Lytle was enthusiastic about Tate's first issue: "It looks very fine, and it certainly is loaded against big and little guns." He thought Tate's editorial "just right" and he was confident that *The Sewanee Review* would not only carry on *The Southern Review*'s programme but would "in many ways be much better".[96] *The Sewanee Review* certainly prospered under Tate's editorship. The number of copies printed of each issue increased dramatically. Of the early issues of 1944, 700 copies had been printed but, as Tate told Lincoln Kirstein on 27 March 1945, "the October (my first) issue was 1200; the January 1700; the current, 2000. So we are going up." [97] Tate's wide connections

[95] "The State of Letters", *SR*, LII, 4 (Autumn 1944), 608, 609.
[96] Letter to Tate, October 16, 1944, Tate papers.
[97] *Sewanee Review* papers. Tate realized that *The Sewanee Review* had "a back-log of libraries and institutions which the Southern Review never achieved", and that his job would be "to build individual subscriptions on this foundation" (Tate to Alexander Guerry, March 29, 1944, Tate papers).

among his literary contemporaries were reflected in his magazine. Among the essayists he published in 1945 were John Peale Bishop, Kenneth Burke, R. P. Blackmur, Malcolm Cowley, Donald Davidson, T. S. Eliot, Robert Heilman, Lincoln Kirstein, Wyndham Lewis, Mark Van Doren, and Morton Zabel; among the fictioneers, Caroline Gordon, Andrew Lytle, and Peter Taylor; among the poets, Randall Jarrell, Wallace Stevens, and Dylan Thomas; and among the book reviewers, John Berryman, Francis Fergusson, Dudley Fitts, John Gould Fletcher, Harry Levin, Arthur Mizener, Henry B. Parkes, and Theodore Spencer. The remuneration of contributors was not very high: $\frac{3}{4}$ cent a word or about $2.60 a page. Because of this low rate, Tate wrote in September 1945, "in the past six months I have missed three or four pieces of first-rate material". He considered five dollars a page "a minimum for a magazine like *The Sewanee Review*." [98]

Tate's editorship lasted for exactly two years but his influence persisted. In the autumn of 1946, he was succeeded by John Palmer, the former managing editor of *The Southern Review*. Palmer recognized that his first editorial duty to the readers of *The Sewanee Review* was "one of reassurance: If under my editorship there should appear to be a break in editorial continuity from the pattern established by Mr. Tate, it will be the result not of intention but of failure of intention." Palmer referred his readers to Tate's editorial of the autumn of 1944: "what little I can say further will be by way of supplement and not of revision." [99] Tate's editorship had indeed set out the future direction of the magazine. He continued to take a close interest in it. He edited, for instance, together with Robert Penn Warren, the Summer 1948 issue which honoured John Crowe Ransom on his sixtieth birthday. After John Palmer had left the *Review* in 1952 to become assistant naval attaché in London, his successor Mon-

---

[98] Tate to Huntingdon Cairns, September 27, 1945, *Sewanee Review* papers. The Rockefeller grant in 1948 enabled *The Sewanee Review* to raise its contributor's rate to two and a half cents a word for prose and fifty cents a line for poetry.

[99] "Editorial", *SR*, LIV, 4 (Autumn 1946), 732.

roe Spears asked Tate to become an advisory editor: "I mean this primarily as public recognition of what you have already done and what you will do. . . ."[100] To celebrate Tate's sixtieth birthday, *The Sewanee Review* devoted its Autumn 1959 issue to an appraisal of his achievements. Monroe Spears opened the issue with the following "Homage to Allen Tate":

Fifteen years ago Allen Tate became editor of *The Sewanee Review*. In less than two years he changed its nature decisively, revolutionized its format, quadrupled its circulation, and brought it into the first rank of American literary quarterlies. Since that time he has retained a special interest in the magazine, has supported it in many crises, and has been generous of advice and help. It is therefore peculiarly fitting that *The Sewanee Review* should do him honor on this occasion.[101]

IV

The foregoing discussion has attempted to demonstrate that the main editorial interests and aims of *The Southern Review, The Kenyon Review*, and *The Sewanee Review* were virtually identical. The personal and ideological bonds between the editors were so close that the differences between their reviews were largely idiosyncratic and accidental; they can be traced to the personalities and the connections of the editors and to the influence of the environment on their magazines. It is much more difficult to explain the position of *Partisan Review* in the tradition of the American literary review. When, in 1948, John Palmer applied for a grant from the Rockefeller Foundation, he claimed *The Kenyon Review* and *Partisan Review* as "our two companion journals".[102] But if there are obvious similarities, the differences are certainly as conspicuous. It will not do to enumerate these similarities and to discard the differences as unfortunate divergencies which do not fit the terms of this discus-

---

[100]   Letter of December 10, 1952, *Sewanee Review* papers.
[101]   *SR*, LXVII, 4 (Autumn 1959), 527.
[102]   Draft of letter to David H. Stevens, n.d., *Sewanee Review* papers.

sion. At the present moment *Partisan Review* might well be seen as the most important critical magazine of this century, just as perhaps ten years ago a similar claim might have been made for *The Kenyon Review*. This would simply mean that today the tradition of *Partisan Review* is more alive and meaningful than the tradition of *The Kenyon Review*. It would mean that *Kenyon Review*'s supremacy during the 'Forties was merely a won battle but that *Partisan Review*'s was the final victory. Such a hypothesis can only be tested by a close inspection of *Partisan Review*.

We may start with a number of bold generalizations which will not tell the entire truth but which will indicate what we are looking for. We have pointed out before that the *Southern, Kenyon, Sewanee* and *Partisan* reviews came together on the matter of critical standards: "we all want to keep them as rigid as possible; that is the reputation we have earned, and the reputation we want to preserve." [103] But at this point it is more profitable to formulate some of the main differences. Firstly, *Partisan Review* was an urban enterprise; in 1941, thirty-five percent of its readers lived in New York City and nine percent in Chicago.[104] *The Southern Review* and *The Sewanee Review* had a considerable regional emphasis, and although *The Kenyon Review* looked upon its local setting as merely accidental, it shared their aversion of "sick" urban culture. New York especially was their image of metropolitan decadence and duplicity. *Partisan Review,* however, was edited from New York by New Yorkers and was most relevant to the position of the liberal New York intellectuals.

Secondly, *Partisan Review* was editorially committed to politics. Although its official alignment with the Communist Party was uneasy and of short duration, it continued to explore and to advocate the possibilities of leftist political action. The scope of its political advocacy, however, was necessarily diminished by the failure of Marxism in the late 'Thirties, by the second World War and by the subsequent political apathy. Many of its earlier

---

[103] *Ibid.*
[104] Only three percent lived in the Southern states but, as we have noted in our discussion of *The Southern Review*, this is not so much a comment on the quality of *Partisan Review* as on the apathy of the South.

admirers felt let down. Irving Howe, for instance, deplored the weakening of its earlier radicalism. He thought it particularly significant that *Partisan Review* had failed to counter McCarthyism with any confidence: "it failed to take the lead on the issue of freedom which could then once more have imbued the intellectuals with some fighting spirit." [105] *Partisan Review* combined an interest in *avant-garde* literature and radical politics, and although its critics felt that these two ingredients did not always mix well, they gave the magazine an unmistakable identity. It condemned the "dangerous American tradition of the 'purely literary' magazine" which *The Dial* had "helped establish".[106] The late 'Thirties and early 'Forties were perhaps the years of its greatest distinction. It was in those years that its political position was most heatedly debated unhampered by a constrictive alliance with the Communist Party.

Thirdly, *Partisan Review*'s attitude towards politics and society was essentially optimistic. Whereas the other reviews were often consciously propagating lost causes in the hope merely of slowing up developments which they abhorred, *Partisan Review* was in accord with the temper of the times. However pessimistic it might be about actual conditions, it did not lose faith in the capacity of the human mind to better these conditions. The trend of the times, it is true, modified its revolutionary optimism to a kind of radical liberalism. It was a political review run by intellectuals for intellectuals. Although before the war it fervently believed in the proletarian revolution, only four percent of its readers actually belonged to the working class. After the outbreak of the war, its politics appeared increasingly unrealistic and Utopian. This led to an editorial crisis in 1943; it had become obvious that the intellectuals could exert very little direct influence on politics. But *Partisan Review* could and did carry on an independent investigation of the world around it, especially of the intellectual's and artist's relation to that world. Richard Hofstadter has called *Partisan Review* "the house organ of the American intellectual

---

[105] "PR", *The New York Review of Books* (special issue, 1963), 20.
[106] William Barrett, "The Resistance", *PR*, XIII, 4 (Sept.-Oct. 1946), 482.

community", and Leslie Fiedler has spoken of its "archetypically highbrow pages".[107]

Fourthly, *Partisan Review* took a rationalistic, secular attitude towards its environment. This attitude was obviously at the root also of its basic political optimism. We may compare it to the essentially defeatist position of its contemporaries. The more detached contributors to the *Southern, Sewanee* and *Kenyon* reviews did not hope to change the modern trend according to their own conceptions; they merely tried to give moribund but worthwhile ideas a new lease of life. Accordingly, they gave a hearing to kinds of "knowledge" other than scientific and "naturalistic" and "positivistic" which were everywhere in evidence. In their thinking certain myths took the place of the increasingly secular and mechanistic world picture. *Partisan Review* was to campaign against this "failure of nerve". It tried to face the new world on its own terms and it deplored the growing tendency of its contemporaries in the 'Forties to seek refuge in aestheticism and mysticism.

The preceding generalized description of the main differences between *Partisan Review* and its fellow quarterlies shows how importantly *Partisan Review* diverged from the tradition of the critical review as it had been consolidated in *The Southern Review* and its direct successors. In some important respects it was indeed the antithesis of these magazines, although they influenced it profoundly – in part indirectly through their influence on the contemporary literary world. A closer inspection of its pages will enable us to delimit its position with greater accuracy.

Partisan Review was first published by the John Reed Club of New York in early 1934 as a "Bi-Monthly of Revolutionary Literature". Its opening editorial was somewhat ambiguous. Like most of its militant Marxist contemporaries it would "combat not only the decadent culture of the exploiting classes but also the debilitating liberalism which at times seeps into our writers through the pressure of class-alien forces". But it would not forget to keep its own house in order: "We shall resist every

---

[107]   Hofstadter, *Anti-Intellectualism in American Life* (New York, 1963), p. 394; Fiedler, *Waiting for the End* (New York, 1964), p. 148.

attempt to cripple our literature by narrow-minded, sectarian theories and practices." *Partisan Review* would publish the best creative work of the members of the John Reed Club as well as of non-members who shared its "literary aims".[108] The first volume was full of the simplistic party rhetoric of most Marxist little magazines. A writer's political convictions were often more closely examined than his literary abilities. For instance, a review, in the first issue, of Archibald MacLeish's *Poems 1924-1933* began ominously: "We know what Archibald MacLeish thinks about Marxism", and the second issue stated that T. S. Eliot's "gods are the caricatures and monsters of fascism".[109] The first issue also featured a discussion of four Marxist little magazines, *Left Front, The Anvil, Blast,* and *Dynamo,* "which prove – despite the sneers and sarcasm of the literary liberals – the growing vitality of revolutionary writing in America." [110] In the fourth issue, Ramon Fernandez, who three years earlier in *The Symposium* had attacked Marxism as a dangerous evil, penitently confessed how "I Came Near Being a Fascist". But a number of contributions, notably those by one of its editors, Philip Rahv, had an air of independent inquiry which was indicative of a growing revolt against party strictness. This new note did not go unnoticed. One influential Marxist critic, Granville Hicks, rebuked the magazine publicly for printing the work of "well-established writers" who did not belong to the John Reed Club, instead of encouraging "the less mature members".[111]

In its second year the magazine waned. Although it continued as a bi-monthly it only published four issues, the last two of which were reduced from ninety-six to sixty-four pages. In its third year it merged with another Marxist magazine, *The Anvil.* The first issue of *Partisan Review and Anvil* appeared in February

---

[108]   "Editorial Statement", *PR,* I, 1 (Feb.-March, 1934).
[109]   Obed Brooks (review of MacLeish's *Poems*), *PR,* I, 1 (Feb.-March 1934), 52; Wallace Phelps, "Eliot Takes His Stand", *PR,* I, 2 (April-May 1934), 54.
[110]   Waldo Tell, *PR,* I, 1 (Feb.-March, 1934), 60-61.
[111]   "Our Magazines and their Function", *New Masses,* XIII (December 1934), 22; quoted by Daniel Aaron, *Writers on the Left* (New York, 1961), p. 297.

1936.[112] The editors described it as a monthly which, "though continuing the traditions of its predecessors", would be "broader in scope and, we believe, more mature".[113] It was certainly more critical of the Communist Party line. The fifth monthly issue announced a summer recess during July and August; the editors intended to take advantage of this interval in order to work out "a program of enlarging the magazine and broadening its appeal", and they announced that the September number would contain "several pieces of unusual interest".[114] But the September number never appeared. The last issue for 1936 came out in October. It was entitled *Partisan Review* with in small letters underneath "Combined with the Anvil". It was the last number of the merger magazine.

It was not till December 1937 that the first number of the reconstructed *Partisan Review* appeared. Its editors were three Yale friends – F. W. Dupee ("who had been literary editor of the *New Masses* just long enough to see through its pretensions"), Dwight Macdonald ("who, having but lately discovered the socialist cause, was ready to devote to it his abundant energies and capacities"), and George L. K. Morris ("a modern painter who was able to undertake the financing of the venture") – and William Phillips and Philip Rahv, who had been on the editorial board of the earlier *Partisan Review*.[115] Its contributors, apart from the editors, included Delmore Schwartz, J. T. Farrell, Ar-

---

[112] "The merger was to be known as *Anvil and Partisan Review*, but something happened, and it appeared as *Partisan Review and Anvil*" (Ben Hagglund, "Akin to Revelation", *Carleton Miscellany*, VI, 1 [Winter 1965], 66).

[113] "This Month", *Partisan Review and Anvil*, III, 1 (February 1936), 2.

[114] "Announcement", *Partisan Review and Anvil*, III, 5 (June 1936), 2. Dwight Macdonald has given the following reasons for the suspension of *Partisan Review* from late 1936 to late 1937: "the Party's heavy-handed 'proletarian-literature' line; the Moscow Trials and other Soviet scandals, which had shaken their [the editors'] political faith; and the turn away from ultra-revolution to a 'popular front' with the New Deal, which had caused the Party to lose interest in *avant-garde* efforts like P.R." (*Memoirs of a Revolutionist* [New York, Meridian Books, 1958 (1957)], p. 12).

[115] William Phillips and Philip Rahv, "In Retrospect: Ten Years of *Partisan Review*", in *The Partisan Reader, 1934-1944* (New York, 1946), pp. 682-683.

thur Mizener, Edmund Wilson, Pablo Picasso, Lionel Abel, James Agee, Mary McCarthy, Sidney Hook, William Troy, and Lionel Trilling. The editors succeeded in making it "a 'strong' issue, for obvious tactical reasons".[116] The opening editorial was a declaration of independence. The editors retained their faith in revolutionary socialism; they still believed that any magazine that "aspires to a place in the vanguard of literature today, will be revolutionary in tendency"; but they were also convinced that any such magazine would be "unequivocally independent. . . . Indeed we think that the cause of revolutionary literature is best served by a policy of no commitments to any political party." Their critical independence was exemplified by their resolution to work within the tradition of the literary magazines of the 1920's which the more orthodox Marxists had dismissed as decadent expressions of a bourgeois culture: "As our readers know, the tradition of aestheticism has given way to a literature which, for its origin and final justification, looks beyond itself and deep into the historic process. But the forms of literary editorship, at once exacting and adventurous, which characterized the magazines of the aesthetic revolt, were of definite cultural value; and these forms *Partisan Review* will wish to adapt to the literature of the new period." The editorial accent would fall "chiefly on culture and its broader social determinants" instead of on party politics, and it would keep an open mind in its judgment of literature. "Conformity to a given social ideology or to a prescribed attitude or technique, will not be asked of our writers. On the contrary, our pages will be open to any tendency which is relevant to literature in our time." [117]

Partisan Review appeared as a "Literary Monthly" till September 1938. After that it continued as "A Quarterly of Literature and Marxism" till the autumn of 1939. From 1940 to the

---

[116] Dwight Macdonald, "Delmore Schwartz (1913-1966)", *The New York Review of Books*, VII, 3 (September 8, 1966), 14.
[117] "Editorial Statement", *PR*, IV, 1 (December 1937), 3, 4. "This insistence upon freedom on the one hand and commitment on the other" was, in the words of Reed Whittemore, "a normally polite paradox made tough and practical by political urgencies" (*Little Magazines*, University of Minnesota Pamphlets on American Writers, No. 32 [1963], p. 17).

end of 1943 it appeared bi-monthly and converted into a quarterly again in 1944. In 1941 Frederick Dupee left *Partisan Review* and Clement Greenberg joined the editorial board. Greenberg, Macdonald, and Morris left in 1943 leaving only William Phillips and Philip Rahv with one new editor, Delmore Schwartz, in charge.

The December 1937 editorial, which announced the break with the Communist Party, had clearly stated that literary contributions would be judged on purely literary merits; the magazine would keep its politics and its literature separate. The theory and practice of this policy would attract considerable criticism. An editor of *The Hudson Review,* for instance, thought that, as a magazine, "P. R. has only rarely managed to resolve its dual nature, part political, part literary." [118] The Autumn 1938 issue, which marks *Partisan Review*'s first appearance as "A Quarterly of Literature and Marxism", contains an eloquent editorial statement in the form of a letter to Malcolm Cowley. In *The New Republic* of 19 October, Cowley had attacked *Partisan Review* as "factional", "anti-Soviet", and as a perpetrator of "literary crimes".[119] His main charge had been that in contrast to its alleged editorial policy, *Partisan Review* used its literature for political ends. The editors answered that Cowley had mistaken their renunciation of the Communist Party for devotion to "an above-the-battle kind of pure Literature, such as the Dial once stood for. . . . But we have never aspired to stand for Pure Literature." They felt that the contemporary writer must concern himself with politics "if his work is to have any deep meaning for our time". In the course of their refutation of Cowley's article, the editors declared themselves to be against Stalinism which had "ceased to be a revolutionary tendency", and in fact was "rapidly turning into the opposite". They considered the influence of the Communist Party "a major threat to both literature and revolution in our time". Against Cowley's charge of

[118] William Arrowsmith, *"Partisan Review* and American Writing", *The Hudson Review*, I, 4 (Winter 1949), 527.
[119] "Partisan Review", *The New Republic*, XCVI (October 19, 1938), 311-312.

low literary standards, they adduced the flattering notices of their *Review* in "such non-political and exclusively literary magazines" as *Poetry, New Directions,* and *The Criterion*.[120] In the following issue, the editors reiterated emphatically that the artist or intellectual could not remain indifferent to the political developments of his time. In their obituary on the death of *The Criterion* they maintained that in later years *The Criterion*'s influence had not been constructive because Eliot had cultivated "abstraction from worldly issues. . . . But to English intellectuals the plea for aloofness came as a dry wind to the drought-stricken. Detachment? They were already perishing of it!" [121]

In the summer of 1939 *Partisan Review* published a statement of the League for Cultural Freedom and Socialism. As all the editors were among the undersigned, this statement had a direct bearing on the political and cultural position of their magazine. It was addressed "to all artists and writers who are concerned about the present drift of the United States to reaction and war". Reaction was threatening not only in Germany, in Italy, and in Russia – "where nationalism and personal dictatorship are replacing the revolutionary ideals of freedom and democracy – but also in the United States:

Increasingly, experimentation is discouraged in the creative arts; a premium is put upon the conventional and the academic. The social sciences are witnessing the revival of various forms of obscurantism, the rise of an intolerant orthodoxy. Educators are being intimidated through loyalty oaths. Government censorship cripples W.P.A. theatre, art, and literary projects. Terrorism is exercised by the Catholic Church over such cultural enterprises as the movies. Covert sabotage hinders the publication of work by independent and revolutionary writers. And in heresy hunting bodies like the Dies Committee, many of these tendencies find official and concentrated expression.

The statement noted a general weakening of the radical positions which the intellectuals had conquered after 1929. The Communist Party could no longer sustain them; indeed the most active forces of reaction were "the so-called cultural organizations"

[120] The Editors, "A Letter to the *New Republic*", *PR*, VI, 1 (Autumn 1938), 124, 125, 126.
[121] The Editors, "T. S. Eliot's Last Words", *PR*, VI, 2 (Winter 1939), 7.

which the Party controlled. But the failure of the Party must not lead intellectuals to abandon "the ideals of revolutionary socialism". Intellectual freedom must be insisted upon and all theories and practices must be rejected which "tend to make culture the creature of politics, even revolutionary politics. We demand COMPLETE FREEDOM FOR ART AND SCIENCE. NO DICTATION BY PARTY OR GOVERNMENT." [122]

During the next few years *Partisan Review* kept a vigilant watch for further signs of reaction. The decline of Marxism and the revolutionary cause was a frequent subject of debate. Another frequently discussed problem was America's attitude to the war in Europe. Generally speaking, *Partisan Review* moved from a militantly revolutionary and anti-war position to the recognition that the chances of revolution were lower than ever before and that American participation in the war was inevitable. This gradual editorial shift was deplored by Dwight Macdonald who in 1943 left the magazine "in high political dudgeon".[123]

In the summer of 1940 Philip Rahv wrote *Partisan Review*'s contribution to the debate of "What Is Living and What Is Dead" in Marxism. Rahv drew attention to the disaster of communist movements everywhere, and to the fact that "everywhere, including in the Soviet Union, it is not the social revolution but the counter-revolution which has triumphed". It was true that events had confirmed the Marxist analysis of bourgeois economy and imperialist wars, but they had failed to confirm the Marxist prognosis of a proletarian revolution once the objective conditions for such a revolution had ripened: "and objective conditions, considered on an international scale, have not only been ripe but at times rotten-ripe". Marxist doctrine had optimistically assumed that as capitalism decayed the revolutionary awareness of the working class would increase. But there was no workers' movement of any size or influence which was "carrying forward the revolutionary tradition" and which could be seriously counted on "to utilize the opportunities for action that will no doubt arise in the near future".

[122] "Statement of the L.C.F.S.", *PR*, VI, 4 (Summer 1939), 125, 126, 127.
[123] Arrowsmith, "*Partisan Review* and American Writing", 527.

Rahv tried to steer a middle course between the revisionists, who were now "in the pink of condition, thriving as they do on routs and defeats" – and the diehards, who mistook "their doctrinal inflexibility for scientific rectitude".[124] Rahv was more interested in the practice than in the theory of Marxism. His emphasis on historical experience and on experimental verification as a rationale for political action profoundly influenced *Partisan Review*. It gave the magazine the necessary flexibility to adapt its ideological position to the rapid changes of its political environment. But it never jeopardized its intellectual independence. In 1941, Dwight Macdonald could justly claim that, "in its three years of existence, the present PARTISAN REVIEW has steadfastly opposed all forms of totalitarian oppression, both red and black".[125] In the spring of 1942 the editors once more demonstrated their intellectual alertness by establishing a new department, "Dangerous Thoughts", which would have the function of "a 'listening post' to give publicity to the more significant instances of suppression of free thought from month to month".[126]

But although the editors were in agreement about the necessity of independent inquiry and freedom of thought, they differed on the issues of revolutionary socialism and American participation in the war. Their disagreements were brought into the open when Philip Rahv challenged the "Ten Propositions on the War" published in the summer of 1941 by Dwight Macdonald and Clement Greenberg, who had once more defended the ideals of revolutionary socialism and of non-participation in the war. These Propositions, Rahv thought, had put his fellow-editors "into a snug sectarian hole". He could not adopt their position because he regarded it "as morally absolutist and as politically representative of a kind of academic revolutionism which we should have learned to discard long ago". Greenberg and Macdonald had been completely impervious to the "shattering surprises of the past two years" and were still advocating the "same

[124] P.R., "Comment: What Is Living and What is Dead", *PR*, VII, 3 (May-June 1940), 175, 176.
[125] Letter to Jocelyn Wagner, *PR*, VIII, 3 (May-June 1941), 254.
[126] "Dangerous Thoughts", *PR*, IX, 2 (March-April 1942), 172.

old orthodox recommendations. Again we read that the social revolution is around the corner and that imperialism is tottering on the edge of the abyss, and again we fail to recognize the world as we know it." Again Rahv's main argument was that the programme put forward by Greenberg and Macdonald was unrealistic, a Utopian vision completely out of touch with actual political developments. Hitler's swift conquests had changed the political picture entirely; his military defeat had become "the indispensable pre-condition of any progressive action in the future". This defeat could only be brought about by "the combined might of the Anglo-American imperialism and Stalin's Red Army". The orthodox Marxists had hoped that the different capitalist camps would exhaust each other and then they would take over. But events had turned out otherwise. All indications were against the possibility of a successful revolutionary movement in America or in England. Rahv was not arguing against a revolutionary policy as such but practical conditions made such a policy illusory. The assertions of Greenberg and Macdonald wholly ignored "the element of time, which is the one element one can least afford to overlook in political calculations". Rahv believed not only in the necessity of American participation in the war, but also in an ultimate Anglo-American victory: "There is every reason to believe that once America is fully drawn into the struggle its offensive power will astound the world." [127]

The extent of the editorial disagreements necessitated a "Statement by the Editors" on the actual entrance of the United States into the war. As *Partisan Review*, "while primarily a cultural magazine", had always been "concerned with politics", a question of its future editorial policy naturally arose:

For some time, as recent issues of the magazine have made clear, the editors have disagreed on major political questions. The complexity

[127] "10 Propositions and 8 Errors", *PR*, VIII, 6 (Nov.-Dec. 1941), 499, 501, 503. Many years after these events, Dwight Macdonald wrote: "After Pearl Harbor Rahv and Phillips had come to feel it was their war and their country, while I had remained disaffected." Editorial dissent on the war, however, was already brewing before Pearl Harbor (*Memoirs of a Revolutionist* [New York: Meridian Books, 1958 (1957)], p. 25).

of the world situation, indeed, is reflected in the fact that no two
editors hold the same position on all major issues. The actual outbreak
of hostilities has not altered this line up. It is clear, therefore, that
PARTISAN REVIEW can have no editorial line on the war. Its editors
will continue to express themselves on the issue as individuals.

But they remained unanimous about the necessity of the "fullest
freedom of expression on political matters".[128] In subsequent
issues this freedom was mainly exercised by Dwight Macdonald.
There was, for instance, his vehement refutation of James Burnham's argument in *The Managerial Revolution*.[129] Burnham had
been a fellow-Trotskyist of Macdonald and his sudden abandon-
ment of doctrinaire Marxism, which he had first embraced in
the pages of *The Symposium,* had amazed many of his revolutionary friends.

But Macdonald's revolutionary zeal was decreasingly relevant
to the trend of *Partisan Review*. The contents pages of the first
issues of 1943 stated once more explicitly that the articles published in the magazine, "whether written by editors or contributors, represent the point of view of the individual author, and
not necessarily of the editors". None of the other literary reviews
had thought such editorial caution necessary, except *The Symposium*. This is symbolic of a distinct resemblance between
Partisan Review and *The Symposium*, especially if we take into
account that they were not edited simultaneously. Firstly, these
two magazines had more regular contributors in common with
each other than with any of the other literary reviews. We may
mention Dwight Macdonald, William Phillips, Philip Rahv, and
Frederick Dupee – in other words, all of the important editors
of *Partisan Review* prior to 1943 – Lionel Trilling, William
Troy, Harold Rosenberg, and James Burnham. Secondly, both
The Symposium and *Partisan Review* were New York magazines
and both took an active interest in Marxism. As *The Symposium*
had first appeared before the leftist political agitation due to the
depression had gained momentum, its turn to Marxism came late
in its career. It was, of course, largely instigated by James Burn-

---

[128]   "A Statement by the Editors", *PR*, IX, 1 (Jan.-Feb. 1942), 2.
[129]   "The Burnhamian Revolution", *PR*, IX, 1 (Jan.-Feb. 1942), 76-84.

ham, and it appears no coincidence that Burnham was a valued contributor to the early *Partisan Review* (in later years, Julian Symons thought he had been an editor [130]), and that Philip Wheelwright contributed regularly to *The Kenyon Review* in a vein very much in accord with Ransom's editorial policy. Indeed, the different interests of the two editors of *The Symposium* point to the two major traditions of the literary review in the 'Thirties and after: we find the radical and secular trend of James Burnham again in *Partisan Review*, and the aesthetic and religious trend of Philip Wheelwright in *The Kenyon Review*. Another way of saying the same thing is that *The Symposium* published work of a number of characteristic contributors both to *Partisan Review* and to *The Criterion*.

The internal dissent among the editors of *Partisan Review* was resolved in the summer of 1943 when Dwight Macdonald tendered his resignation. As it had been an editorial habit to publish the more significant letters to the editors in a special section of the magazine – a habit which added liveliness to its pages and which gave the editors ample scope to clarify their positions – Macdonald's letter was printed in the July-August issue of 1943. Macdonald felt that the divergence between his own opinions and those of the other editors could no longer be bridged: "This divergence is partly cultural: I feel *Partisan Review* has become rather academic, and favor a more informal, dis-respectable and chance-taking magazine, with a broader and less exclusively 'literary' approach." But the divergence was mainly political. The value of *Partisan Review,* according to Macdonald, had been its "Marxian socialist cultural" direction. This had distinguished it "from other literary organs like *Southern Review* and *Kenyon Review*", and had accounted for much of its in-tellectual success. But the interest in Marxism had been reduced

---

[130] "James Burnham, another of the early editors, left the magazine at about the same time as Macdonald, after publishing *The Managerial Revolution*" ("Woofers and Tweeters", *The Spectator* [February 22, 1963], 232). Burnham was on the Advisory Board of *Partisan Review* from 1948 to 1953. According to Leslie Fiedler, Burnham's resignation was a result of *Partisan Review*'s political discussion of McCarthyism. (" 'Partisan Review': Phoenix or Dodo", *Perspectives U.S.A.*, No. 15 [Spring 1956], 90).

to "a minority of one", and since Pearl Harbor, the editors had tended to discourage all political discussion.[131] The remaining editors answered that they naturally regretted Macdonald's resignation but regretted even more that Macdonald had "allowed himself to be carried away by political passions." They maintained that he had left because he had failed to transform *Partisan Review* into a "political magazine with literary trimmings". *Partisan Review*, "which from its very inception has been edited mainly by literary men",[132] never wanted to put itself forward as a substitute for a political movement.

Macdonald's resignation forced the editors once more to clarify their views concerning the selection of the political and the literary subject-matter of their magazine: "We could never agree to 'subordinate' art and literature to political interests. It is precisely this sort of disagreement which led, in 1937, to our break with the Stalinists. . . . Macdonald speaks of the magazine's 'intellectual success'; but he shows his bias in ascribing it largely to the Marxist slant rather than to the specific modulation achieved in combining socialist ideas with a varied literary and critical content. This will continue to be the policy of the magazine." [133] The reconciliation of the political and the literary contents of their magazine had always been an awkward problem for the editors. About two years before Macdonald's resignation, Julian Symons had suggested to them that "a statement of editorial attitude, with regard to the relation between your political views and the creative work you publish, would be useful". *Partisan Review* had then just published Eliot's *East Coker*.[134]

[131] "Letters", *PR*, X, 4 (July-Aug. 1943), 382. Soon afterwards (February 1944) Macdonald edited his own magazine appropriately called *Politics*, which had a skirmish with *Partisan Review* towards the end of 1946.
[132] William Arrowsmith, however, could not "believe that Rahv or Phillips or William Barrett are generally regarded as being primarily men-of-letters; they are editors, neither more nor less . . ." (*"Partisan Review* and American Writing", 534).
[133] "Letters", *PR*, X, 4 (July-Aug. 1943), 382-383. Martin Greenberg left *Partisan Review* before Macdonald in early 1943, and George L. K. Morris after Macdonald at the end of the same year. Their departures did not call forth editorial comments.
[134] *PR*, VII, 3 (May-June 1940). One year later *Partisan Review* published another Quartet, *The Dry Salvages* (*PR*, VIII, 3 [May-June 1941]).

The editors retorted that Symons's question had "always been a hard one" for them to answer, but that they had "always felt that literary values must come first in judging literature".[135]

As the political situation worsened, these literary values became more and more prominent. When Macdonald resigned one of the reasons certainly was, as the editors wrote, that his political interests tended to eliminate his literary interests, but it was equally true, as Macdonald maintained, that *Partisan Review* was becoming increasingly literary and less political. In this connection it is significant that Macdonald's successor was a purely literary man, Delmore Schwartz, who had been one of the most regular and esteemed young contributors to *The Southern Review,* but who had also, in 1938, won the prize of $100 which *Partisan Review* had offered in a contest for the best short story.[136]

Partisan Review's campaign for literary independence had started in 1937 with its break with the Communist Party, which also meant a break with other Marxist little magazines. It differed from non-Marxist little magazines in its emphasis upon "ideas and intellectual attitudes".[137] Its new ideological independence and the contemporary literary and political situation naturally led to a closer identification with its fellow literary quarterlies. The first issue of the reconstructed *Partisan Review* in 1937 contained contributions by Delmore Schwartz, Wallace Stevens and Arthur Mizener, and its first quarterly issue (Winter 1939)

Partisan Review did of course not subscribe to Eliot's cultural views. In the spring of 1944 it published Eliot's "Notes Towards the Definition of Culture", but it gave an opportunity to several writers – R. P. Blackmur, Clement Greenberg, William Phillips and I. A. Richards – to comment on his ideas. Many years later, William Phillips would write that Eliot's "ideological conservatism automatically made him taboo in official leftist circles, but to the group around *Partisan Review* he was a major poet, and a revolutionary one, who – as Edmund Wilson put it in *Axel's Castle* – had accomplished in the area of sensibility a breakthrough analogous to Marxism in political thought" ("What Happened in the 30's", *Commentary*, XXXIV, 3 [September 1962], 207).

[135] "P.R.'s Literary Principles", *PR*, VIII, 6 (Nov.-Dec. 1941), 518.

[136] Schwartz shared the prize with Mary King who soon afterwards also contributed to *The Southern Review.*

[137] Lionel Trilling, *The Liberal Imagination* (New York, 1950), p. 97.

featured R. P. Blackmur's review of "Nine Poets". The group book review which was carried on in the next few issues by such critics as Philip Rahv, Randall Jarrell and David Daiches, may well have been inspired by the example of *The Southern Review*. Philip Rahv for one was greatly impressed by *Southern Review*'s performance: "I think the recent numbers of your Review have been excellent", he wrote to Robert Penn Warren in 1939; "Its varied and bountiful content and the freedom and independence of its general approach make it all the more valuable at a time when almost all the intellectual organs have lost all sense of their real function." [138]

In the autumn of 1940 the editors intended to underline their political independence and, perhaps also, their waning revolutionary optimism, by publishing *Partisan Review* under a new name, *The Forties,* beginning with the first issue of 1941. "We are making this change because the old name, pertinent when the magazine first appeared in 1934, has more recently led to many misunderstandings of the magazine's purpose and character." [139] But the reactions of their readers were so unfavourable – somebody suggested, as an alternative name, *The American Criterion* – that the editors decided to continue as *Partisan Review*. Most of its readers, however, sympathized with its gradual turn to literary matters. This was illustrated by the results of the questionnaire which the *Review* sent out to its subscribers in early 1941; nine out of ten wanted more articles, and again nine out of ten of these wanted more articles on writers and writing; the number of those who wanted more political articles was considerably smaller.[140]

We have noted previously that *Partisan Review,* like its fellow quarterlies, took a very sombre view of the contemporary literary situation. Indeed, in their retrospect of the first ten years of the

---

[138] February 23, 1939, *Southern Review* papers, Yale University Library. One year earlier Eleanor Clark had described *The Southern Review* in *Partisan Review* – as "one of the few magazines in this country worth serious attention" ("No More Swans", *PR*, IV, 4 [March 1938], 58).
[139] "To Our Readers", *PR*, VII, 5 (Sept.-Oct. 1940), inside front cover.
[140] "Results of the P.R. Questionnaire", *PR*, VIII, 4 (June-Aug. 1941), 346.

magazine, the editors Phillips and Rahv prided themselves on their percipience in this matter:

Long before the popular critics acknowledged the slump in contemporary writing, we repeatedly noted in editorial articles, that, compared with the high level achieved in the twenties, the literature of the thirties and forties has shown a decline in originality, integrity, and creative power. Hence it seemed to us that in this period a magazine dedicated solely to experiment and innovation could not but turn into a futile undertaking, as the paucity of material on which such a magazine must subsist would eventually compel it to adopt meretricious standards, permitting the souvenirs of past experimentation to be passed off as the vital discoveries of the present.[141]

Perhaps the most famous indictment of the literary situation by an editor of *Partisan Review* appeared in *The Kenyon Review* in 1939: Philip Rahv's "Paleface and Redskin". Rahv's discussion of the "split personality" of American literature, exemplified in the persons and the works of Henry James and Walt Whitman, will be familiar. "At present", Rahv wrote, "the redskins are in command of the literary situation, and seldom has the literary life in America been as intellectually impoverished as it is today".[142]

The literary reviews were undoubtedly representatives of the waning paleface tradition. Their fight was against the lowbrow writer and critic and their hold on the reading public. But whereas Rahv had written an indictment in terms of a theory of American literature, *Partisan Review*, like its fellow quarterlies, chose for its specific adversaries Van Wyck Brooks and Archibald MacLeish and, later on, Bernard DeVoto. In late 1941 Dwight Macdonald led off with an attack on Van Wyck Brooks's lecture "Primary Literature and Coterie Literature." [143] Brooks had built

---

[141]   *The Partisan Reader, 1934-44*, p. 685. Two years earlier Philip Rahv had written to Malcolm Cowley: "God knows how we get the stuff together for the *Partisan*; there's so little being done nowadays; but somehow the magazine keeps coming out. We hope that the end of the war will bring about a radical change in the situation. Once the pressure relaxes writers will have the courage to determine their own fate" (May 12, 1944, Cowley papers, Newberry Library).

[142]   *KR*, I, 3 (Summer 1939), 254.

[143]   A paper delivered at the Second Annual Conference on Science, Philosophy and Religion, at Columbia University on September 10, 1941.

his argument around an antithesis between "primary" and "secondary" writers. The former was "a great man writing", "one who bespeaks the collective life of the people" by celebrating "the great themes . . . by virtue of which the race has risen – courage, justice, mercy, honor, love". The work of the "secondary", or "coterie" writer only reached "a mere handful of readers". His work had brilliant "form" but lacked "content". He was "a mere artificer or master of words", who perversely celebrated the "death-drive" instead of the "life-drive".[144] Brooks's examples of primary writers included Tolstoi, Milton, Dostoievsky, Goethe, Whitman, and Whittier. His secondary writers included Joyce, Proust, Valéry, Pound, Eliot, James, Rimbaud, and Hemingway. Among his "secondary" critics were Eliot, Richards, Winters, Pound, Tate, and Ransom, in contrast to such "primary" critics as Arnold, Taine, and Sainte-Beuve.

Macdonald called Brooks's lecture "the boldest statement to date of that cultural counter-revolution opened by Archibald MacLeish's attack on the 'irresponsibles' ".[145] Unlike his literary contemporaries, he saw Brooks's and MacLeish's positions as manifestations of political decline. Indeed, he mentioned Brooks's lecture in one breath with James Burnham's *The Managerial Revolution*. Brooks, according to Macdonald, had no use for modern writers because they exposed the weaknesses and absurdities of a dying bourgeois culture. But he had to admit that, for all his boldness, Brooks nowhere dared to "assert that bourgeois society in this century is in a flourishing condition. He simply *assumes* this crucial point – or, more accurately, doesn't seem aware it *is* crucial, and that writers can be expected to

[144] Quoted by Macdonald, "Kulturbolschewismus Is Here", *PR*, VIII, 6 (Nov.-Dec. 1941), 443.

[145] *Ibid.*, 444. MacLeish had commented on the dangerous split between writers and scholars. "The men of intellectual duty, those who should have been responsible for action, have divided themselves into two castes, two cults – the scholars and the writers. Neither accepts responsibility for the common culture or for its defense." The writer's irresponsibility was of a different kind from the scholar's. "Where the modern scholar escapes from the adult judgements of the mind by taking the disinterested man of science as his model, the modern writer escapes by imitation of the artist" (*A Time To Speak* [Cambridge, Mass., 1940], pp. 113, 118).

exhibit his 'primary' virtues only in a 'primary' historical period."
According to Macdonald, Brooks's values and methods were
"the specific cultural values of Stalinism and the specific methods
of the Moscow Trials". Brooks was representative of the drift of
totalitarianism which after the Hitler-Stalin pact had deserted
Stalinism to support the official government line. His was the
"*official* approach to culture" which had for its aim "the protec-
tion of a historically reactionary form of society against the free
inquiry and criticism of the intelligentsia." He had become the
"leading mouthpiece for totalitarian cultural values".[146]

Macdonald's article served as an opening for a much wider
debate. It was sent to some twenty writers with a request for
comments on it. Seven writers reacted to this request, among
them Allen Tate, the future editor of *The Sewanee Review*, and
John Crowe Ransom, the editor of *The Kenyon Review*. If the
editors of *The Southern Review* were invited to comment, they
failed to do so. It was of course at this time – late 1941 – that
they were planning their own editorial on MacLeish and Brooks
which never appeared. But the trend of their editorial policy and
their earlier attack on the position of Howard Mumford Jones
permit one to surmise that their reactions would have been very
similar to Tate's.[147] Tate was as radical as Macdonald in his
rejection of the "Brooks-MacLeish Thesis", but on cultural rather
than on political grounds:

Mr. Macdonald seems to feel that the great writers of our time were
consciously exposing the evils of capitalism; yet I believe that the most
we can say, if we are not going to succumb to special pleading, is that
they have written out of a vision of life in our time, or out of a vision
of the evils of life which are common to all times; and it is this tragic
view which Mr. Brooks cannot understand, because he holds the

[146]   "Kulturbolschewismus Is Here", 446, 450, 451.
[147]   This opinion is reinforced by Warren's satirical review of V. W.
Brooks's *The Opinions of Oliver Allston* ("Homage to Oliver Allston",
KR, IV, 2 [Spring 1942], 259-263) published at the time of *Partisan
Review*'s discussion, and by Cleanth Brooks's "Mrs. Colum and Mr. Jones"
which appeared four years later (*SR*, LIV, 2 [Spring 1946], 335-343) and
which once more attacked Howard Mumford Jones who commanded "a
division of the army currently drawn up under the banners of Mr. Van
Wyck Brooks" (p. 337).

moralistic and didactic view which can be extended, as he has extended it, into the nationalist and patriotic view.

Brooks had always seen literature as chiefly a symptom, but Tate had "an uneasy suspicion" that Macdonald was defending the moderns as symptoms also. He wondered whether they would not become unnecessary after "the triumph of Mr. Macdonald's socialism".[148]

Ransom's reception of Macdonald's article illustrates how in *The Kenyon Review* the Brooks-MacLeish affair was to some extent overschadowed by other priorities, particularly the attack on science. Ransom accepted "a good deal of the substance" of Brooks's generalization as Macdonald had reported it. He too felt that the moderns were not "primary" or "great" writers: "Our literature with its brilliance is less creative and positive than other literatures have been." But he did argue "in defense of the greatness of a few moderns, such as James, Yeats, and Proust". He did not explain the direction of contemporary fiction and poetry in cultural or political terms but in terms of the rise of science:

I find myself more and more imagining that the epochal thing that has happened to us is a sudden crisis of language and expression. For the first time in human history we have pure science, which is pure prose, and that means that we have pushed language to the point where it is the perfect instrument for science. The esthetic and imaginative elements of language that used to clutter it – the figures of speech for example – have been spotted and thrown out. The consequence is that literature, with its imaginative order of knowing, is homeless. It has to make up its own occasions, and it becomes factitious and technical in a degree that was never known before.[149]

---

[148] "On the 'Brooks-MacLeish Thesis' ", *PR*, IX, 1 (Jan.-Feb. 1942), 38.
[149] *Ibid.*, 40-41. At about the same time Brooks wrote: "the 'new criticism' was not really criticism; and, as it evaded the whole world of values, which is justly the concern of criticism, it lay outside the field of literature. It was properly a discipline in the field of science" (*The Opinions of Oliver Allston* [London, 1942 (1941)], pp. 164, 165). Compare also Brooks's later statement that literature for the new critics "had no public function; they had entirely relinquished, as Ransom said, the notion of the poet as a prophet or a priest; whereas the great writers who had formed our minds had felt it was part of their task 'to improve the prevailing order of the world' " (*Days of the Phoenix* [New York, 1957], p. 118).

The lowbrow attitude to literature and the growing literary nationalism remained frequent topics of the editorial interest in *Partisan Review*. Their increasing prestige was deplored by William Phillips in early 1944. The "rediscovery of America" had become "practically an occupational disease not only of popular writers and reviewers but also of people who once had at least one foot in the movements of literary revolt". This literary nationalism had been accompanied by "a wave of anti-intellectualism" which threatened to wipe out the remaining traces of earlier experimentation and of the former radical spirit. But what was "perhaps even more remarkable" was the absence of a new generation of writers with a common direction.[150] The publication of Bernard DeVoto's *The Literary Fallacy* only confirmed the editors' gloomy predictions. Philip Rahv called the book "as vicious and mindless a tract as any so far produced by those who have set themselves the task of subverting the critical spirit of modern art and thought."[151]

The preceding remarks will go to show that the literary reviews were unanimous in their condemnation of the activist anti-intellectualism and literary nationalism of the early 'Forties, but *Partisan Review* differed greatly from its contemporaries in the explanations it offered and in the remedies it proposed. This was due to its secular, rationalistic, positivistic attitude towards the contemporary world. Although it was highly critical of specific abuses, it tried to expose them without rejecting the world in which they occurred. It opposed the numerous contemporary myths which had been propagated to throw light on the complexity of the modern scene and often also to obstruct the devel-

---

[150] "Variety: Portrait of the Artist as a Middle Aged Man", *PR*, XI, 1 (Winter 1944), 120.

[151] "Variety: the Progress of Cultural Bolshevism (cont'd)", *PR*, XI, 3 (Summer 1944), 361. During that same summer Rahv told Malcolm Cowley that Brooks and DeVoto made "the same mistakes that the vulgar Marxists did, only from a (sometimes well concealed) rightist angle: the same extra-literary pressure and presumption; instead of worshipping the 'proletariat' they worship 'America' – an object of adoration and pompous reference which in their sense of it is quite as mythical as the Marxist object" (August 4, 1944, Cowley papers, Newberry Library).

opment of its most characteristic traits. It was probably this secular, positivistic quality of *Partisan Review* which led John Palmer, the editor of *The Sewanee Review,* to describe it, in a letter to T. S. Eliot in 1946, as "morally suspect". Palmer remembered the great disappointment of the editors of *The Southern Review* – he himself had been managing editor at the time – when Eliot's *Four Quartets* began to appear in *Partisan Review.* "Perhaps this will appear as nothing else than underhand remarks about a rival publication: but I do regard the *Partisan Review* as morally suspect, and I worried over what explanations there might be for your choice of it for so very important an occasion." [152]

Partisan Review's attitude was most clearly formulated in a series of essays entitled "The New Failure of Nerve" which was started in early 1943. The title of this series had been derived from Gilbert Murray's *Four Stages of Greek Religion.* Murray had characterized the period from 300 B.C. to the first century of the Christian era as marked by "a failure of nerve". This failure of nerve had exhibited itself in "a rise of asceticism, of mysticism, in a sense, of pessimism; a loss of selfconfidence, of hope in this life and of faith in normal human efforts; a despair of patient inquiry, a cry for infallible revelation: an indifference to the welfare of the state, a conversion of the soul to God".[153] Surveying the cultural tendencies of the early 'Forties, Sidney Hook, whose essay opened the new series, noticed many signs pointing to a new failure of nerve in Western civilization. Although its manifestations were more complex and sophisticated and characteristic of a secular culture, at bottom they betrayed "the same flight from responsibility, both on the plane of action and on the plane of belief, that drove the ancient world into the shelters of pagan and Christian supernaturalism". Liberalism, not as a nineteenth-century economic doctrine, but as an intellectual temper, as "faith in intelligence, as a tradition of the free market in the world of ideas" was everywhere on the defensive.

---

[152] Palmer to Eliot, December 12, 1946, *Sewanee Review* papers.
[153] Quoted by Sidney Hook, "The New Failure of Nerve", *PR*, X, 1 (Jan.-Feb. 1943), 2.

Hook noticed signs of intellectual panic in almost all fields of "theoretical life", but there was a primary attitude underlying them all. It exhibited itself as "a loss of confidence in scientific method, and in varied quests for a 'knowledge' and 'truth' which, although they give us information about the world, are uniquely different from those won by the process of scientific inquiry." These truths were often regarded as superior to truths of science and common sense, but Hook considered them "gateways to intellectual and moral irresponsibility".[154]

Hook's essay was accompanied in the same issue by contributions of John Dewey and Ernest Nagel which were in essential agreement with Hook's defence of scientific methods against the increasing "obscurantism". I. A. Richards, who was asked to comment on these three essays in a later issue, tried to steer a middle course. He felt that representatives of both sides in this "old intellectual war" were more interested in warfare itself than in ultimate solutions. "They belong already to one party or the other, their reading serves to stiffen their necks, inflame their hearts and anneal their colours." Neither party would admit to any doubt. But Richards wondered "whether the thinker, if we separate him from the polemist, does not need both the language of religion and the language of science".[155] Richards did not expect, however, that his intermediary solution would be acceptable, and the continuing polemics between the two opposing camps in *Partisan Review* and in *The Kenyon Review* proved that his mediation was indeed as illusory as he himself considered it.

---

[154] *Ibid.*, 2, 3, 4, 5.
[155] "The Two Rings: A Communication", *PR*, X, 4 (July-Aug. 1943), 380, 381. The same issue featured as "The New Failure of Nerve, IV" Dwight Macdonald's "The Future of Democratic Values", a final statement of his political position before he left *Partisan Review*. Another contributor who discussed the "new failure of nerve" in political terms was Julian Symons. He felt that the term applied "perfectly to the English intellectual scene". It was to him "obvious that a conscious exaltation of the power of myth, a deliberate obsession with the 'romantic' and religious as opposed to the reasonable and logical, *any* victory of rhetoric over good sense, is finally a score for reaction" ("In the Desert: a 'Fascism of the Intellectuals' ", *PR*, X, 5 [Sept.-Oct. 1943], 425).

V

In 1960 Allen Tate wrote: "It is generally supposed that the utmost span of usefulness for a literary magazine is about seven years." [156] Tate was talking about *The Fugitive* and his statement may well be more relevant to a little magazine than to a literary quarterly. The *Kenyon, Sewanee,* and *Partisan* reviews have far exceeded the seven years age limit and they are still performing valuable literary services. But their survival is largely due to the stability of the institutions backing them. Even the combatively independent *Partisan Review* is now edited from Rutgers University. It was to some extent the influence on the literary scene of the reviews themselves which made their survival possible. They have created a public, mainly in the universities, for whom they have become indispensable in one form or another.

The literary quarterlies had their heyday in the 'Forties when they consolidated the revolution in criticism and in the teaching of literature which they had begun in the later 'Thirties. But towards the end of the 'Forties observant critics registered the first persistent signs of discontent. In 1949, for instance, Alan Swallow noticed a "restiveness" which he interpreted as an indication "that the critical review is at its zenith. No one, I suppose, would wish the complete downfall of the pattern of the review, since these magazines have great abilities. But the restiveness indicates that the critical review does not by any means perform the many functions of the noncommercial magazines." [157] This restiveness increased during the 'Fifties when the reviews were among the official intellectual export products of the Rockefeller Foundation, and when up-and-coming American universities, aware of the kudos they conveyed, put out their own usually more academic imitations. In 1957, an ex-editor of *Partisan Review*, William Barrett, traced the "Declining Fortunes of the Literary Review 1945-57".[158] Barrett shared Swallow's feeling

---

[156] "Random Thoughts on the 1920's", *Minnesota Review*, I, 1 (Autumn 1960), 50.
[157] "Postwar Little Magazines", *The Prairie Schooner*, XXIII, 2 (Summer 1949), 153.
[158] *The Anchor Review*, No. 2 (1957), 145-160.

that the reviews suffered from inbreeding and from a lack of new ideas and inspiring causes; from a lack, as Swallow put it, of "a powerful sense", which the earlier reviews had had, that "some new ideas were being developed into literary significance".[159]

The literary reviews were increasingly criticized as institutionalized, unenterprising and dull. At the end of the 'Fifties *The Massachusetts Review* was founded because the editors' vision of the literary reviews was, in the words of John Hicks, "of a situation which left a vacuum that a new and energetic publication might try to fill". Hicks described this situation as follows:

There was, for example, *Partisan Review*, which had introduced American audiences to European literature and existentialist thought, and had as its animating impulse politics. Or there was the widely influential *Kenyon Review* with its great achievement in critical theory and practical criticism. But by 1959, with the ending of an era, these forces had in large measure diminished into coterie groups and interests. The journals we had thought of as being beacons over the land had suddenly shrunk to something like mouthpieces – for the propagation of the New Criticism, for example, or for the partisans of a shrinking concept of the left.

The editors of *The Massachusetts Review* modelled their magazine on "a courageous, outspoken, and elegant journal of the 1930's: *Hound & Horn*", because they saw in it "an avant-garde publication in which an acute aesthetic sensibility was not incompatible with advanced thought in politics, literature, and public affairs".[160]

---

[159] "Postwar Little Magazines", 154.
[160] John H. Hicks, "Literary Quarterlies of the 1960's", *College English*, XXVII, 2 (November 1965), 153, 154, 155. For a similar description of the decline of the literary reviews, cf. Reed Whittemore, *Little Magazines*, University of Minnesota Pamphlets on American Writers, No. 32 (1963), p. 29. Whittemore also notes that by the end of the 'Forties, the ideological war between *Partisan Review* and its contemporaries had largely spent itself: "certainly it is true that the old combatants were exhausted and that the hot war turned tepid" (p. 22). Another complaint that was frequently directed against the quarterlies was that they, in the words of Randall Jarrell, "print far too much criticism, and far too much of the criticism that they print is of a kind that is more attractive to critics and to lovers of criticism than it is to poets and fiction-writers and to lovers of poetry and fiction" (*Poetry and the Age* [New York, 1953], p. 65).

The growing dissatisfaction with the literary quarterlies was soon also voiced in the pages of the quarterlies themselves. It is characteristic that *Partisan Review* was most alive to it. It repeatedly drew a parallel between the decline of the literary review and the decline of the *avant-garde*. Valuable representatives of the *avant-garde* were, in the words of William Barrett, "the snotty young men". Barrett did not use the term in any derogative sense:

indeed the snotty young men are very valuable for the literary review, and a certain number of them are indispensable to keep the bounce in its pages: they can be counted on to throw bricks when and where needed, and generally to remind readers how awful things really are. Of course, they do get tiresome and strident, and there is a certain monotony in their targets; but if they were not around to remind us, we might forget that things are often even worse than the snotty young men make them out to be.[161]

In the 'Twenties, these young men moved in a still relatively open society and could live in Europe on very few dollars. In the 'Thirties, they were Marxists; during that decade:

The leisure of a Bohemia (though a much grubbier one) was still possible: there were gaps, open spaces, in the social life, and indeed one great big gap of national unemployment. With the forties and the War there ensued a gradual closing down of horizons. The snotty young men inherited from their forebears the social values of rebels, but the positive content of the two previous decades was gone: the revolution in letters of the twenties had been assimilated, and revolutionary politics was no longer possible ... the highest calling left seemed to be to denounce the fake, to keep a steady eye on the high and serious even if the period could not quite produce these itself – in short, the dreary war upon the middlebrow.[162]

It is ironic that the dissatisfaction of the quarterlies themselves was often aimed at critical practices for whose recognition they had fought in earlier years. The progress of *The Kenyon Review* is representative. A good example is the following passage from a review by Howard Nemerov in *The Kenyon Review* in early 1956:

[161] *The Anchor Review* (see note 158 on page 308), p. 151.
[162] *Ibid.*, p. 152.

The dominant criticism of the day is a criticism which explains things; it seems to have appeared as a response to a few difficult poems, and to have proceeded on the presumption that poems are very difficult matters, or that they would be from now on, or that, if they were not, they could be made so by judicious explanations. The habit of such criticism has produced some odd effects both good and bad, of which the good have perhaps been often enough surveyed. As to the bad: certain sorts of difficulty are taken as signs of excellence, and the explanation of them as preeminently the business of criticism; poetic illiteracy has mightily increased not for one reason alone, no doubt, but this species of criticism has done its share, with the best intentions in the world, toward producing the situation as we have it. The habit of reading poetry seems largely lost, replaced by the school room habit of 'analysing' it.[163]

In the following issue of *The Kenyon Review,* in an essay on Samuel Johnson, Emerson R. Marks wrote that Johnson's very errors could be beneficial at a time "when the relative neatness of our theory and the precision of our critical techniques may threaten to dehumanize the arts".[164]

The Kenyon Review made a conscious effort to adjust itself to the altered literary situation. In the summer of 1958 when, after twenty years, John Crowe Ransom retired, Robie Macauley was appointed the new editor. Because of a year's leave of absence, Macauley only took up his editorial duties in the summer of 1959. Five years later he wrote that, although *The Kenyon Review* inherited Ransom's "good principles and the tradition of printing good criticism", yet he hoped that, in the 1960's, "we are coming into a somewhat different literary era that calls for a somewhat

---

[163] "Just a Good Poet", *KR*, XVIII, 1 (Winter 1956), 131. In 1959 R. P. Blackmur wrote: "... whenever any of my work is attacked I am attacked as a new critic. Usually when people wish to make more pleasant remarks about me they say how it is that I have departed from the new criticism" (*New Criticism in the United States* [Tokyo, 1959], p. 1). Already in 1954, Philip Blair Rice of *The Kenyon Review* had tried to formulate a "justification of the egghead quarterlies" ("The Intellectual Quarterly in a Non-Intellectual Society", *KR*, XVI, 3 [Summer 1954], 423). In 1960, Monroe Spears of *The Sewanee Review* defended the quarterlies as "necessary evils, produced by the peculiar cultural situation of our time" ("The Present Function of the Literary Quarterlies", *Texas Quarterly*, III, 1 [Spring 1960], 33).
[164] "The Uses of Dr. Johnson", *KR*, XVIII, 2 (Spring 1956), 317.

different kind of magazine. It may well be the time for a new show of talent in poetry, drama, and fiction: a new creative burst like that of the 20's." [165]

Although the 'Fifties, then, witnessed an increasing opposition to the quarterlies, their position was not effectively challenged by new publications, although a number of Beat magazines like *Big Table* and *Evergreen Review* made some impact. This was perhaps not so much due to the ineptitude or scarcity of little magazines in the 'Fifties – after all, Felix Pollak has counted more than two hundred of them [166] – as to the changed literary and cultural climate. Little magazines were typical and influential voices in the 'Twenties, but it was ironically their very success which lessened the influence of their successors. In the 'Fifties, Bohemia had become more closely allied to the universities, and even to the New York publishing houses, than ever before. Or as Irving Howe described it: "Bohemia gradually disappears as a setting for our intellectual life, and what remains of it seems willed or fake." [167] Many poets taught in the universities and the university quarterlies published their poetry. On the other hand,

---

[165] Long and Burr, p. 49. In his first editorial, in the Spring 1960 issue, Macauley had made much the same point: "The new *Kenyon Review* will print a larger variety and a greater amount of fiction than in the past. This may seem an eccentric policy – but imagine the day when the Age of Criticism will have devoured itself ... There will be nothing to read but literature then" ("Standpoint", *KR*, XXII, 2 [Spring 1960], 312).

[166] "Landing in Little Magazines", *Arizona Quarterly*, XIX, 3 (Summer 1963), 101-115.

[167] *A World More Attractive* (New York, 1963), p. 254. The quotation is from a reprinted essay which Howe originally contributed to the *Partisan Review* symposium "Our Country and Our Culture" (May-June 1952). Philip Rahv noticed a similar development: "We are witnessing a process that might well be described as that of the *embourgeoisement* of the American intelligentsia ..." (reprinted in *Image and Idea: Twenty Essays on Literary Themes* [London, 1957], p. 225; see also Richard Chase, "The Fate of the Avant-Garde", *PR*, XXIV, 3 [Summer 1957], 363-375). In 1964, *The Times Literary Supplement* organized a symposium called "The Changing Guard". The introductory editorial stated: "We have come to a point where the very concept of an avant-garde is beginning to be questioned, and to be questioned most keenly by those who most respect its achievements ... The whole scene has been transformed since 1945. Already before the war it was plain that the truly spectacular avant-garde movements had all run their course ..." (August 6, 1964: 675).

such unlikely magazines as *Playboy* and *Esquire* began to publish an occasional story or article which a decade earlier might have found its way into a highbrow literary magazine.[168] A typical little magazine topic like censorship, which had engaged *The Dial* in the 'Twenties, now made headlines in the popular press. Indeed, if the love or the direct knowledge of literature had not increased greatly, literary sophistication had.

The democratization of literary culture – which mainly affects young people, primarily students – has gained momentum in the 1960's, when such valued contributors to the literary quarterlies as Mary McCarthy and Saul Bellow have become bestsellers. But the power of the popular press has increased proportionally. The 'Sixties would seem to provide young people with a number of challenging, non-ideological causes – social and political perhaps rather than literary; the issues ranging from civil rights and pacifism to drugs and sex – but they no sooner take them up than the popular press is on their trail to vulgarize their idealism or to exploit their exhibitionism. The *avant-garde* is indeed "one of the great success-stories of this century".[169] Its achievement was most revolutionary when it acted as a rebellious minority in a hostile or indifferent society, but today it shows tabloid journalists the way to fresh thrills for their readers. What is most needed today therefore is critical journalism in the best sense, rather than academic criticism. This the literary reviews which came of age in the 'Forties have been unable to provide. Their early influence was revolutionary but on the whole they have failed to keep step with the changing times. Also, their quarterly appearance was a distinct advantage in earlier decades when the number of good critics who were possible contributors was smaller than it is today, and when these critics were carrying

---

[168] In the summer of 1966, Robie Macauley, the editor of *The Kenyon Review*, was appointed fiction editor of *Playboy*. The following quotation is interesting in a number of ways: " 'I was familiar with *Playboy*', says Macauley. 'The students at Kenyon read it – so did the clergy. Besides, a magazine like this matures as it goes along' " ("Magazines", *Time* [Atlantic Edition, March 3, 1967], 38).

[169] Dwight Macdonald, *Against the American Grain* (New York, 1962), p. 20.

through a definite, even revolutionary programme. Today it has turned into a disadvantage. It prohibits a rapid exchange of opinion and renders it impossible for the quarterlies to give the kind of critical guidance and stimulus readers have come to expect from them.

The influence of the quarterlies has indeed drastically decreased. If they are still occasionally attacked, such attacks are plainly anachronistic, because they no longer represent the influence they used to. They are important historical landmarks and their backfiles are indispensable for an understanding of the literary developments of the past few decades. But a much more representative publication of the 1960's is *The New York Review of Books,* which appears twice monthly, except during the summer, and which covers more books and topics and reaches a much wider, informed audience than the quarterlies ever did. It was started during the New York newspaper strike in late 1963, because the editors were dissatisfied with the critical standards of the weekly literary supplements of *The New York Times* and of *The New York Herald Tribune* (which were, in due course, considerably affected by it). Its temper is very reminiscent of *Partisan Review* in its more polemic days. Its reviews are often aggressively critical and frequently develop into independent articles. It is the organ of an urban, politically engaged, liberal intelligentsia.

We have indeed entered into a completely different literary era. The recent revival of *The Southern Review* at Louisiana State University may serve as an illustration; it is a pious monument to the achievement of Brooks and Warren some thirty years ago, but it lacks the sense of excitement and purposeful direction of the earlier magazine. Whatever their continuing services to letters, the old formula for the literary review as it was consolidated by the *Southern, Kenyon,* and *Sewanee* reviews in the 'Forties, does not represent the salient characteristics of the present era. Their representative achievement belongs to the past.

LIST OF WORKS CITED

I. PRIMARY SOURCES

a. *The complete files of the following magazines*

The Dial (1920-1929)
The Hound & Horn (1927-1934)
The Kenyon Review (1939–)
Partisan Review (1934–)
The Sewanee Review (1892 [1939]–)
The Southern Review (1935-1942)
The Symposium (1930-1933)

b. *The following manuscript collections*

Richard Aldington collection at the Academic Centre Library of the University of Texas at Austin, letters of T. S. Eliot and Ezra Pound to Aldington.

Sherwood Anderson collection at the Newberry Library, Chicago, selected readings.

Ronald Bottrall collection at the Academic Centre Library of the University of Texas at Austin, letters of F. R. Leavis to Bottrall.

Malcolm Cowley collection at the Newberry Library, Chicago, selected readings.

The Dial collection at the Beinecke Rare Book and Manuscript Library of Yale University, complete files.

The Hound & Horn collection at the Beinecke Library of Yale University, complete files.

Ronald Latimer collection at the Library of the University of Chicago, selected readings.

Merrill Moore collection at the Library of Congress, Washington, D.C., selected readings.

Poetry collection at the Library of the University of Chicago, selected readings.

Samuel Putnam collection at the Princeton University Library, correspondence between Ezra Pound and Samuel Putnam.

The Sewanee Review collection at the office of *The Sewanee Review* and at the Library of the University of the South, Sewanee, Tenn., selected readings.

The Southern Review collection at the Beinecke Library of Yale University, complete files.

Alfred Stieglitz collection at the Beinecke Library of Yale University, letters of Scofield Thayer to Stieglitz.

Allen Tate collection at the Princeton University Library, selected readings.

Louis Zukofsky collection at the Academic Centre Library of the University of Texas at Austin, letters of Ezra Pound to Zukofsky.

II. SECONDARY SOURCES

a. *Books*

Aaron, Daniel, *Writers on the Left* (New York, 1961).

Aldington, Richard, *Life for Life's Sake: Reminiscences* (New York, 1941 [1940]).

Anderson, Margaret, *My Thirty Years' War* (New York, 1930).

Arnold, Willard B., *The Social Ideas of Allen Tate* (Boston, 1955).

Beach, Sylvia, *Shakespeare and Company* (New York, 1959).

Beatty, Richard Croom (ed.), *A Vanderbilt Miscellany* (Nashville, Tenn., 1944).

Blackmur, R. P., *New Criticism in the United States* (Tokyo, 1959).

Bourne, Randolph, *War and the Intellectuals: Essays 1915-1919*, edited and with an Introduction by Carl Resek (Harper Torchbook, 1964).

Bradbury, John, *The Fugitives: A Critical Account* (Chapel Hill, N.C., 1958).

Brooks, Cleanth, *The Well Wrought Urn* (New York, 1947).

Brooks, Cleanth and Robert Penn Warren (eds.), *Stories from the Southern Review* (Baton Rouge, La., 1953).

Brooks, Van Wyck, *Days of the Phoenix* (New York, 1957).

——, *The Opinions of Oliver Allston* (London, 1942 [1941]).

——, *Writers at Work: The Paris Review Interviews*, edited and with an Introduction by Van Wyck Brooks (New York, 1963).

Cash, W. J., *The Mind of the South* (New York, 1941).

Colum, Mary, *Life and the Dream* (New York, 1947).

Couch, W. T. (ed.), *Culture in the South* (Chapel Hill, N.C., 1934).

Cowley, Malcolm, *Exile's Return* (Compass Books, 1962 [1951]).

——, *The Literary Situation* (New York, 1954).

Cummings, E. E., *Six Non-Lectures* (Cambridge, Mass., 1953).

Damon, S. Foster, *Amy Lowell: A Chronicle* (Boston and New York, 1935).

Davidson, Donald, *Southern Writers in the Modern World* (Athens, Ga., 1958).

Eliot, T. S., *After Strange Gods* (New York, 1934).

Ellmann, Richard, *James Joyce* (New York, 1959).

Ezell, John Samuel, *The South Since 1865* (New York, 1963).

Fiedler, Leslie, *Waiting for the End* (New York, 1964).

Fishman, Solomon, *The Disinherited of Art* (Berkeley and Los Angeles, 1953).

Foerster, Norman, *Humanism and America* (New York, 1930).

Ford, Ford Madox, *Collected Poems* (Oxford, 1936).

Frank, Waldo, *The New America* (London, 1922).

——, *The Re-Discovery of America* (New York, 1929).

Gallup, Donald, *T. S. Eliot: A Bibliography* (London, 1952).

Greenbaum, Leonard, *The Hound & Horn: The History of a Literary Quarterly* (= *Studies in American Literature*, VI, The Hague, 1966).

Gregory, Alyse, *The Day is Gone* (New York, 1948).

Hoffman, Frederick, Charles Allen, and Caroline Ulrich, *The Little Magazine: A History and a Bibliography*, 2nd ed. (Princeton, 1947).

Hofstadter, Richard, *Anti-Intellectualism in American Life* (New York, 1963).

Howarth, Herbert, *Notes on Some Figures behind T. S. Eliot* (Boston, 1964).

Howe, Irving, *A World More Attractive* (New York, 1963).

Jarrell, Randall, *Poetry and the Age* (New York, 1953).

Jones, Howard Mumford and Walter Rideout (eds.), *Letters of Sherwood Anderson*, selected and edited with an Introduction and Notes (Boston, 1953).

Joost, Nicholas, *Scofield Thayer and 'The Dial': An Illustrated History* (Carbondale and Edwardsville, 1964).

——, *Years of Transition: 'The Dial', 1912-1920* (Barre, Mass., 1967).

Josephson, Matthew, *Life among the Surrealists: A Memoir* (New York, 1962).

Joyce, James, *Letters of James Joyce*, Vol. I, ed. Stuart Gilbert (London, 1957); Vols. II & III, ed. Richard Ellmann (London, 1966).

Karanikas, Alexander, *Tillers of a Myth: Southern Agrarians as Social and Literary Critics* (Madison, Wis., 1966).

Langton, Lawrence, *The Magic Curtain* (London, 1952).

Loeb, Harold, *The Way It Was* (New York, 1959).

Lovett, Robert Morss, *All Our Years* (New York, 1948).

Macdonald, Dwight, *Against the American Grain* (New York, 1962).

——, *Memoirs of a Revolutionist* (New York, Meridian Books, 1958 [1957]).

MacLeish, Archibald, *A Time to Speak* (Cambridge, Mass., 1940).

MacShane, Frank, *The Life and Work of Ford Madox Ford* (London, 1965).

Meiners, R. K., *The Last Alternatives: A Study of the Works of Allen Tate* (Denver, Col., 1963).

Mellquist, Jerome and Lucie Wiese (eds.), *Paul Rosenfeld: Voyager in the Arts* (New York, 1948).

Muller, Herbert, *Science and Criticism: The Humanistic Tradition in Contemporary Thought* (New Haven, Conn., 1943).

Mullins, Eustace, *This Difficult Individual, Ezra Pound* (New York, 1961).

Munson, Gorham, *Destinations: A Canvas of American Literature since 1900* (New York, 1928).

Norman, Charles, *E. E. Cummings: The Magic-Maker* (New York, 1964).

——, *Ezra Pound* (New York, 1960).

Nowell, Elisabeth (ed.), *The Letters of Thomas Wolfe* (New York, 1956).

Opotowsky, Stan, *The Longs of Louisiana* (New York, 1960).

Oppenheim, James, *The Solitary* (New York, 1919).

Orage, A. R., *Readers and Writers (1917-1921)* (New York, 1922).

Paige, D. D. (ed.), *The Letters of Ezra Pound, 1907-1941* (New York, 1950).

Phillips, William and Philip Rahv (eds.), *The Partisan Reader, 1934-1944* (New York, 1946).

Pound, Ezra, *ABC of Reading* (London, 1934).

Powys, Llewelyn, *The Verdict of Bridlegoose* (New York, 1926).

Purdy, Rob Roy (ed.), *Fugitives' Reunion – Conversations at Vanderbilt, May 3-5, 1956* (Nashville, Tenn., 1959).

Putnam, Samuel, *Paris Was Our Mistress* (New York, 1947).

Rahv, Philip, *Image and Idea: Twenty Essays on Literary Themes* (London, 1957).

Ransom, John Crowe (ed.), *The Kenyon Critics: Studies in Modern Literature from the Kenyon Review* (New York, 1951).

Read, Herbert, *Annals of Innocence and Experience* (London, 1940).

Richards, I. A., *Practical Criticism* (London, 1929).

Rodman, Selden, *Portrait of the Artist as an American. Ben Shahn: A Biography with Pictures* (New York, 1956).

Rogers, W. G., *Wise Men Fish Here: The Story of Frances Steloff and the Gotham Book Mart* (New York, 1965).

Rosenfeld, Paul, *Port of New York*, edited and with an Introduction by Sherman Paul (Urbana, Ill., 1961).

Russell, Francis, *The Great Interlude* (New York, 1964).

Smith, Bernard, *Forces in American Criticism* (New York, 1939).

Stewart, John L., *The Burden of Time: The Fugitives and Agrarians* (Princeton, 1965).

Stock, Noel, *Poet in Exile: Ezra Pound* (Manchester, 1964).

Tambimuttu and Richard March (eds.), *T. S. Eliot: A Symposium* (London, 1965 [1948]).

Taper, Bernhard, *Balanchine* (New York, 1963).

Tate, Allen, *Collected Essays* (Denver, Col., 1959).

—— (ed.), *The Language of Poetry* (Princeton, 1942).

—— (ed.), *A Southern Vanguard* (New York, 1947).

Thirlwall, John C. (ed.), *The Selected Letters of William Carlos Williams* (New York, 1957).

Trilling, Lionel, *The Liberal Imagination* (New York, 1950).

Turner, Susan, *A History of 'The Freeman'* (New York, 1963).

Twelve Southerners. *I'll Take My Stand* (New York, 1930).

Wagner, Geoffrey, *Wyndham Lewis: Portrait of the Artist as the Enemy* (London, 1957).

Wasserstrom, William, *The Time of 'The Dial'* (Syracuse, N.Y., 1963).

Weber, Brom (ed.), *Letters of Hart Crane* (New York, 1952).

Weber, Brom, *Sherwood Anderson* (= *University of Minnesota Pamphlets on American Writers*, No. 43, Minneapolis, 1964).

Whittemore, Reed, *Little Magazines* (= *University of Minnesota Pamphlets on American Writers*, No. 32, Minneapolis, 1963).

Widdemer, Margaret, *Golden Friends I Had* (New York, 1964).

Williams, William Carlos, *The Autobiography of William Carlos Williams* (New York, 1951).

Wilson, Edmund, *The American Earthquake: A Documentary of the Twenties and Thirties* (Garden City, N.J., 1958).

Winters, Yvor, *In Defense of Reason* (Denver, Col., 1947).

b.   *Articles and Dissertations*

Aldington, Richard, "Notes: Literature and the 'Honnête Homme' ", *Criterion*, I, 4 (July 1923), 421-422.

Allen, Charles, "The Dial", *University Review*, X, 2 (Winter 1943), 101-108.

——, "*Glebe* and *Others*", *College English*, XV, 8 (May 1944), 418-423.

Anon. (editorial), *American Oxonian*, XXVIII, 1 (January 1941), 35.

——, "Books: Obit in Baton Rouge", *Time* (February 2, 1942), 74, 76.

——, "The Changing Guard", *Times Literary Supplement* (August 6, 1964).

——, "Chronicle and Comment", *Bookman*, LXXI, 1 (March 1930), 76; LXXIV, 3 (November 1931), 253.

——, "Don't Bury the Hatchet", *Times Literary Supplement* (February 13, 1964), 127.

——, "Editorial: The New Magazines", *Nation*, CXXX (January 29, 1930), 116.

——, "Editorial Note", *Magazine*, II, 1 (July-August 1934), inside front cover.

——, "Editorial", *Seven Arts*, I, 1 (November 1916), 52-56.

——, "Editorials: The Magazine in America", *Double Dealer*, I, 3 (March 1921), 82-87.

——, "Memento", *Nouvelle Revue Française*, X, 111 (Nouvelle Série, December 1922), 762.

——, "Literary Intelligence", *London Mercury*, I, 4 (February 1920), 392.

——, "Magazines", *Time* (Atlantic Edition, March 3, 1967), 36-40.

—— (editorial), *Nation*, CLII, 1 (January 4, 1941), 22-23.

——, "Notes", *Nouvelle Revue Française*, VI, 69 (Nouvelle Série, June 1919), 143.

——, "Sic Transit", *This Quarter*, II, 1 (Summer 1929), 175-176.

——, "Some Periodicals", *Adelphi*, II, 5 (August 1931), inside front cover.

—— (editorial), *Time*, I, 1 (March 3, 1923), 12.

——, "To Our Readers", *Little Review*, III, 7 (November 1916), 21.

Arrowsmith, William, "*Partisan Review* and American Writing", *Hudson Review*, I, 4 (Winter 1949), 526-537.

Auden, W. H., "Private Poet", *New York Review of Books*, III, 7 (November 5, 1964), 8-10.

Barrett, William, "Declining Fortunes of the Literary Review: 1945-1955", *Anchor Review*, No. 2 (1957), 145-160.

Benét, William Rose, "Phoenix Nest", *Saturday Review of Literature*, X, 45 (May 26, 1934), 720.

Bradbury, Malcolm, "*The Criterion*: A Literary Review in Retrospect", *London Magazine*, V, 2 (February 1958), 41-54.

Bridson, D. G., "American Periodicals", *Criterion*, XIV, 57 (July 1935), 727-729.

Brooks, Obed, "The Literary Front", *Modern Monthly*, VII, 2 (March 1933), 115-117.

Brooks, Van Wyck, "A Reviewer's Notebook", *Freeman*, II, 27 (September 15, 1920), 22.

—— (editorial), *Seven Arts*, I, 3 (January 1917), 272.

Burke, Kenneth, "Correspondence: *The Dial*'s Policy", *Literary Review* of *The New York Evening Post*, III, 31 (April 7, 1923), 594.

Canby, Henry Seidel, "Longfellow Junior", *Literary Review* of *The New York Evening Post*, III, 26 (March 13, 1923), 497.

Chesterton, G. K. (editorial), *New Witness*, XIX, 483 (February 10, 1922), 94.

Collins, Seward, "Criticism in America", *Bookman*, LXXII, 2 (October 1930), 145-164.

Cowley, Malcolm, "The Little Magazines Growing up", *New York Times Book Review*, LII (September 14, 1947), 5, 35.

——, "Midsummer Medley", *New Republic*, LXXX (August 15, 1934), 24-25.

——, "Partisan Review", *New Republic*, XCVI (October 19, 1938), 311-312.

——, "Ten Little Magazines", *New Republic*, CXVI (March 31, 1947), 30-33.

Cunard, Nancy, "The Hours Press", *Book Collector*, XIII, 4 (Winter 1964), 488-496.

Dahlberg, Edward, "The Fastidious Movement", *Nation*, CXXXIV (April 6, 1932), 402.

D[avies], H[ugh] S[ykes], "American Periodicals", *Criterion*, XI, 43 (January 1932), 361-363; XI, 48 (April 1933), 540-544.

DeJong, David Cornel, "Money and Rue", *Carleton Miscellany*, VI, 1 (Winter 1965), 50-52.

D[obree], B[onamy], "American Periodicals", *Criterion*, IX, 35 (January 1930), 369-373; X, 40 (April 1931), 587-590.

Eliot, T. S., "A Commentary", *Criterion*, XII, 49 (July 1933), 642-647.

——, "Communications", *Transatlantic Review*, I, 1 (January 1924), 95-96.

——, "The Idea of a Literary Review", *Criterion*, IV, 1 (January 1926), 1-6.

——, "Last Words", *Criterion*, XVIII, 71 (January 1939), 269-275.

——, "Notes: The Function of a Literary Review", *Criterion*, I, 4 (July 1923), 421.

Fiedler, Leslie, " 'Partisan Review', Phoenix or Dodo?", *Perspectives U.S.A.*, No. 15 (Spring 1956), 82-97.

Frank, Waldo, "How I Came to Communism", *New Masses*, VIII, 3 (September 1932), 6-7.

——, "Symposium on the Little Magazines", *Golden Goose*, III, 1 (1951), 11-28.

Gold, Michael, "Notes of the Month", *New Masses*, VI, 2 (July 1930), 4-5.

Grattan, C. Hartley, "Composite Photograph", *New Republic*, LXXIX (June 13, 1934), 133-134.

Greenbaum, Leonard, "The *Hound & Horn* Archive", *Yale University Library Gazette*, XXXIX, 3 (January 1965), 137-146.

——, "*The Hound & Horn*: Episodes in American Literary History, 1927-1934" (doctoral dissertation), University of Michigan, 1963.

Hackett, Francis, "A Letter from America", *London Mercury*, II, 10 (August 1920), 472.

Hagglund, Ben, "Akin to Revelation", *Carleton Miscellany*, VI, 1 (Winter 1965), 62-68.

Heap, Jane [jh], "The 'Art Season' ", *Little Review*, VIII, 2 ("Picabia Number", Spring 1922), 58-60.

Hemingway, Ernest, "Chroniques III: And to the United States", *Transatlantic Review*, I, 5 (May 1924), 355.

Hicks, Granville, "The Crisis in American Criticism", *New Masses*, VIII, 7 (February 1933), 3-5.

——, "Hounds and Horns", *New Republic*, LXXI (May 25, 1932), 49.

——, "Inheritance Tax", *New Republic*, LXX (April 20, 1932), 278-279.

Hicks, John H., "Literary Quarterlies of the 1960's", *College English*, XXVII, 2 (November 1965), 153-156.

Howe, Irving, "PR", *New York Review of Books* (special issue, 1963), 20.

Janssens, G. A., "*The Dial* and the 'Twenties", *Yale Review*, LIV, 2 (Winter 1965), 282-284.

——, "*The Dial* and *The Seven Arts*", *Papers on Language and Literature* (to appear in 1968).

Jolas, Eugene and Eliott Paul, "A Review", *transition*, No. 12 (March 1928), 139-147.

Kirstein, Lincoln, "*The Hound & Horn*, 1927-1934" (with a Letter from Varian Fry as a Note), *Harvard Advocate*, CXXI, 2 (Christmas 1934), 6-10, 92-94.

Knickerbocker, William S., "The Dilemma of the Fugitives", *Contempo*, II, 1 (May 25, 1932), 1-2.

Leavis, F. R., " 'The Kenyon Review' and 'Scrutiny' ", *Scrutiny*, XIV, 2 (December 1946), 134-136.

Leavis, Q. D., "Hardy and Criticism", *Scrutiny*, XI, 3 (Spring 1943), 230-237.

Long, David and Michael Burr (eds.), "John Crowe Ransom: A Tribute from the Community of Letters", *Kenyon Collegian* (Supplement to vol. LXXXX, 7, Gambier, 1964).

Lowell, Robert, "Randall Jarrell, 1914-1965", *New York Review of Books*, V, 8 (November 25, 1965), 3-4.

Macdonald, Dwight, "Delmore Schwartz (1913-1966)", *New York Review of Books*, VII, 3 (September 8, 1966), 14-16.

MacShane, Frank, "The Transatlantic Review", *Dalhousie Review*, XLI, 3 (Autumn 1961), 303-313.

M[angan], S[herry], "Final Remarks on Criticism", *Pagany*, II, 1 (Winter 1931), 101-103.

Mather, Margaret Wright, review of *Poems* of Archibald MacLeish, *New Masses*, X, 3 (January 1934), 26.

Mirsky, D. S., "Joyce and Irish Literature", *New Masses*, XI, 1 (April 3, 1934), 31-34.

M[onroe], H[arriet], "The Arrogance of Youth", *Poetry*, XXXVII, 6 (March 1931), 328-333.

Montesi, Albert J., "*The Southern Review* (1935-1942): A History and an Evaluation" (unpublished doctoral dissertation), Pennsylvania State University, 1955.

Moore, Marianne, "The Dial", *Life and Letters Today*, XXVII, 40 (December 1940), 175-183; XXVIII, 41 (January 1941), 3-9.

——, "Symposium on the Little Magazine", *Golden Goose*, III, 1 (1951), 11-28.

Mosher, Frederic J., "Chicago's 'Saving Remnant': Francis Fisher Browne, William Morton Payne, and the *Dial* (1880-1892)" (unpublished doctoral dissertation), University of Illinois, 1950.

Muller, Herbert, "The Function of a Critical Review", *Arizona Quarterly*, IV, 1 (Spring 1948), 5-20.

Mumford, Lewis, "The Image of Randolph Bourne", *New Republic*, LXIV (September 24, 1930), 151-152.

——, "On The Dial" (review of William Wasserstrom's *The Time of 'The Dial'*), *New York Review of Books*, II, 1 (February 20, 1964), 3-5.

Munson, Gorham, "The Artist's Stone", *Pagany*, I, 1 (Winter 1930), 3.

M[unson], G[orham] B., "Exposé No. 1", *Secession*, No. 1 (Spring 1922), 22-24.

Munson, Gorham, "Greenwich Village That Was: Seedbed of the Twenties", *Literary Review: An International Journal of Contemporary Writing*, V, 3 (Spring 1962), 313-335.

——, "Herald of the Twenties", *Forum*, III, 8 (Autumn 1961), 4-14.

Murry, John Middleton, "Flaubert and Flaubart", *Yale Review*, XIII, 2 (January 1924), 347-364.

North, Richel (pseudonym for A. D. Emmart), "The Limitations of American Magazines", *Modern Quarterly*, I, 1 (March 1923), 2-12; I, 3 (September 1923), 17-25.

Oppenheim, James, "The Story of *The Seven Arts*", *American Mercury*, XX, 78 (June 1930), 156-164.

Phillips, William, "What Happened in the 30's", *Commentary*, XXXIV, 3 (September 1962), 204-212.

Pollak, Felix, "Landing in Little Magazines – Capturing (?) a Trend", *Arizona Quarterly*, XIX, 3 (Summer 1963), 101-115.

P[orteus], H[ugh] G[ordon], "Significant Journals", *Purpose*, X, 4 (Autumn 1938), 237-248.

Pound, Ezra, "After Election", *New Review*, I, 1 (January-February 1931), 53-55.

P[ound], E[zra], "The Exile", *Exile*, I, 1 (Spring 1927), 88-92.

Pound, Ezra, "The First Year of 'Pagany' and the Possibility of Criteria", *Pagany*, II, 1 (Winter 1931), 104-111.

——, "Historical Survey", *Little Review*, VIII, 1 ("Brancusi Number:" Autumn 1921), 39-42.

——, "The Reader Critic", *Little Review*, III, 2 (April 1916), 36.

——, "Simplicities", *Exile*, No. 4 (Autumn 1928), 1-2.

——, "Small Magazines", *English Journal*, XIX, 9 (November 1930), 689-704.

——, "Terra Italica", *New Review*, I, 4 (Winter 1932), 386-389.

Ransom, John Crowe, "An Age of Criticism", *New Republic*, CXXVI (March 31, 1952), 18-19.

R[ead], H[erbert], "Periodical Reviews", *Criterion*, V, 3 (June 1927), 372.

R[ivers], H., "Editorial: Literature without Money", *Direction* (special issue), I, 3 (1938), 6-10.

Rivière, Jacques, "La Nouvelle Revue Française", *Nouvelle Revue Française*, VI, 69 (Nouvelle Série, June 1919), 1-10.

——, review of Julien Benda's *Belphégor*, *Nouvelle Revue Française*, VI, 69 (Nouvelle Série, June 1919), 146-153.

Rolland, Romain, "America and the Arts", *Seven Arts*, I, 1 (November 1916), 47-51.

S., K., review of Lincoln Kirstein's *Flesh Is Heir*, *Boston Evening Transcript* (March 23, 1932), Part IV, 2.

Salter, Paul, "Fascist Philosophers", *New Masses*, VIII, 11 (July 1933), 13-14.

Schwartz, Delmore, "*The Criterion*, 1922-1939", *Purpose*, XI, 4 (Autumn 1939), 225-237.

——, "An Unpleasant and Important Fact: The Misery and Necessity of the Quarterly", *American Scholar*, XV, 4 (Autumn 1946), 553-554.

Spears, Monroe, "The Present Function of the Literary Quarterlies", *Texas Quarterly*, III, 1 (Spring 1960), 33-50.

Stone, Albert E., Jr., "Seward Collins and the *American Review*: Experiment in Pro-Fascism, 1933-1937", *American Quarterly*, XII, 1 (Spring 1960), 3-19.

Sühnel, Rudolf, "The Marxist Trend in Literary Criticism in the USA in the Thirties", *Jahrbuch für Amerikastudien*, Band 7 (Heidelberg, 1962).

Swallow, Alan, "Postwar Little Magazines", *Prairie Schooner*, XXIII, 2 (Summer 1949), 152-157.

Symons, Julian, "Woofers and Tweeters", *Spectator* (February 22, 1963), 232.

Tate, Allen, "Miss Emily and the Bibliographer", *American Scholar*, IX, 1 (Winter 1940), 449-460.

——, "Random Thoughts on the 1920's", *Minnesota Review*, I, 1 (Autumn 1960), 46-56.

——, "The Unliteral Imagination; Or, I, Too, Dislike It", *Southern Review* (New Series), I, 3 (Summer 1965), 530-542.

——, "What Is Creative Writing?", *Wisconsin Studies in Contemporary Literature*, V, 2 (Autumn 1964), 181-184.

T[itus], E[dward] W., "Editorially", *This Quarter*, IV, 1 (Summer 1931), 7-10.

Titus, Edward, "The Flying Column", *This Quarter*, III, 4 (Spring 1931), 747-749.

Troy, William, "The Story of the Little Magazines", *Bookman*, LXX, 5 (January 1930), 476-481.

Vivas, Eliseo, "Criticism and the Little Mags", *Western Review*, XVI, 3 (Autumn 1951), 9-19.

——, review of Philip Wheelwright's *The Burning Fountain, Perspectives U.S.A.*, No. 14 (Winter 1956), 167-175.

Warren, Austin, "Some Periodicals of the American Intelligentsia", *New English Weekly*, I, 25 (October 6, 1932), 595-597.

Wasserstrom, William, Letter to Lewis Mumford, *New York Review of Books*, II, 5 (April 16, 1964), 19.

Whittemore, Reed, "Foundations and Magazines: A Symposium", *Carleton Miscellany*, IV, 2 (Spring 1963), 45-83.

Williams, William Carlos, "The Advance Guard Magazine", *Contact*, I, 1 (February 1932), 86-90.

Wilson, Edmund, "An Imaginary Conversation: Mr. Paul Rosenfeld and Mr. Matthew Josephson", *New Republic*, XXXVIII (April 9, 1924), 179-182.

Winters, Yvor, "The Critiad: A Poetical Survey of Recent Criticism", *This Quarter*, III, 4 (Spring 1931), 738-743.

Woodward, Daniel, "Notes on the Publishing History and Text of 'The Waste Land' ", *Papers of the Bibliographical Society of America*, LVIII (Third Quarter 1964), 252-269.

Z[abel], M[orton] D[auwen], "Recent Magazines", *Poetry*, XXXVIII, 3 (June 1931), 170-173; XXXIX, 6 (March 1932), 345-349; XLIII, 4 (January 1934), 168-173; XLIV, 3 (June 1934), 170-171; XLVIII, 1 (April 1936), 51-52.

Zabel, Morton Dauwen, "The Way of Periodicals", *Poetry*, XXXIV, 6 (September 1929), 330-334.

INDEX

STUDIES IN AMERICAN LITERATURE

MOUTON · PUBLISHERS · THE HAGUE